FLOYD CLYMER - 2025 EDITION
OSSA
WORKSHOP MANUAL
1971 to 1978

Motocross - Enduro - Trials
125cc - 175cc - 250cc - 310cc

A Floyd Clymer Publication - 2025 VelocePress.com

PREFACE

TRADEMARKS & COPYRIGHT

OSSA® was the registered trademark of the original manufacturer from 1924 to 1982. After that time it passed through a series of owners ending in 2015 at which time the OSSA motorcycle division was discontinued. This publication is not sponsored by or endorsed by the trademark owner. We recognize that some words, model names and designations, for example, mentioned herein are the property of the trademark holder. We use them for identification purposes only. This is not an official publication however; it may include non-copyright works of the trademark holder.

INTRODUCTION

Welcome to the world of digital publishing ~ the book you now hold in your hand was printed using the latest state of the art digital technology. The advent of print-on-demand has forever changed the publishing process, never has information been so accessible and it is our hope that this book serves your informational needs for years to come. If this is your first exposure to digital publishing, we hope that you are pleased with the results. Many more titles of interest to the classic automobile and motorcycle enthusiast, collector and restorer are available via our website at www.VelocePress.com. We hope that you find this title as interesting as we do.

NOTE FROM THE PUBLISHER

The information presented is true and complete to the best of our knowledge. All recommendations are made without any guarantees on the part of the author or the publisher, who also disclaim all liability incurred with the use of this information.

INFORMATION ON THE USE OF THIS PUBLICATION

This manual is an invaluable resource for those interested in performing their own maintenance. However, in today's information age we are constantly subject to changes in common practice, new technology, availability of improved materials and increased awareness of chemical toxicity. As such, it is advised that the user consult with an experienced professional prior to undertaking any procedure described herein. While every care has been taken to ensure correctness of information, it is obviously not possible to guarantee complete freedom from errors or omissions or to accept liability arising from such errors or omissions. Therefore, any individual that uses the information contained within, or elects to perform or participate in do-it-yourself repairs or modifications acknowledges that there is a risk factor involved and that the publisher or its associates cannot be held responsible for personal injury or property damage resulting from the use of the information or the outcome of such procedures.

WARNING!

One final word of advice, this publication is intended to be used as a reference guide, and when in doubt the reader should consult with a qualified technician.

CONTENTS

QUICK REFERENCE DATA

CHAPTER ONE
GENERAL INFORMATION 1

    Manual organization
    Service hints
    Safety hints
    Parts replacement
    Tools
    Expendable supplies
    Serial numbers
    Location of controls

CHAPTER TWO
LUBRICATION, PERIODIC MAINTENANCE AND TUNE-UP 7

    Maintenance/lubrication schedule
    Tools
    Oil changing
    Drive chain
    Rear sprocket
    Changing fork oil
    Control cables
    Speedometer cable
    Brake lever
    Engine tune-up
    Air cleaner
    Fuel strainer
    Battery
    Electrical equipment
    Spark plug
    Compression test
    Ignition timing
    Carburetor
    Decarbonization
    Miscellaneous
    Storage

CHAPTER THREE
TROUBLESHOOTING 21

    Operating requirements
    Troubleshooting instruments
    Starting difficulties
    Idling
    Misfiring
    Flat spots
    Power loss
    Overheating
    Engine noises
    Piston seizure
    Excessive vibration
    Clutch
    Transmission
    Handling
    Brakes
    Electrical
    Ignition system
    Ignition switch
    Charging system
    Lights
    Short circuits
    Horn
    Fuse
    Troubleshooting guide

CHAPTER FOUR
FUEL SYSTEM 30

    Carburetor operation   Air filter
    Carburetor overhaul   Fuel strainer
    Carburetor adjustment   Gas tank

CHAPTER FIVE
ELECTRICAL SYSTEM 45

    Battery   Ignition switch
    Wiring diagram   Headlight
    Ignition system   Taillight, indicator light and horn
    Ignition coil

CHAPTER SIX
ENGINE 57

    Engine operation   Splitting the crankcase
    Servicing engine in frame   Primary cover
    Engine removal/installation   Clutch, cush drive shaft and kickstarter
    Cylinder and piston   Clutch and engine sprockets
    Magneto   Primary chain inspection
    Carburetor and air cleaner   Breaking in a rebuilt engine

CHAPTER SEVEN
TRANSMISSION, CRANKSHAFT AND BEARINGS 81

    Transmission   Crankshaft and bearings

CHAPTER EIGHT
CHASSIS 109

    Frame   Spokes
    Front fork and steering components   Wheel bearings
    Swing arm   Brakes
    Rear shocks   Tire
    Wheels   Exhaust pipe

APPENDIX
SPECIFICATIONS 140

SUPPLEMENT
1977-1978 SERVICE INFORMATION 145

    General information   Frame
    Engine   Front fork and steering components
    Chassis   Wheels

INDEX 159

QUICK REFERENCE DATA

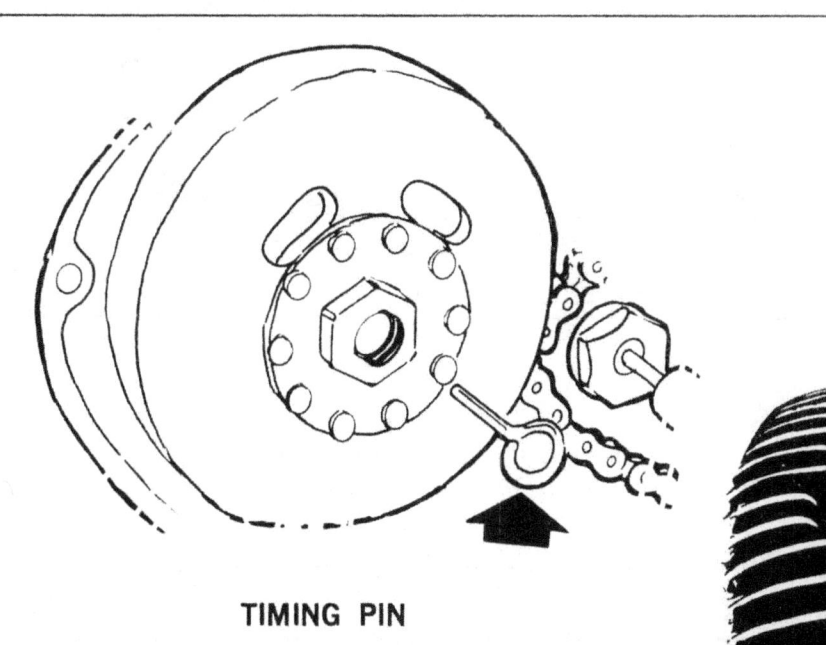

TIMING PIN

DIAL INDICATOR

IGNITION TIMING[1]

Model	Inches[2]	Millimeters[2]
Phantom 125, 175, and 250	0.116	(2.95)
Stiletto 175	0.098-0.108	(2.50-2.75)
Stiletto 250	0.118	(3.00)
Pioneer 175	0.088-0.098	(2.25-2.50)
Super Pioneer 125, 175, and 250	0.108-0.116	(2.75-2.95)
Plonker 250, 310	0.102	(2.60)
GP III	0.08	(2.00)

1. Refer to Chapter Two, **Ignition Timing** section, for procedure.
2. Measured with dial indicator through spark plug hole.

NOTE: While the above figures are those recommended by Ossa, several top Ossa tuners recommend 0.124 in. (3.15mm) for ALL Ossa engines for optimum performance.

CARBURETOR ADJUSTMENTS

Throttle Opening	Adjustment	If too Rich	If too Lean
0-1/8	Air screw	Turn out	Turn in
1/8-1/4	Throttle valve cutaway	Use larger cutaway	Use smaller cutaway
1/4-3/4	Jet needle	Raise clip	Lower clip
3/4-full	Main jet	Use smaller number	Use larger number

ADJUSTMENTS

Clutch lever free play	½-¾ in. (13-19mm)
Drive chain play	
Short travel models	¾-1 in. (19-25mm)
Long travel models	2-2½ in. (51-64mm)
Rear brake pedal travel	¾-1⅛ in. (19-30mm)
Front brake lever travel	¾-1⅛ in. (19-30mm)

SPARK PLUGS

Models	Spark plug type	Spark plug gap
Stiletto 175, 250TT, and 250MX	NGK B10EN or equivalent	0.020 in. (0.5mm)
Pioneer 175 and 250	NGK B9ES or equivalent	0.020 in. (0.5mm)
Plonker/Explorer 250	NGK B8ES or equivalent	0.020 in. (0.5mm)
Super Pioneer 125, 175, and 250, Phantom 125, 175 and 250	NGK B8EN, B9EN, or equivalent	0.020 in. (0.5mm)
Mountaineer 310 and BLT Plonker 310; Six-Day; and GP III	NGK B9EN or B10EN, or equivalent	0.020 in. (0.5mm)

RECOMMENDED TRANSMISSION OIL

Temperature	Viscosity	Capacity
All temperatures	80W racing gearbox oil or SAE 30 W motor oil	1 qt. (0.9 liter) all models
Optional:		
Above 59°F (15°C)	SAE 30W	
32-59°F (0-15°C)	SAE 20W	
Below 32°F (0°C)	SAE 10W	

TIRE PRESSURE

Model	Pressure (psi)[1]
All models	
Front	8-10
Rear	10-15

1. Adjust pressure up or down from these figures, according to your personal requirements, the type of tires used, etc.

FRONT FORK CAPACITY

Model	Viscosity	Capacity
All short travel (6½ in.) front models	5W fork oil	6.7 fl. oz. (200cc)
All long travel front fork models	5W fork oil	8.1 fl. oz. (240cc)

CHAPTER ONE

GENERAL INFORMATION

This manual provides maintenance and repair information for all 5-speed 175cc and 250cc Ossa motorcycles. It can also be used as a guide for servicing the 125cc engine since procedures are identical.

Dimensions and capacities are expressed in English as well as metric units.

MANUAL ORGANIZATION

This chapter, in addition to providing general information, discusses equipment and tools useful both for preventive maintenance and troubleshooting. The section on safety reminders should be read very carefully.

Chapter Two explains all periodic lubrication and routine maintenance necessary to keep a motorcycle in proper running condition. Chapter Two also includes recommended tune-up procedures which eliminate the need to constantly consult chapters on the various subassemblies.

Chapter Three provides methods and suggestions for quick and accurate diagnosis and repair of problems. Troubleshooting procedures discuss typical symptoms and logical methods to pinpoint trouble spots.

Subsequent chapters described specific systems, such as the engine, transmission, and electrical system. Each chapter provides disassembly, repair, and assembly procedures in simple step-by-step form. If a repair is impractical for an owner/mechanic, it is so indicated. It is usually faster and less expensive to take such repairs to a dealer or competent repair shop.

The Supplement at the end of this handbook covers all 1977-1978 models.

The terms NOTE, CAUTION, and WARNING have specific meanings in this manual. A NOTE provides additional information to make a step or procedure easier or clearer. Disregarding a NOTE could cause inconvenience but would not cause damage or personal injury.

A CAUTION emphasizes areas where equipment damage could result. Disregarding a CAUTION could cause permanent mechanical damage; however, personal injury is unlikely.

A WARNING emphasizes areas where personal injury, or even death, could result from negligence. Mechanical damage may also occur; WARNINGS are to be taken seriously. In some cases, serious injury or death has been caused by mechanics disregarding similar warnings.

Throughout this manual, keep in mind 2 conventions. The front of any component, such as the engine, is that end which faces toward the front of the bike. The left and right side refer to a person sitting on the bike facing forward. For example, the clutch lever is on the left side. These conventions are simple, but even experienced mechanics occasionally become disoriented.

SERVICE HINTS

Most service procedures covered are straightforward and can be performed by anyone reasonably handy with tools. It is suggested, however, that you consider your own capabilities carefully before attempting any operation involving major disassembly of the engine.

Some operations, for example, require the use of a press. It would be wiser to have these performed by a shop equipped for such work, rather than to try to do the job at home with makeshift equipment. Other procedures require precision measurements. Unless you have the skills and equipment required, it would be better to have a qualified repair shop make the measurements.

Special tools are required for some repair procedures. These may be purchased from an Ossa dealer (or borrowed if you are on good terms with the service department personnel) or fabricated by a mechanic or machinist; often at considerable savings.

Repairs go much faster and easier if the bike is clean before beginning work. Special cleaners are available for washing the engine and related parts. Just brush or spray on the cleaning solution, let it stand, then rinse away with a garden hose. Clean all oily or greasy parts with cleaning solvent as they are removed.

WARNING
Never use gasoline as a cleaning agent. It presents an extreme fire hazard. Be sure to work in a well-ventilated area while using cleaning solvent. Keep a fire extinguisher, rated for gasoline and oil fires, handy at all times.

Much of the labor charge for repairs made by dealers is for the removal and disassembly of other parts to reach a defective unit. It is frequently possible to perform the preliminary operations first and then take the defective unit to a dealer for repair.

Once having decided to tackle a job at home, read the entire section which pertains to it. Make sure to identify the proper section. Study the illustrations and text to gain a good idea of what is involved in completing the job satisfactorily. If special tools are necessary, make arrangements to get them before starting. It is frustrating and a waste of time to get partly into a job and then be unable to complete it.

Simple wiring checks are easily made at home; but knowledge of electronics is almost a necessity for performing tests with complicated electronic test gear.

During disassembly of parts, keep a few general cautions in mind. Force is rarely needed to get things apart. If parts are a tight fit, as a magneto on a crankshaft, there is usually a tool designed to separate them. Never use a screwdriver to pry apart parts with machined surfaces such as crankcase halves and valve covers. It will mar the surfaces and cause leaks.

Make diagrams wherever similar-appearing parts are found. For example, case cover screws are often of various lengths. Do not rely on remembering where everything came from—mistakes are costly. There is also the possibility of being sidetracked and not returning to work for days or weeks; meanwhile, carefully laid out parts may have become disarranged.

Tag all similar internal parts for location and mark all mating parts for position. Record the number and thickness of shims as they are removed. Small parts, such as several identical bolts, can be identified by placing them in plastic sandwich bags and sealing and labeling the bags with masking tape.

Wiring should be tagged with masking tape and marked as each wire is removed. Do not rely on memory alone.

Disconnect the battery ground cable before working near electrical connections and before disconnecting wires. Never run the engine with the battery disconnected; the electrical system could be seriously damaged.

Protect finished surfaces from physical damage or corrosion. Keep gasoline and cleaning solvent off painted surfaces.

Frozen or very tight bolts and screws can often be loosened by soaking with penetrating oil, then sharply striking the bolt head a few times with a hammer and punch (or screwdriver for screws). Do not use heat unless absolutely necessary, because it may melt, warp, or remove the temper from parts.

Avoid flames or sparks while working near a battery being charged or near flammable liquids such as cleaning fluids or gasoline.

No parts, except those assembled with a press fit, require unusual force during assembly. If a part is hard to remove or install, find out why before proceeding.

Cover all openings after removing parts to keep dirt, small tools, and other foreign matter from falling in.

While assembling 2 parts, start all fasteners and then tighten evenly to avoid warpage.

Clutch plates, wiring connections, and brake shoes and drums should be kept clean and free of grease and oil during assembly.

While assembling parts, be sure that all shims and washers are replaced exactly as they were before disassembly. Wherever a rotating part butts against a stationary part, look for a shim or washer.

Use new gaskets if there is any doubt about the condition of old ones. Generally, apply gasket cement to one mating surface only so that the parts may be easily disassembled in the future. A thin coat of oil on gaskets helps them seal effectively.

Heavy grease can be used to hold small parts in place if they tend to fall out during assembly. However, keep grease and oil away from electrical components or brake shoes and drums.

High spots may be sanded off a piston dome with sandpaper, but emery cloth and oil do a much more professional job.

Carburetors are best cleaned by soaking the disassembled parts in a commercial carburetor cleaner. Never soak gaskets or rubber parts in cleaner. Never use wire to clean jets and air passages; they are easily damaged. Use compressed air to blow out the carburetor only if the float has been removed first.

A baby bottle is a good measuring device for adding oil to forks and transmissions. Obtain one which is graduated in ounces and cubic centimeters.

Take sufficient time to do the job right. Do not forget that a newly rebuilt motorcycle engine must be broken in the same as a new one. Keep rpm's within the limits given in the owner's manual.

SAFETY HINTS

Professional motorcycle mechanics can work for years and never sustain a serious injury. Observing a few rules of common sense and safety lets one enjoy many safe hours servicing one's own machine. You can hurt yourself or damage the bike if you ignore the following rules.

1. Never use gasoline as a cleaning solvent.

2. Never smoke or use a torch in the vicinity of flammable liquids such as cleaning solvent in open containers.

3. Never smoke or use a torch in an area where batteries are being charged. Highly explosive hydrogen gas is formed during the charging process.

4. If welding or brazing is required on the machine, remove the fuel tank to a safe distance (at least 50 feet away). Welding on gas tanks requires special safety procedures and must be performed only by someone skilled in the process.

5. Use the proper sized wrenches to avoid personal injury and damage to nuts.

6. While loosening a tight or stuck nut or bolt, be guided by what would happen if the wrench should slip.

7. Keep the work area clean and uncluttered.

8. Wear safety goggles during all operations involving drilling, grinding, or use of a chisel.

9. Never use worn tools.

10. Keep a fire extinguisher handy and be sure it is rated for gasoline and electrical fires.

PARTS REPLACEMENT

When ordering parts from a dealer or other parts distributor, always order by engine and frame number. Write the numbers down and carry them in your wallet. Compare new parts to old before purchasing. If they are not alike, have the parts personnel explain the difference.

TOOLS

Tool Kit

Most new bikes are equipped with fairly complete tool kits. These tools are satisfactory for most small jobs and emergency roadside repairs. A tool kit, widely available and suitable for most minor servicing, is shown in **Figure 1**.

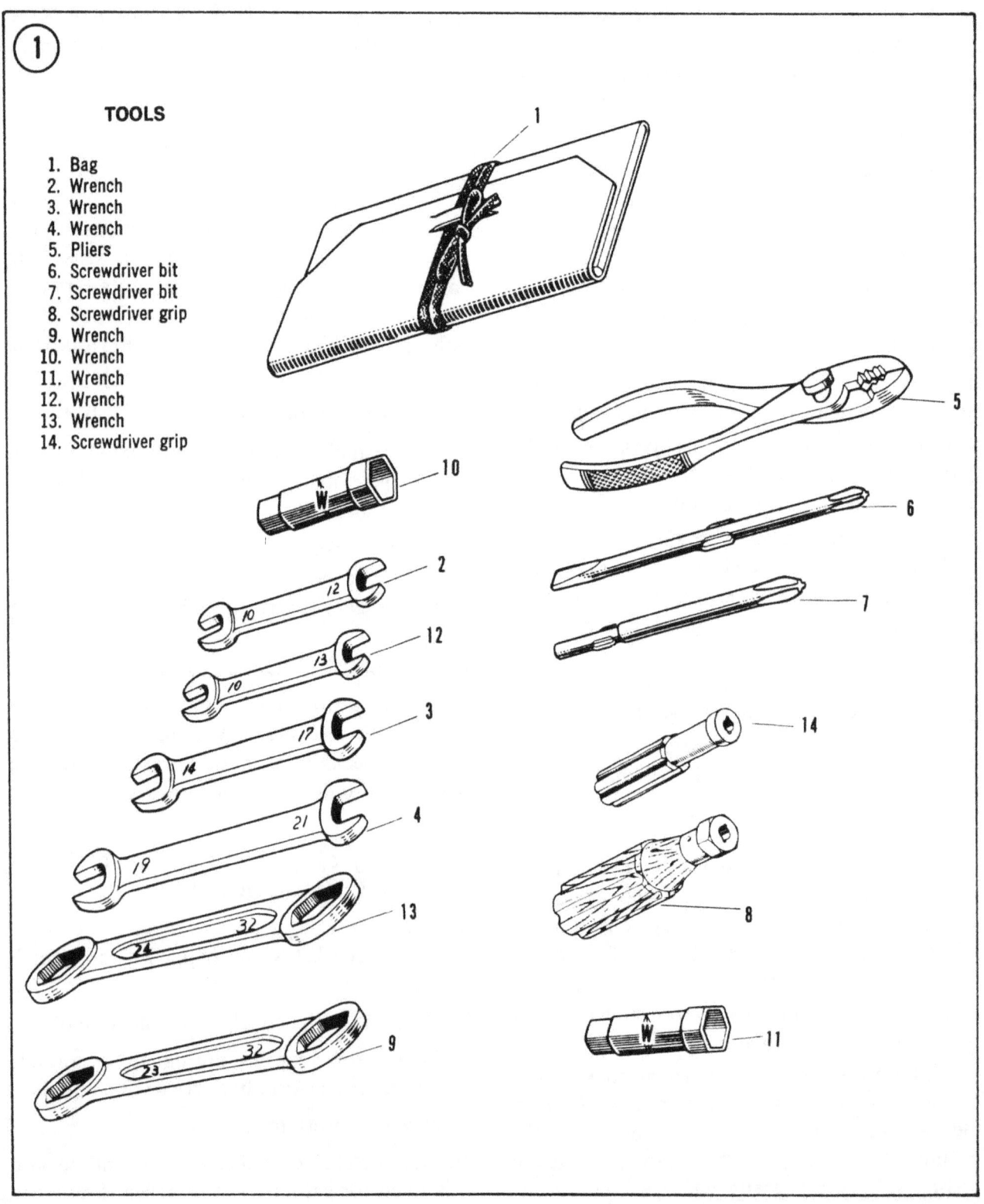

TOOLS

1. Bag
2. Wrench
3. Wrench
4. Wrench
5. Pliers
6. Screwdriver bit
7. Screwdriver bit
8. Screwdriver grip
9. Wrench
10. Wrench
11. Wrench
12. Wrench
13. Wrench
14. Screwdriver grip

Shop Tools

For proper servicing, an assortment of ordinary hand-tools is needed. As a minimum, these include:

1. Combination wrenches
2. Socket wrenches
3. Plastic mallet
4. Small hammer
5. Snap ring pliers
6. Pliers
7. Phillips screwdrivers
8. Slot (common) screwdrivers
9. Feeler gauges
10. Spark plug gauge
11. Spark plug wrench
12. Dial indicator

Special tools necessary are designated in the chapters covering the particular repair in which they are used.

Electrical system servicing requires a voltmeter, ohmmeter or other device for determining continuity, and a hydrometer for battery equipped machines.

Advanced tune-up and troubleshooting procedures require the additional tools listed below.

1. *Timing gauge* (**Figure 2**). By screwing this instrument into the spark plug hole, piston position may be determined. The tool shown costs approximately $20 and is available from larger dealers and mail order houses. Less expensive ones, which utilize a vernier scale instead of a dial indicator, are also available. They are satisfactory but are not quite so quick and easy to use.

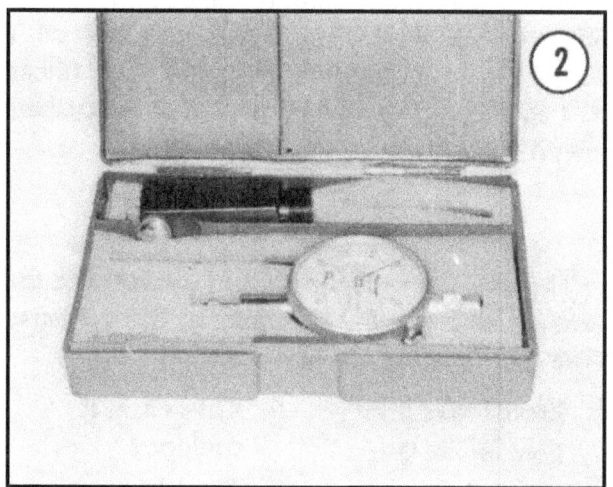

2. *Hydrometer* (**Figure 3**). This instrument measures the state of charge of the battery and tells much about battery condition. Such an instrument is available at any auto parts store and through most larger mail order outlets. A satisfactory one costs approximately $3.

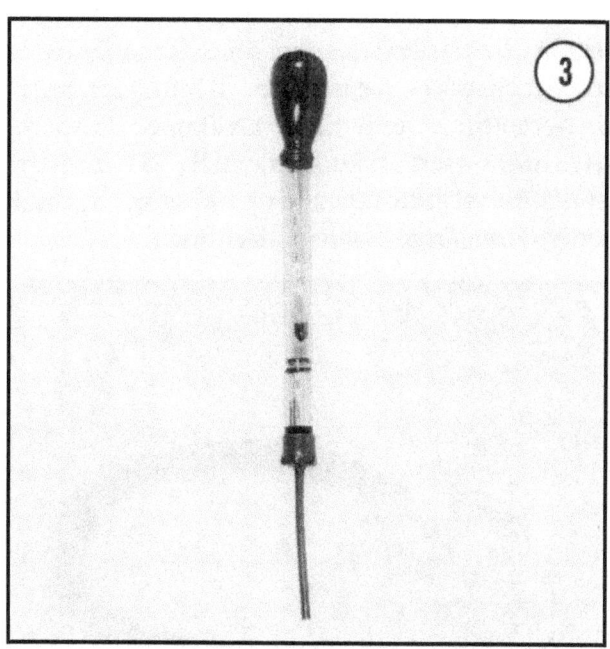

3. *Multimeter or VOM* (**Figure 4**). This instrument is invaluable for electrical system troubleshooting and service. A few of its functions may be duplicated by locally fabricated substitutes but for the serious hobbyist it is a must. Its uses are described in the applicable sections of this manual. Prices start at around $10 at electronics hobbyist stores and mail order outlets.

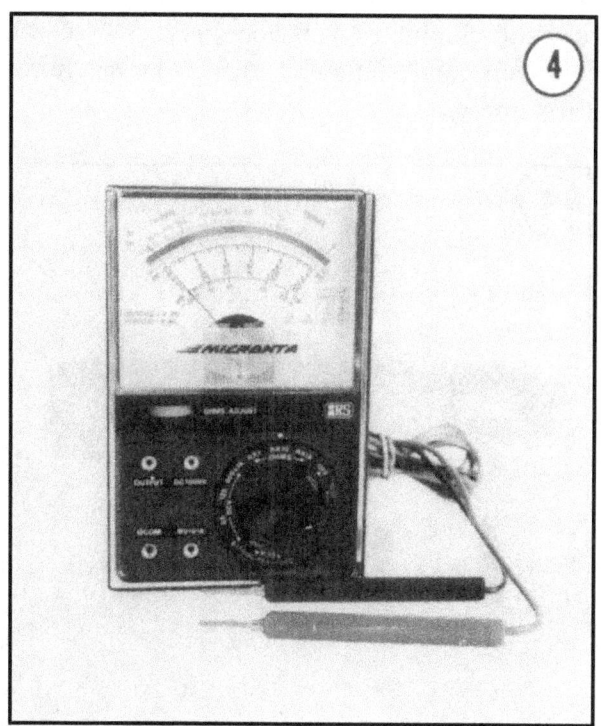

4. *Compression gauge* (**Figure 5**). An engine with low compression cannot be properly tuned and will not develop full power. A compression gauge measures engine compression. The one shown has a flexible stem which enables it to reach cylinders where there is little clearance between the cylinder head and frame. Inexpensive ones start at approximately $3 and are available at auto accessory stores or by mail order from large catalog order firms.

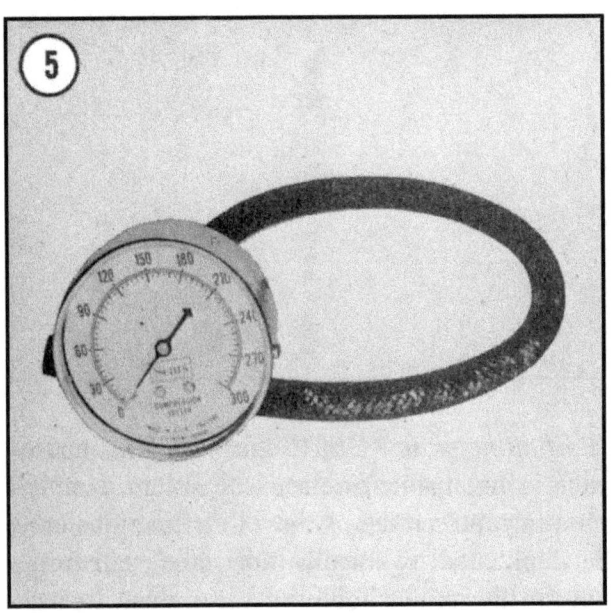

5. *Impact driver* (**Figure 6**). This tool might have been designed with the motorcyclist in mind. It makes removal of engine cover screws easy and eliminates damaged screw slots. Good ones run approximately $12 at larger hardware stores.

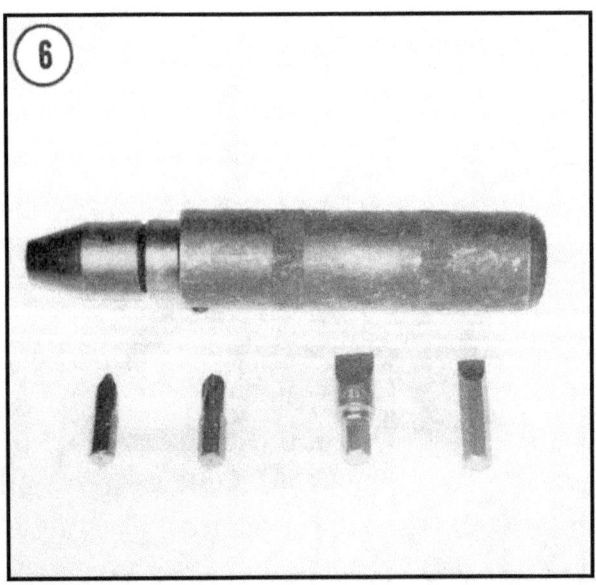

6. *Ignition gauge* (**Figure 7**). This tool measures spark plug gap and breaker point gap.

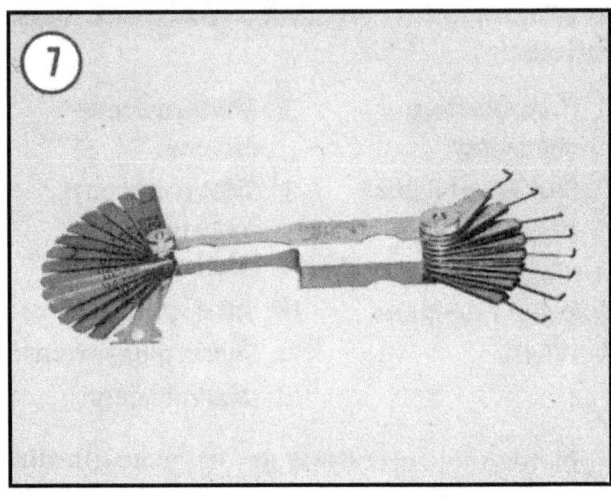

EXPENDABLE SUPPLIES

Required expendable supplies include grease, oil, gasket cement, wiping rags, cleaning solvent, and distilled water. Ask a dealer for the special locking compounds, silicone lubricants, and commercial chain lube products. Solvent is available at most service stations. Distilled water for the battery may be obtained at almost any supermarket.

SERIAL NUMBERS

The model serial number must be available for the sake of registration and when ordering parts. These numbers can be permanently recorded by placing a sheet of paper over the imprinted area and rubbing with the side of a pencil. Some motor vehicle registration offices will accept such evidence in lieu of inspecting the bike in person.

LOCATION OF CONTROLS

The new rider must become familiar with the location and use of the controls, listed below, prior to riding for the first time.

1. Front brake lever
2. Rear brake lever
3. Clutch lever
4. Gearshift lever
5. Ignition
6. Kill switch, if equipped
7. Throttle
8. Kickstarter
9. Lights
10. Horn

CHAPTER TWO

LUBRICATION, PERIODIC MAINTENANCE, AND TUNE-UP

Regular maintenance is the best guarantee of a trouble-free motorcycle. An afternoon spent cleaning and adjusting can minimize costly mechanical problems and unexpected breakdowns on the road.

This chapter provides a guide for all required preventive maintenance and procedures for a tune-up. Anyone with average mechanical ability can perform the procedures.

MAINTENANCE/LUBRICATION SCHEDULE

Maintenance and lubrication intervals are shown in **Table 1**. In addition to the items listed in the table, the following parts should be carefully inspected after the first 24 months.
 a. Brake cable
 b. Brake light switches
 c. Fuel lines

TOOLS

The basic tools needed for maintenance are listed in Chapter One. In addition, equipment required for a complete tune-up include a stroboscopic timing light, a dial indicator, and sets of flat and round feeler gauges.

OIL CHANGING

Transmission oil should be drained while the engine is warm.

1. Remove the drain plug beneath the crankcase. Allow the oil to drain for approximately 10 minutes.

2. Tilting the engine helps the oil to flow around obstacles inside the transmission to the drain hole.

3. Check the plug and gasket for wear or damage. Replace if necessary.

4. Use a good grade of SAE 30 motor oil to refill. Add oil through the inspection plate on the primary cover.

5. Change oil the first time for a new bike at 600 miles (960 km) and every 2,000 miles (3,200 km) thereafter (or every 6 months, whichever occurs first). Off-road use dictates more frequent intervals based on use and severity of road conditions.

DRIVE CHAIN

The chain is one of the most neglected parts of a motorcycle. It is seldom adjusted properly and only rarely lubricated. Special foaming lubes are available which can enter and lubri-

Table 1   LUBRICATION AND MAINTENANCE

		Months or miles (Km), whichever comes first				
	Months	—	6	12	18	24
Service Required	Miles Km	600 1,000	3,000 5,000	6,000 10,000	9,000 15,000	12,000 20,000
Engine						
Service spark plug			X	X	X	X
Adjust ignition timing		X	X	X	X	X
Check ignition wiring				X		X
Service air cleaner			X	X	X	X
Adjust carburetor			X	X	X	X
Check throttle operation			X	X	X	X
Clutch						
Adjust clutch		X	X	X	X	X
Battery						
Service battery		X	X	X	X	X
Fuel System						
Clean fuel valve filter			X	X	X	X
Check fuel tank and fuel lines			X	X	X	X
Steering and Front Suspension						
Check steering head bearings				X		X
Check steering handle lock				X		X
Check handlebar holder			X	X	X	X
Check front fork top plate			X	X	X	X
Check front fork bottom case			X	X	X	X
Change front fork oil				X		X
Rear Suspension						
Grease swing arm			X	X	X	X
Check rear suspension mounting bolts			X	X	X	X
Wheels and Brakes						
Check front and rear wheel spokes		X	X	X	X	X
Check front and rear wheel rims and hubs			X	X	X	X
Check front and rear wheels, bearings, and axles				X		X

(continued)

Table 1   LUBRICATION AND MAINTENANCE   (continued)

Service Required		600 Miles / 1,000 Km	6 Months / 3,000 Miles / 5,000 Km	12 Months / 6,000 Miles / 10,000 Km	18 Months / 9,000 Miles / 15,000 Km	24 Months / 12,000 Miles / 20,000 Km
Wheels and Brakes (continued)						
Check front and rear tires			X	X	X	X
Check and adjust brake pedal		X	X	X	X	X
Check front and rear brake shoe linings				X		X
Check rear brake stopper arm			X	X	X	X
Chassis and Final Drive						
Check frame			X	X	X	X
Check exhaust system			X	X	X	X
Check side stand			X	X	X	X
Service and adjust final drive chain		X	X	X	X	X
Check final drive and driven sprockets				X		X
Lights and Accessories						
Check lights and switches			X	X	X	X
Check horn			X	X	X	X
Check speedometer and tachometer			X	X	X	X

cate the inner rollers and are less likely to fly away due to centrifugal force.

Inspection/Service

1. Periodically inspect the chain for dryness and lubricate with the special foaming lube or with an oil soaked brush. Wipe off excess oil.

2. Every 1,000 miles (1,600 km), remove the chain. If a piece of old chain is available, connect it to the chain on the bike before it is removed and leave the old chain around the driving sprocket to make chain installation easier.

3. Clean the chain thoroughly with kerosene or solvent; use a wire brush to loosen grit and grease deposits. Hang up the chain and allow it to air dry.

4. Inspect the chain for wear and try to work out any kinks. Place the chain alongside a 12-inch scale and compress the links together. See **Figure 1**. Then stretch the chain while holding

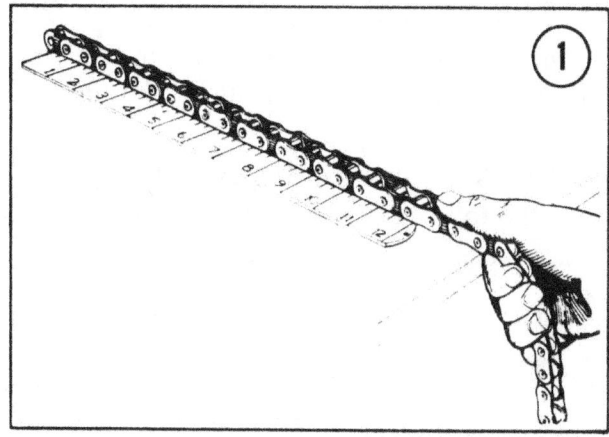

one end fixed. If more than ¼ inch movement in the 12 inch length of chain is possible, it is too worn to be used again. Replace if necessary.

5. Place the chain in a container of motor oil for 24 hours or more. Hang the chain up by one end and allow it to drip for several hours.

6. Apply a good quality chain lube and install the chain.

7. Install the master link so that the clip opening faces opposite to the direction of chain movement. See **Figure 2**. Failure to do so may result in the loss of the clip and damage to the chain.

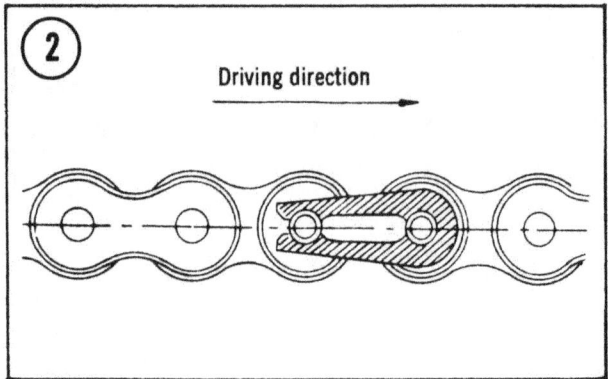

Adjustment

1. Support the motorcycle so the rear wheel is free to rotate.
2. Place the transmission in neutral and rotate the rear wheel to take up the slack in the top loop of the chain.
3. Check the up-and-down play in the lower loop of the chain at a point midway between the sprockets and with a rider on the bike. The movement should be approximately one inch. See **Figure 3**.
4. Loosen axle nut.
5. Turn the adjusters, which bear against the axle, to obtain the recommended play in the chain.
6. Check straightness of the chain by sighting along the top run of the chain from a few feet behind the bike. Adjust as necessary and check free play of the chain again.
7. Check the sprocket and its alignment as detailed below.

REAR SPROCKET

Check the sprocket for wear or damaged teeth. **Figure 4** shows how a worn gear may appear. Proper chain lubrication and proper tightness of the mounting bolts can prolong sprocket life.

A misaligned sprocket can be detected by sighting along the top run of the drive chain from a few feet behind the bike.

CHANGING FORK OIL

Front forks must have the same amount of oil in each fork leg to operate properly. Leakage may mean that the fork seals and O-rings need to be replaced. Fork oil generally should be changed twice yearly. Change more frequently if the bike is used off-road or in racing. If the forks begin to malfunction, check first to see that each has the proper amount of oil.

1. Remove the drain plug and fiber washer from the bottom rear of each fork leg (see **Figure 5**).
2. Apply the front brake and pump repeatedly on the handlebars to pump the oil out of the forks.
3. Check the drain plugs and fiber washers for wear or damage. Replace if necessary and install them in the fork legs.

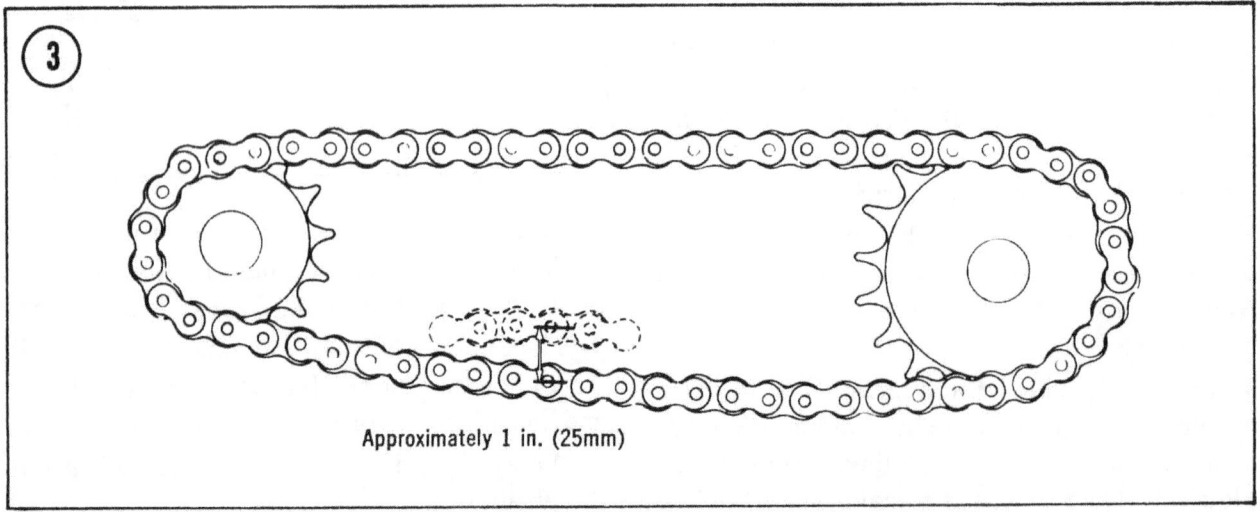

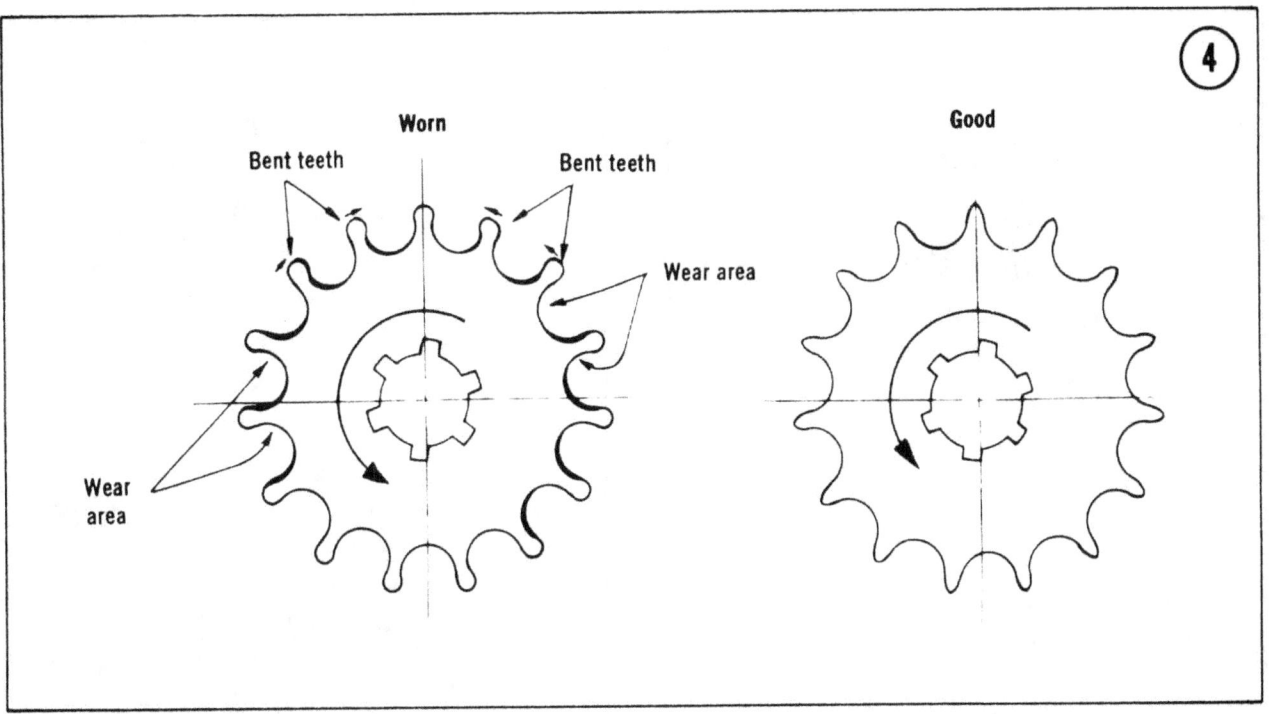

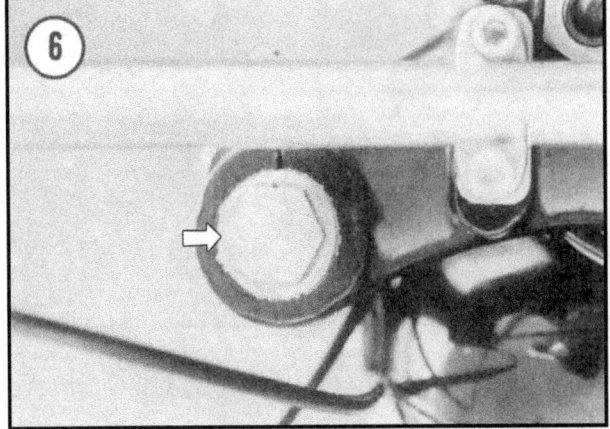

5. Pour 190-200cc of SAE 30 motor oil into each fork tube, for riding temperatures of 30-90°F (0-32°C). Above or below these temperatures or for unusual riding conditions, use a heavier or lighter oil for proper damping.

6. Remove the nut on the bottom of each fork tube cap nut (see **Figure 7**) and remove the ball and spring inside.

7. Carefully clean all parts in solvent, blow dry with air, and reassemble. Check the O-ring on each cap nut for wear or damage and replace if necessary.

8. Screw the cap nuts into the fork tubes by hand as far as possible. Torque to 50 ft.-lb.

9. Put the front wheel on the ground and pump the forks up and down. If oil comes out of the hole in the cap nut, or if you can hear air leaking,

4. Prop up the motorcycle with the front wheel off the ground. Remove the cap nuts from the top of the fork tubes (see **Figure 6**).

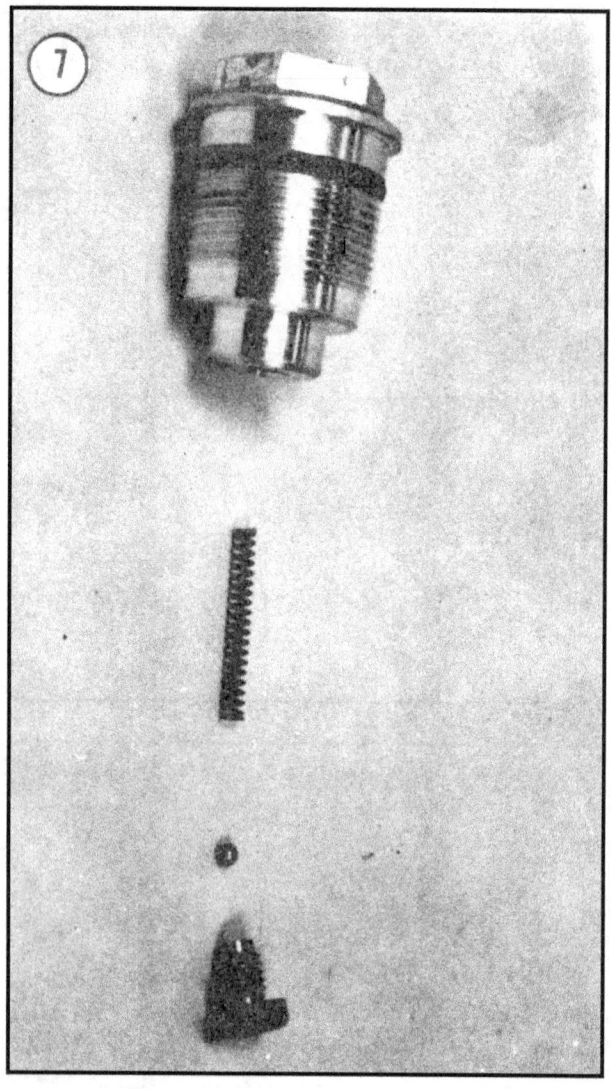

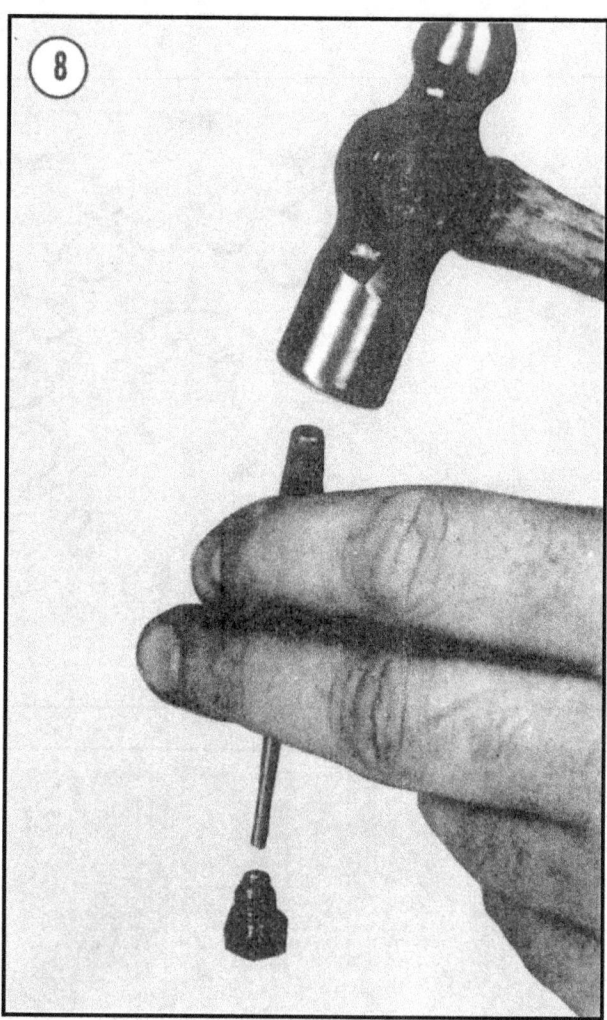

prop the front wheel off the ground and remove the cap nut.

10. Remove the nut, ball, and spring from the cap nut and check again for wear or damage.

11. Lay the nut on a bench and place the ball on it. See **Figure 8**.

12. Tap the ball lightly with a soft metal punch to reseat it. Be sure to use a brass, copper, or aluminum punch; not steel.

13. Install the components again and torque the cap nut to 50 ft.-lb.

14. Pump the forks up and down. If there is still an oil or air leak, remove the bottom nut, ball, and spring, and replace them.

CONTROL CABLES

Control cables should be lubricated at their exposed ends every 1,000 miles (1,600 km) with light oil. Occasionally remove them and soak in oil so their entire length is properly lubricated. Place in a pan filled with 30 weight motor oil for at least 8 hours.

SPEEDOMETER CABLE

Lubricate the speedometer cable by disconnecting it from the speedometer and removing the inner cable. Clean and grease it lightly along its entire length except for the top 6 inches. Replace the inner cable, turning it to ensure that its end is inserted in the drive mechanism and reconnect the outer cable at the speedometer. A jumping or vibrating speedometer needle usually means that lubrication is needed.

BRAKE LEVER

Remove the brake lever occasionally. Remove rust with emery cloth. Clean the spindle and lever bore and grease them.

ENGINE TUNE-UP

When a tune-up is needed, the following guide will be helpful. Check the engine carefully and proceed systematically. Consult Chapter Three for troubleshooting any suspected malfunction.

A thorough tune-up should also include a check of the power head and complete lubrication of moving parts. The first 4 steps of the following procedure may be skipped during a minor tune-up if the components listed are known to be in good shape from a previous overhaul. Complete and detailed procedures for Steps 5-9 are included in this manual.

1. Remove the cylinder head. See *Cylinder and Piston,* Chapter Six.

2. Slowly rotate the flywheel and check for scored cylinder walls, cracked rings, carbon deposits, and excessive wear. Correct as necessary.

3. Clean carbon from the piston crown and cylinder head, being careful not to damage the piston or alter its shape.

4. Inspect the battery and all wiring.

5. Check the timing; adjust if necessary.

6. Drain and refill the crankcase; lubricate all moving parts.

7. Inspect the fuel lines, air cleaner, filter screens on petcocks and carburetor banjo, and the breather tube on the fuel tank. Clean if necessary.

8. Inspect, clean, and regap or replace the spark plug as needed.

9. Inspect the carburetor. Refer to *Idle Test and Adjustment* and *Final Test and Adjustment* under *Carburetor Adjustment* in Chapter Four. Check performance at high, medium, and low speeds and while idling; adjust the carburetor if necessary.

10. Clean the carbon out of the exhaust pipe with a wire brush. If the deposits are too heavy to remove with a brush, heat the baffle tube with a torch and tap the tube lightly. Clean the carbon from the exhaust pipe by running a used drive chain through the pipe.

11. Tighten all screws, nuts, and bolts to the torque values specified in the Appendix.

AIR CLEANER

A clogged air cleaner can decrease the efficiency and the life of the engine. Even minute particles of dust can cause severe wear, so never run without a filter.

Check the air filter every 2,000 miles or more often. Dirt riding will make it necessary to check the filter after every ride.

Replace the element if it is clogged with dirt, caked with oil, or if it shows deterioration.

Light dust can be shaken off the element by tapping it while using a soft brush on the outside. If necessary, carefully blow compressed air through the element from the inside.

If the bike has a wet foam filter, clean it in kerosene. Allow the foam filter to air dry, dip it in lightweight oil, squeeze out the excess oil, and insert it in the stock housing.

FUEL STRAINER

The fuel strainer filters out particles which might otherwise enter the carburetor and cause the float needle valve to remain open. Such particles also tend to get into the engine and cause damage.

Remove the fuel strainer and clean during each tune-up. Clean the strainer with solvent and blow dry with compressed air.

BATTERY

The battery should be serviced as part of every tune-up. Complete battery service procedures are given in Chapter Five. As a minimum, the following points should be checked at every tune-up (preferably more often).

1. Test state of battery charge. Recharge if at half charge (1.220 specific gravity) or less.

2. Add distilled water if required.

3. Clean the battery and battery holder with baking soda and water.

4. Clean and tighten terminals. Coat the terminals lightly with Vaseline or a silicone grease to retard corrosion.

ELECTRICAL EQUIPMENT

Lights

Check periodically for satisfactory operation of the lights. Be sure that stoplight switches are adjusted so that the stoplight is on before braking action begins. Check to see that all connections, particularly ground connections for all electrical equipment, are tight and free of corrosion.

See Chapter Five for procedure on headlight adjustment.

Horn

The tone may be adjusted by turning the adjustment screw on the rear of the horn.

SPARK PLUG

Spark plugs are available in various heat ranges hotter or colder than the plug originally installed at the factory.

Select a plug of a heat range designed for the loads and temperature conditions under which the engine will run. Incorrect heat range can cause a seized piston, scored cylinder wall, or damaged piston crown.

In general, use a lower-numbered plug for low speeds, low loads, and low temperatures. Use a higher-numbered plug for high speeds, high engine loads, and high temperatures.

> NOTE: *Use the highest numbered plug that will not foul.. In areas where seasonal temperature variations are great, the factory recommends a high-numbered plug for slow winter operation.*

The reach (length) of a plug is also important. A longer than normal plug could interfere with the piston, causing permanent and severe damage. Refer to **Figures 9 and 10**.

Testing

A quick and simple test can be made to determine if the plug is correct for your type of use. Accelerate hard and maintain a high, steady speed. Shut the throttle off and kill the engine simultaneously; allow the bike to slow (out of gear). Do not allow the engine to slow the bike.

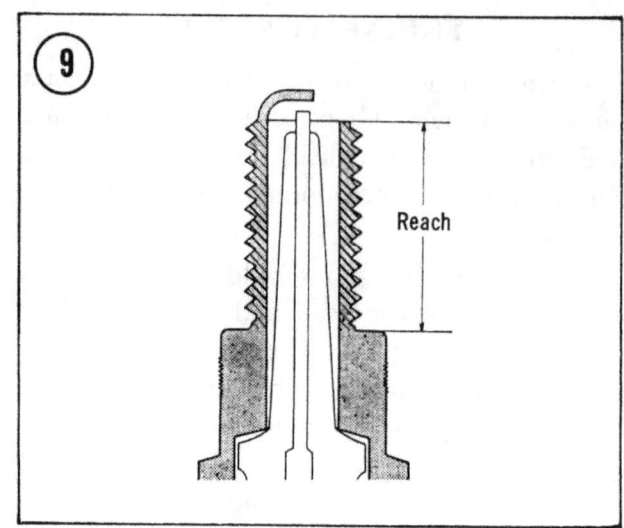

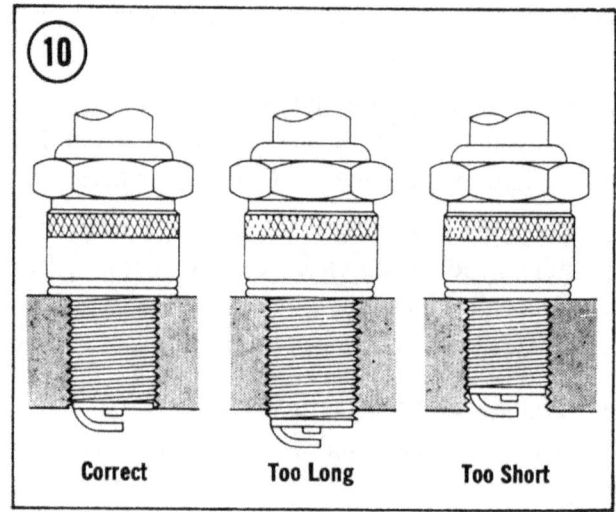

Remove the plug and check the condition of the electrode area. A spark plug of the correct heat range, with the engine in a proper state of tune, will appear light tan. See **Figure 11**.

If the insulator is white or burned, the plug is too hot and should be replaced with a colder one. Also, check the setting of the carburetor, it may be too lean.

A too-cold plug will have sooty deposits ranging in color from dark brown to black. Replace with a hotter plug and check for too-rich carburetion.

Removal/Installation

Remove and clean the spark plug frequently. Inspect the plug for worn or eroded electrodes. Replace it if there is any doubt about its condition. If the plug is found to be serviceable, file the center electrode square and adjust the gap by bending the outer electrode only. Measure

Normal plug appearance noted by the brown to grayish-tan deposits and light electrode wear. This plug indicates the correct plug heat range and proper air/fuel ratio.

Red, brown, yellow, and white coatings caused by fuel and oil additives. Such additives should not be used or damage will result.

Carbon fouling distinguished by dry, fluffy black carbon deposits which may be caused by an over-rich air/fuel mixture, excessive hand choking, clogged air filter, or excessive idling.

Shiny yellow glaze on insulator cone is caused when the powdery deposits from fuel and oil additives melt. Melting occurs during hard acceleration after prolonged idling. This glaze conducts electricity and shorts out the plug. Avoid the use of additives at all times.

Oil fouling indicated by wet, oily deposits caused by too much oil in the mix. A hotter plug temporarily reduces oil deposits, but a plug that is too hot leads to preignition and possible engine damage.

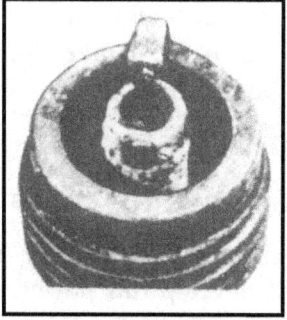

Overheated plug indicated by burned or blistered insulator tip and badly worn electrodes. This condition may be caused by preignition, cooling system defects, lean air/fuel ratios, low octane fuel, or over advanced ignition timing.

the gap with a round wire spark plug gauge only; a flat gauge will yield an incorrect reading. Set the gap at 0.02 in. (0.5mm). See **Figure 12**.

If there is difficulty in removing the spark plug, apply penetrating oil to the base of the plug and allow time for the oil to work in. Be sure to clean the seating area on the cylinder head and use a new gasket when replacing the spark plug. Install the plug finger-tight, then tighten it an additional ½ turn. Remember that a faulty spark plug is the greatest cause of starting failures in 2-stroke engines.

COMPRESSION TEST

If compression is low for any reason, the engine will not develop full power. Proceed as follows for a compression test:

1. Warm up the engine to operating temperature. Stop the engine.
2. Remove the spark plug.
3. Screw a compression gauge into the spark plug hole. If a press-in type gauge is used, hold it firmly in position.
4. Keep the ignition in the OFF position, crank the engine with the kickstarter and read the compression gauge. The compression gauge reading will increase with each operation of the kickstarter for the first few operations. Record the reading.

5. Repeatedly crank the engine until the compression gauge reading is the same for succcessive readings; for example:

1st kick	75 psi
2nd kick	105 psi
3rd kick	120 psi
4th kick	125 psi
5th kick	125 psi

Because of differences in engine design, carbon deposits and other factors, definite compression readings cannot be specified for any one engine. A series of measurements made over a period of time, however, may reveal an indication of trouble ahead, long before the engine exhibits other serious symptoms. Make and record the first compression reading when the bike is new and every 2,000 miles thereafter. An example is given in **Table 2**.

Table 2 COMPRESSION

Mileage (miles)	Compression Pressure (psi)
Zero	130
2,000	125
4,000	125
6,000	120
8,000	95

A difference of 20% between successive compression test readings over a period of time, if made under identical conditions, is an indication of trouble. If the compression reading for the bike was taken for the first time at 8,000 miles (see Table 2), a reading of 95 psi might be considered normal but, compared with the engine's history, it is an indication of trouble.

For the tests outlined, the serious motorcyclist will want to own and use his own compression gauge and also keep a permanent record of the test readings.

NOTE: *Readings taken with different gauges are not necessarily conclusive, because of production tolerances, calibration errors, and other factors.*

IGNITION TIMING

Timing Adjustment (Static)

1. Remove the magneto side cover. Two guide pins on the engine case may hold onto the cover after the screws have been removed. If so, push the clutch actuating arm inward to force the cover off the guide pins. Be sure to retrieve the clutch actuating plunger in removing the cover. The plunger is a small round part which fits into the clutch actuating assembly.

2. Rotate the flywheel to position the small hole in the face of the flywheel approximately at the 5 o'clock position. See **Figure 13**.

3. Insert a timing pin (obtainable from an Ossa dealer) and move the flywheel back and forth until the pin is also inserted into the matching hole in the stator. This is the flywheel position at which the spark plug fires.

4. Obtain a dial indicator kit. See **Figure 14**. Remove the spark plug and screw the adapter into the spark plug hole. Insert the plunger through the adapter and install the dial indicator in the adapter.

5. Push the dial indicator down until the needle has completed approximately one revolution.

Tighten the lock screw on the adapter to lock the indicator in place.

6. Rotate the dial face so the large needle reads zero. See **Figure 15**.

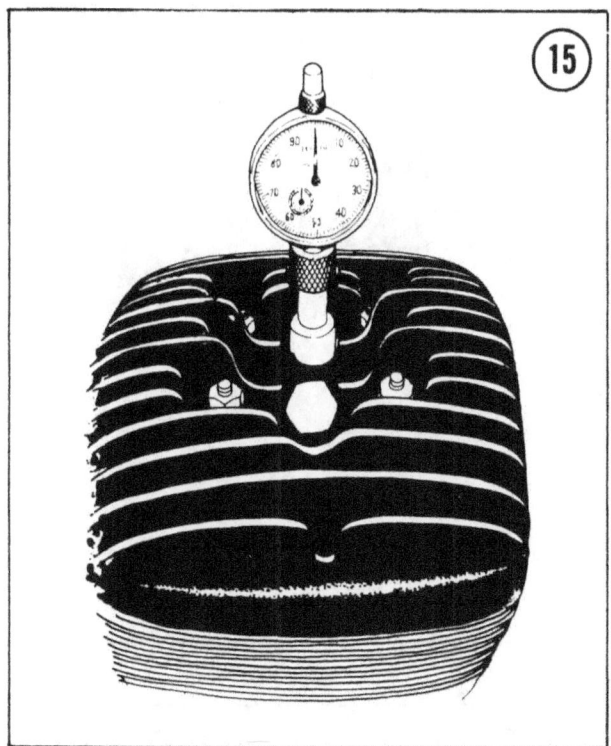

7. Remove the timing pin from the flywheel and rotate the flywheel both ways slightly. If the needle does not move every time the flywheel does, the dial gauge plunger is too short and must be replaced.

8. Put the timing pin back into the flywheel and stator. Check to see that dial needle is at zero.

9. Remove the timing pin and turn the flywheel clockwise until the dial gauge needle stops moving. Count the number of complete revolutions the needle makes before it stops moving. The flywheel position then corresponds to top dead center (TDC) for the piston.

10. At TDC, read the fraction showing on the dial gauge and add to it the number of complete revolutions the flywheel made. For example, if the needle made 2 complete revolutions and stopped at 0.72 (metric scale), the ignition timing is 2.72mm BTDC.

Refer to **Table 3** for correct timing for 1971 and later Ossa motorcycles.

11. If the measured timing is not within the tolerance, remove the flywheel following procedures given in the *Magneto* section, Chapter Six.

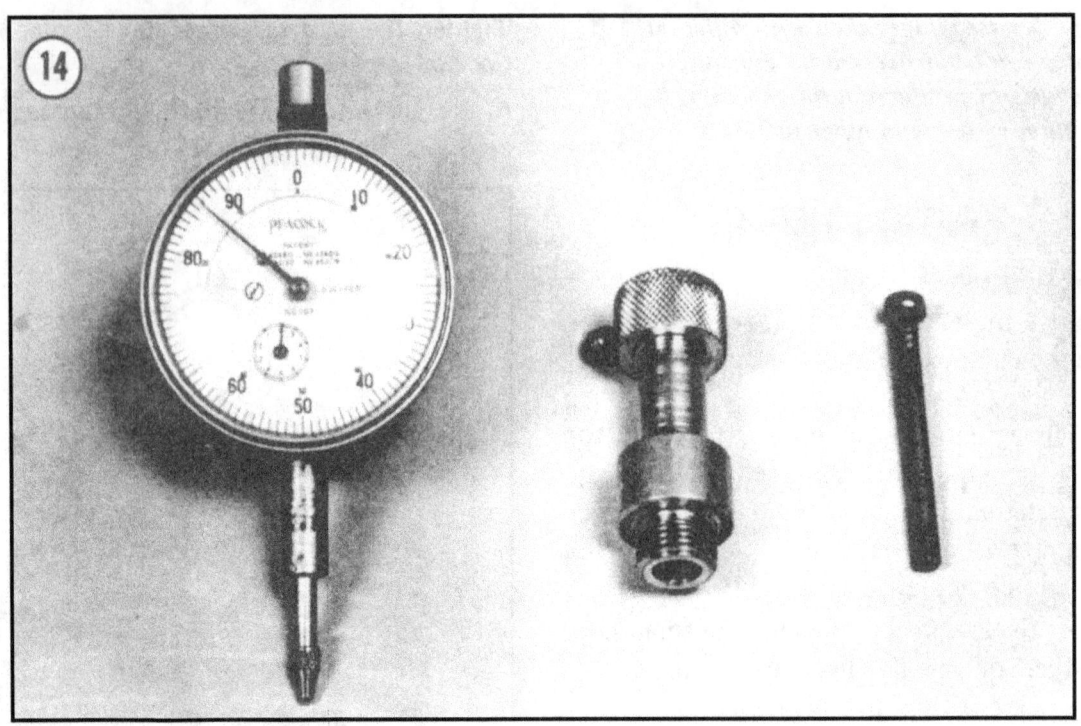

Table 3 TIMING

Model	Timing
250 Pioneer	2.75-3.0mm BTDC
250 Stiletto, TT, & D.M.R.	3.0mm BTDC
250 Plonker	2.5-3.0mm BTDC
175 Plonker	2.25-2.5mm BTDC
175 Stiletto	2.5-2.75mm BTDC

12. Loosen the stator mounting screws.

13. If the measured timing is less than given in the table, rotate the stator counterclockwise slightly. If it is more, rotate the stator clockwise.

14. Tighten the stator mounting screws and install the flywheel following procedures given in the *Magneto* section of Chapter Six.

15. Check the timing again. Repeat this procedure until the timing is within the tolerance.

16. Remove the dial indicator, plunger, and adapter.

17. Follow Steps 6-16 of *Magneto Installation* section, Chapter Six, to complete installation.

Timing Adjustment (Strobe)

If the ignition is erratic and spark plug readings are not consistent, and the motorcycle is lacking in power, it is possible that the magneto is producing the spark at the wrong time even though properly timed using the timing pin and dial indicator. Use of a stroboscopic timing light gives a definitive answer as to whether the timing is correct. Set the timing as described above before stroboscopically checking as detailed below:

1. Follow Steps 1-3 under *Ignition Timing* above.

2. With the timing pin still in place, make a reference line on the flywheel and engine case. See **Figure 16**. Remove the timing pin.

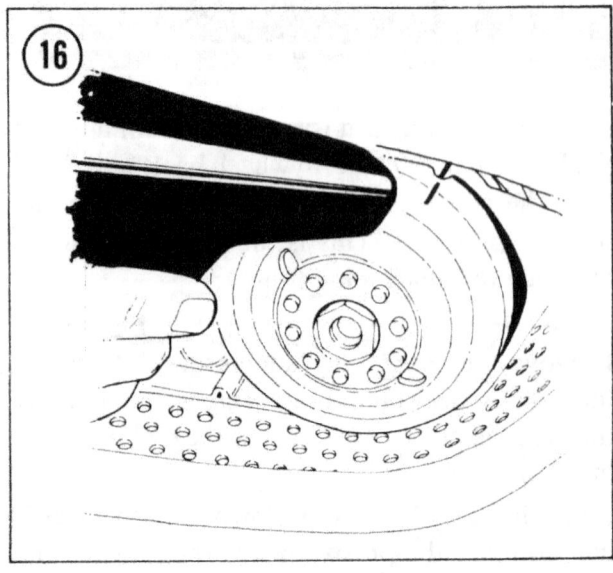

3. Connect the strobe timing light to the plug wire following the manufacturer's instructions.

4. Run the engine at idling speed.

5. Observe the relative position of the 2 marks as the timing light illuminates the marks. The flywheel mark should consistently appear to be slightly to the right of the case mark.

6. Increase engine speed to approximately 6,000 rpm and hold. The timing is fully advanced at this engine speed and the marks should now appear to be aligned.

7. If the marks do not align, remove the flywheel and rotate the position of the stator as detailed previously. Turn the stator left or right an equivalent distance as the flywheel mark was left or right of the case mark. Install the flywheel as detailed previously and check the marks again with the timing light.

8. If the mark alignment is erratic, i.e., if firing is occurring at varying relative positions of the 2 marks, replace the magneto and recheck timing.

9. Follow Steps 6-16 of *Magneto Installation* section, Chapter Six, to complete installation.

CARBURETOR

The carburetor normally will not require adjustment during a tune-up, except possibly at idling speed, unless it is disassembled. It should be worked on only as a last resort when all other possible causes of such problems as rough idling or misfiring have been checked out. See Chapter Four for detailed procedures for the carburetor. For adjustment at idling speed:

1. Warm up engine to operating temperature.

2. Reduce the engine speed to idling speed. Adjust the carburetor idle mixture and speed. Turn the low-speed air screw clockwise for richer and counterclockwise for leaner mixture.

DECARBONIZATION

After an engine has been run for many hours it will probably require the removal of carbon from the piston crown and cylinder head. The best way to detect this need is if the engine has shown progressively worsening preignition or a gradual loss of power. Several new products are now being marketed to allow a simple approach to decarbonizing without the need of dismantling the engine. These products will not be as thorough, but can be used periodically. The procedure for their use is given on the container. If this fails to completely decarbonize the cylinder then you will have to remove the head as outlined in Chapter Six.

MISCELLANEOUS

Inspect the entire bike carefully, examining it for loose spokes, bent wheels, damaged or worn tires, oil leaks, or anything else which could result in unsafe riding conditions or cause major problems later. Correct any such condition at once.

STORAGE

Several months of inactivity can cause serious problems and a general deterioration of the bike. This is especially true in areas of weather extremes. During the winter months it's advisable to specially prepare the bike for lay-up.

Selecting a Storage Area

Most cyclists store their bikes in their home garage. If you do not have a garage, facilities suitable for long-term motorcycle storage are readily available for rent or lease in most areas. In selecting a building, consider the following points:

1. The storage area must be dry, free from dampness and excessive humidity. Heating is not necessary but the building should be well insulated to minimize extreme temperature variations.

2. Buildings with large window areas should be avoided, or such windows should be masked (also a good security measure) if direct sunlight can fall on the bike.

3. Buildings in industrial areas, where factories are liable to emit corrosive fumes, are not desirable, nor are facilities near bodies of salt water.

4. The area should be selected to minimize the possibility of loss by fire, theft, or vandalism. The area should be fully insured, perhaps with

a package covering fire, theft, vandalism, weather, and liability. The advice of your insurance agent should be solicited on these matters. The building should be fire-proof and items such as the security of doors and windows, alarm facilities and proximity of police should be considered.

Preparing for Storage

Careful pre-storage preparation will minimize deterioration and will ease restoring the bike to service in the spring. The following procedure is recommended:

1. Wash the bike completely making certain to remove any accumulation of road salt that may have collected during the first weeks of winter. Wax all painted and polished surfaces.

2. Run the engine for 20-30 minutes to stabilize oil temperature. Drain transmission oil regardless of mileage since last oil change and replace with normal quantity of fresh oil.

3. Remove battery and coat cable terminals with petroleum jelly. If there is evidence of acid spillage in the battery box, neutralize with baking soda, wash clean, and repaint. Batteries should be kept in an area where they will not freeze, and where they can be recharged every 2 weeks.

4. Drain all gasoline from fuel tank, settling bowl, and carburetor float bowls. Leave fuel cock on the RESERVE position.

5. Remove spark plug and add a small quantity of oil to the cylinder. Turn the engine a few revolutions by hand. Install spark plug.

6. Check tire pressure. Move bike to storage area and place on center stand. If preparation is performed in an area remote from the storage facility, the bike should be trucked, not ridden, into storage.

Inspection During Storage

Try to inspect the bike weekly while it is in storage. Any deterioration should be corrected as soon as possible. For example, if corrosion of bright metal parts is observed, coat with a light film of grease or silicone spray.

Restoring to Service

A bike that has been properly prepared, and stored in a suitable area, requires only light maintenance to restore it to service. It is advisable, however, to perform a tune-up.

1. Before removing the bike from the storage area, re-inflate tires to the correct pressures. Air loss during the storage period may have nearly flattened the tires, and moving the bike can cause damage to tires, tubes, or rims.

2. When the bike is brought to the work area, immediately install the battery (fully charged) and fill the fuel tank. (The fuel cock should be on the RESERVE position; do not move yet.)

3. Check the fuel system for leaks. Remove the carburetor float bowl or open the float bowl drain cock and allow several cups of fuel to pass through the system. Move the fuel cock slowly to the CLOSE position, remove the settling bowl and empty any accumulated water.

4. Perform a normal tune-up and while checking the spark plug add a few drops of oil to the cylinder.

5. Check safety items, i.e., lights, horn, etc., as oxidation of switch contacts and/or sockets during storage may make one or more of these critical devices inoperative.

6. Test ride and clean the motorcycle.

CHAPTER THREE

TROUBLESHOOTING

Diagnosing mechanical problems is relatively simple if orderly procedures are used and a few basic principles are kept in mind.

The troubleshooting procedures in this chapter analyze typical symptoms, and show logical methods of isolating causes. These methods are not the only ones. There may be several ways to solve a problem, but only a systematic, methodical approach can guarantee success.

Never assume anything. Do not overlook the obvious. If, while riding along, the engine suddenly quits, check the easiest, most accessible problem spots first. Is there gasoline in the tank? Is the gas petcock in the ON or RESERVE position? Has a spark plug wire fallen off? Check the ignition switch. Sometimes the weight of keys on a key ring may turn the ignition off suddenly.

If nothing obvious turns up in a cursory check, look a little further. Learning to recognize and describe symptoms wlil make repairs easier at home or by a mechanic at the shop. Describe problems accurately and fully. Saying that "it won't run" isn't the same as saying "it quit on the highway at high speed and wouldn't start," or that "it sat in my garage for 3 months and then wouldn't start."

Gather as many symptoms together as possible to aid in diagnosis. Note whether the engine lost power gradually or all at once, what color smoke (if any) came from the exhaust, and so on. Remember that the more complicated a machine is, the easier it is to troubleshoot because symptoms point to specific problems.

After the symptoms are defined, areas which could cause the problems are tested and analyzed. Guessing at the cause of a problem may provide the solution, but it can easily lead to frustration, wasted time, and a series of expensive, unnecessary replacement of parts.

Neither fancy equipment nor complicated test gear is needed to determine whether repairs can be attempted at home. A few simple checks could save a large repair bill and time lost while the bike sits in a dealer's service department. On the other hand, be realistic and don't attempt repairs beyond your abilities. Service departments tend to charge heavily for putting together a disassembled engine that may have been abused. Some won't even take on such a job—so use common sense, do not get in too deeply.

OPERATING REQUIREMENTS

An engine needs 3 basics to run properly; correct gas/air mixture, compression, and a spark at the right time. If one or more are missing, the engine will not run. The electrical system is the weakest link of the three. More problems result from electrical breakdowns than from any other source. Keep that in mind before you begin tampering with carburetor adjustments and the like.

If a bike has been sitting for any length of time and refuses to start, check the battery (if so equipped) for a charged condition first, and then inspect the gasoline delivery system. This includes the tank, fuel petcock, lines, and carburetor. Rust may have formed in the tank, obstructing fuel flow. Gasoline deposits may have gummed up carburetor jets and air passages. Gasoline tends to lose its potency after standing for long periods. Condensation may contaminate it with water. Drain old gas and try starting with a fresh tankful.

TROUBLESHOOTING INSTRUMENTS

Chapter One lists many of the instruments needed and gives detailed instructions on their use.

STARTING DIFFICULTIES

Check gas flow first. Remove the gas cap and look into the tank. If gas is present, pull off a fuel line at the carburetor and see if gas flows freely. If none comes out, the fuel tap may be shut off, blocked by rust or other foreign matter, or the fuel line may be stopped up or kinked. If the carburetor is getting usable fuel, inspect the electrical system next.

Check that the battery (if so equipped) is charged by turning on the lights or by beeping the horn. Refer to your owner's manual for starting procedures with a dead battery. Recharge the battery if necessary.

Pull off a spark plug cap, remove the spark plug, and reconnect the cap. Lay the plug against the cylinder head so its base makes a good connection, and turn the engine over with the kickstarter (engine rotation of at least 500 rpm). A fat, blue spark should jump across the electrodes. If there is no spark, or only a weak one, there is electrical system trouble. Check for a defective plug by replacing it with a known good one. Do not assume a plug is good just because it is new.

Once the plug has been cleared of malfunctioning but there is still no spark, start backtracking through the system. If the contact at the end of the spark plug wire can be exposed, it can be held about 1/8 inch from the head while the engine is turned over to check for a spark. Remember to hold the wire only by its insulation to avoid a nasty shock. If the plug wire is dirty, greasy, or wet, wrap a rag around it so you do not get shocked. If you do feel a shock or see sparks along the wire, clean or replace the wire and/or its connections.

If there is no spark at the plug wire, look for loose connections at the coil and battery. Refer to *Ignition System* section of this chapter for checkout procedures for the entire system and individual components. Refer to Chapter Two for checking and setting ignition timing.

Note that a spark plug of the incorrect heat range (too cold) may cause hard starting. Set gap to specification. If you have just ridden through a puddle or washed the bike and it won't start, dry off the plug and plug wire. Water may have entered the carburetor and fouled the fuel under these conditions, but a wet plug and wire are the more likely problem.

If a healthy spark occurs at the right time, and there is adequate gas flow to the carburetor, check the carburetor itself. Make sure all jets and air passages are clean. Check float level and adjust if necessary. Shake the float to check for gasoline inside it, and replace or repair as indicated. Check that the carburetor is mounted snugly and that no air is leaking past the manifold. Check for a clogged air filter.

Compression, or the lack of it, usually occurs only in the case of older bikes. Worn or broken pistons, rings, and cylinder bores could prevent starting. Generally, a gradual power loss and harder starting will be readily apparent in this case.

Compression may be checked in the field by turning the kickstarter by hand and noting that an adequate resistance is felt.

An accurate compression check gives a good idea of the condition of the basic working parts of the engine. See Chapter Two for detailed instructions on perofrming a compression test.

IDLING

Poor idling may be caused by incorrect carburetor adjustment, incorrect timing, or ignition system defects. Check the gas cap vent for an obstruction.

MISFIRING

Misfiring can be caused by a weak spark or a dirty plug. Check for fuel contamination. Run the machine at night to check for spark leaks along the plug wire and under spark plug cap.

WARNING
Do not run engine in closed garage to check for spark leaks. There is considerable danger of carbon monoxide poisoning, fire, or explosion.

If misfiring occurs only at certain throttle settings, refer to the fuel system chapter for the specific carburetor circuits involved. Misfiring under heavy load, as when climbing hills, or accelerating, is usually caused by a bad spark plug.

FLAT SPOTS

If the engine seems to die momentarily when the throttle is opened and then recovers, check for a dirty main jet in the carburetor, water in the fuel, or an excessively lean mixture.

POWER LOSS

Poor condition of rings, piston, or cylinder will cause a lack of power and speed. Ignition timing should be checked.

OVERHEATING

If the engine seems to run too hot all the time, be sure you are not idling it for long periods. Air-cooled engines are not designed to operate at a standstill for any length of time. Heavy stop-and-go traffic or slow hill-climbing is hard on a motorcycle engine. A spark plug of the wrong heat range can burn a piston. An excessively lean gas mixture may cause overheating. Check ignition timing. Do not ride in too high a gear. Broken or worn rings may permit compression gases to leak past them, heating the head and cylinder excessively. Check oil level and use the proper grade lubricants.

ENGINE NOISES

Experience is needed to diagnose accurately in this area. Noises are hard to differentiate and harder yet to describe. Deep knocking noises usually mean main bearing failure. A slapping noise generally comes from a loose piston. A light knocking noise during acceleration may be a bad connecting rod bearing. Pinging should be corrected immediately or damage to the piston will result. Compression leaks at the head-cylinder joint will sound like a rapid on-and-off squeal.

PISTON SEIZURE

Piston seizure is caused by incorrect piston clearances when fitted, fitting rings with improper end gap, too thin an oil being used, incorrect spark plug heat range, or incorrect ignition timing. Overheating from any cause may result in seizure.

EXCESSIVE VIBRATION

Excessive vibration may be caused by loose motor mounts, worn engine or transmission bearings, loose wheels, worn swinging arm bushings, a generally poor running engine, broken or cracked frame, or one that has been damaged in a collision. See also *Poor Handling*.

CLUTCH

Clutch slip may be due to worn plates, improper adjustment, or glazed plates. A dragging clutch could result from damaged or bent plates, improper adjustment, or even clutch spring pressure.

All clutch problems, except adjustments or cable replacement, require removal to identify the cause and make repairs.

1. *Slippage*—This condition is most noticeable when accelerating in high gear at relatively low speed. To check slippage, drive at a steady speed in fourth or fifth gear. Without letting up the accelerator, push in the clutch long enough

to let engine speed increase (1 or 2 seconds). Then let the clutch out rapidly. If the clutch is good, engine speed will drop quickly or the bike will jump forward. If the clutch is slipping, engine speed will drop slowly and the bike will not jump forward.

Slippage results from insufficient clutch lever free play, worn friction plates, or weak springs. Riding the clutch can cause the disc surfaces to become glazed, resulting in slippage.

2. *Drag or failure to release*—This trouble usually causes difficult shifting and gear clash especially when downshifting. The cause may be excessive clutch lever free play, warped or bent plates, stretched clutch cable, or broken or loose disc linings.

3. *Chatter or grabbing*—Check for worn or misaligned steel plate and clutch friction plates.

TRANSMISSION

Transmission problems are usually indicated by one or more of the following symptoms:

   a. Difficulty in shifting gears
   b. Gear clash when downshifting
   c. Slipping out of gear
   d. Excessive noise in neutral
   e. Excessive noise in gear

Transmission symptoms are sometimes hard to distinguish from clutch symptoms. Be sure the clutch is not causing the trouble before working on the transmission.

HANDLING

Poor handling may be caused by improper tire pressures, a damaged frame or swing arm, worn shocks or forks, weak springs, a bent or broken steering stem, misaligned wheels, loose or missing spokes, worn tires, bent handlebars, worn wheel bearings, or dragging brakes.

BRAKES

Sticking brakes may be caused by broken or weak return springs, improper cable or rod adjustment, or dry pivot and cam bushings. Grabbing brakes may be caused by greasy linings which must be replaced. Brake grab may also be due to out-of-round drums or linings which have broken loose from the brake shoes. Glazed linings or glazed brake pads will cause loss of stopping power.

ELECTRICAL

Bulbs which continuously burn out may be caused by excessive vibration, loose connections that permit sudden current surges, poor battery connections, or installation of the wrong type bulb.

A dead battery or one which discharges quickly may be caused by a faulty alternator. Check for loose or corroded terminals. Shorted battery cells or broken terminals will keep a battery from charging. Low water level will decrease a battery's capacity. A battery left uncharged after installation will sulphate, rendering it useless.

A majority of light and horn, or other electrical accessory, problems are caused by loose of corroded ground connections. Check these first, and then substitute known good units for easier troubleshooting. See specific systems following.

IGNITION SYSTEM

Troubleshooting the ignition system should be undertaken in an orderly sequence, as detailed below. Troubleshooting is best accomplished by substitution. There are, however, several checks which may be made with an ohmmeter. Because resistance readings will vary (depending on ohmmeter type, range used, and battery voltage), check the ohmmeter's accuracy by measuring the resistance of a known resistor.

1. Check the spark plug and its connector as described previously under *Starting Difficulties* section of this chapter.

2. Clean and tighten *all* connections in the ignition system. Be particularly sure that the connection between the coil mounting bracket and the motorcycle is clean, free of corrosion, and tight. Check the spark itself, as described under *Starting Difficulties* in this chapter.

3. Disconnect the blue wire from the ignition switch (if fitted) and check the spark. If the spark is good, test the switch further by following procedure in *Ignition Switch Test* section of this chapter.

4. Disconnect the blue and black leads at the high voltage coil. Connect the 2 leads of the ohmmeter to the terminals of the coil and read the resistance. Reverse the leads and read again. If either reading is less than 16 ohms or more than 38 ohms, install a new coil and check the spark.

5. Connect the negative lead from the ohmmeter to ground. Connect the positive lead in turn to the blue and black wires which are from the magneto stator. Both readings should be 235-280 ohms.

6. Reverse the ohmmeter leads and repeat the measurements made in Step 4. Both resistance readings should be essentially infinite.

7. Measure the resistance between the blue and black leads. Reverse the ohmmeter leads and read again. For the Pioneer and Plonker models, each reading should be 17-20 ohms. For the Stiletto, TT, and DMR, each reading should be 9-12 ohms.

8. Connect either ohmmeter lead to the coil mounting bracket. Connect the other lead to the spark plug lead. Resistance should be approximately 10,000 ohms.

9. Connect one ohmmeter lead to the mounting bracket. Set the ohmmeter to its highest range. While carefully observing the meter, connect the other test lead to the blue terminal. The ohmmeter needle should flick downscale momentarily, then settle at infinity.

10. Repeat Step 9 by connecting to the black terminal instead of the blue one.

11. If any readings in Steps 4, 5, or 6 are not within specified tolerances and if the wiring is good and the mounting of the stator is properly grounded, then remove the flywheel and stator following procedures given in Chapter Six.

12. Install a new magneto assembly.

13. Determining the flux of the peraiment magnets in the magneto flywheel is beyond the scope of the home mechanic. An approximate test can be made by carefully and gently placing a steel bar on the face of each magnet in turn and pulling it away from the magnet. The pull for all 6 magnets on the Pioneer and Plonker models should be equal. For the Stiletto, TT, and DMR models, the pull should be equal for 5 of the magnets and considerably greater for the 6th one. Install a new magneto assembly if these criteria are not met. Do not strike or jar the magneto flywheel; damage to the magnets may result.

14. If the ignition is still not performing satisfactorily, try substituting a new coil for the old one and retesting. If this last step does not yield improvement, reinstall the old coil and substitute a new magneto assembly for the old one and retest. Any further testing will require taking the bike to a competent repair shop which is equipped with sophisticated test equipment. Also see the *Ignition Timing* section of Chapter Two for additional tests.

IGNITION SWITCH

Test

1. Disconnect the black wire which comes from the battery.

2. Remove the fuse.

3. Connect the ohmmeter to the terminal from which the black wire was disconnected and to ground.

4. Turn the ignition switch to the ON position; the meter should read zero.

5. Turn the ignition switch to the OFF position; the meter should read infinity.

6. If the switch fails the above tests, check to see that the switch is wired correctly. If wired correctly, install a new ignition switch. See instructions given in Chapter Five for removal and installation of the ignition switch.

CHARGING SYSTEM

Troubleshooting the charging system involves checking the electrical continuity (including all connections), the output of the magneto, and the condition of each component. Use the following procedure.

Check and service the battery as detailed in the *Battery* section of Chapter Five prior to testing the charging system.

Wiring

1. Check all connections to be sure they are clean and tight.

2. Refer to Figures 5, 6, and 7 in Chapter Five for the wiring diagrams and illustrations of the wiring system. Check that the wiring is correctly connected.

Magneto

1. Disconnect the connector which connects the red wire (which comes from the magneto through a black tube) to the purple wire.

2. Connect an ohmmeter between the red wire and ground. Read the resistance. Reverse the ohmmeter leads and read again. One reading should be 12-15 ohms and the other infinity.

3. If readings in Step 2 are not as specified, check the red wire for damage and continuity between its disconnected end and the stator. If the red wire checks satisfactorily, install a new magneto assembly following procedures given in Chapter Six under *Magneto*.

Magneto Output

If the readings in Step 2 of the previous section, *Magneto*, are as specified, check the output of the magneto using the following procedure.

1. Connect the positive lead of a DC voltmeter to the end of the (disconnected) red wire and the other lead to ground.

2. Run the engine at approximately 6,000 rpm and read the meter. It should read approximately 30-34 volts.

3. If the reading in Step 2 is not as specified, check the red wire for damage and continuity between its disconnected end and the stator. If the red wire checks satisfactorily, install a new magneto assembly following procedures given in Chapter Six.

LIGHTS

1. With all wiring connected, locate the connector which connect a red wire (which comes from the magneto through a black tube) to a purple wire. Attach the positive lead of a DC voltmeter to the connector and the other lead to ground.

2. Put the light switch at OFF position and run the engine at approximately 6,000 rpm. Read the meter. It should read approximately 30-32 volts.

3. Turn on the lights and read the meter again with the engine still at 6,000 rpm. It should read approximately 7-9 volts.

4. If the readings in Steps 2 and 3 were not within the approximate ranges specified, check the individual components of the lighting system using the following procedures.

Resistor

1. Disconnect the wires attached to the resistor but leave the resistor in place.

2. Connect an ohmmeter across the resistor and read the meter. If it does not read 14.5-15.5 ohms, install a new resistor.

3. Reposition one of the ohmmeter leads onto a mounting nut. If the meter reading is other than infinity, install a new resistor.

Light Switch

1. Disconnect both connectors from the terminals of the 15 ohm resistor (see Figure 5, Chapter Five).

2. Remove the fuse.

3. Connect the ohmmeter leads to the 2 connectors.

4. Turn the light switch to OFF and read the meter. It should read infinity.

5. Turn the light switch to ON and read the meter. It should read zero.

6. If the readings in Steps 4 and 5 are not as specified, the switch is faulty. Remove the switch and examine its operation. Turning the switch ON should provide electrical continuity between terminals 3 and 8.

7. Disassemble the switch, clean it, and reassemble. If it still malfunctions, install a new switch.

SHORT CIRCUITS

An internal short in one of the electrical components, as well as a shorted wire, can excessively load the electrical system. Check for an internal short by the following procedure.

1. Locate the connector between the fuse and battery and disconnect the wire from the positive side of the battery.

2. Connect a DC ammeter in the gap in the circuit thus created (with the negative lead of the ammeter attached to the wire from the battery).

3. Turn the light switch OFF and the ignition switch ON but do not start the engine.

4. Read the meter. If it reads other than zero, there is a short.

5. Apply the footbrake to turn on the brake light and read the ammeter; it should read approximately 3 amps. Release the footbrake.

6. Apply the front brake to turn on the brake light and read the ammeter; it should read approximately 3 amps. Release the brake.

7. Sound the horn; the ammeter reading should be approximately 3 amps.

8. Turn on the lights. With either beam of the headlight, the ammeter should read approximately 6 amps.

9. If any component in Steps 5-8 caused a *high* reading, the component or its wiring is faulty. Install a new component and check the ammeter reading again.

10. To pinpoint an electrical short, disconnect each component in sequence while observing the reading on the ammeter. When the reading drops to normal, something associated with the last wire caused the abnormal reading.

11. To determine the proper current (amperes) for components on a battery equipped motorcycle, divide the wattage of the component by the battery voltage (6 volts).

HORN

If the horn fails to operate, check the mounting bolts and wiring (see Figure 5, Chapter Five). A partially discharged battery may also cause a malfunction of the horn. If all connections are good, limited adjustment is possible by loosening the large locknut found in the center of the back of the horn and turning the small screw in the center of the nut. Try turning the screw in both directions to obtain the desired tone. Tighten the locknut.

If the desired tone cannot be obtained and if an original part is not available, virtually any 6V horn is a good substitute.

FUSE

A 20 amp fuse is fitted in the red wire leading from the battery. Most electrical troubleshooting should start by checking the fuse, fuse holder, and connections to the holder.

TROUBLESHOOTING GUIDE

Table 1 is a quick reference guide which summarizes part of the troubleshooting process. Use it to outline possible problem areas, then refer to the specific chapter or section involved.

Table 1   TROUBLESHOOTING GUIDE

Item	Problem or Cause	Things to Check
Loss of power	Poor compression	Piston rings and cylinder Head gasket Crankcase leaks
	Overheated engine	Lubricating oil supply Clogged cooling fins Ignition timing Slipping clutch Carbon in combustion chamber
	Improper mixture	Dirty air cleaner Restricted fuel flow Gas cap vent hole
	Miscellaneous	Dragging brakes Tight wheel bearings Defective chain Clogged exhaust system
Steering	Hard steering	Tire pressures Steering damper adjustment Steering stem head Steering head bearings
	Pulls to one side	Unbalanced shock absorbers Drive chain adjustment Front/rear wheel alignment Unbalanced tires Defective swing arm Defective steering head
	Shimmy	Drive chain adjustment Loose or missing spokes Deformed rims Worn wheel bearings Wheel balance
Gearshifting difficulties	Clutch	Adjustment Springs Friction plates Steel plates Oil quantity
	Transmission	Oil quantity Oil grade Return spring or pin Change lever or spring Drum position plate Change drum Change forks

(continued)

Table 2　TROUBLESHOOTING GUIDE　(continued)

Item	Problem or Cause	Things to Check
Brakes	Poor brakes	Worn linings Brake adjustment Oil or water on brake linings Loose linkage or cables
	Noisy brakes	Worn or scratched lining Scratched brake drums Dirt in brakes
	Unadjustable brakes	Worn linings Worn drums Worn brake cams

CHAPTER FOUR

FUEL SYSTEM

The fuel system comprises the carburetor, air cleaner, and fuel tank.

For proper operation, a gasoline engine must be supplied with fuel and air which is mixed in the proper proportions of 15:1. A mixture which contains an excess of fuel is said to be rich. A lean mixture is one which contains insufficient fuel. It is the function of the carburetor to supply the proper mixture to the engine under all operating conditions.

Ossa motorcycles are equipped either with IRZ or Bing carburetors. The IRZ carburetor may be either the double-needle or single-needle type. Service procedures are similar for the 2 types. Differences are pointed out where they exist. See **Figure 1** for an exploded view of a typical IRZ carburetor.

The Bing carburetor is used on Ossa's later model competition bikes.

The essential functional parts of a carburetor are a float and float valve mechanism for maintaining a constant fuel level in the float bowl, a pilot system for supplying fuel at low speeds, and a main fuel system which supplies the engine at medium and high speeds. The operation of each system is discussed in the following paragraphs.

Separate dismantling procedures for the IRZ and Bing carburetors are given in this chapter.

CARBURETOR OPERATION

Float Mechanism

Figure 2 illustrates a typical float mechanism. Proper operation of the carburetor is dependent on maintaining a constant fuel level in the carburetor bowl. As fuel is drawn from the float bowl, the float level drops. When the float drops, the float valve moves away from its seat and allows fuel to flow past the valve and seat into the float bowl. As this occurs, the float rises and presses the valve against its seat, thereby shutting off the flow of fuel. It can be seen from this discussion that a small piece of dirt trapped between the valve and seat can prevent the valve from closing and allow fuel to rise beyond the normal level, resulting in flooding. **Figures 3 and 4** illustrate this condition.

Pilot System

Under idle or low speed conditions, at less than 1/8 throttle, the engine doesn't require much fuel or air, and the throttle valve is almost closed. A separate pilot system is required for operation under such conditions. **Figure 5** illustrates the operation of the pilot system. Air is drawn through the pilot air inlet and controlled by the pilot air screw. The air is then mixed with fuel drawn through the pilot jet. The air/fuel

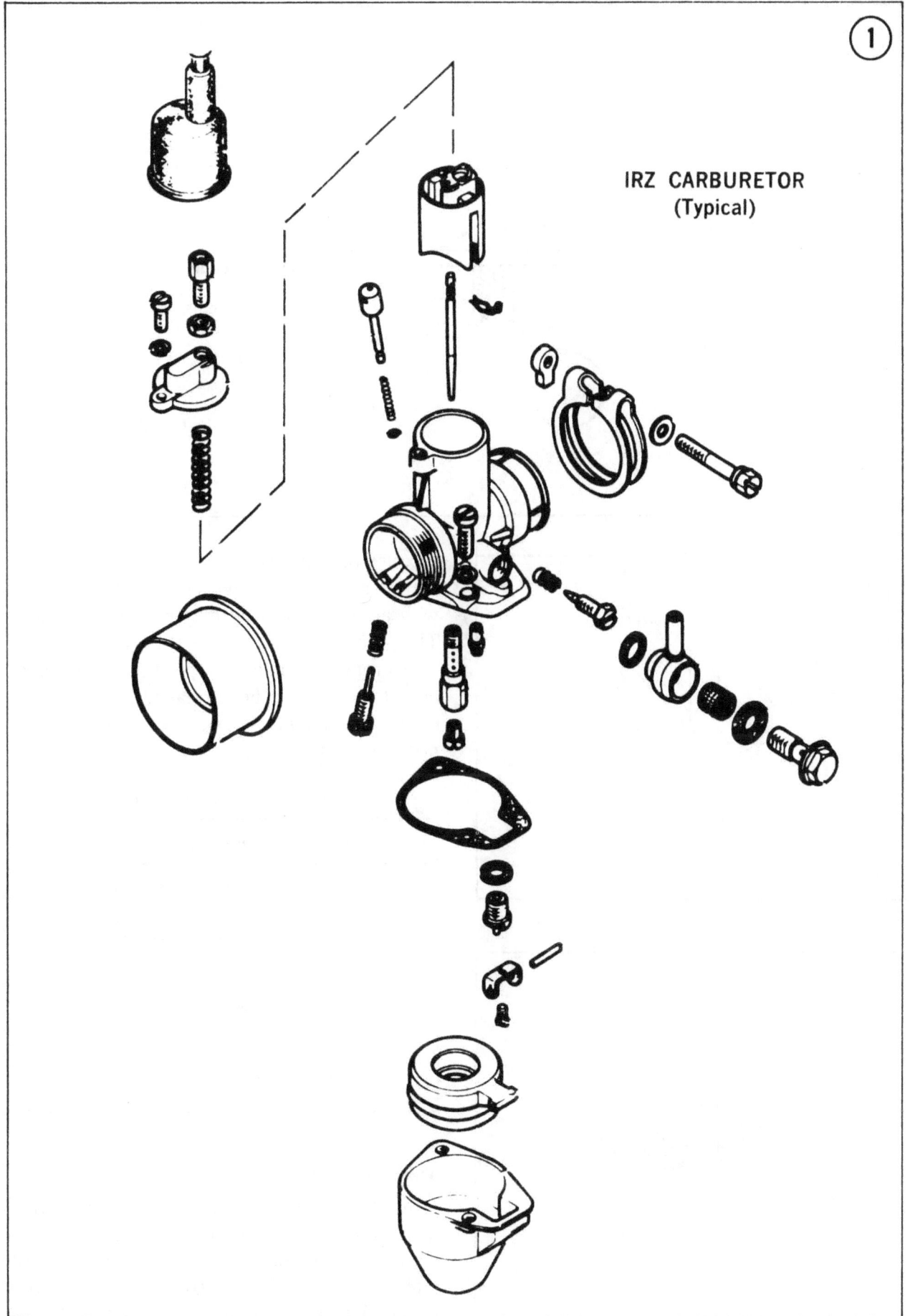

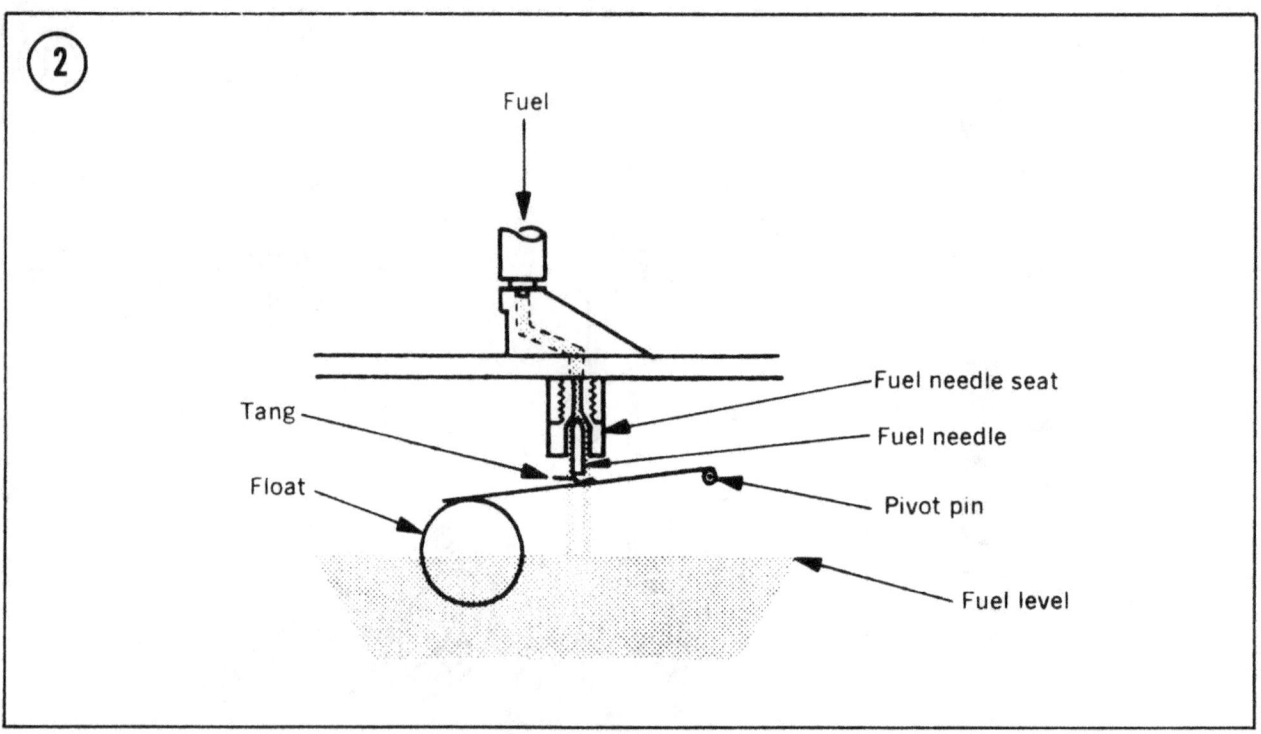

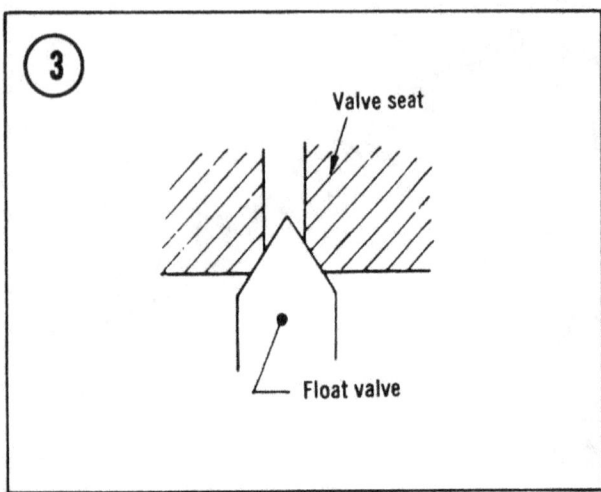

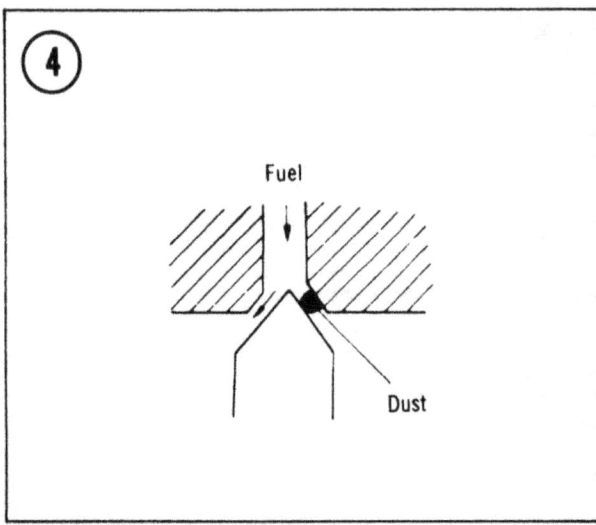

mixture then travels from the pilot outlet into the main air passage, where it is further mixed with air prior to being drawn into the engine. The pilot air screw controls the idle mixture.

If proper idle and low speed mixture cannot be obtained within the normal adjustment range of the idle mixture screw, refer to **Table 1** for possible causes.

Table 1   IDLE MIXTURE

Mixture:	Caused by:
Too rich	Clogged pilot intake
	Clogged air passage
	Clogged air bleed opening
	Pilot jet loose
Too lean	Obstructed pilot jet
	Obstructed jet outlet
	Worn throttle valve
	Carburetor mounting loose

Main Fuel System

As the throttle is opened more (up to approximately ¼ open) the pilot circuit begins to supply less of the total mixture to the engine as the main fuel system, illustrated in **Figure 6**, begins to function. The main jet, the needle jet, the jet

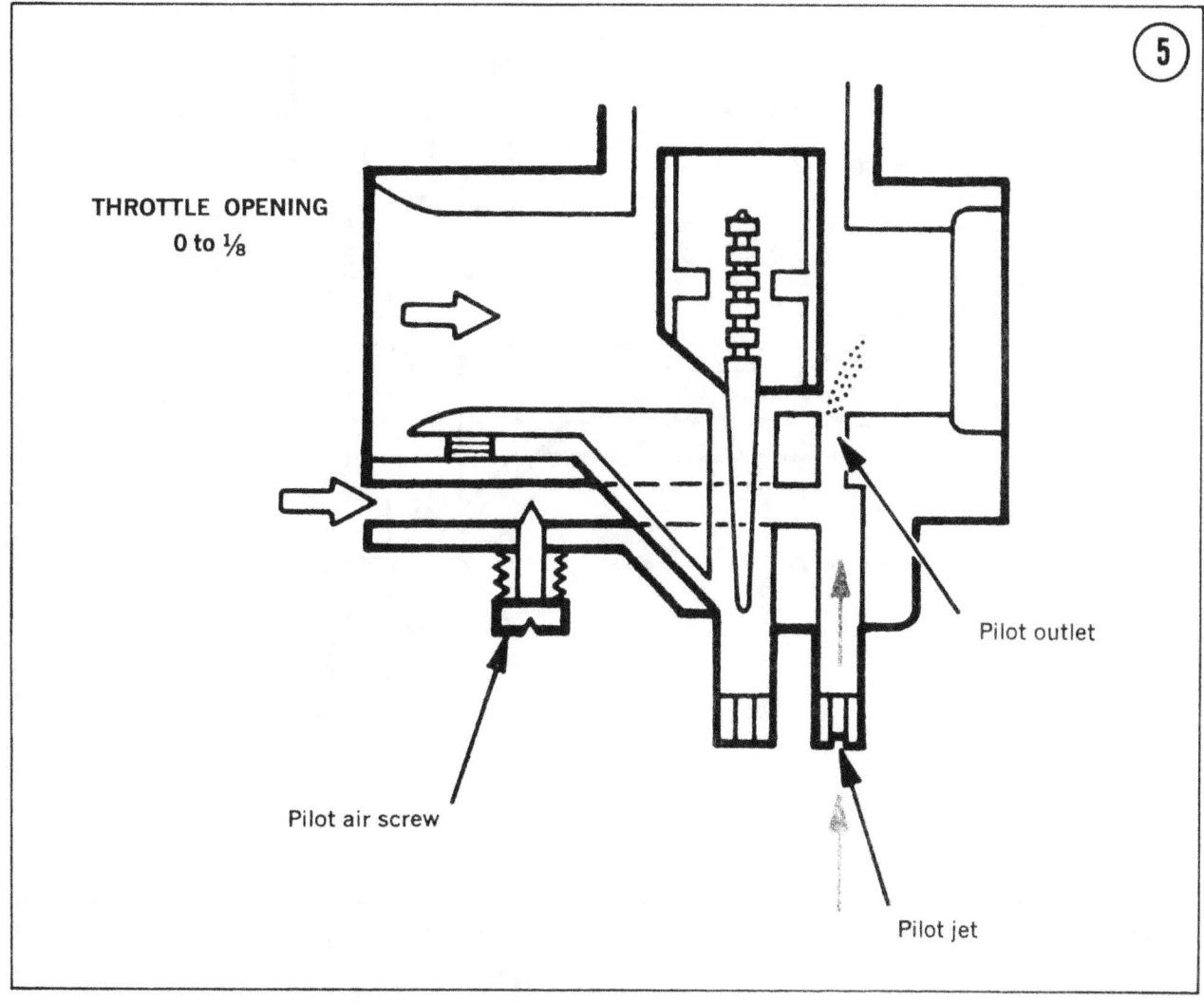

needle, and the air jet make up the main fuel circuit.

As the throttle valve opens more than approximately ⅛ of its travel, air is drawn through the main port, and passes under the throttle valve in the main bore. The velocity of the air stream results in reduced pressure around the jet needle. Fuel then passes through the main jet, past the needle jet and jet needle, and into the air stream where it is atomized and sent to the cylinder. As the throttle valve opens, more air flows through the carburetor. The jet needle, which is attached to the throttle slide, rises to permit more fuel to flow.

A portion of the air bled past the jet needle is mixed with the main air stream and atomized.

Airflow at small throttle openings is controlled primarily by the cutaway on the throttle slide.

As the throttle is opened still more, up to approximately ¾ open, the circuit draws air from 2 sources, as shown in **Figure 7**. The first source of air is through the venturi; the second source is through the air jet. Air passing through the venturi draws fuel through the needle jet. The jet needle is tapered, and therefore allows more fuel to pass. Air passing through the air jet passes to the needle jet to aid atomization of the fuel there.

Figure 8 illustrates the circuit at high speeds. The jet needle is withdrawn almost completely from the needle jet. Fuel flow is then controlled by the main jet. Air passing through the air jet continues to aid atomization of the fuel as described in the foregoing paragraphs.

Any dirt which collects in the main jet or in the needle jet obstructs fuel flow and causes a lean mixture. Any clogged air passage, such as the air bleed opening or air jet, may result in an overrich mixture. Other causes of a rich mix-

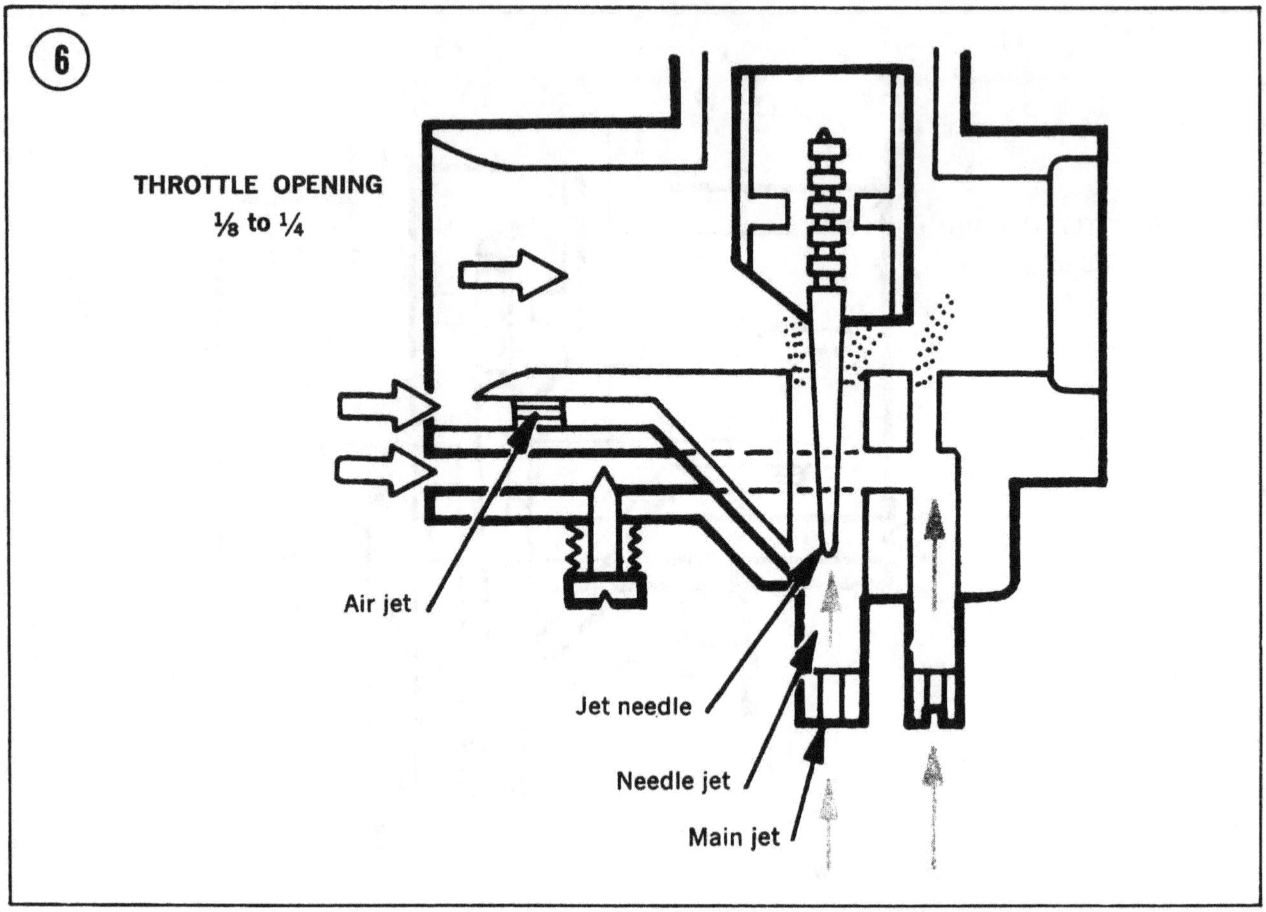

6

THROTTLE OPENING
⅛ to ¼

- Air jet
- Jet needle
- Needle jet
- Main jet

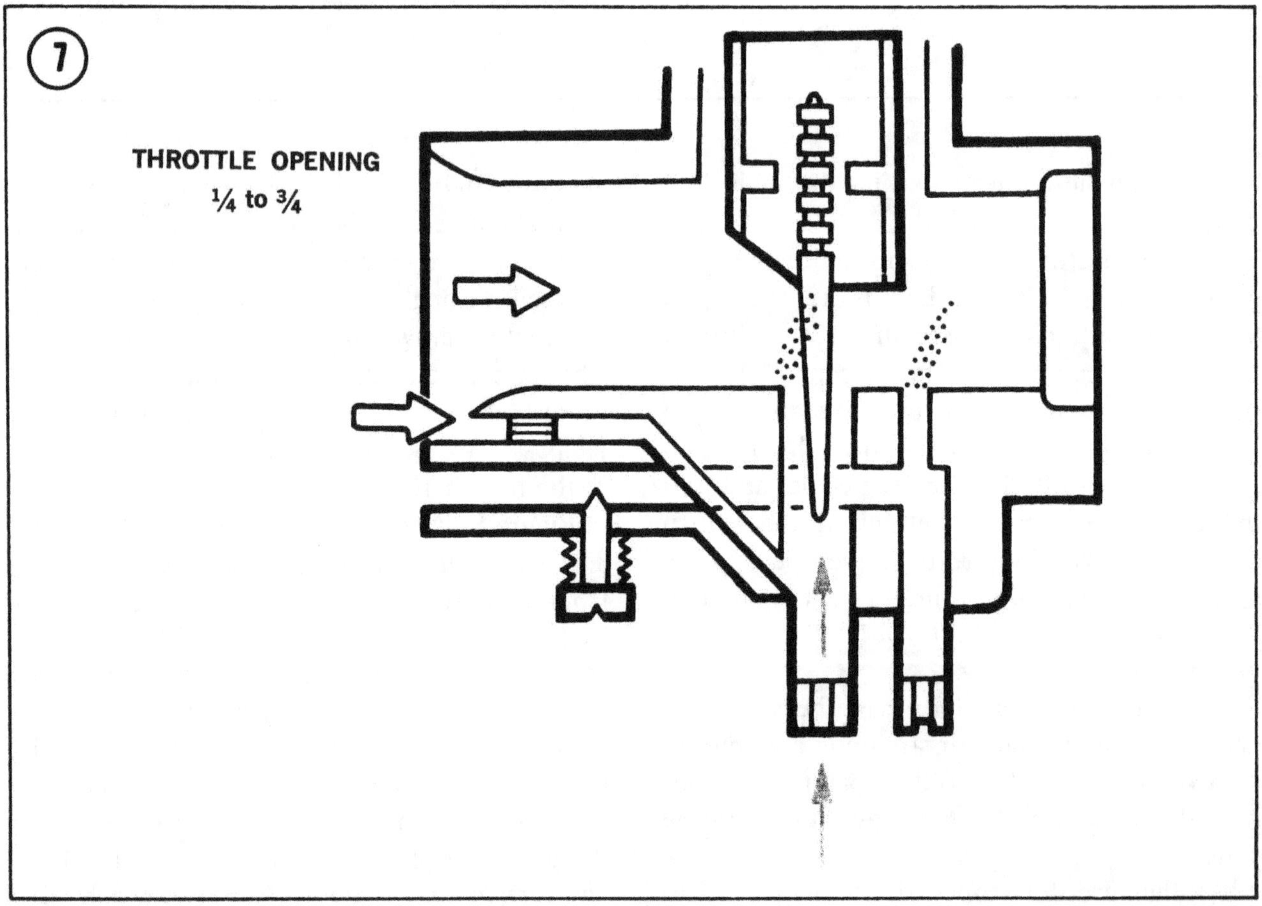

7

THROTTLE OPENING
¼ to ¾

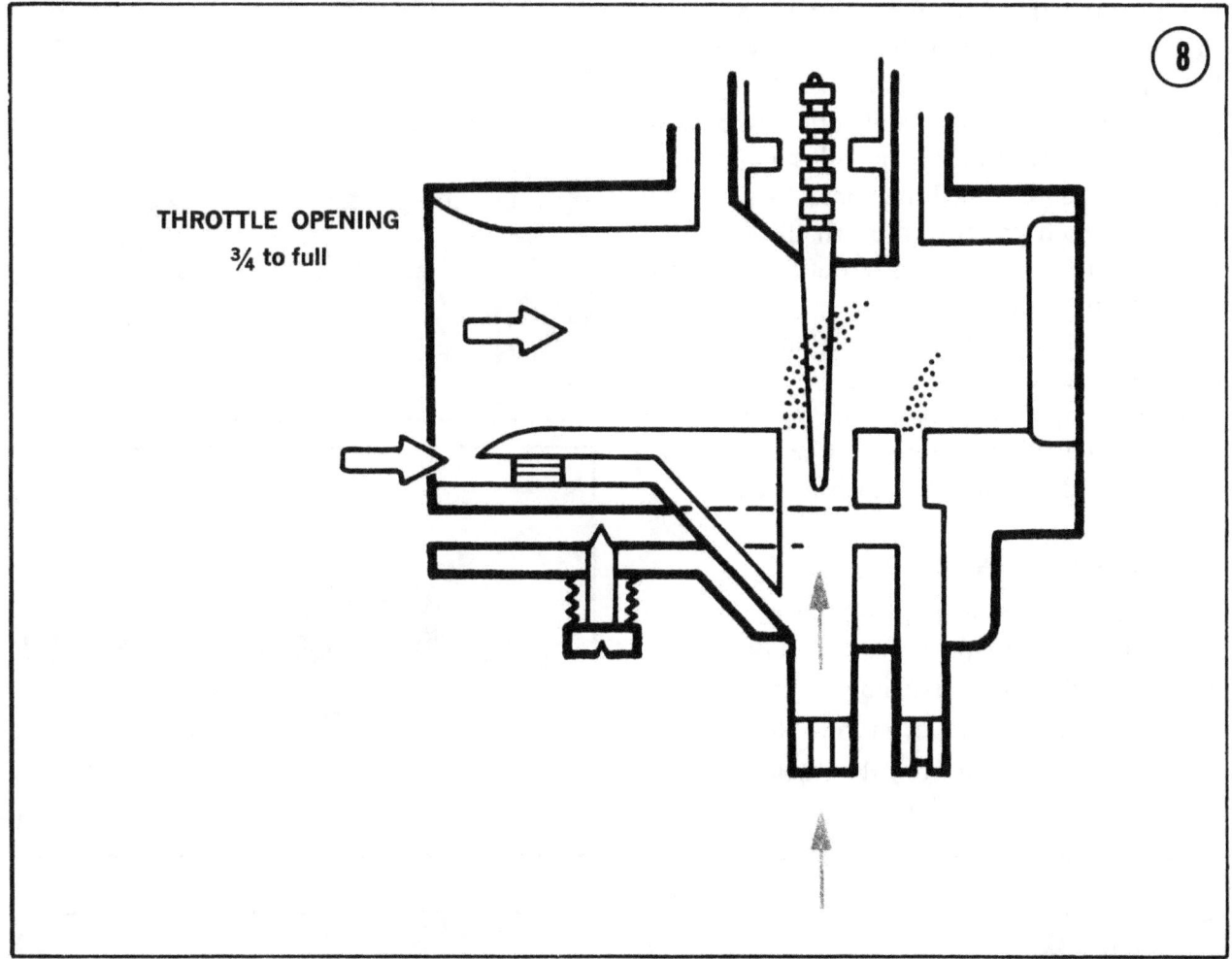

THROTTLE OPENING
¾ to full

ture are a worn jet needle, a worn needle jet, loose needle jet, or loose main jet. If the jet needle is worn, it should be replaced. However, it may be possible to effect a temporary repair by placing the jet needle clip in a higher groove.

Double-needle Model (IRZ)

The preceding description of carburetor operation pertains to single-needle carburetors in general. The double-needle model of the IRZ has a second needle jet and needle usually called the "high-speed needle"; it is the longer needle jet inside the carburetor. The mid-range needle begins to function to control the fuel flow in the ⅛ to ¼ throttle opening range. The high-speed needle begins to function similarly in the ½ to ¾ throttle opening range and it controls the fuel flow for higher throttle openings.

The needle in single-needle model carburetors similarly begins to function to control fuel flow at approximately the ⅛ throttle setting and gradually increases its functioning to fully control the fuel flow as the throttle opening is increased. The single-needle IRZ carburetor also utilizes air entering the booster hole into the needle jet through holes halfway up it to increase the fuel flow at throttle openings beyond approximately the halfway setting.

Tickler System

A cold engine requires a mixture which is far richer than normal. The tickler system provides this rich mixture. When the rider presses the tickler button, the float is forced downward, causing the float needle valve to open, and thereby allowing extra fuel to flow into the float chamber.

CARBURETOR OVERHAUL

There is no set rule regarding frequency of carburetor overhaul. A carburetor used primarily for street riding may go 5,000 miles

(8,000 km) without attention. If the bike is used in dirt, the carburetor might need an overhaul in less than 1,000 miles (1,600 km). Poor engine performance, hesitation, and little response to idle mixture adjustment are all symptoms of possible carburetor malfunctions. As a general rule, it is good practice to overhaul the carburetor each time you perform a routine decarbonization of the engine.

If the carburetor is to be overhauled, follow the instructions given separately below for the IRZ and Bing carburetors. If the carburetor is merely to be adjusted, refer to *Carburetor Adjustment* in this chapter for each model.

IRZ Disassembly/Assembly

Figure 1 shows an exploded illustration of a typical IRZ carburetor. Refer to this figure during disassembly and reassembly.

1. Remove the carburetor at the cylinder.

2. Remove the screw from the carburetor top, then remove the top (**Figure 9**).

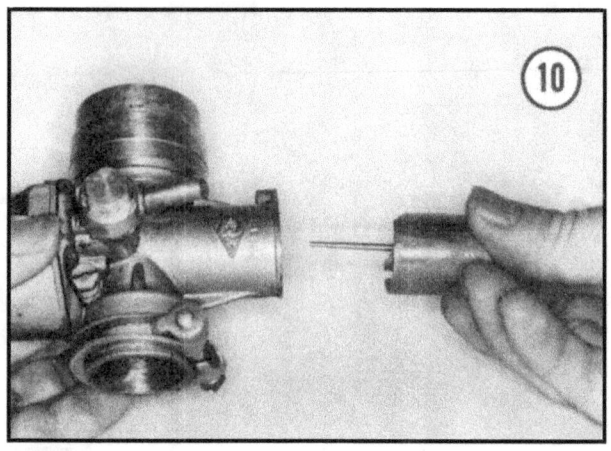
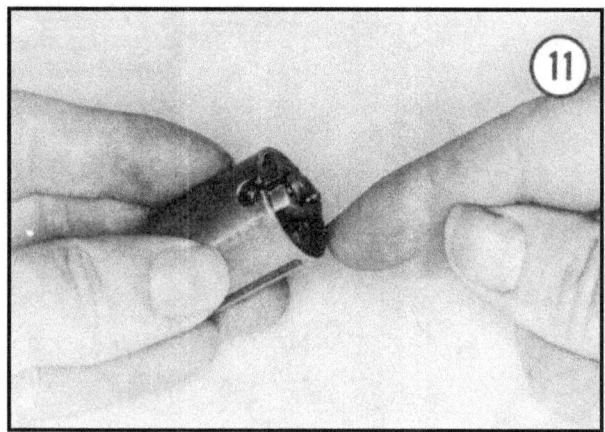
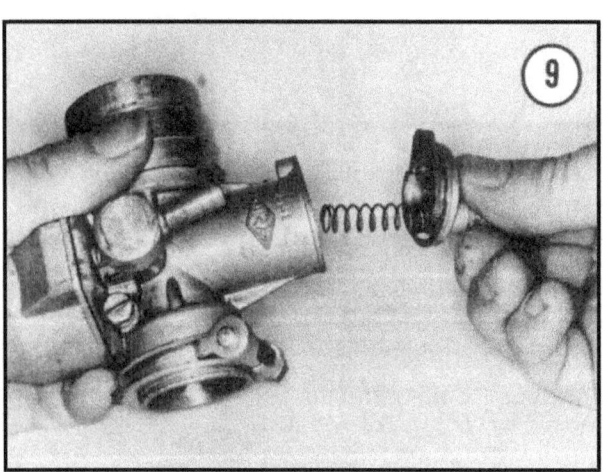
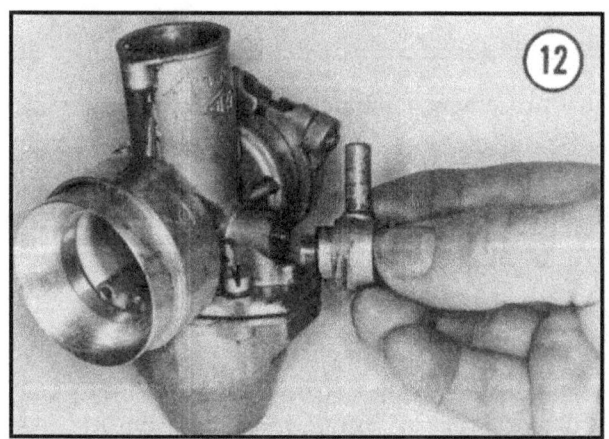

3. Withdraw the throttle slide (**Figure 10**).

4. Compress the slide return spring, then unhook the cable end from the slide.

5. Note which groove the jet needle clip is in, then remove the clip and pull the jet needle from the throttle valve (**Figure 11**).

6. Remove the fuel inlet banjo bolt, then the banjo and filter element (**Figure 12**).

7. Remove the pilot air screw and its associated spring (**Figure 13**).

8. Remove the 2 float bowl attaching screws, then the float bowl (**Figure 14**).

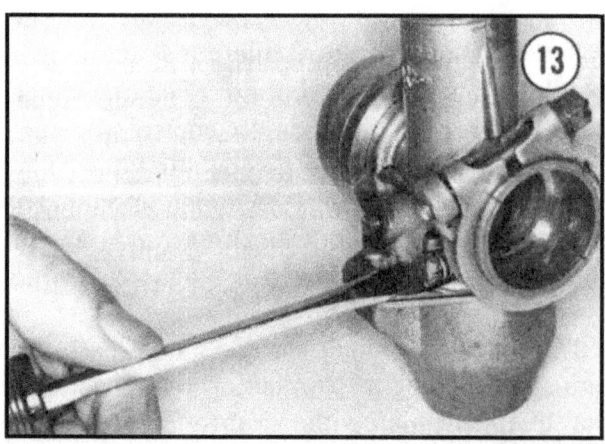

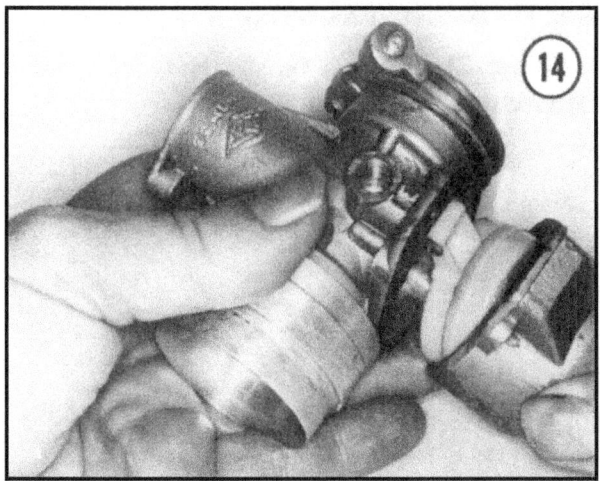

9. Press out the float pivot shaft, then remove the float (**Figure 15**).

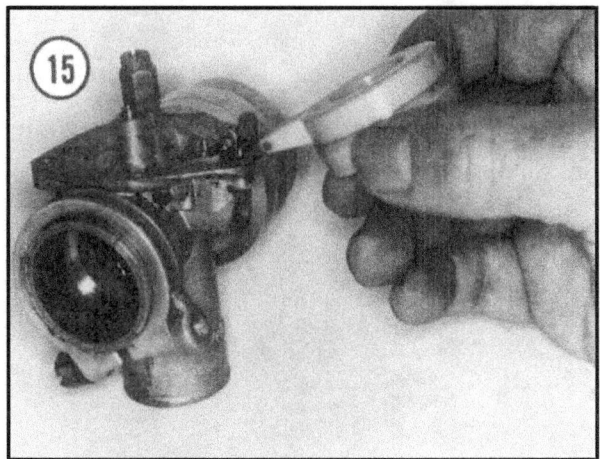

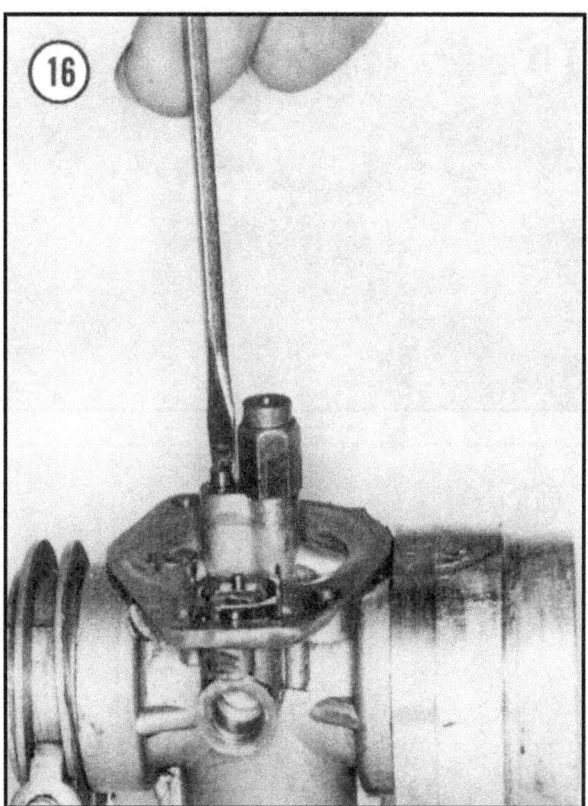

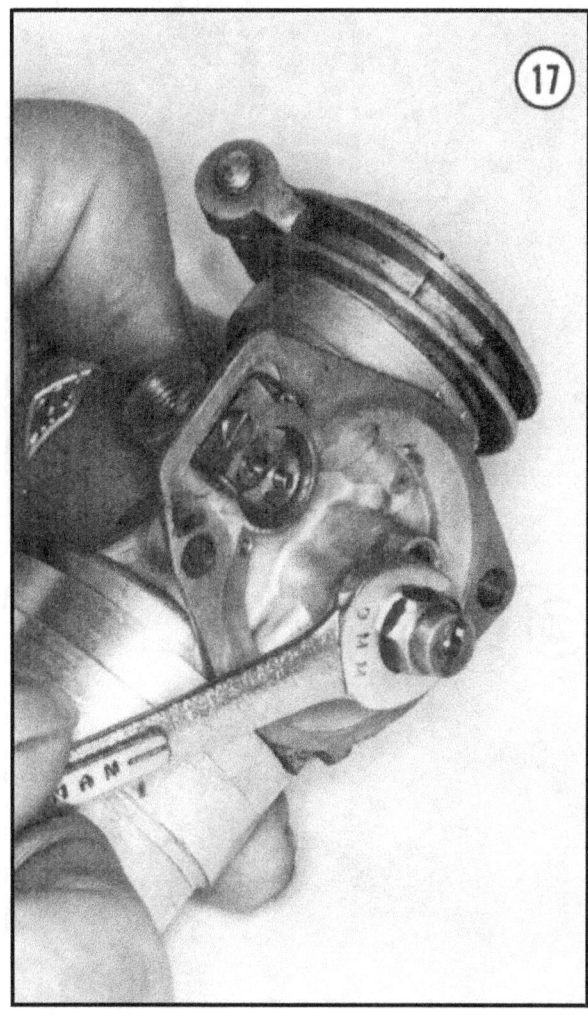

10. Unscrew the pilot jet (**Figure 16**).

11. Remove the needle jet from the jet holder (**Figure 17**).

12. Unscrew the main jet from the needle jet (**Figure 18**).

13. Unscrew the float needle assembly, using a pair of duckbill pliers on the ridge running across the center (**Figure 19**). Do not squeeze the ridge too tightly.

14. With a pair of pliers, twist the mounting clip on the tickler button, then remove the clip. Pull out the tickler button and spring.

15. Remove the idle stop screw and spring (**Figure 20**).

16. Clean all parts as described below.

17. Reverse the disassembly procedure to reassemble the carburetor.

> NOTE: *Always install new gaskets during assembly.*

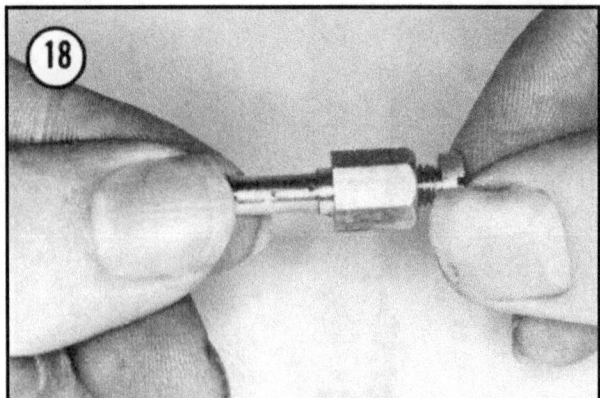

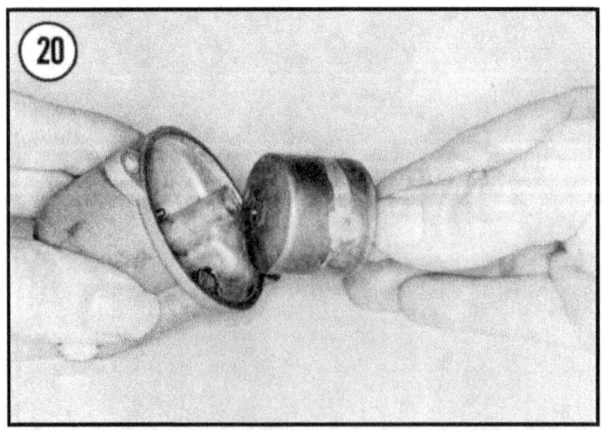

Bing Disassembly/Assembly

Figure 21 shows a typical Bing slide valve carburetor.

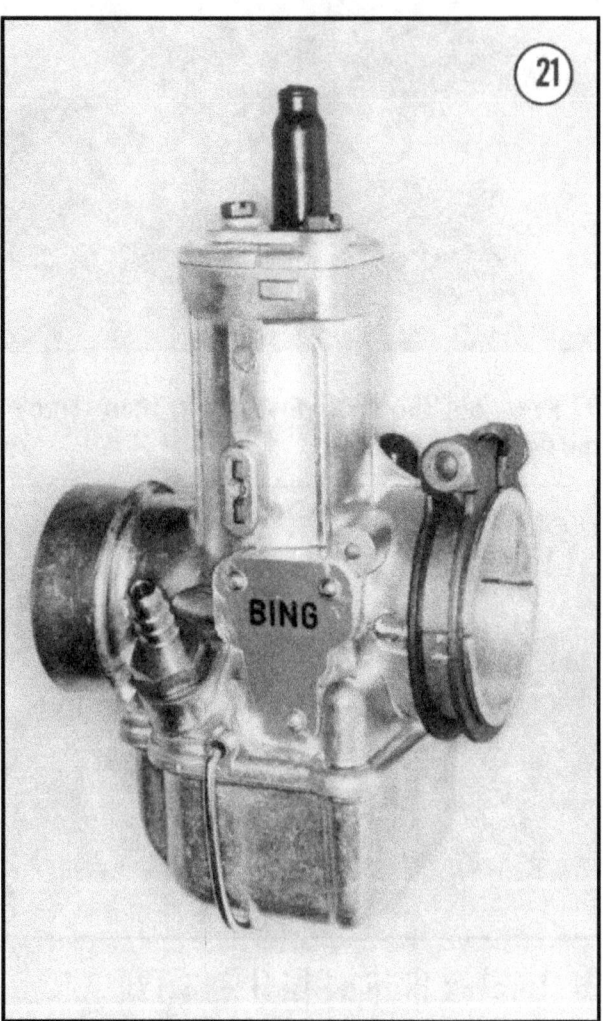

1. Remove the retaining screws, then the mixing chamber top (**Figure 22**). Be careful; the cover is under spring pressure.

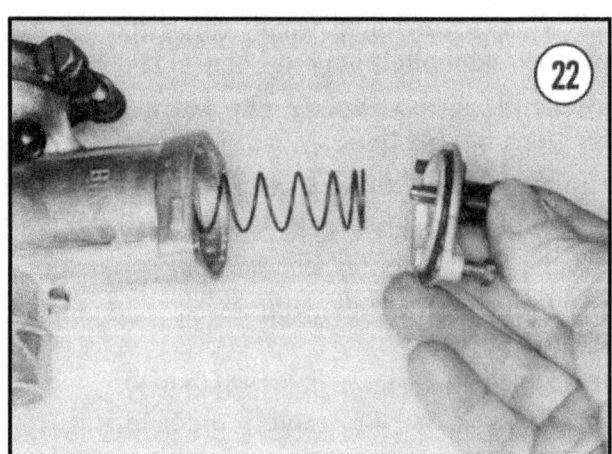

2. Remove the spring, then the throttle slide (**Figure 23**).

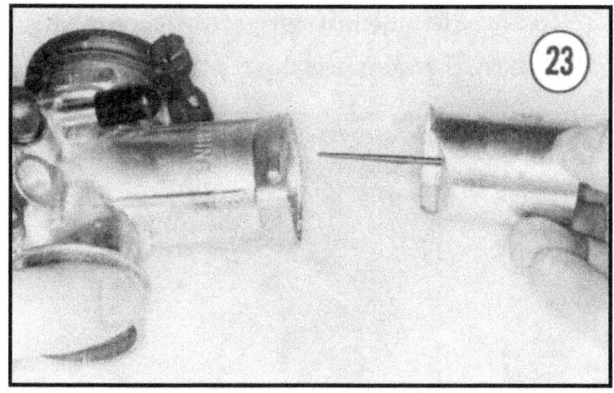

3. Push the float bowl retaining bail toward the carburetor inlet (**Figure 24**).

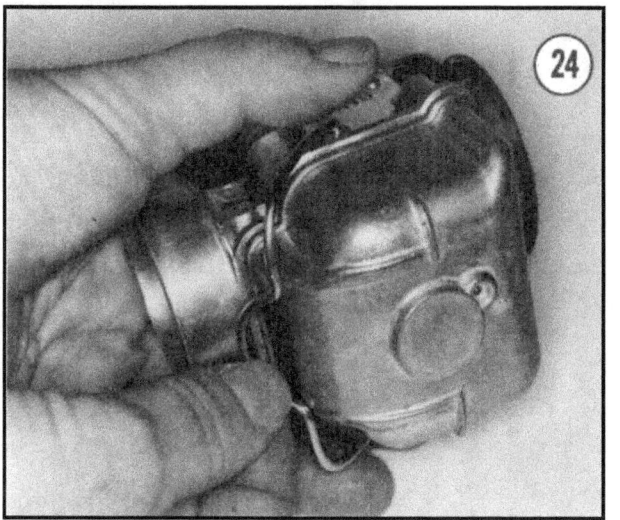

4. Remove the float bowl (**Figure 25**).
5. Pull out the float pivot pin (**Figure 26**), then gently remove the float assembly.

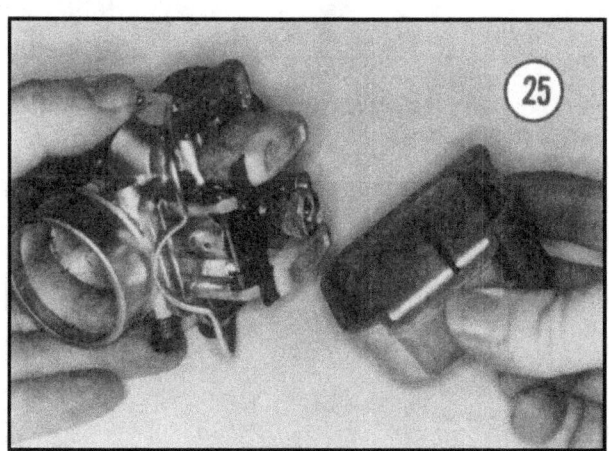

6. Pull out the float needle (**Figure 27**).
7. Carefully remove the strainer from the main jet (**Figure 28**).

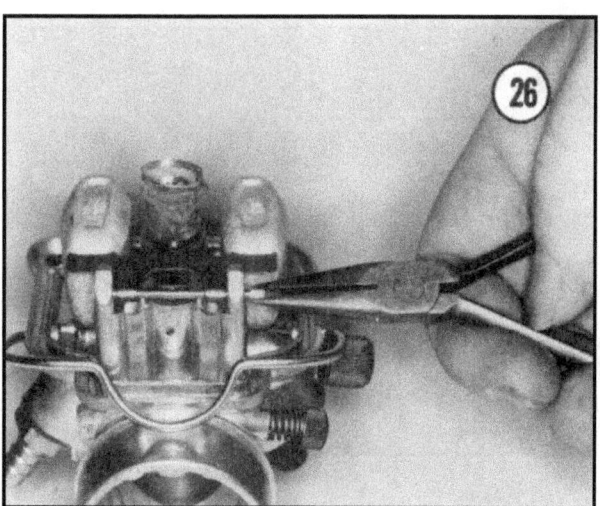

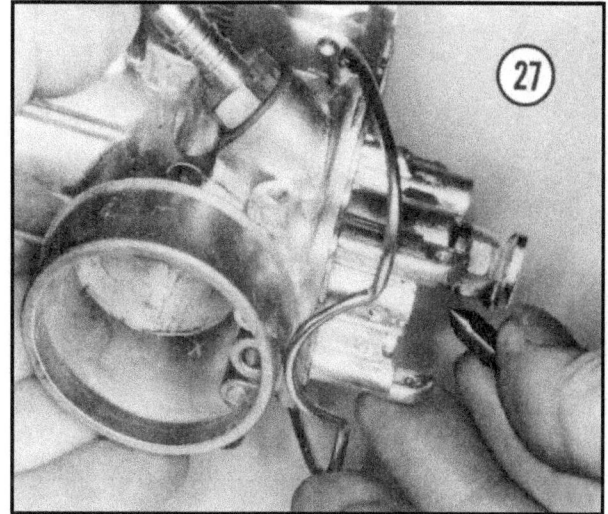

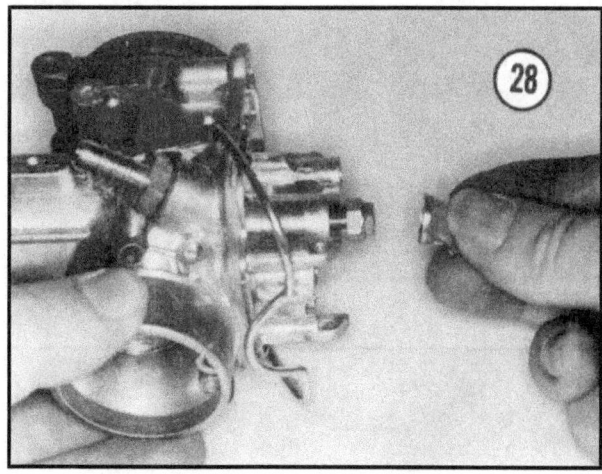

8. Remove the jet holder (**Figure 29**).
9. Turn the carburetor upright. The needle jet will drop out (**Figure 30**). Push it out with a plastic rod if necessary.
10. Remove the pilot jet (**Figure 31**).
11. Remove the fuel inlet fitting (**Figure 32**).

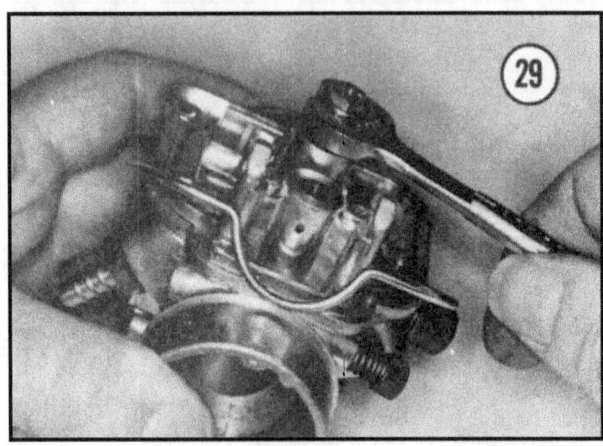

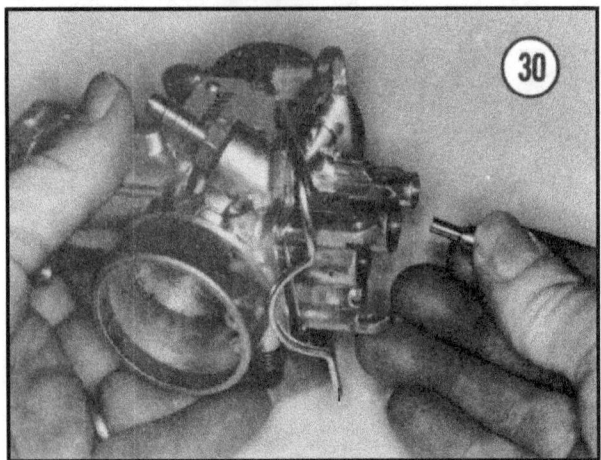

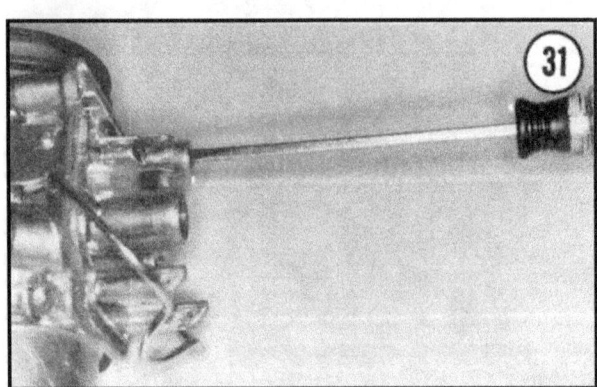

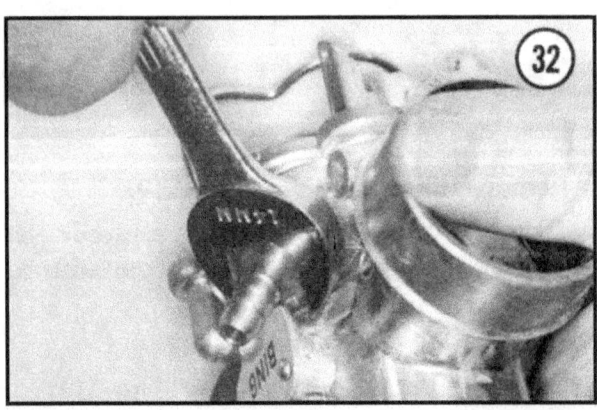

12. Remove the idle mixture screw (**Figure 33**).
13. Remove the idle speed screw (**Figure 34**).

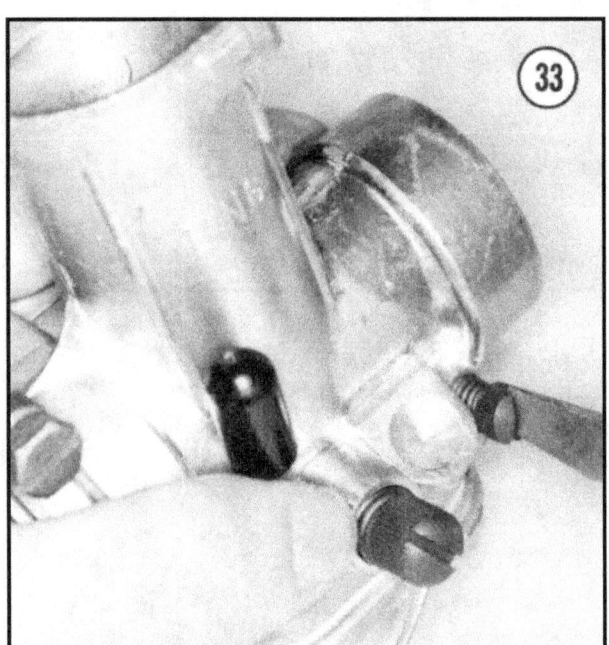

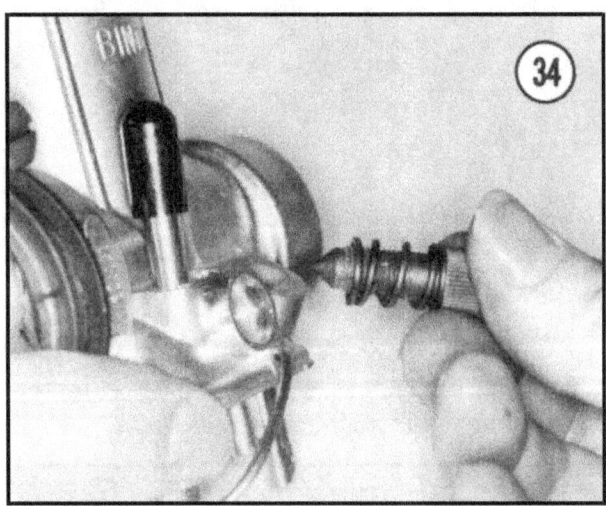

14. Remove the jet needle from the throttle valve (**Figure 35**).

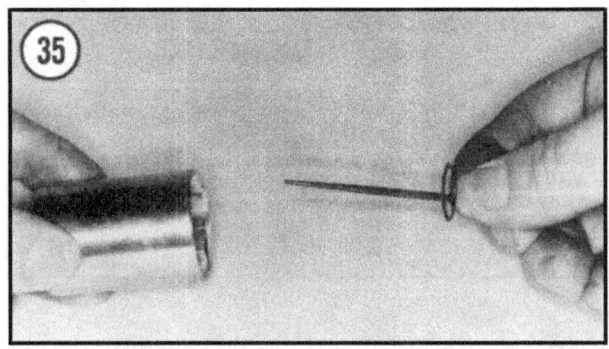

15. Unscrew the main jet from the jet holder (**Figure 36**).

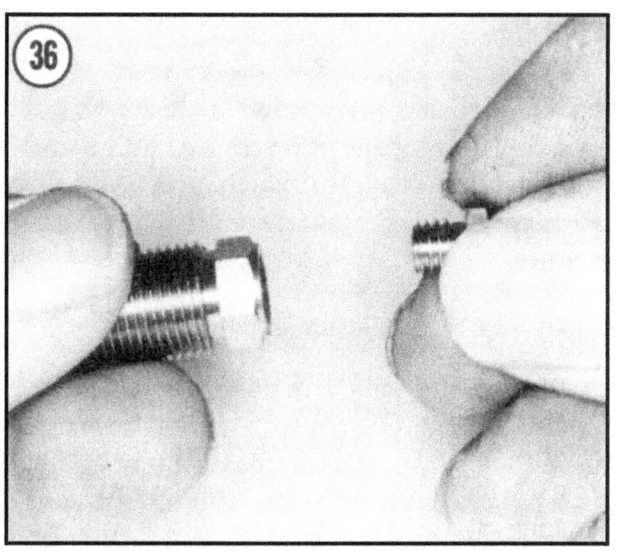

16. Clean all parts as described below.
17. Assemble in reverse order of disassembly.

NOTE: *Always install new gaskets during assembly.*

Cleaning Carburetor Parts

Clean all parts in carburetor cleaning solvent. Dry the parts with compressed air. Clean the jets and other delicate parts with compressed air after the float bowl has been removed. Never attempt to clean jets or passages by running a wire through them. To do so will cause damage and destroy their calibration. Do not use compressed air to clean an assembled carburetor because the float and float valve can be damaged.

CARBURETOR ADJUSTMENT

The carburetor should be adjusted *only* after all other tune-up procedures have been completed. Check the items listed below and correct deficiencies *before* deciding to adjust the carburetor. A summary of carburetor adjustments is given in **Table 2**.

1. Check the air cleaner, the filter screens on the petcock, and the carburetor banjo for clogging.
2. Check the breather tube on the fuel tank for clogging.
3. Check the spark plug for type and heat range.
4. Check the ignition components and timing.
5. Check all gaskets and nuts for fit and tightness.
6. Check the piston, rings, and cylinder clearance for wear or damage.
7. Check the carburetor for cleanliness and fuel or air leaks.
8. Check the exhaust system for freedom from restrictions.

The following paragraphs describe the various components of the carburetor which may be changed to vary performance characteristics.

Throttle Valve

The throttle valve cutaway (**Figure 37**) controls air flow at small throttle openings. Cutaway sizes are numbered. Large numbers permit more air to flow at a given throttle opening and result in a leaner mixture. Conversely, smaller numbers result in a richer mixture.

Jet Needle

The jet needle (**Figure 38**), together with the needle jet, controls the mixture at medium speeds. As the throttle valve rises to increase air flow through the carburetor, the jet needle rises with it. The tapered portion of the jet needle rises from the needle jet and allows more fuel to flow, thereby providing the engine with the proper mixture at up to about ¾ throttle opening. The grooves at the top of the jet needle

Table 2   CARBURETOR ADJUSTMENTS

Throttle Opening	Adjustment	If too Rich	If too Lean
0 - ⅛	Air screw	Turn out	Turn in
⅛ - ¼	Throttle valve cutaway	Use larger cutaway	Use smaller cutaway
¼ - ¾	Jet needle	Raise clip	Lower clip
¾ - full	Main jet	Use smaller number	Use larger number

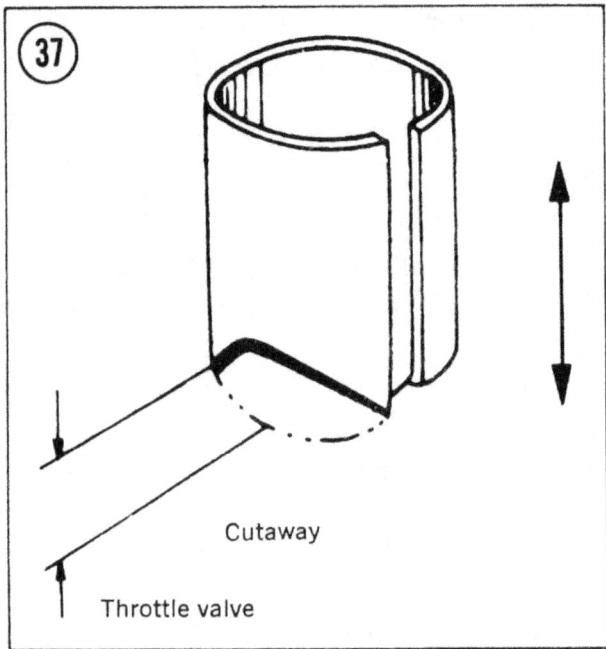

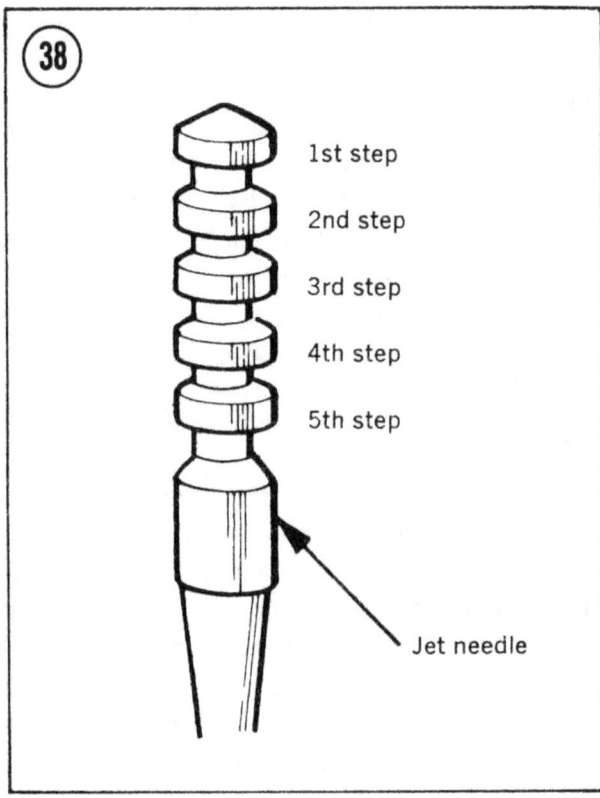

Main Jet

The main jet controls the mixture at full throttle, and has some effect at lesser throttle openings. Each main jet is stamped with a number. Fuel flow is approximately proportional to the number. Larger numbers provide a richer mixture.

Initial Test and Adjustment

1. Wrap white tape around the twistgrip (see **Figure 39**) and divide it with marks designating throttle openings. Mark the throttle housing seam as the reference point with an arrow. By glancing at the throttle, you know what the throttle opening is where the symptoms occur.

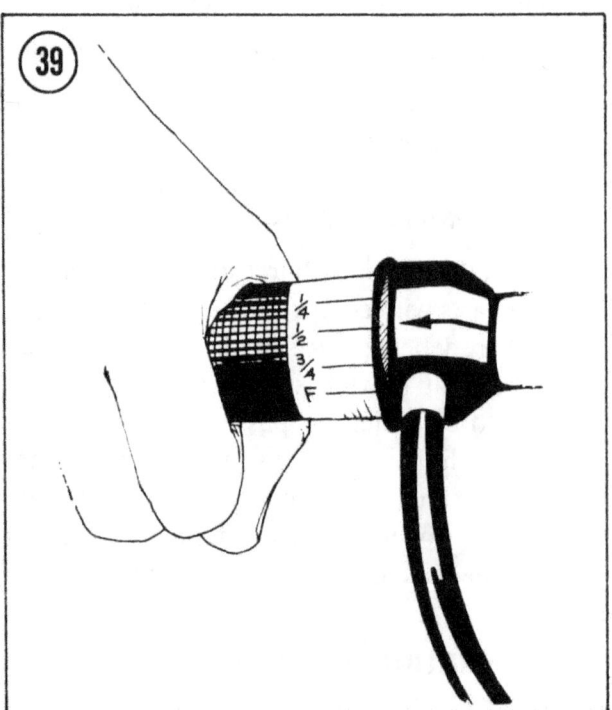

2. Warm up the engine to operating temperature. On a level or slightly uphill grade, run the engine up to peak rpm by opening the throttle slowly and smoothly while listening carefully. Then close it slowly and smoothly while listening carefully.

3. If the engine pings or rattles, the mixture is too lean. If it dies or loses rpm while opening the throttle, it is very lean. Note at what throttle opening these symptoms occur.

4. If the engine 4-strokes, firing every other revolution, or accelerates poorly, the mixture is too rich. If the exhaust has excessive smoke when the fuel/oil ratio is correct, the mixture

permit adjustment of the mixture ratio in the medium speed range.

Needle Jet

The needle jet operates with the jet needle. Several holes are drilled through the side of the needle jet. These holes meter the air flow from the air jet. Air from the air jet is bled into the needle jet to assist in atomization of the fuel.

is too rich. Note at what throttle opening these symptoms occur.

5. If the engine runs lean at *all* throttle settings, remove the float bowl and check the float for proper operation. The float must pivot freely and the needle must seat in the metering jet properly.

6a. *IRZ double-needle carburetors*: Hold the float bowl with the float toward you (see **Figure 40**). Pass a ¼ in. rod between the small rib of the float bowl at one o'clock and the float body. With the float upside down, the rod should pass between the rib and the float without moving the float. Adjust the float level by bending the tab of the hinge and test again. Continue until the proper float level is attained.

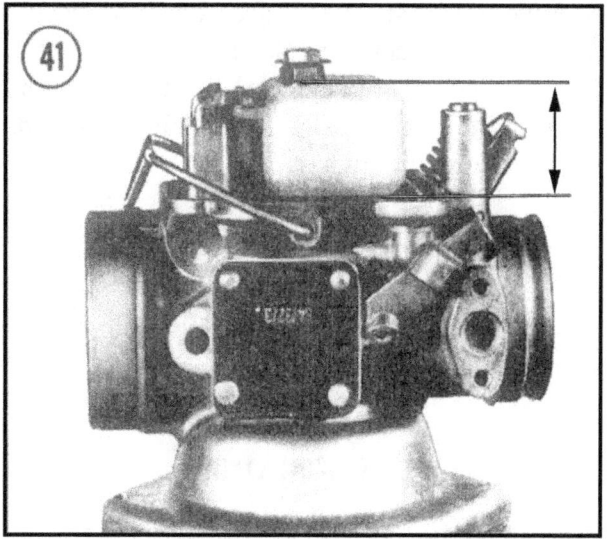

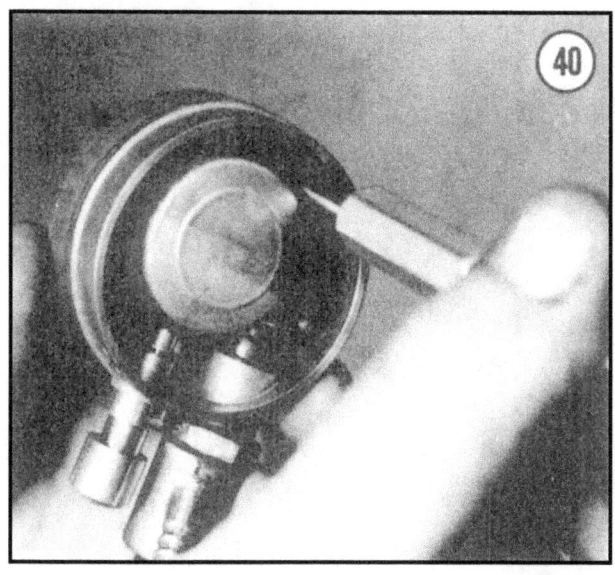

6b. *IRZ single-needle carburetors*: The float is not adjustable. If it leaks or breaks, replace it.

6c. *Bing carburetor*: Adjust the float so that the bottom side of the float is parallel to the float bowl mounting surface when the float assembly is resting against the needle valve. See **Figure 41**.

7. If the engine runs rich at *all* throttle settings, check the float as detailed above. Carefully check the seating of the float needle and float metering jet, as fuel may enter the float after the needle closes. Be sure the float is airtight so it does not contain fuel. These conditions cause fuel to spill over into the carburetor, flooding the engine.

NOTE: *When adjusting more than one metering system in the carburetor, always start with the smallest throttle opening and finish with the largest. This ensures a smooth blending of systems as the throttle is opened. This precaution will prevent the necessity of changing the larger opening adjustments more than once.*

8. If the engine runs lean (or rich) at one or more throttle settings, refer to Table 2 and adjust accordingly.

Final Test and Adjustment

1. After the initial test is complete, ride the bike ¼ mile at ⅛ throttle setting. Hold the throttle steady, turn off the ignition and immediately disengage the clutch. Remove the spark plug and check it.

2. If the bike has no ignition switch, set the idle speed screw so the engine will not idle. Ride at full throttle position and simultaneously pull the clutch and turn off the throttle. Do not use the compression release to slow the engine, it will alter the carburetion and plug reading.

3. Check the spark plug. The spark plug insulator should be light brown. If the color is very light or almost white, the mixture is too lean. If the plug is dark or oily, the mixture is too rich. See *Spark Plug*, Chapter Three.

4. Refer to Table 2 to adjust the carburetor for that throttle opening.

5. Repeat Steps 1 through 4 for ¼, ½, ¾, and full throttle openings.

6. When all adjustments are complete, repeat these tests at each throttle opening again, beginning with the smallest throttle opening through the largest, to be sure each one blends with the next fine tune.

AIR FILTER

See Chapter Two for maintenance and service under *Air Filter*.

FUEL STRAINER

See Chapter Two for maintenance and service under *Fuel Strainer*.

GAS TANK

Removal/Installation

1. Shut off the petcocks.
2. Disconnect the fuel lines.
3. Remove the tank.

WARNING
Welding a gas tank requires special safety procedures and must be performed only by someone skilled in the process. If any welding or brazing is required on the bike, remove the gas tank to a safe distance (at least 50 feet away).

4. Installation is the reverse of these steps.

CHAPTER FIVE

ELECTRICAL SYSTEM

The electrical system comprises the battery, ignition system, charging system, lighting, and horn. A typical wiring diagram is given in this chapter. Specifications and data for service and for replacement are given in the Appendix.

Any part of the electrical system may be repaired with a minimum of special tools by following the procedures described in this manual.

BATTERY

Specifications for the battery are given in **Table 1**. Construction details of a battery are shown in **Figure 1**.

Table 1   BATTERY

Type	6N6-1D
Voltage	6V
Capacity	6Ah (at 10 hour rate)
Charging current	1.0A
Specific gravity of electrolyte when fully charged	1.260-1.280 at 20°C (68°F)

Be sure to check battery electrolyte level frequently, especially during hot weather.

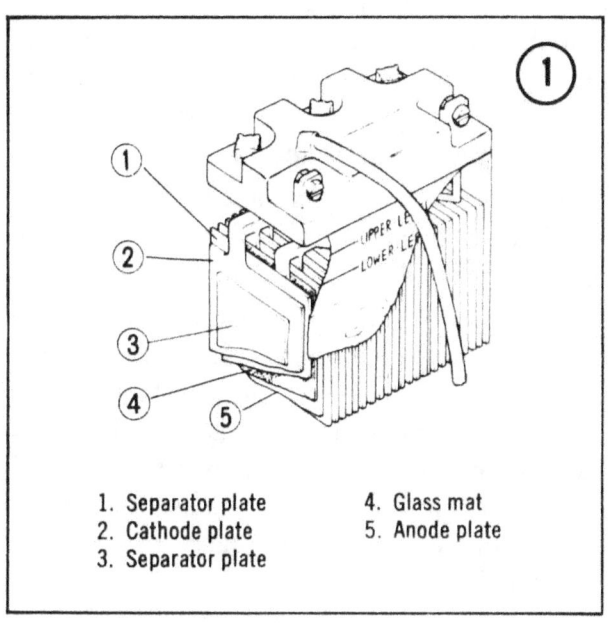

1. Separator plate
2. Cathode plate
3. Separator plate
4. Glass mat
5. Anode plate

Removal

Remove the foam rubber insulator, if necessary. Disconnect the ground, or negative (—) cable first and then the positive (+) cable. Lift the battery out.

Safety Precautions

While working with batteries, use extreme care to avoid spilling or splashing electrolyte. Electrolyte is sulphuric acid which can destroy clothing and cause serious chemical burns. If any electrolyte is spilled or splashed on clothing or body, or other surfaces, neutralize it immediately with a solution of baking soda and water, then flush with plenty of clean water.

> **WARNING**
> *Electrolyte splashed into the eyes is extremely dangerous. Safety glasses should always be worn when working with batteries. If electrolyte is splashed into the eye, call a physician immediately, force the eye open, and flood with cool, clean water for about 5 minutes.*

While batteries are being charged, highly explosive hydrogen gas forms in each cell. Some of this gas escapes through the filler openings and may form an explosive atmosphere around the battery. This explosive atmosphere may exist for several hours. Sparks, open flame, or even a lighted cigarette can ignite this gas, causing an internal explosion and possible serious personal injury. The following precautions should be taken to prevent an explosion.

1. Do not smoke or permit any open flame near any battery being charged or which has been recently charged.

2. Do not disconnect live circuits at battery terminals, because a spark usually occurs when a live circuit is broken. Care must always be taken while connecting or disconnecting any battery charger; be sure its power switch is off before making or breaking connections. Poor connections are a common cause of electrical arcs whcih cause explosions.

Inspection and Service

1. Measure the specific gravity of the battery electrolyte with a hydrometer. The specific gravity is calibrated on the hydrometer float stem. The reading is taken at the fluid surface level with the float buoyant in the fluid. See **Figure 2**.

2. If the reading is less than 1.20 with the temperature corrected to 68°F, recharge the battery. See **Figure 3** for a graph of specific gravity vs. residual capacity.

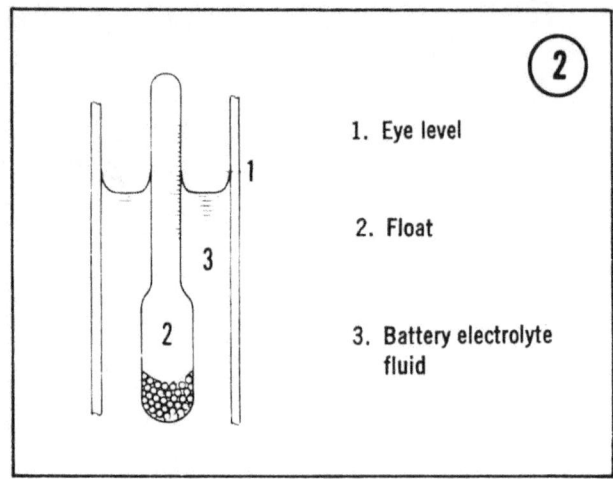

1. Eye level
2. Float
3. Battery electrolyte fluid

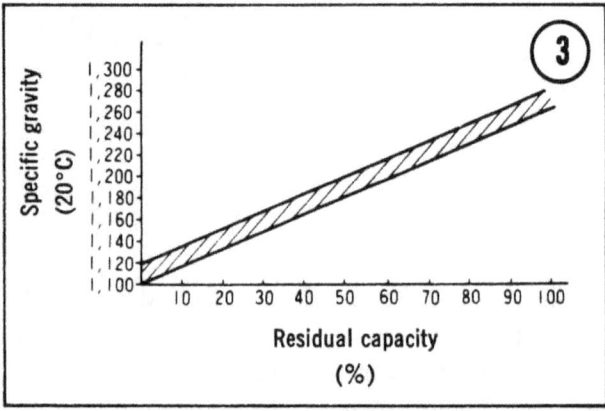

3. If any cell electrolyte level is below the lower mark on the battery case, fill with distilled water to the upper mark.

4. Replace the battery if the case is cracked or damaged. Corrosion on the battery terminals causes leakage of current. Clean with a wire brush or with a solution of baking soda and water.

5. Check the battery terminal connections. If corrosion is present, the connection is poor. Clean the terminal and connector. Coat with Vaseline and reinstall.

6. Vibration causes the corrosion of the battery plates to flake off, forming a paste on the bottom (see **Figure 4**). Replace the battery when paste builds up considerably (clear case battery) or when it fails to hold a charge (black case).

Charging

Batteries are not designed for high charge or discharge rates. For this reason, it is recommended that a battery be charged at a rate not exceeding 10 percent of its ampere-hour capac-

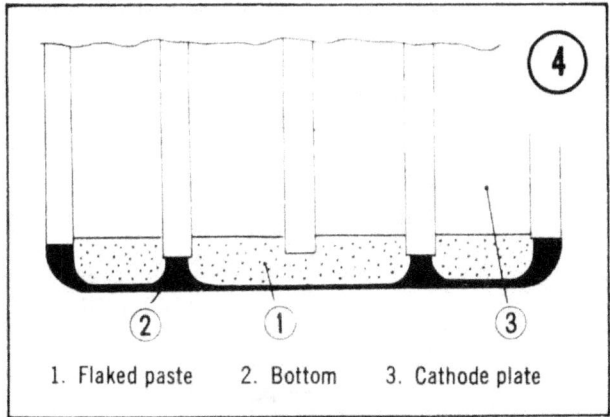

1. Flaked paste 2. Bottom 3. Cathode plate

ity. That is, do not exceed 0.5 ampere charging rate for a 5 ampere-hour battery, or 1.5 amperes for a 15 ampere-hour battery. This charge rate should continue for 10-13 hours if the battery is completely discharged, or until specific gravity of each cell is up to 1.260-1.280, corrected for temperature. If after prolonged charging, specific gravity of one or more cells does not come up to at least 1.230, the battery will not perform as well as it should, but may continue to provide satisfactory service for a time.

Some temperature rise is normal as a battery is being charged. Do not allow the electrolyte temperature to exceed 110°F (43.3°C). Should temperature reach that figure, discontinue charging until the battery cools, then resume charging at a lower rate.

If possible, always slow-charge a battery (see **Table 2**). Quick-charging will shorten the battery service life. Use a quick-charge only if *absolutely necessary*.

Table 2 BATTERY CHARGE

Charging current rate	Maximum of 10% of ampere-hour rating
Checking for full charge	① Specific gravity: 1.260-1.280 at 20°C (68°F) maintained constant for one hour ② 7.5V-8.3V maintained constant at terminals, checked with voltmeter
Charging duration	By the above method, a battery with specific gravity of electrolyte below 1.220 at 20°C (68°F) will be fully charged in approximately 10-13 hours

1. Hook the battery to a charger by connecting the positive lead to the positive (red) terminal on the battery and the negative lead to the negative (black) terminal. To do otherwise could cause severe damage to the battery and could result in injury if the battery explodes.

2. The electrolyte will begin bubbling, signifying that explosive hydrogen gas is being released. Excessive bubbling indicates that the charging rate is too high. Make sure the area is adequately ventilated and that there are no open flames.

3. It will normally take at least 8 hours to bring the battery to full charge. Test the electrolyte periodically with a hydrometer to see if the specific gravity is within the standard range of 1.26-1.28. If the reading remains constant for more than an hour, the battery is charged.

Installation

1. Wash the battery with water to remove spilled electrolyte. Coat the terminals with Vaseline or light grease before installing.

2. When replacing the battery, be careful to route the vent tube so that it is not crimped. Connect the positive terminal first, then the negative one. Don't overtighten the clamps.

3. Remeasure the specific gravity of the electrolyte with a bulb hydrometer.

WIRING DIAGRAM

A typical wiring diagram for Ossa motorcycles is given in **Figure 5**. Refer to it when servicing the electrical system.

See **Figures 6 and 7** for the way the electrical and exhaust systems are fitted on the Ossa motorcycle.

IGNITION SYSTEM

The Motoplat solid state electronic ignition system is used on all Ossa motorcycles. This system uses no breaker points, cams, or other moving parts. Because of the extremely fast rise time of the generated high voltage, effects of spark plug fouling are minimized.

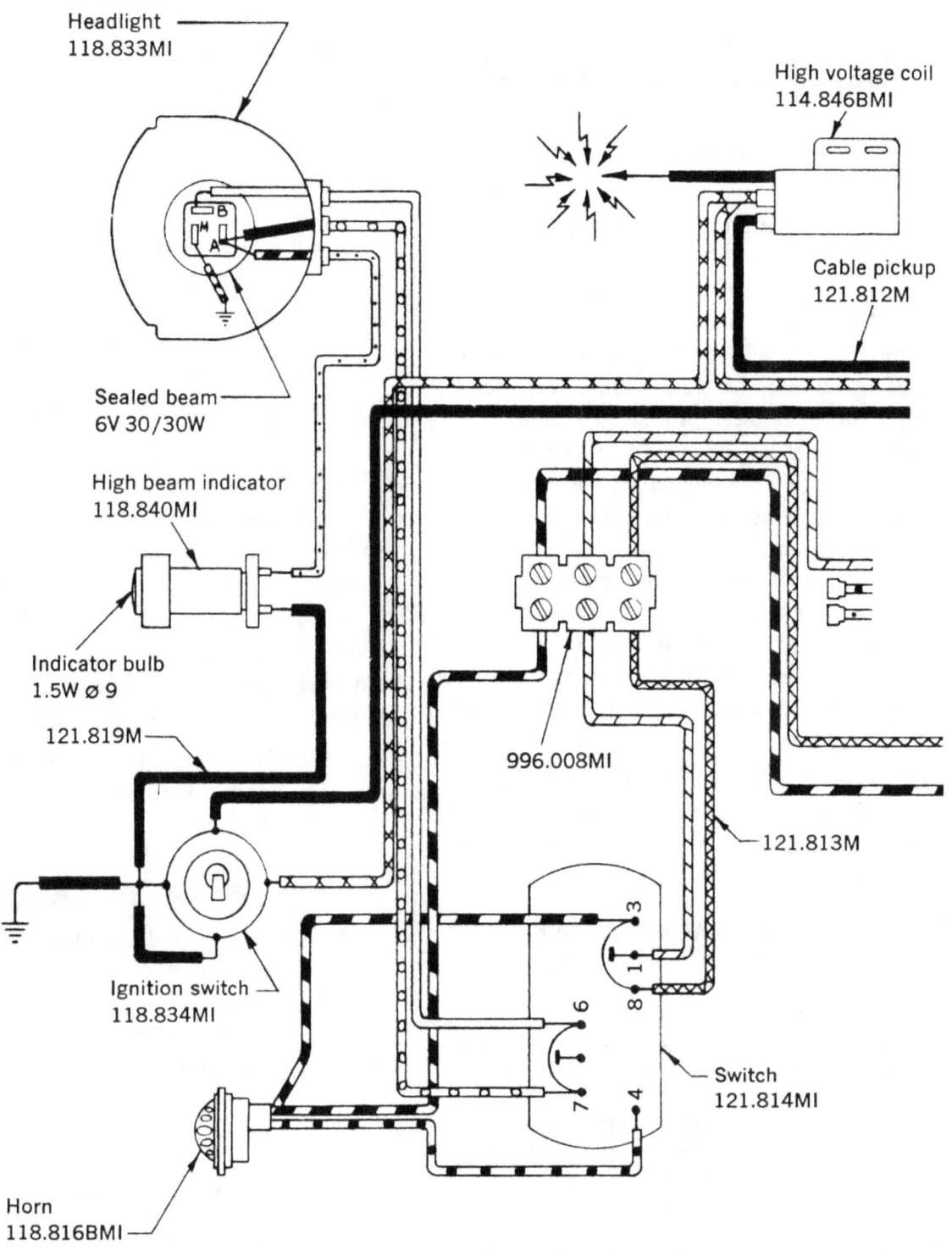

WIRING DIAGRAM — TYPICAL 250

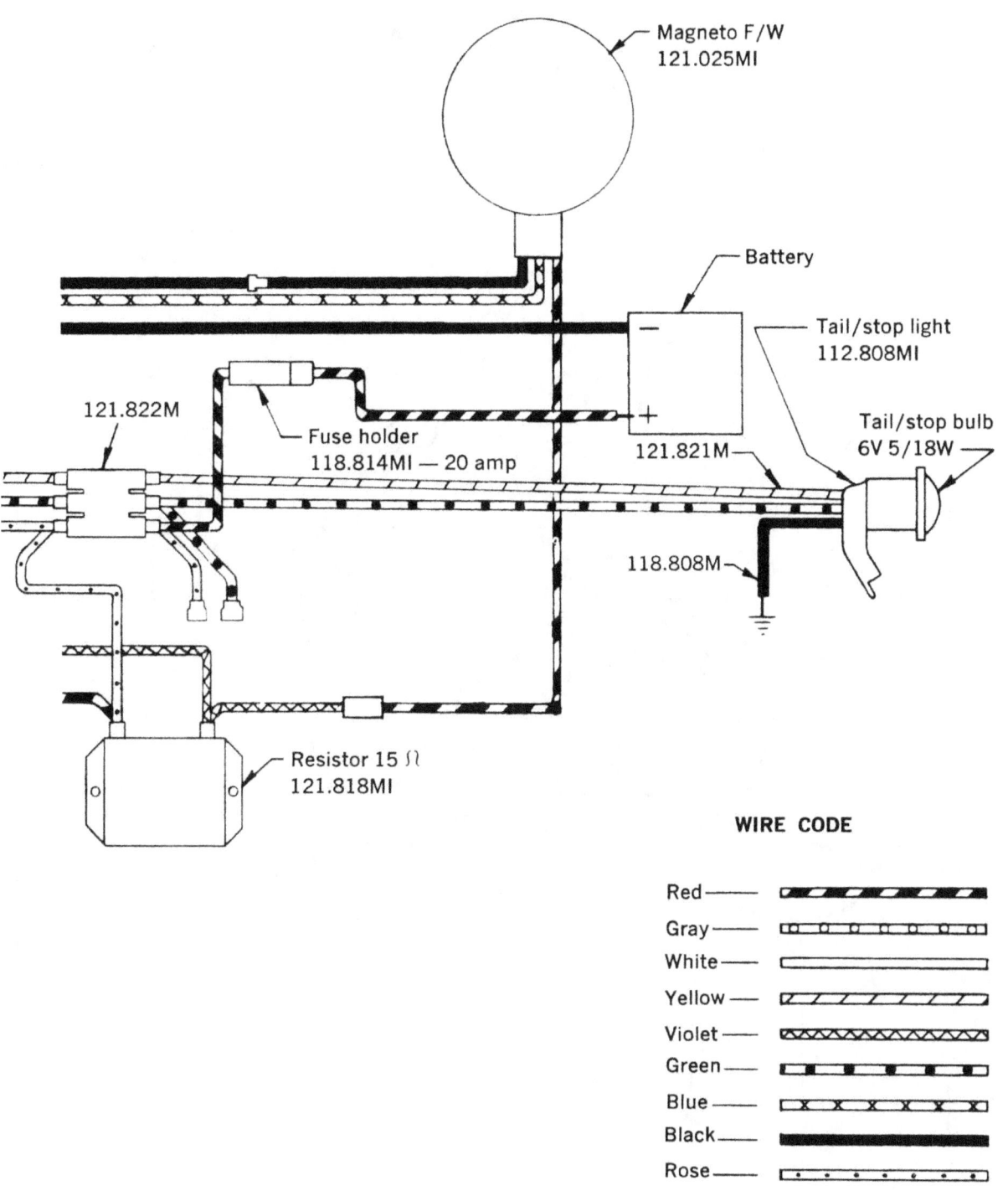

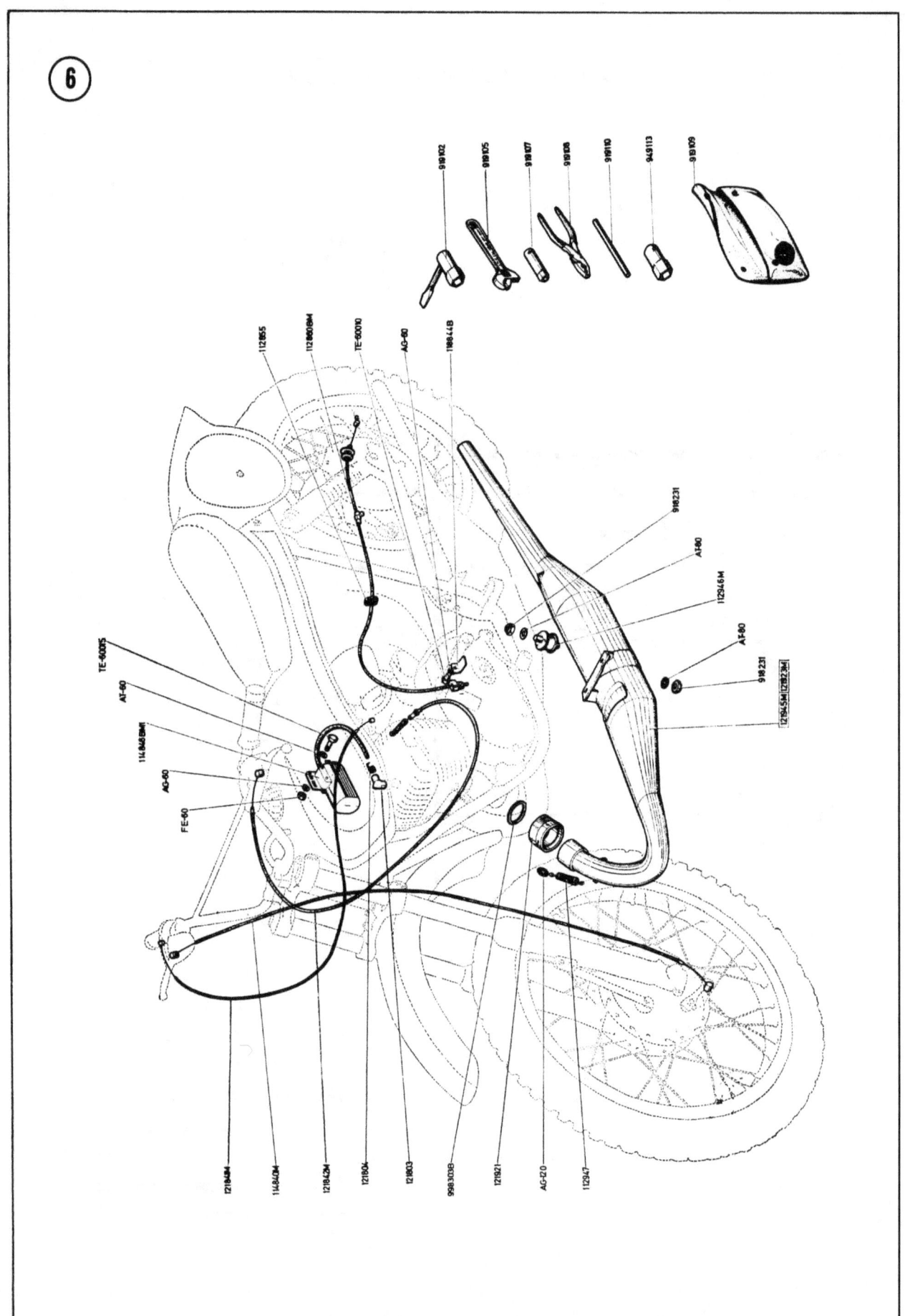

ELECTRICAL AND EXHAUST SYSTEM (TYPICAL)

Part Number	DESCRIPTION	Quantity
112.855	Rubber ring rear brake	2
112.860 BM	Rear cable assembly	1
112.946 M	Exhaust silent block	2
112.947	Spring exhaust mount	2
114.840 M	Front cable assembly	1
114.846 BMI	H.T. coil	1
118.844 B	Cable guide	1
121.803	Spark plug cap	1
121.804	Spring spark plug cap	1
121.841 M	Throttle cable assembly	1
121842 M	Clutch cable assembly	1
121.921	Exhaust nut	1
121.923 M	Expansion chamber (for 175 AS)	1
121.945 M	Expansion chamber (for 250 AS)	1
918.231	Exhaust nut mount	4
996.028 MI	Junction block	1
998.303 B	Gasket exhaust nut	1

COMMON PARTS

Part Number	DESCRIPTION	Quantity
AG-60	Washer H.T. coil, cable guide	3
AG-120	Washer exhaust spring	2
AT-60	Washer H.T. coil	2
AT-80	Washer expansion chamber	4
FE-60	Nut H.T. coil	2
TE-60010	Bolt cable guide	1
TE-60015	Bolt H.T. coil	2

TOOLS

Part Number	DESCRIPTION	Quantity
919.102	Spark plug socket	1
919.105	Adjustable wrench	1
919.107	12 mm. socket	1
919.108	Pliers	1
919.109	Tool bag	1
919.110	T. Handle	1
949.113	23 mm. socket	1

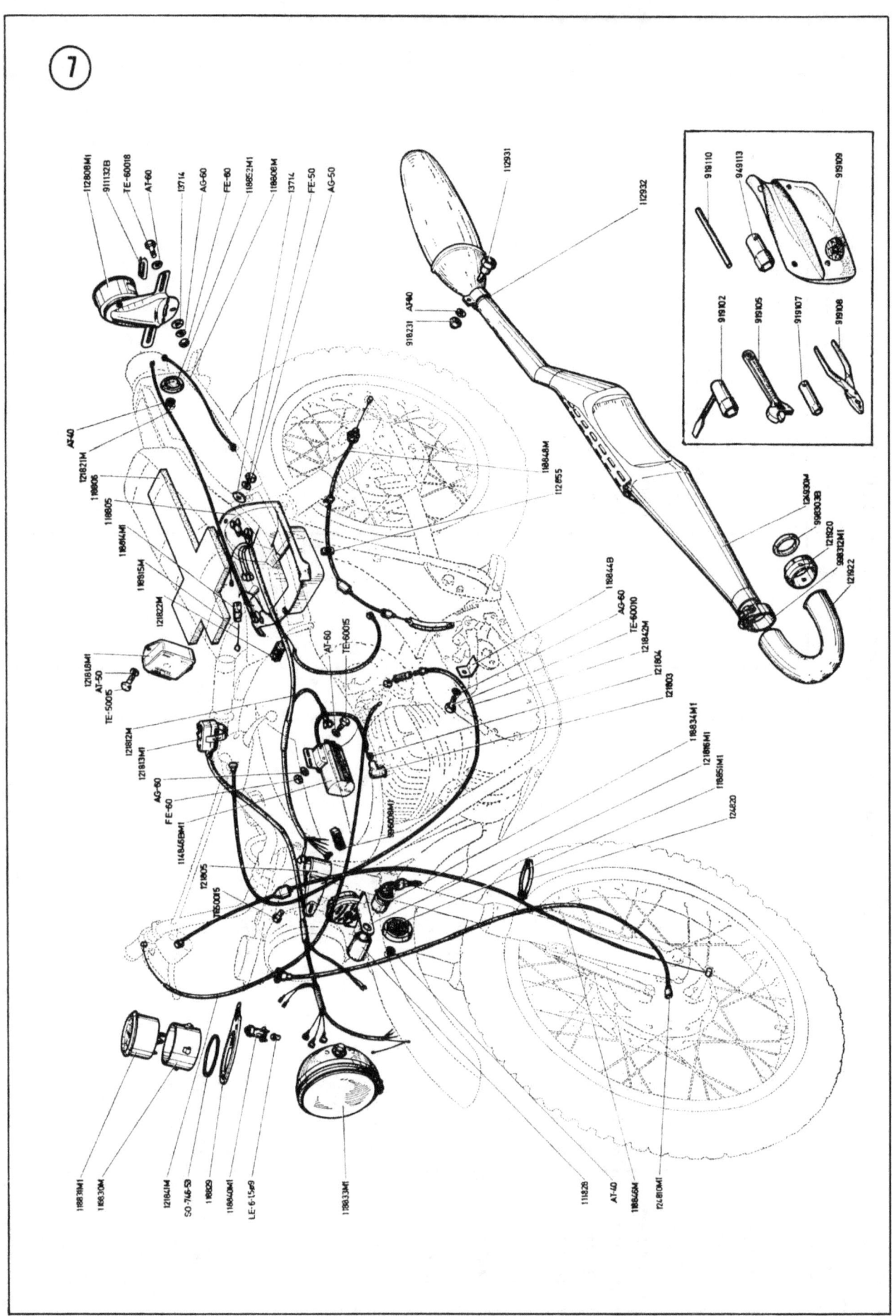

WIRING AND EXHAUST COMPONENTS — 250 AE-72 PIONEER

Part Number	Description	Quantity
13.714	Washer, Regulator and taillight	5
111.828	Rubber protector	1
112.808 MI	Bracket taillight	1
112.855	Guide rear cable	1
112.931	Nut, shockabsorbers and exhaust pipe	1
112.932	Clamp, muffler	1
114.846 BMI	H. T. coil	1
118.804 M	Wiring regulator and battery	1
118.805	Bracket regulator and battery	1
118.806	Battery box foam	1
118.808 M	Ground wiring taillight	1
118.814 MI	Fuse box	1
118.815 M	Wiring, fuse to battery	1
118.829	Bracket speedometer mount	1
118.830 M	Bracket assembly speedometer	1
118.831 MI	Speedometer assembly	1
118.833 MI	Headlight assembly	1
118.834 MI	Switch assembly	1
118.840 MI	High beam indicator	1
118.844 B	Cable guide	1
118.846 M	Front brake cable assembly	1
118.848 M	Rear brake cable assembly	1
118.851 MI	Front reflector	2
118.852 MI	Rear reflector	2
121.803	Spark plug cap	1
121.804	Spring spark plug cap	1
121.805	Bracket headlight mount	2
121.812 M	Wiring harness	1
121.813 MI	Horn assembly	1
121.816 MI	Wiring headlight with switch box	1
121.818 MI	Regulator	1
121.821 M	Wiring taillight	1
121.822 M	Junction box	1
121.841 M	Throttle cable assembly	1
121.842 M	Clutch cable assembly	1
121.920	Exhaust nut	1
121.922	Exhaust pipe	1
124.810 MI	Speedometer cable	1
124.820	Clamp cable guide	2
124.930 M	Muffler assembly	1

Part Number	Description	Quantity
911.132 B	Rubber wiring protector	1
918.231	Nut muffler clamp	1
996.008 MI	Junction box	1
998.303 B	Gasket exhaust pipe	1
998.312 MI	Clamp muffler	1
	COMMON PARTS	
AG-50	Spring washer, regulator	2
AG-60	Washer H. T. coil taillight bracket, and cable guide	6
AG-120	Washer, spring mount.	2
AT-40	Washer, horn reflectors	4
AT-50	Washer, regulator	6
AT-60	Washer, H. T. coil, taillight bracket	5
AT-80	Washer, Exhaust pipe	1
FE-50	Nut, regulator	2
FE-60	Nut, H. T. coil, taillight bracket	5
LE-6-1,5 Ø 9	Bulb, high beam indicator	1
SO-746-53	O Ring speedometer mount	1
TE-50015	Bolt regulator and headlight bracket	6
TE-60010	Bolt, cable guide	1
TE-60015	Bolt, H. T. coil	2
TE-60018	Bolt, taillight bracket	3
	TOOLS	
919.102	Spark plug socket	1
919.105	Adjustable wrench 6 mm.	1
919.107	12 mm. socket	1
919.108	Pliers	1
919.109	Tool bag	1
919.110	T. handle	1
949.113	23 mm. socket	1

System Operation

Figure 8 is a schematic diagram of the electronic ignition system. Alternating current is developed in the source coil (1) as magnets within the flywheel rotate past the coil. This current is rectified by diode (2), and then charge capacitor (3). Thyristor (4) is normally in a non-conducting state, and prevents discharge of the capacitor. A small magnet attached to the magneto flywheel moves past signal coil (7) as the piston approaches firing position, and thereby induces a small voltage in the signal coil. This voltage is applied to the trigger electrode in the thyristor, which then immediately conducts, providing a discharge path for the capacitor through the primary winding of ignition coil (8). Ignition voltage is stepped up in the ignition coil to a value sufficient to fire spark plug (5). Resistor (6) acts as a limiter.

Figure 9 illustrates system connections. Note that a kill button must be connected to the blue terminal only.

The source coil (magneto stator) is also wired to provide charging current for the lighting system, if fitted.

Electronic Ignition Maintenance

No maintenance is required on the electronic ignition system other than occasional checks to be sure that all connections are clean and secure. Be sure that the mounting bracket on the electronic converter unit makes good electrical contact with the motorcycle frame. Failure to maintain a good connection at this point may result in ignition system malfunction.

Ignition Timing

Refer to Chapter Two for timing specifications and procedures.

Electronic Ignition Cautions

The electronic ignition is simple and should give no trouble. Damage can occur, however, if certain precautions are not observed.

1. Never stop the machine by disconnecting the spark plug lead. Connect a kill button, if required, to the blue wire only.
2. Do not interchange the blue and black wires.
3. Keep all connections clean and tight, including mounting bracket to frame connection.

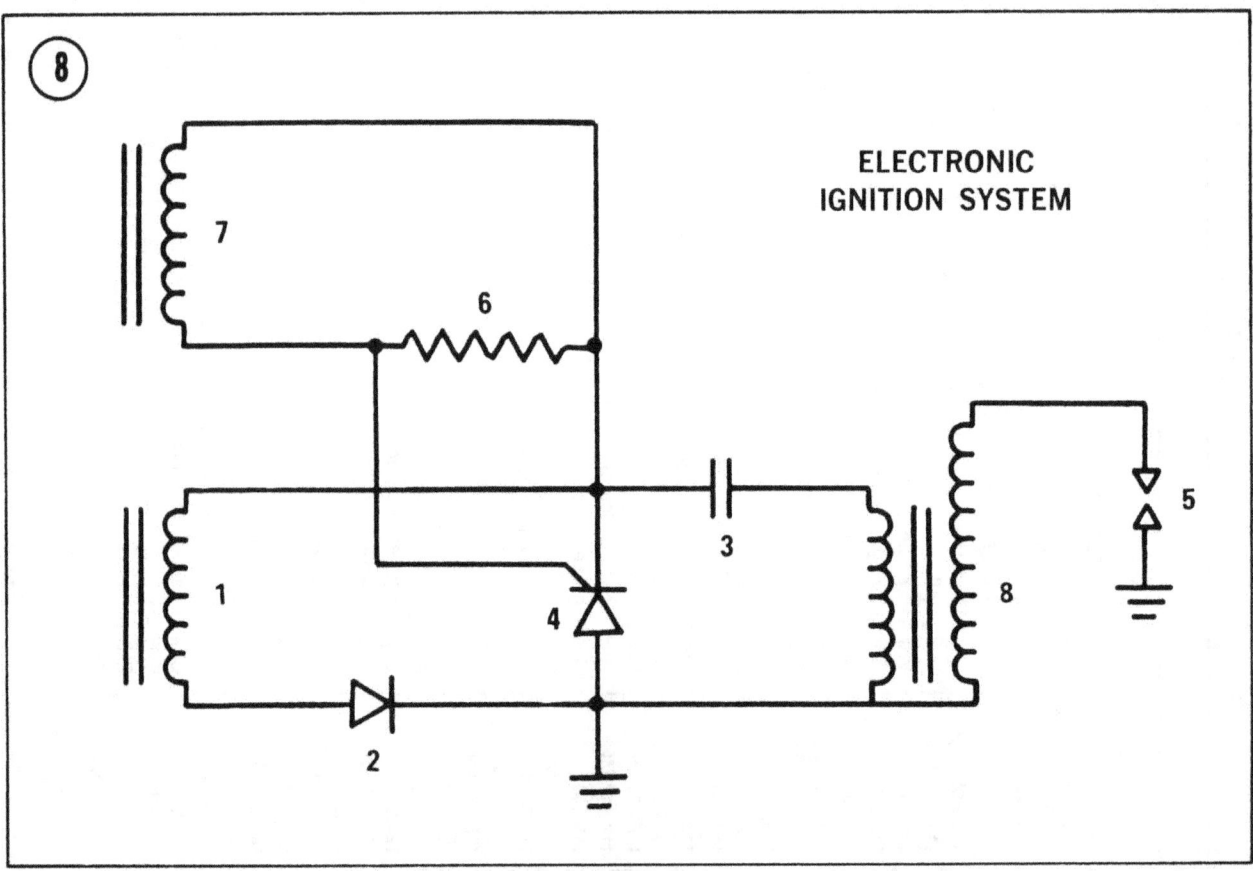

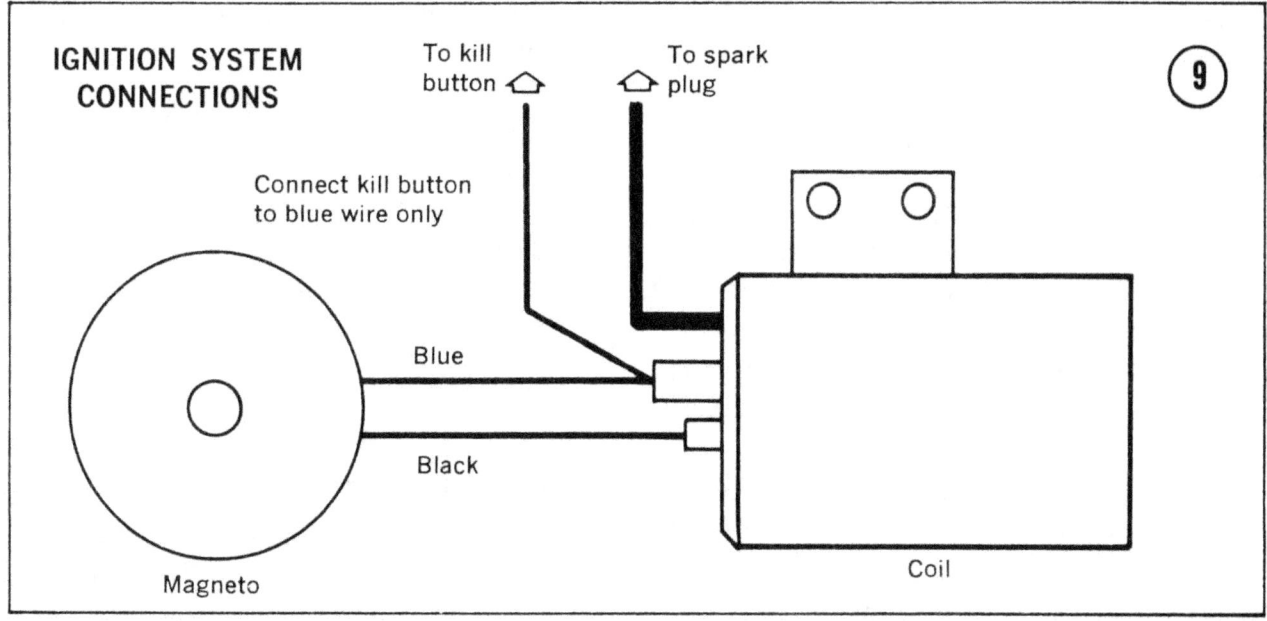

Troubleshooting

Refer to Chapter Three for troubleshooting the ignition system.

IGNITION COIL

Removal/Installation

1. Disconnect the ground lead to the battery, if equipped.
2. Disconnect leads to the coil.
3. Detach coil from mounting bracket and remove.
4. Install in reverse order of removal.

IGNITION SWITCH

Removal/Installation

1. Disconnect the ground lead to the battery, if equipped.
2. Remove the fuse.
3. Disconnect leads to the switch.
4. Detach the switch from the mounting bracket and remove.
5. Install in reverse order of removal.

HEADLIGHT

Replacement

Early models of the Pioneer use a 6-volt bulb instead of the sealed beam found in more current machines. If the bulb or sealed beam is burned out, service is the same, since the bulb should be replaced with the sealed beam for better lighting.

1. Loosen the screw clamping the chrome ring on the front of the headlight unit and spread the ends as shown in **Figure 10**.

2. Disconnect the wiring connector and remove the defective unit.
3. Replace the sealed beam with a 40/20 unit available from a dealer.
4. Reconnect the wiring.
5. Fit the rubber ring securely around the unit and replace in the headlight shell. If both chrome rings have been removed, note that they fit properly with their flat edges facing each other.

Adjustment

Proper headlight adjustment is essential to safe night riding. If the lights are set too low, the road will not be visible. If set too high, they will blind oncoming vehicles. Adjustment is very simple and should be a part of routine maintenance. Specifications vary from state to state, so get a dealer's advice if there is any doubt. The procedure is as follows.

1. Place the motorcycle approximately 16 feet from a white or light colored wall. Refer to **Figure 11**.
2. Make sure the motorcycle and wall are on level, parallel ground and that the motorcycle is pointing directly ahead.
3. Measurements should be made with one rider sitting on the seat and both wheels on the ground.
4. Draw a cross on the wall equal in height to the center of the headlight.
5. Put on the high beam. The cross should be centered in the concentrated beam of light.
6. If the light does not correspond to the mark, adjust the headlight by loosening the bolts holding the headlight shell to the mounts on the fork tubes. Tighten the bolts and recheck positioning.

TAILLIGHT, INDICATOR LIGHT, AND HORN

Removal/Installation

Removal of the taillight, indicator lights, and horn are straightforward tasks. See Figures 6 and 7 for typical illustrations of the way electrical components and wiring are fitted to the Ossa motorcycle.

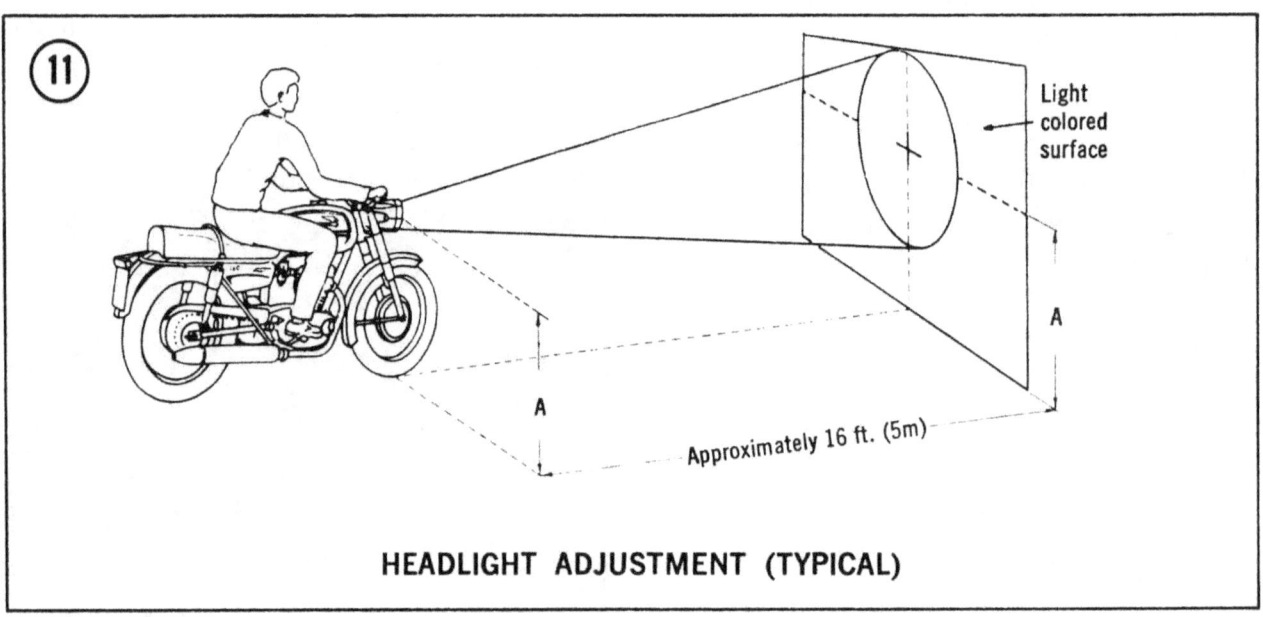

HEADLIGHT ADJUSTMENT (TYPICAL)

CHAPTER SIX

ENGINE

This chapter provides procedures for removal, disassembly, replacement, reassembly, and installation of Ossa motorcycle engines. Much work can be performed on the engine while it is in the frame. Find the section which specifically applies to the repair or replacement needed and read it carefully to determine the extent of work required and whether or not it will be necessary to remove the engine from the frame.

Illustrations are included to show differences between the engines and to aid in performing the work. Study them carefully to avoid confusion. **Figures 1 and 2** are exploded illustrations of typical Ossa engines.

Operating principles of the piston port, 2-stroke engine is discussed in this chapter.

ENGINE OPERATION

Figures 3 through 6 illustrate the operation of a piston port engine.

During this discussion, assume that the crankshaft is rotating counterclockwise.

In Figure 3, as the piston travels downward, a scavenging port (A) between the crankcase and the cylinder is uncovered. The exhaust gases leave the cylinder through the exhaust port (B), which is also opened by the downward movement of the piston. A fresh fuel/air charge, which has previously been compressed slightly, travels from the crankcase (C) to the cylinder through the scavenging port (A) as the port opens. Since the incoming charge is under pressure, it rushes into the cylinder quickly and helps to expell the exhaust gases from the previous cycle.

Figure 4 illustrates the next phase of the cycle. As the crankshaft continues to rotate, the piston moves upward, closing the exhaust and scavenging ports. As the piston continues upward, the air/fuel mixture in the cylinder is compressed. Notice also that a low pressure area is created in the crankcase at the same time. Further upward movement of the piston uncovers the intake port (D). A fresh fuel/air charge is then drawn into the crankcase through the intake port because of the low pressure created by the upward piston movement.

The third phase is shown in Figure 5. As the piston approaches top dead center, the spark plug fires, igniting the compressed mixture. The piston is then driven downward by the expanding gases.

When the top of the piston uncovers the exhaust port, the fourth phase begins, as shown in Figure 6. The exhaust gases leave the cylinder through the exhaust port. As the piston con-

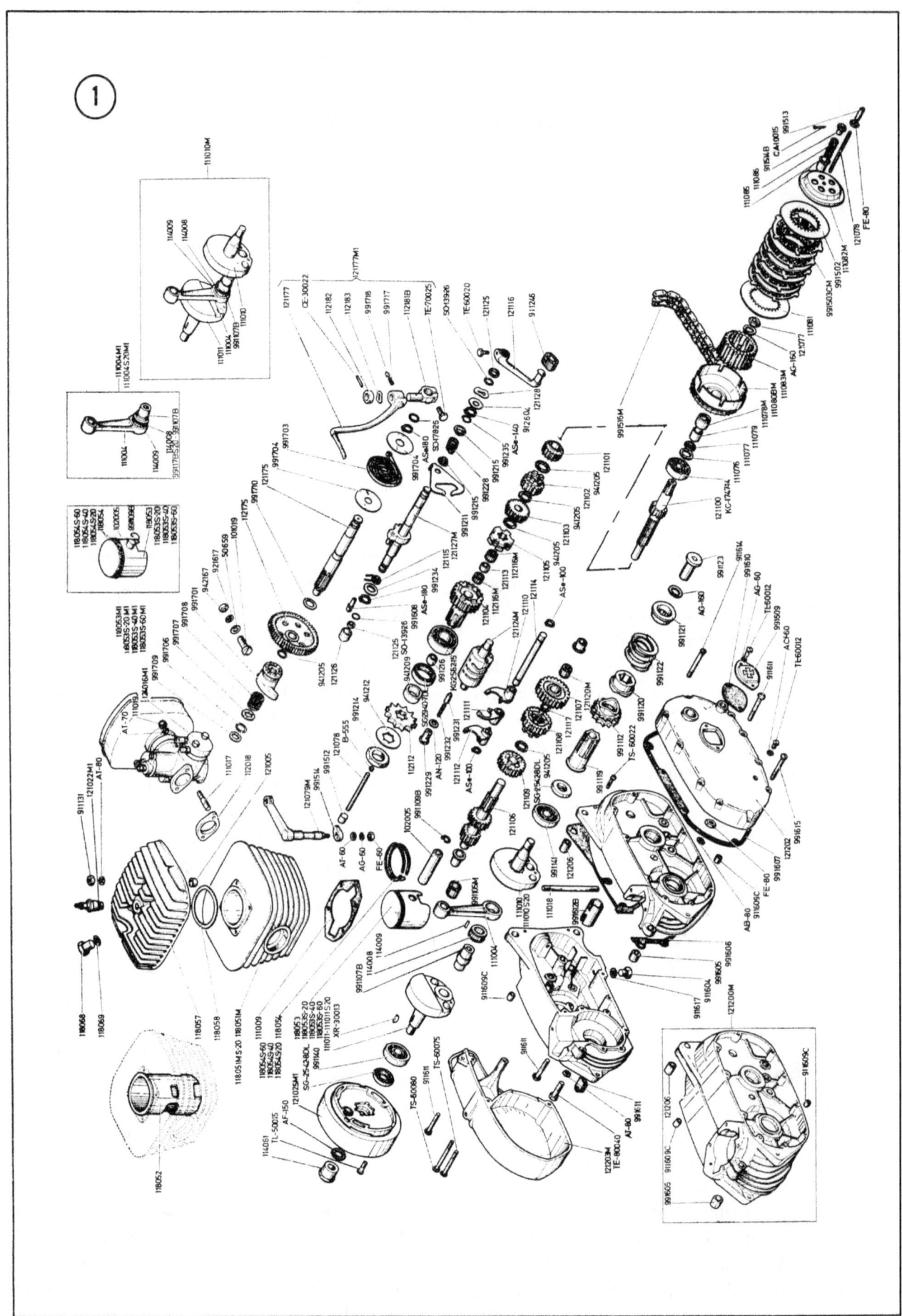

250 PIONEER (250 PHANTOM SIMILAR)

Part Number	DESCRIPTION	Quanti.	Part Number	DESCRIPTION	Quanti.	Part Number	DESCRIPTION	Quanti.
124.001 MI	Engine assembly	1	121.104	Gear 5th. main shaft	1	991.235	Retaining ring	1
33.176 I-II-IV	Shim washer lay shaft	—	121.105	Dog wheel 4th. and 5th. gear	1	991.502	Clutch plate	5
33.292 I-II-IV-X	Shim washer lay shaft	—	121.106	Lay shaft	1	991.503 CM	Clutch plate	5
50.404 I-II-IV-X	Shim washer selector	—	121.107	Gear 1st lay shaft	1	991.512	Plunger clutch arm	1
50.659	Washer stop bolt kick	1	121.108	Gear 2nd lay shaft	1	991.513	Clutch regulating screw	1
101.019	Stop bolt kick	1	121.109	Gear 3rd lay shaft	1	991.514	Clutch cam	1
102.005	Wristpin	1	121.110	Shifting fork 1st. and 3rd.	1	991.516 M	Chain primary	1
111.004 MI	Connecting rod assembly	1	121.111	Shifting fork 2nd.	1	991.605	Locating dowel engine case	2
111.004 S-20MI	Connecting rod assembly 1st. oversize	1	121.112	Shifting fork 4th. and 5th.	1	991.606	Gasket center case	1
111.004	Connecting rod	1	121.113	Spacer 5th. gear	1	991.607	Gasket clutch cover	1
111.009	Crankshaft assembly	1	121.114	Shifting fork shaft	1	991.608	Anchor pin	1
111.010 M	Flywheel clutch side	1	121.115	Spring selector	1	991.609	Inspection cover	1
111.010	Flywheel magneto	1	121.116	Footshift lever	1	991.610	Inspection cover gasket	1
111.010 S-20	Flywheel clutch side 1st. oversize	1	121.117	Washer 1st. gear	1	991.611	Grommet rubber	1
111.010 S-20	Flywheel magneto 1st. oversize	1	121.120 M	Needle brg. 1st. gear	2	991.612 B	Tube breather	1
111.017	Stud, cylinder head	4	121.124 M	Selector body assembly	1	991.615	Screw engine cover primary side	1
111.018	Nut. intake manifold	2	121.125	Dust cover selector shaft	1	991.701	Ratchet Kickstarter	1
111.019	Thrust washer	1	121.126	Plug selector shaft	1	991.703	Spring	1
111.076	Spacer	1	121.127 M	Selector shaft assembly	1	991.704	Washer kickstarter spring	1
111.077	Needle brg.	1	121.128	Washer selector shaft spring	1	991.706	Circlip kickstarter shaft	1
111.078 M	.O. ring	2	121.175	Shaft Kickstarter	1	991.707	Stop kickstarter spring	1
111.079	Clutch hub assembly	1	121.177 MI	Kickstarter lever assembly	1	991.708	Spring kickstarter engage	1
111.080 BM	Clutch plate inner	1	121.200 M	Engine cases assembly	1	991.709	Thrust washer kickstarter shaft	1
111.081	Clutch plate outer	1	121.202	Clutch cover	1	991.710	Thrust washer kickstarter gear	1
111.082 M	Clutch hub assembly	1	121.203 M	Magneto cover	1	991.717	Spring, lever kickstarter	1
111.083 M	Cup clutch spring	1	121.206 M	Bushing	1	991.718	Pin kick lever	1
111.085	Clutch spring	5	124.016 MI	Carburetor	1			
111.086	Gasket manifold	5	911.131	Nut cylinder head	4		COMMON PARTS	
112.018	Countershaft sprocket	1	911.139 II-IV-X	Shim washer	—			
112.112	Needle brg. cage 5th. gear	2	911.514 B	Rubber footshift lever	1	AB-80	Spring washer engine cases	1
112.175	Kickstarter driving gear	1	911.604	Slotted nut clutch spring	5	ACf-60	Washer oil lever screw	1
112.182 B	Kick lever suport	1	911.609 C	Drain plug	4	AF-150	Washer magneto	1
112.183	Suport kick lever ring	1	911.611	Locating dowel	15	AG-60	Lock washer clutch arm, inspection cover	3
114.008	Spring washer lever	14	911.614	Bolt, engine cases	4	AG-160	Washer cush drive hub	1
114.009	Cage big end bearing	1	911.617	Screw	1	AN-120	Flat washer	2
114.081	Roller big end bearing	1	912.604	Gasket drain plug	1	ASe-100	Snap, ring fork shaft	1
118.051 M	Nut magneto flywheel	1	921.111	Washer selector shaft		ASe-140	Snap, ring selector	2
118.051 MS-20	Cylinder assembly	2	921.112	Shim washer main shaft 0.05	5	ASe-180	Snap, ring selector and kickstarter	5
118.052	Cylinder Assembly 1st oversize		921.113	Shim washer main shaft 0.1	5	AT-60	Clutch arm washer	5
118.053	Cylinder sleeve	1	921.617	Shim washer main shaft 0.2	2	AT-70	Carburetor mounting washer	1
118.053 S-20-2MI	Piston assembly	1	941.205	Washer	1	AT-80	Washer head and engine cases	1
118.053 S-40 MI	Piston assembly 2nd oversize	1	941.209	Circlip	5	B-555	Clutch rod ball	1
118.053 S-60 MI	Piston assembly 3rd oversize	1	941.212	Spacer countershaft sprocket	1	CA.10.015	Clutch bolt cotter pin	2
118.053	Piston	1	942.167	Washer countershaft sprocket	1	CE-30.022	Kick suport pin	1
118.053 S-20	Piston 1st oversize	1	991.105 M	Nut stop bolt	1	FE-60	Clutch arm nlt	1
118.053 S-40	Piston 2nd oversize	1	991.107 BS-20	Rod brg. cage	1	FE-80	Nut clutch and engine	1
118.053 S-60	Piston 3rd oversize	1	991.107	Crankshaft pin	2	KC-17-47-14	Gearbox bearing	2
118.054	Piston ring	2	991.109 B	Crankshaft pin 1st oversize		KC-25-52-15	Gearbox bearing	2
118.054 S-20	Piston ring 1st oversize	2	991.112	Piston circlip	2	SG-25-42-8-DL	Oil seal	1
118.054 S-40	Piston ring 2nd oversize		991.119	Engine sprocket	1	SG-29-40-7-DL	Oil seal	1
118.054 S-60	Piston ring 3rd oversize		991.120	Shaft cush drive	1	SO-139-26	.O. ring selector shaft	1
118.057	Cylinder head	1	991.121	Coupling cush drive	1	SO-178-26	.O. ring kickstarter	1
118.058	Gasket cylinder head	1	991.122	Stop spring	1	TE-60.020	Bolt gear lever	1
118.068	Compression release plug	1	991.123	Spring cush drive	1	TE-70.025	Engine bolt	2
118.069	Compression release gasket	1	991.139 II-IV-X	Allen nut cush drive		TE-80.040	Bolt kickstarter lever	1
121.005	Stud, protection tube	4	991.140	Right main brg.	1	TL-50.015	Engine bolt	1
121.022 MI	Spark plug	1	991.141	Left main brg.	1	TL-60.012	Screw magneto back-plate	3
121.025 MI	Magneto assembly	1	991.214	Selector fork	1	TS-60.075	Clutch cover and oil level bolt	2
121.077	Nut clutch hub	1	991.216	Spring stop selector	2	TS-60.080	Engine case bolt	2
121.078	Clutch arm assembly	2	991.228	Oil seal	1	XR.30.013	Bolt magneto cover	2
121.079 M	Clutch hub	1	991.229	Spring	1		Bolt magneto cover	2
121.100	Main shaft	1	991.231	Guide selector	1		Magneto key	1
121.101	Gear 2nd main shaft	1	991.232	Anchor pin selector				
121.102	Gear 3rd main shaft	1	991.234	Spring				
121.103	Gear 4th main shaft	1		Washer selector shaft				

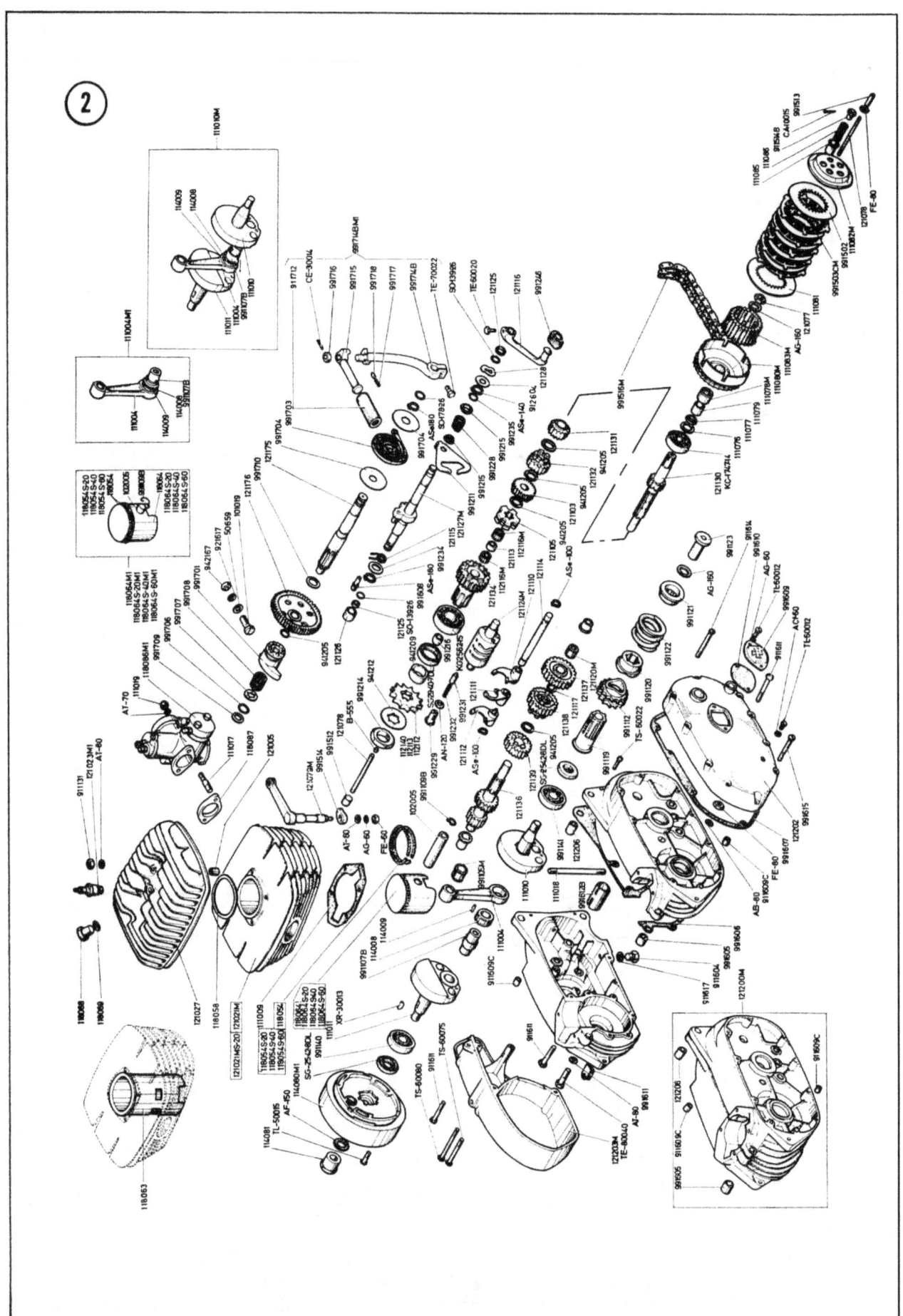

ENGINE – 250 STILETTO

Part Number	DESCRIPTION	Quanti.	Part Number	DESCRIPTION	Quanti.	Part Number	DESCRIPTION	Quanti.
121.021 MI	Engine assembly	1	121.117	Washer 1st gear	1	991.606	Gasket center case	1
33.176 I-II-IV	Shim washer lay shaft	–	121-120 M	Needle brg. 1st gear	1	991.607	Gasket clutch cover	1
33.292 I-II-IV	Shim washer lay shaft	–	121-124 M	Selector body assembly	2	991.605	Anchor pin	1
50.404 I-II-IV-X	Shim washer selector	–	121.125	Dust cover selector shaft	1	991.609	Inspection cover	1
50.659	Washer, stop bolt kick	1	121.126	Plug selector shaft	1	991.610	Inspection cover gasket	1
101.019	Stop bolt kick	1	121.127 M	Selector shaft assembly	1	991.611	Grommet rubber	1
102.005	Wristpin	1	121.128	Washer selector shaft spring	1	991.612 B	Tube breather	1
111.004	Connecting rod assembly	1	121.130	Main shaft	1	991.615	Screw engine cover primary side	1
111.004 MI	Connecting rod	1	121.131	Gear 2nd main shaft	1	991.701	Ratchet kickstarter	1
111.009	Cylinder gasket	1	121.132	Gear 3rd main shaft	1	991.703	Spring kickstarter	1
111.010	Crankshaft assembly	1	121.134	Gear 5th main shaft	1	991.704	Washer kickstarter spring	2
111.010 M	Flywheel clutch side	1	121.136	Lay shaft	1	991.706	Circlip kickstarter shaft	1
111.011	Flywheel magneto side	1	121.137	Gear 1st lay shaft	1	991.707	Stop kickstarter spring	1
111.017	Stud, carburetor	2	121.138	Gear 2nd lay shaft	1	991.708	Spring kickstarter engage	1
111.018	Nut, intake manifold	4	121.139	Gear 3rd lay shaft	1	991.709	Thrust washer kickstarter shaft	1
111.019	Washer thrust	2	121.175	Shaft kickstarter	1	991.710	Thrust washer kickstarter gear	1
111.076	Washer spacer	1	121.176	Kickstarter driving gear	1	991.714 BMI	Kickstarter lever assembly	1
111.077	Needle brg	1	121.200 M	Engine cases assembly	1	991.714 B	Kickstarter arm	1
111.078 M	-O- Ring	1	121.202	Clutch cover	1	991.715	Kickstarter lever	1
111.079	Clutch hub assembly	1	121.203 M	Magneto cover	1	991.716	Stop lever ring	1
111.080 M	Clutch plate inner	–	121.131	Nut cylinder head	4	991.717	Kick pin spring	1
111.081	Clutch plate outer	–	911.131	Shim washer	–	991.718	Kick pin	1
111.082 M	Clutch hub assembly	–	911.139 II-IV-X	Bushing	1			
111.033 M	Cup clutch spring	–	911.246	Rubber footshift lever	1		**COMMON PARTS**	
111.085	Clutch spring	5	911.514 B	Slotted nut clutch spring	1			
111.086	Countershaft sprocket	–	911.609 C	Drain plug	1	AB-80	Spring washer engine case	5
112.112	Countershaft sprocket z=11	–	911.611	Locating dowel	4	ACf-60	Washer oil level screw	1
112.113	Countershaft sprocket z=13	–	911.614	Bolt engine cases	15	AF-150	Washer magneto	1
112.116 M	Needle bg. cage 5th gear	2	911.617	Screw Drain Plug	1	AC-60	Lockwasher clutch arm, inspection cover	3
112.140	Cage big end bearing	1	911.712	Gasket Drain Plug	1	AG-160	Washer cush drive, hub	2
114.009	Roller big end bearing	14	912.604	Rubber kickstarter	1	AN-120	Flat washer	1
114.080 MI	Nut magneto flywheel	1	921.111	Washer selector shaft	–	ASe-100	Snap rink, fork shaft	2
114.081	Piston ring	2	921.112	Shim washer main shaft 0.05	–	ASe-140	Snap ring selector shaft	2
118.054	Piston ring 1st oversize	–	921.113	Shim washer main shaft 0,1	–	ASe-18U	Snap ring selector and kickstarter	2
118.054 S-20	Piston ring 2nd oversize	–	921.617	Shim washer main shaft 0,2	–	AT-60	Clutch arm washer	2
118.054 S-40	Piston ring 3rd oversize	–	941.205	Circlip	1	AT-70	Carburetor mounting washer	2
118.054 S-60	Gasket cylinder head	1	941.209	Spacer countershaft sprocket	–	AT-80	Washer head and engine case	5
118.058	Cylinder sleeve	1	941.212	Washer countershaft sprocket	–	B-555	Clutch rod ball	1
118.063	Piston assembly	1	942.167	Nut stop bolt	1	CA-10.015	Clutch bolt cotter pin	5
118.064 MI	Piston assembly 1st oversize	–	991.105 M	Rod brg. cage	1	CE-30.014	Cotter pin kickstarter	1
118.064 S-20 MI	Piston assembly 2nd oversize	–	991.107 B	Crankshaft pin	1	FE-80	Clutch arm nut	1
118.064 S-40 MI	Piston assembly 3rd oversize	–	991.109 B	Piston circlip	2	KC-17-47-14	Nut clutch and engine case	2
118.064 S-60 MI	Piston 1st oversize	–	991.112	Engine sprocket	1	KC-25-52-15	Gearbox bearing	1
118.064 S-20	Piston 2nd oversize	–	991.119	Shaft cush drive	1	SG-25-47-8 DL	Gearbox bearing	1
118.064 S-40	Piston 3rd oversize	–	991.120	Coupling cush drive	1	SG-29-40-7 DL	Oil seal	1
118.064 S-60	Compression release plug	1	991.121	Stop spring	1	SO-139-26	Oil seal	1
118.068	Compression release gasket	1	991.122	Allen nut cush drive	1	SO-178-26	-O- ring selector shaft	1
118.069	Carburetor	1	991.123	Shim washer	–	TE.70.020	-O- ring kickstarter	1
118.086 MI	Carburetor manifold spacer	1	991.139 II-IV-X	Right main brg.	1	TE.70.022	Bolt gear lever	1
118.087	Stud, protection tube	4	991.140	Left main brg.	1	TL.50.015	Bolt kickstarter lever	1
121.005	Cylinder assembly	1	991.141	Selector fork	1	TL.60.012	Engine bolt	3
121.021 M	Cylinder assembly 1st oversize	–	991.211	Nut countershaft sprocket	1	TS.60.022	Screw, magneto back plate	3
121.023 MI	Spark plug	1	991.214	Spring stop selector	2	TS.60.075	Clutch, cover and oil level bolt	2
121.027	Cylinder head	1	991.215	Washer selector shaft	1	TS.60.080	Engine case bolt	2
121.077	Nut clutch hub	1	991.228	Retaining ring	1	XR.30.013	Bolt magneto cover	1
121.078	Clutch rod	1	991.229	Clutch plate	5		Magneto key	1
121.079 M	Clutch arm assembly	1	991.231	Clutch plate	5			
121.103	Gear 4th main shaft	1	991.232	Plunger clutch arm	1			
121.105 M	Dog wheel 4th and 5th gear	1	991.234	Clutch regulating screw	1			
121.110	Shifting fork 1st and 3rd	1	991.235	Clutch cam	1			
121.111	Shifting fork 2nd	1	991.502	Chain primary	1			
121.112	Shifting fork 4th and 5th	1	991.503 CM	Locating dowel engine cases	1			
121.113	Spacer 5th gear	1	991.512					
121.114	Shifting fork snaft	1	991.513					
121.115	Spring selector	1	991.514					
121.116	Footshift lever	1	991.516 CM					
			991.605					

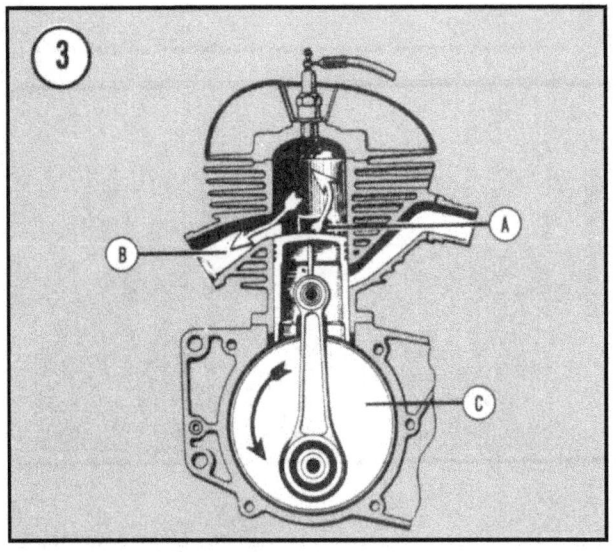

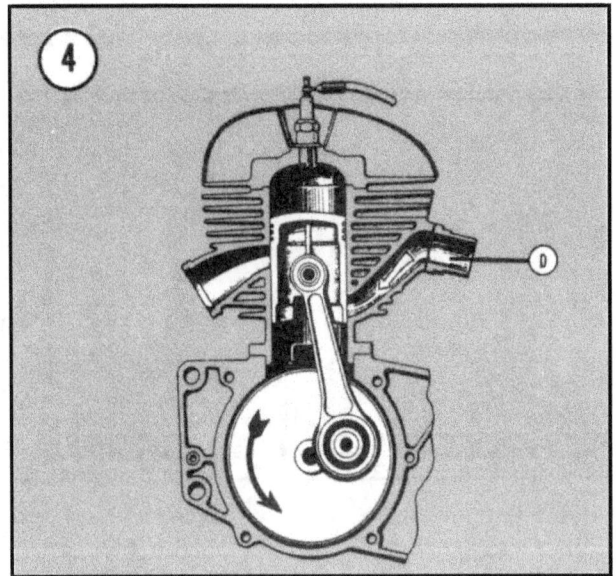

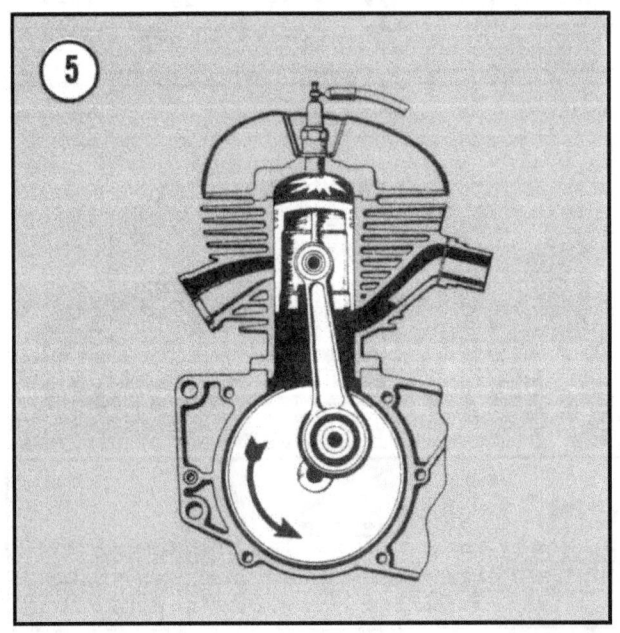

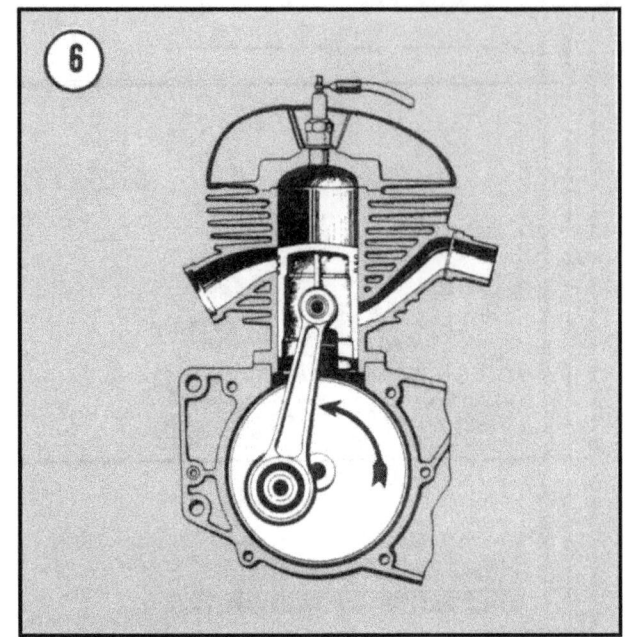

tinues downward, the intake port is closed and the mixture in the crankcase is compressed in preparation for the next cycle. Every downward stroke of the piston is a power stroke.

SERVICING ENGINE IN FRAME

The following parts can be serviced with the engine mounted in the frame:

    a. Cylinder head

    b. Cylinder and piston

    c. Electrical system

    d. Gearshift mechanism

    e. Clutch

    f. Carburetor

ENGINE REMOVAL/INSTALLATION

The engine area should be carefully cleaned with a suitable solvent to simplify work. Kerosene or a commercial product, such as Gunk, can be used. Be careful not to use a heavy concentration on painted surfaces. Rinse and wipe dry or blow dry with compressed air.

1. Shut off the fuel and disconnect the line.

2. Remove the seat (and battery, if fitted). Pause to top up the battery with distilled water; check it and charge, if necessary, according to Chapter Five under *Battery*.

3. Disconnect the ignition system wires. Disconnect any other wire which may interfere with engine removal. Mark wires for identification during assembly.

4. Disconnect the carburetor.

5. Turn the rear wheel until the master connecting link in the chain is accessible. Remove the clip and chain. Replace the master link so that it will not be lost. Place the chain in a container large enough to allow oil to cover every link and allow it to soak in standard 30-weight oil for a few days. Several hours prior to reassembly, hang the chain by one end and allow excess oil to drip off.

6. Remove the muffler if necessary. If removed, wrap the muffler in cloth to protect the finish.

> NOTE: *Parts are easier to locate and match up later if kept with their respective components when disassembled. For instance, a clamp can be replaced on a component and set aside. Bolts can be replaced in their holes after a component has been removed.*

7. Disconnect the clutch control cable.

8. Remove the kickstarter lever.

9. Examine the engine area carefully and disconnect or remove any remaining obstacles to the removal of the engine.

10. Starting at the top rear of the engine, remove all engine mounting nuts and bolts. Remove the engine and place it on a work stand. A homemade engine work stand can be fabricated out of scrap lumber. Form a box of 2 x 4 in. boards on edge, approximately 10 inches wide, 14 inches long, and set the engine on it. The engine can now be maneuvered for convenience in further work.

11. Install the engine in the frame by reversing the removal procedure.

12. After the engine is installed, be sure to adjust the clutch, drive chain, and carburetor following procedures given in Chapter Two.

CYLINDER AND PISTON

Removal

1. Thoroughly clean the engine as detailed previously.

2. If the engine is to be completely disassembled, remove the drain plug from the crankcase and drain the transmission oil. Drain thoroughly by leaning the engine in various directions while the oil is draining.

3. Inspect the drain plug gasket. Replace with a new one, if necessary.

4. Install the drain plug and gasket.

5. Loosen the cylinder head nuts ¼ turn each in a sequence such that loosening one nut by ¼ turn is followed by loosening the opposite (non-adjacent) nut by ¼ turn. Follow this sequence, loosening each nut another ¼ turn, until all nuts are completely loose. Loosening an individual nut fully in one operation or loosening adjacent nuts in sequence may cause warpage of the cylinder head. See **Figure 7**.

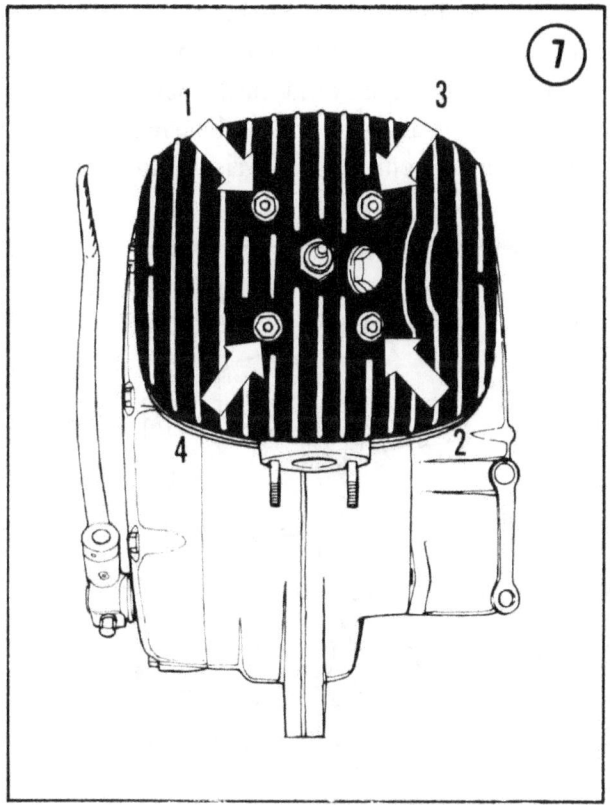

6. Remove the cylinder head.

7. Remove the cylinder head gasket. Be careful not to damage cylinder head mating surfaces.

8. If there is a suspicion that there may be rust or sediment in the holes containing the cylinder studs, turn the engine upside down to remove the cylinder. Otherwise, proceed as follows.

9. Slowly and carefully raise the cylinder from the cylinder base gasket to avoid breaking the

gasket. The gasket will not be reused but breaking it in this step could mean that pieces would fall down into the crankcase.

10. Stuff a clean rag into the crankcase opening under the cylinder to prevent any debris from falling into the crankcase.

11. Remove the cylinder from the cylinder studs. Support the piston so it cannot fall against the crankcase or cylinder studs when the cylinder clears it.

12. Check to see that the rag is snug around the connecting rod before removing the wrist pin circlips; otherwise, they may fall into the crankcase.

13. Remove and discard the wrist pin circlips.

14. Remove the wrist pin with a drift by pushing on the drift while holding the piston stationary. See **Figure 8**. If pushing by hand does not free the wrist pin, do *not* use impact force on the drift. The force could easily bend the connecting rod or damage the rod bearing. Instead, use a tool to remove the wrist pin as shown in **Figure 9**.

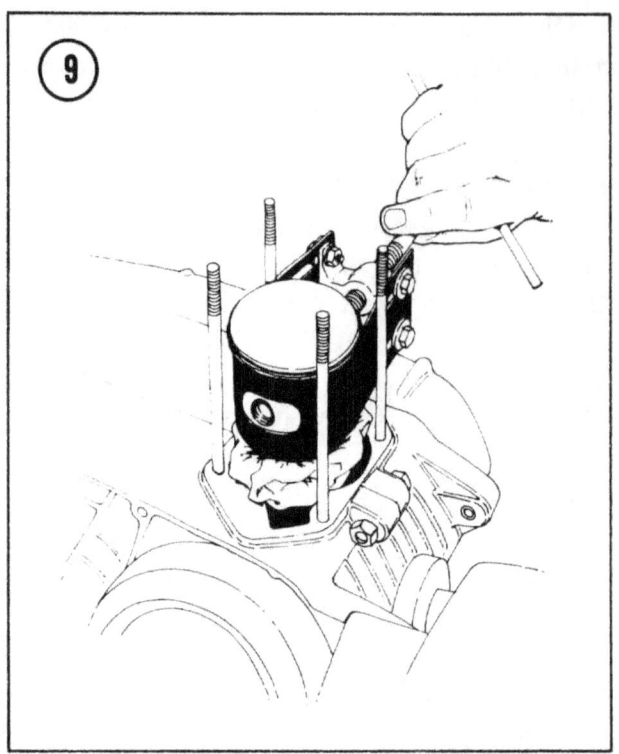

3. Measure the piston from front to back, at the bottom of the skirt, with a micrometer. See **Figure 10**.

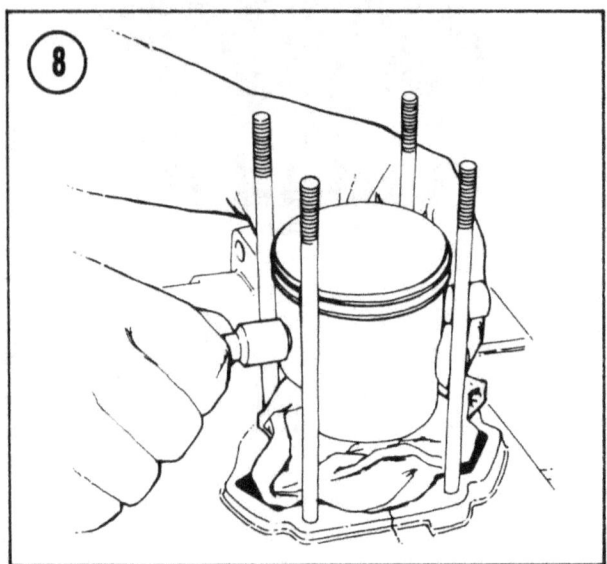

15. Remove the piston and needle bearing from the connecting rod.

16. Remove and discard cylinder base gasket.

Inspection/Installation

1. Clean the piston and cylinder in solvent and dry with compressed air.

2. Check the piston and cylinder for wear, damage, or cracks.

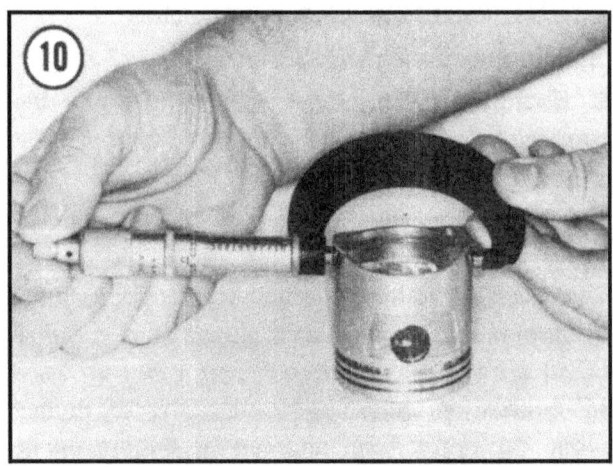

4. Measure the front to back distance on the inside of the cylinder at a point approximately one inch from the bottom of the liner. See **Figure 11**. Determine piston clearance from these 2 measurements. See **Tables 1 and 2** for piston size and clearance information.

5. If the piston and cylinder pass inspection and if the piston clearance is within tolerances given in Table 2, then the piston is suitable for reinstallation. Proceed to Step 13 below.

6. If piston clearance exceeds the specified tolerance, then determine whether a new piston

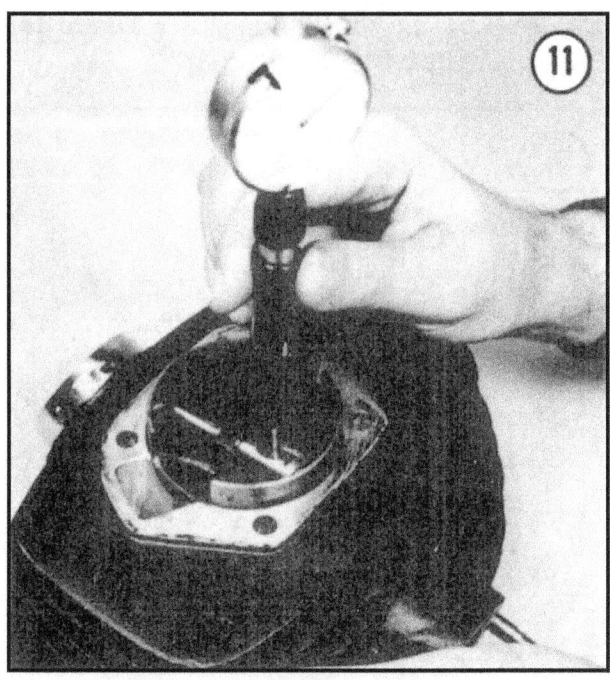

Table 1   NEW PISTON MEASUREMENT DATA

	250 PISTONS	
	Size (mm)	Size (inch)
Standard	72mm	2.8334-2.8344
1st oversize	72.20mm	2.8414-2.8424
2nd oversize	72.40mm	2.8492-2.8502
3rd oversize	72.60mm	2.8570-2.8580
	175 PISTONS	
Standard	60.90mm	2.3960-2.3968
1st oversize	61.10mm	2.4040-2.4048
2nd oversize	61.30mm	2.4118-2.4126
3rd oversize	61.50mm	2.4200-2.4208

Table 2   PISTON CLEARANCE DATA

Model	Piston To Cylinder Clearance (Inch)	Rebore Cylinder If Clearance Exceeds: (Inch)
250 Pioneer	0.00175-0.002	0.0045-0.005
250 Plonker	0.001-0.0015	0.0035-0.004
250 Stiletto	0.002-0.0025	0.0045-0.005
250 TT & D.M.R.	0.0025-0.003	0.005-0.0055
175 Pioneer	0.002-0.0025	0.0035-0.004
175 Stiletto	0.0025-0.003	0.0045-0.005

will suffice, or that reboring the cylinder will be necessary by the following steps.

7. Read the number and letter stamped on top of the old piston. See **Figure 12**. This will give the piston size.

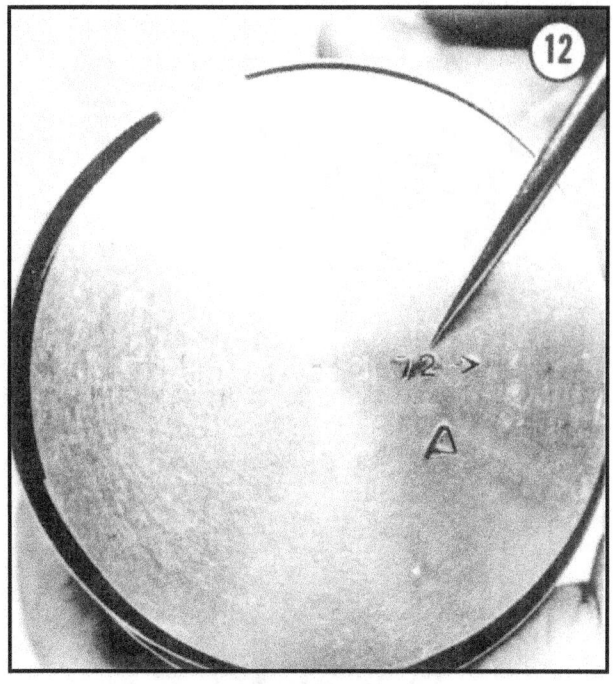

8. Compare the measured size of the old piston with the size of an equivalent new piston as given in Table 1.

9. If the measured size is less than that of a new piston, determine the resulting clearance for a new piston and the measured distance of the old cylinder per Step 4 above. If the clearance is within the tolerance given in Table 2, the cylinder does not need reboring if the new piston is installed.

10. If clearance with a new piston would still be too great, rebore the cylinder to the next oversize and install an oversize piston. Severe scoring or wear may necessitate boring to an even larger diameter or replacement of the liner (see following section, *Cylinder Liner Removal/Installation*). Because too little piston clearance can cause piston seizure and too much can seriously affect performance, it is important that the above measurements be precise and the decision a correct one. If there is the slightest doubt, take the cylinder and piston to a dealer.

11. After boring, hone the cylinder.

12. Bevel the ports to a radius of 0.020 in. with

a small grinder or file. An unbevelled port may cause a ring to catch and break. See **Figure 13**.

13. If the decision is to reinstall the old piston, check the rings for freedom of movement in their grooves. If free, remove the rings and mark them so that each ring can be replaced in its original groove and with the same side of the ring facing upward. Clean the rings.

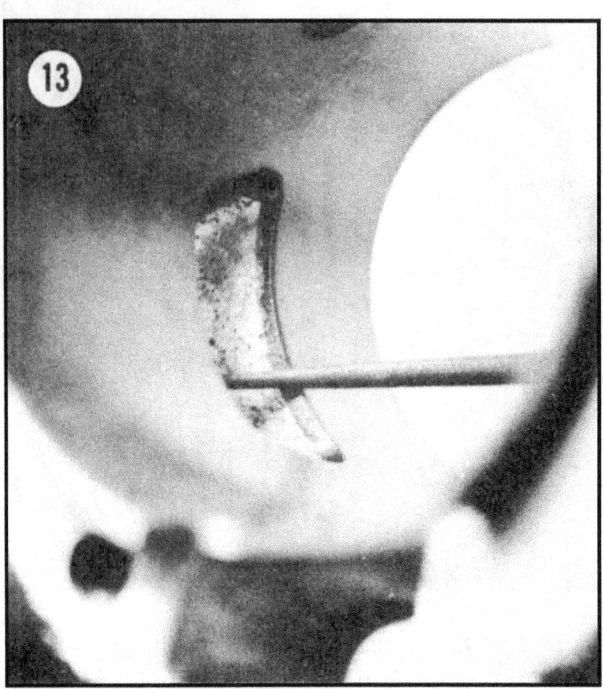

14. Put a ring into the top of the cylinder. See **Figure 14**.

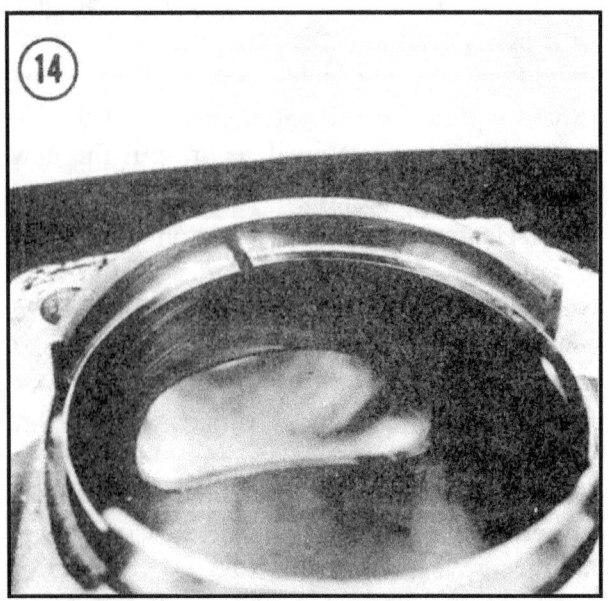

15. Use the piston to push the ring down approximately one inch from the top of the cylinder.

16. Measure the ring end gap. See **Figure 15**. Gap should be 0.019 in. (0.5mm).

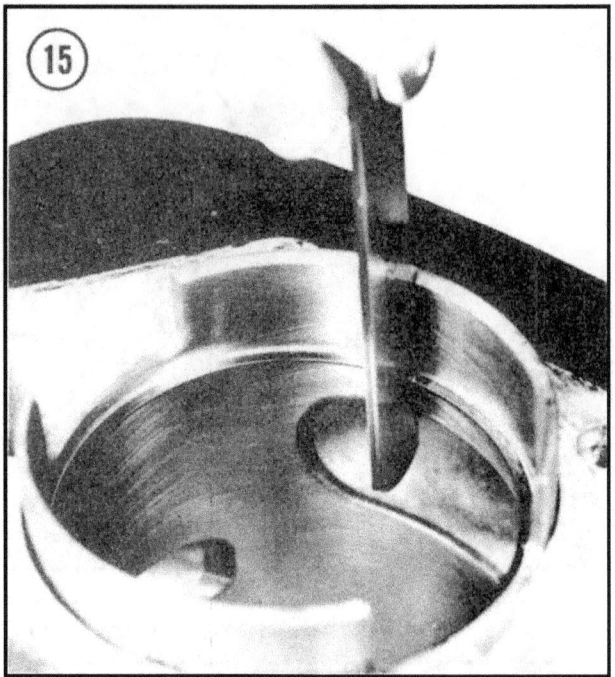

17. Use the piston to push the ring halfway down into the cylinder. Measure the end gap.

18. Repeat Steps 14 through 17 with the other ring.

19. If either measurement for either ring exceeds the specified tolerance, both rings must be replaced with new ones.

20. If new rings are to be installed, hone the cylinder to remove the glaze from the wall in order to allow proper seating of the new rings. If the old rings are to be installed, it is not necessary.

21. Remove only a small amount of material by honing. The only purpose of honing is to remove the glaze.

22. Check the end gap of the rings again, after honing.

Cylinder Liner Removal

If the decision in Step 10 of *Cylinder and Piston, Inspection/Repair*, is to install a new cylinder liner, proceed as follows.

1. Put the cylinder in an oven set at 550°F (306°C). Place it upside down with the fins resting on 2 blocks in such a manner as to allow the liner to drop out. See **Figure 16**.

2. If the liner does not drop out when the cylinder reaches 550°F, tap it very lightly on the lower edge. Do not force it out. Do not heat it to more than 750°F (416°C) or permanent distortion of the cylinder may result. If this procedure does not remove the liner, take it to a machine shop for removal.

3. Clean the inside of the cylinder with solvent.

4. Check for any damage or score marks caused by removing the liner. Sand lightly if necessary. Do not remove much metal.

5. Heat the cylinder in the oven to approximately 425°F (218°C).

6. Remove it from the oven and support it right side up by the fins so that a new liner can be inserted without touching the bench.

7. Insert the new liner one or 2 inches into the cylinder with the liner's ports approximately lined up with the ports in the cylinder. Drop the liner; it will fall into place.

8. Grasp the bottom of the liner and align the ports. See **Figure 17**. There will be approximately 6-10 seconds available to effect alignment, after the liner drops into place.

9. Put a heavy weight on top of the liner while the cylinder cools to room temperature; leave the cylinder supported by the bottom fins while it cools.

10. Again check the alignment of the ports. If

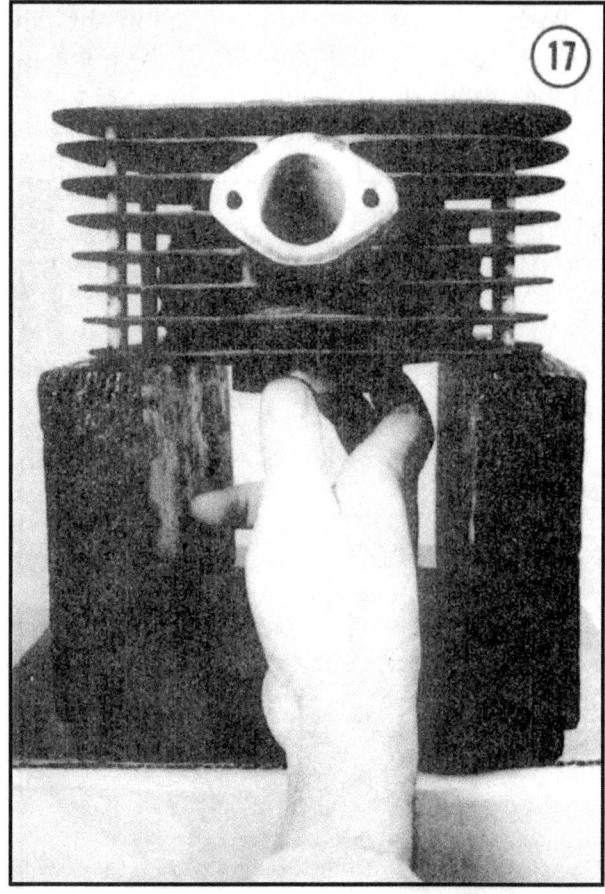

necessary, correct any minor misalignment with a grinding tool. Start over if alignment is too far off.

11. Bore and hone the new liner to the correct piston clearance as detailed previously.

Cylinder Liner Installation

1. Turn the crankshaft to position the connecting rod at top dead center.

2. Wrap a rag around the connecting rod to cover the crankcase opening.

3. Put a new cylinder base gasket into place on the crankcase.

4. If the gasket protrudes into the port cutouts, trim it.

5. Oil the wrist pin bearing and install it in the connecting rod.

6. Position the piston on the rod with the arrow on top pointing forward.

7. Use the wrist pin drift to align the piston and rod by pushing the drift into the piston and through the wrist pin bearing until it touches the wrist pin.

8. Push the wrist pin into place; allow the pin to eject the drift. See **Figure 18**. If the pin cannot be installed by hand, do not use force. Instead, use the tool shown in Figure 8.

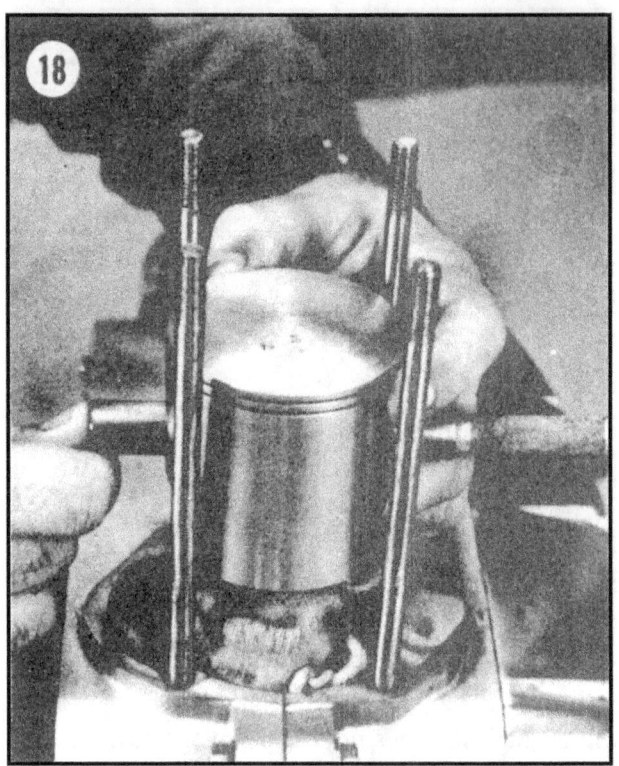

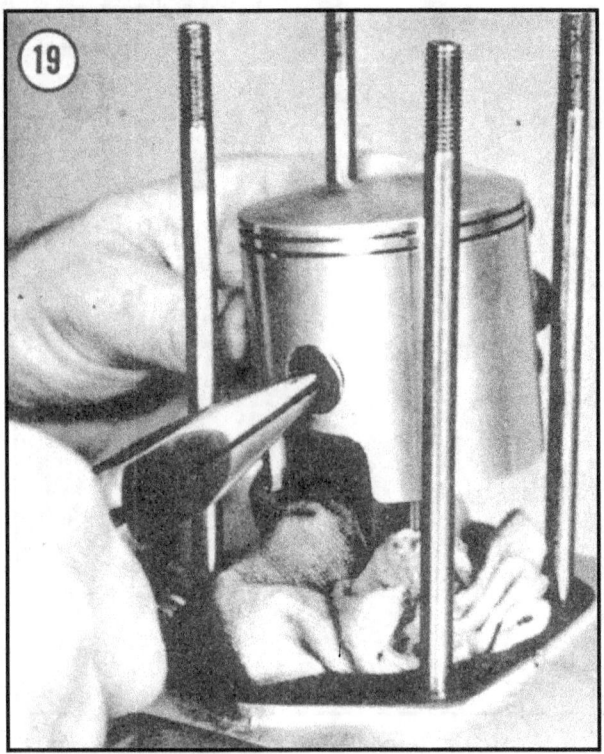

9. Install a new circlip on each end of the wrist pin. See **Figure 19**.

10. Coat each piston ring with oil and install both on the piston, with the peg in the ring groove centered between the ends of the ring. Check to see that neither ring binds in its groove.

11. Remove the rag and turn the engine until the piston is at bottom dead center.

12. Position the cylinder on the studs and let the bottom of the cylinder rest on the top piston ring.

13. Compress each ring in turn with your fingers and slide the cylinder down over the piston until the cylinder is seated. See **Figure 20**.

14. If there is difficulty in compressing the rings by hand, use a large hose clamp as a ring compressor. Compress the ring the minimum required amount with the hose clamp. See **Figure 21**. Slide the cylinder down over the piston and let it push the hose clamp off the ring as the cylinder slides past the ring. Remove the hose clamp.

15. Install the kickstarter lever.

16. Push the kickstarter lever down while observing the movement of the piston within the cylinder. Be sure that it moves freely.

17. Again, check mating surfaces of cylinder and head for smoothness and cleanliness.

18. The 250cc TT and DMR and all 175cc engines use a 1mm thick head gasket. The 250cc Pioneer and Stiletto engines use a 2mm thick gasket. The 250cc Plonker uses a 3mm thick

gasket. Install a new head gasket on the cylinder during assembly.

19. Install the head with the higher ends of the fins toward the front. Torque the nuts, in the sequence described in Step 5, *Cylinder and Piston Removal*, to 5 ft.-lb. (0.7 mkg). Repeat the sequence and torque to 10 ft.-lb. (1.4 mkg). Repeat sequence and torque to 15 ft.-lb. (2.1 mkg).

20. Install a new spark plug, finger-tight.

21. Cover the intake and exhaust ports to protect the interior of the engine and reassemble as described in *Cylinder and Piston*.

MAGNETO

Removal

1. Remove the side cover. Two guide pins on the engine case may hold the cover on after the screws have been removed. If so, push the clutch actuating arm inward to force the cover off the guide pins. Be sure to retrieve the clutch actuating plunger in removing the cover. The plunger is a small round part which fits into the clutch actuating assembly.

2. Use of a special holding tool is recommended to hold the flywheel stationary while removing the magneto flywheel nut. Remove the nut. See **Figure 22**.

3. A flywheel puller is needed to remove the flywheel. An Ossa dealer should have the proper

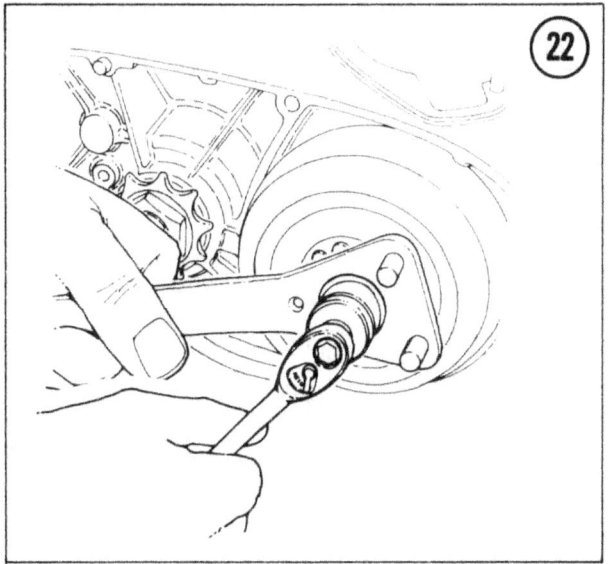

one. Back out the center bolt of the puller to allow the puller to be screwed fully in. Screw the puller into the flywheel threads. Be careful not to damage any threads.

4. Turn the center bolt of the puller clockwise until the flywheel is free and remove the flywheel from the crankshaft. See **Figure 23**. Remove the puller from the flywheel.

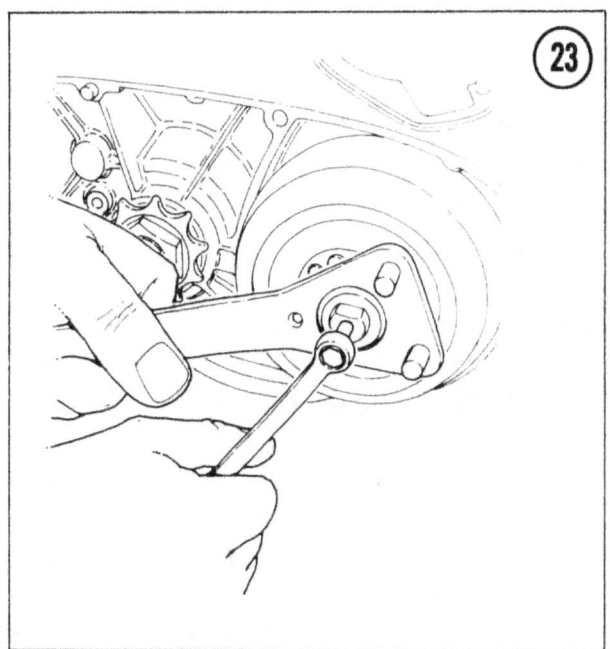

5. Scribe a line across the edge of the magneto stator plate and on a mounting boss with a chisel. Use this line for reference during reassembly. See **Figure 24**.

6. Remove the screws and bolts holding the stator to the engine case and the magneto wire securing strap. Remove the strap.

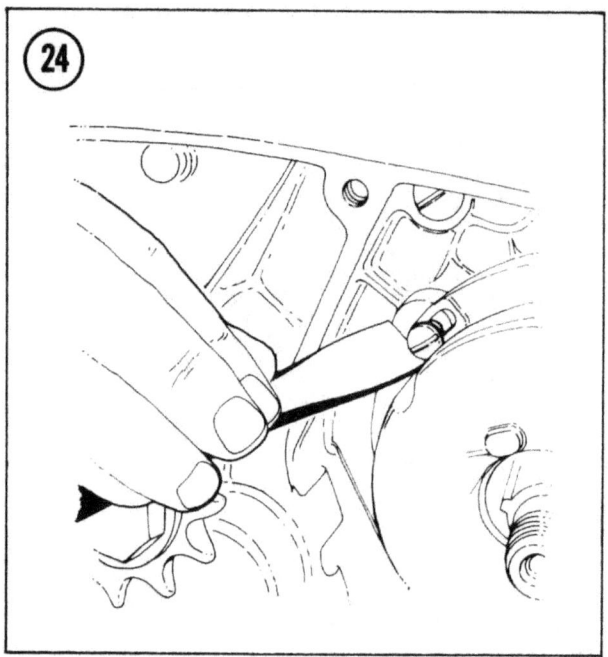
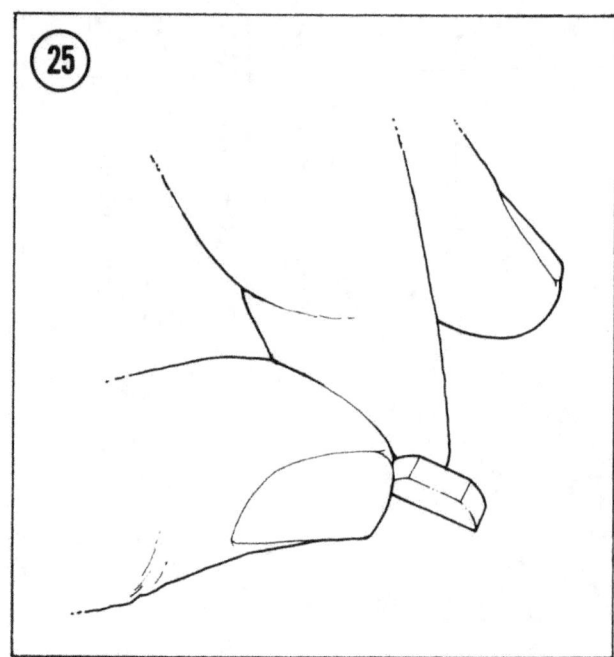

7. Remove the stator and temporarily store it inside the flywheel.

8. Remove the Woodruff key from the crankshaft with a screwdriver and hammer. Tap the screwdriver gently while removing the key to avoid damaging either component.

9. Check the key for wear or damage; replace it if necessary.

10. Store the key on the flywheel at a point where the magnetic field is strong.

11. Remove the rubber selector shaft cover (located at the right hand end of the shaft) and the felt washer.

12. Position the crankshaft Woodruff key upside down and tap the rounded surface with a hammer to widen it for a snug fit in the crankshaft groove. Install the key; tap it in place. See **Figure 25**.

13. Clean the stator with a mild solvent and blow dry with compressed air.

14. Examine the stator carefully for damage; pay particular attention to the condition of the wire windings in the stator. Be sure that there are no metal filings on the stator.

Installation

1. Install the stator on the engine with the scribed lines matching.

2. Install the rubber grommet on the magneto wires in the slot located at the bottom of the case.

3. Install the magneto wire securing strap; use Loctite on the bolt threads.

4. Align the magneto flywheel slot with the Woodruff key in the crankshaft and push the flywheel onto the crankshaft by hand until it is seated; do not install the nut.

5. Turn to the section, *Ignition Timing*, in Chapter Two, and follow the procedure given for setting ignition timing.

6. Install the flywheel nut; use Loctite on the threads. Tighten the nut by hand.

7. Hold the flywheel with the holding tool and torque the flywheel nut to 60 ft.-lb. (8.3 mkg).

8. Check the timing once more to be sure it is correct after the flywheel nut is tight.

9. Install the spark plug; torque to 18 ft.-lb. (2.5 mkg).

10. Put sufficient grease on the clutch actuating plunger to hold it in place and install.

11. Coat the magneto cover face with silicone sealer since there is no gasket.

12. Install the magneto side cover.

13. Check the clutch actuating arm for ½-⅝ in. movement. If necessary, remove the inspection cover in the primary case to gain access to the pushrod adjusting screw in the clutch pressure plate.

14. Loosen the locknut and turn the adjusting screw clockwise until it starts to bind. See **Figure 26**.

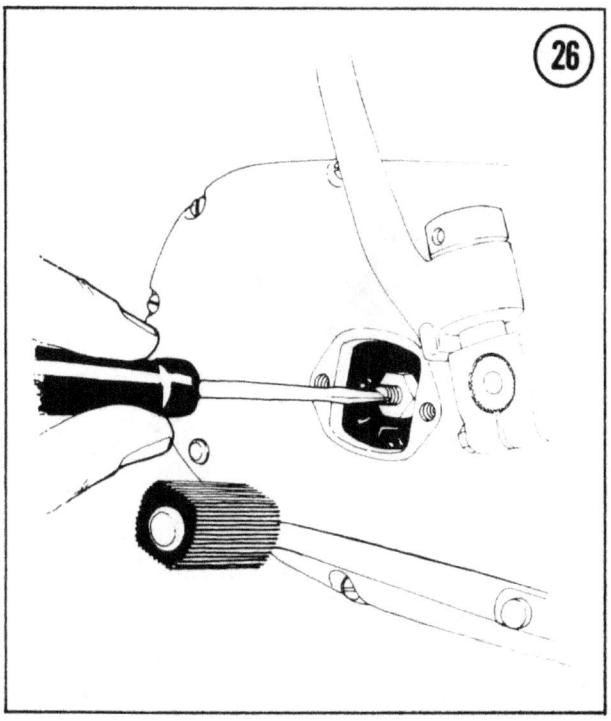

15. Turn the adjusting screw counterclockwise until there is approximately ½-⅝ in. movement in the actuating arm. Tighten the locknut. Check the movement again.

16. Install the inspection cover plate.

CARBURETOR AND AIR CLEANER

Carburetor service is detailed in Chapter Four and air cleaner service in Chapter Two.

SPLITTING THE CRANKCASE

1. Remove the engine as detailed under *Engine Removal/Installation* in this chapter.

2. Remove the outer cover and magneto flywheel as detailed in this chapter under *Magneto*.

3. Turn the engine to gain access to the right side. Loosen the engine case screws ¼ turn each in sequence; start at the center of the case, alternate between screws at the top and bottom of the case, and work toward both ends. The recommended sequence of loosening is shown in **Figure 27**.

4. Remove the screws, following the sequence in Step 3.

5. Remove the shift drum detent screw (it is the screw with a large head, has a nylon washer behind it, and is located at the lower right side of the engine).

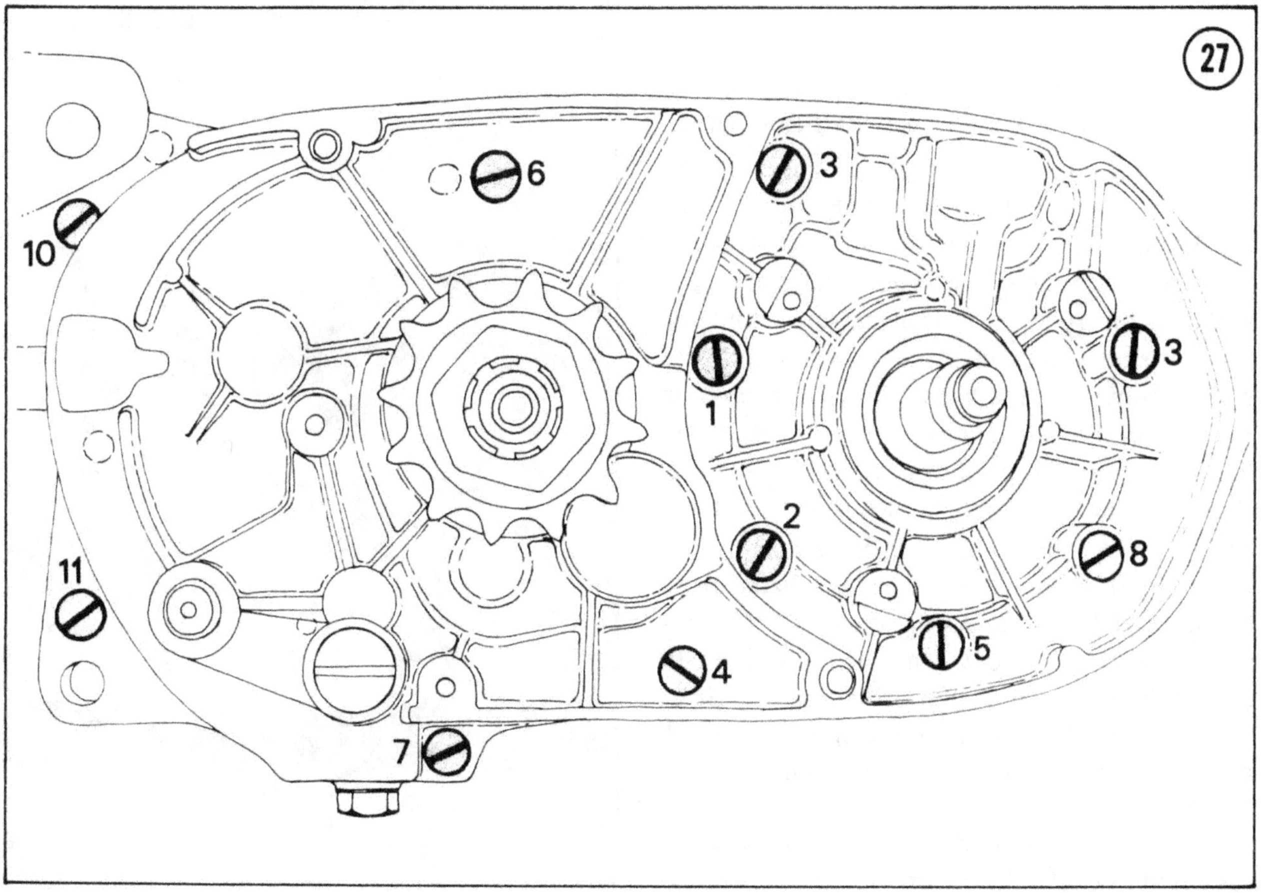

6. Remove the shift spring and plunger.

7. Lay the engine on its right side with the left side facing upward. Remove the front nut and bolt.

8. Typically, there are 3 positioning dowels used to position the cases relative to each other; one at the front and one each at the rear engine mounting holes. Use a drift pin and hammer to tap these dowels out of their holes from the left side. See **Figure 28**. Short pieces of ⅜ in. and ½ in. rods can be used as drifts for removing the dowels.

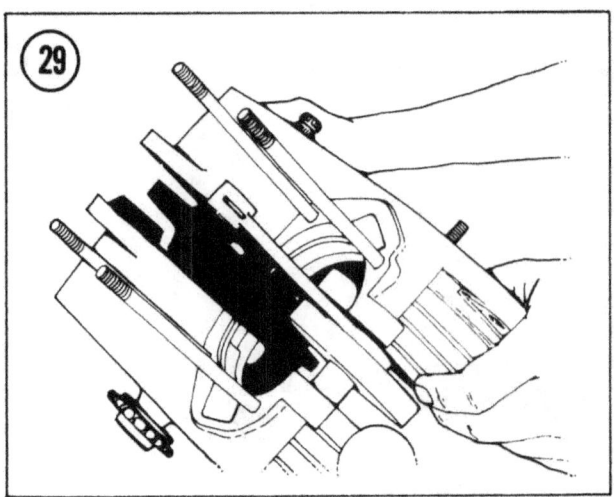

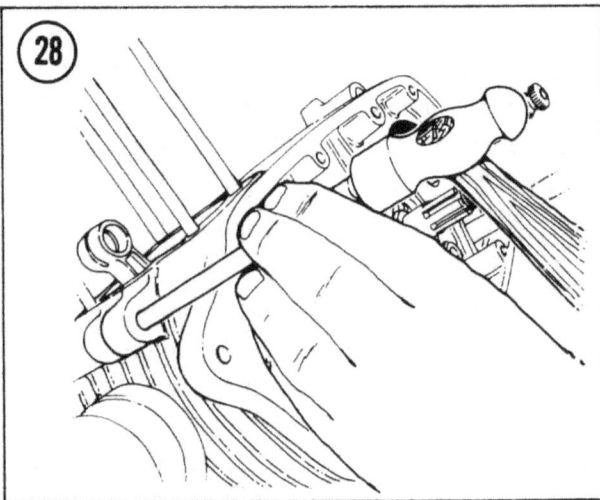

9. Tap the right end of the crankshaft with a soft mallet until the crankcases start to separate.

10. Lay the engine on its right side and remove the left case with both hands. See **Figure 29**. The crankshaft will come off with the left case; check to be sure that the transmission shafts are staying with the right case. If necessary, hold the transmission shafts in place in the right case while removing the left case. If the transmission shafts are allowed to move more than ¼ in. from their initial positions in the right case, shims may fall off the right ends of the shafts.

11. Remove any shims which stick to the mounting bosses of the various shafts from inside the left case and store them on their respective shafts. The crankshaft shimming washers will be on the right end of the crankshaft or the right main bearing. Remove them and attach an identifying tag. These various shims provide for the correct end play and proper gear engagement; it is very important that each be reinstalled in its original position during reassembly.

12. Before reassembling the engine cases, be sure that all gearbox components have been lightly coated with SAE 30 motor oil.

13. Install the transmission fifth driven gear into the right transmission bearing by tapping lightly, if necessary, to seat it against the bearing. See **Figure 30**.

14. Use a special sprocket holding tool and sprocket nut wrench to install the sprocket spacer, transmission sprocket, tab washer, and sprocket nut on the magneto side. The sprocket nut has a left hand thread. See **Figure 31**. Bend the tabs of the washer against 2 flats of the nut.

15. Install all transmission components in the right case as detailed in Chapter Seven.

16. Install the breather tube in the boss at the top of the case. Be sure the slots in the tube are facing forward. See **Figure 32**.

17. Install a new center case gasket, coated with grease (not cement) on both sides, on the right case.

18. Install the positioning dowels in the right case.

19. Put grease on the right hand crankshaft shims (to hold them in place) and position them on the inner race of the right main bearing.

20. Position the right case with the open side facing upward. Install the left engine case, with crankshaft assembly, on the right case; it may be necessary to assist the ends of the crankshaft and kickstarter shaft to their correct positions. See **Figure 33**.

21. Tap the cases together with a soft mallet.

22. Install the front engine case bolt with Loctite on the threads. Turn nut only finger-tight.

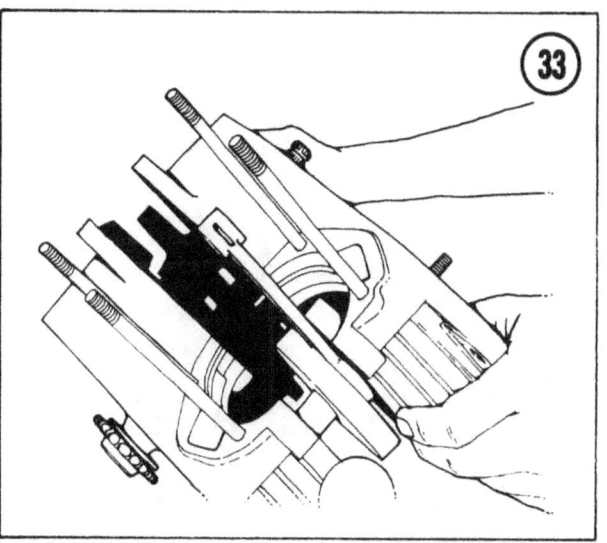

23. Install the engine case screws in the magneto side. Turn them until they are snug, but not tight.

24. Follow the sequence described in Step 3 of this section and tighten each screw firmly. See Figure 27.

25. Torque the front engine case to 12 ft.-lb. (1.7 mkg).

26. Install the shift drum detent assembly and turn it in with your fingers. Tighten with a screwdriver.

27. Install the felt washer and rubber cap on the right end of the transmission selector shaft.

PRIMARY COVER

Removal

1. Remove the foot shift lever and felt washer from the shaft.
2. Remove the kickstarter lever from the shaft.
3. Remove the screws which hold the primary case to the engine case.
4. Insert the blade of a large screwdriver under the edge of the primary cover inspection cover and over the end of the kickstarter shaft. Pry until the primary cover separates from the engine case. See **Figure 34**. Remove the primary cover.

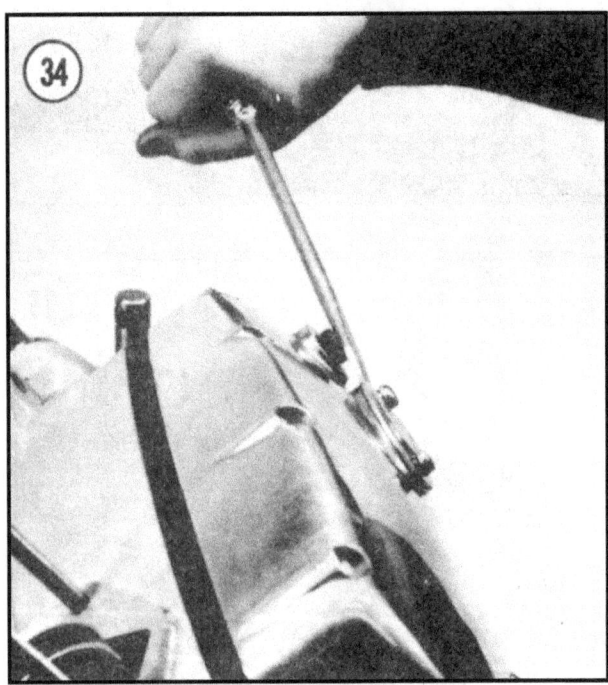

5. Remove the primary cover gasket.
6. If the positioning dowels are loose, remove them. Otherwise they may be left in place but be careful not to damage them while working on the engine.

Installation

1. Clean the primary cover and other removed parts.
2. Check the condition of the O-rings in the primary case. If in doubt, replace them.
3. Grease both sides of the new primary cover gasket and install it.
4. If the engine was removed from the motorcycle, position it so that the primary drive faces upward. Pour a quart of SAE 30 motor oil into the engine. Be sure to thoroughly cover the primary drive components so they will have lubrication when the engine is started.
5. Two special tools may be used to protect the O-rings from damage by the shaft splines during installation of the primary cover. They are obtainable from an Ossa dealer along with instructions for their use. See **Figures 35 and 36**.

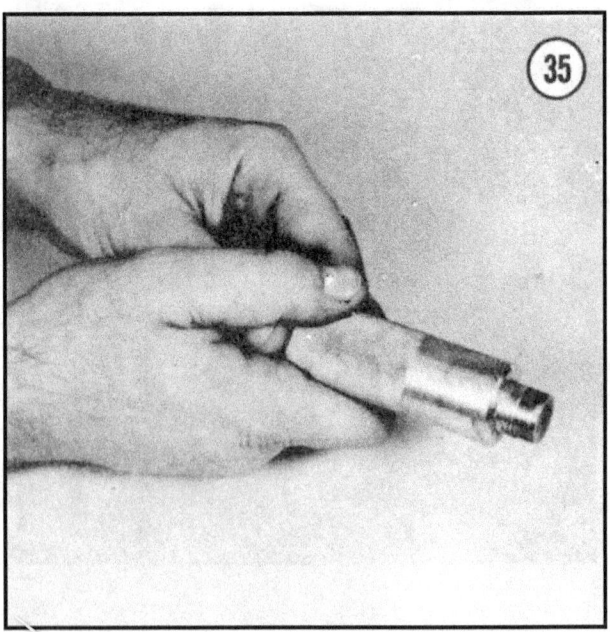

6. Install the primary cover on the engine and tap with a soft mallet to seat it.
7. Install the screws into their original holes and turn them until they are snug, but not tight.
8. Tighten the screws securely in sequence. Start at the left-right center of the cover, alternate in crisscross fashion between screws at the top and bottom of the case, and work toward both ends. The recommended sequence of tightening is shown in **Figure 37**.
9. Install the kickstarter lever.
10. Install the felt washer and foot shift lever; use Loctite on the bolt threads.

CLUTCH, CUSH DRIVE SHAFT, AND KICKSTRTER

Clutch Removal

1. Remove the engine and primary cover as detailed in this chapter.
2. Remove the washers from the selector shaft.

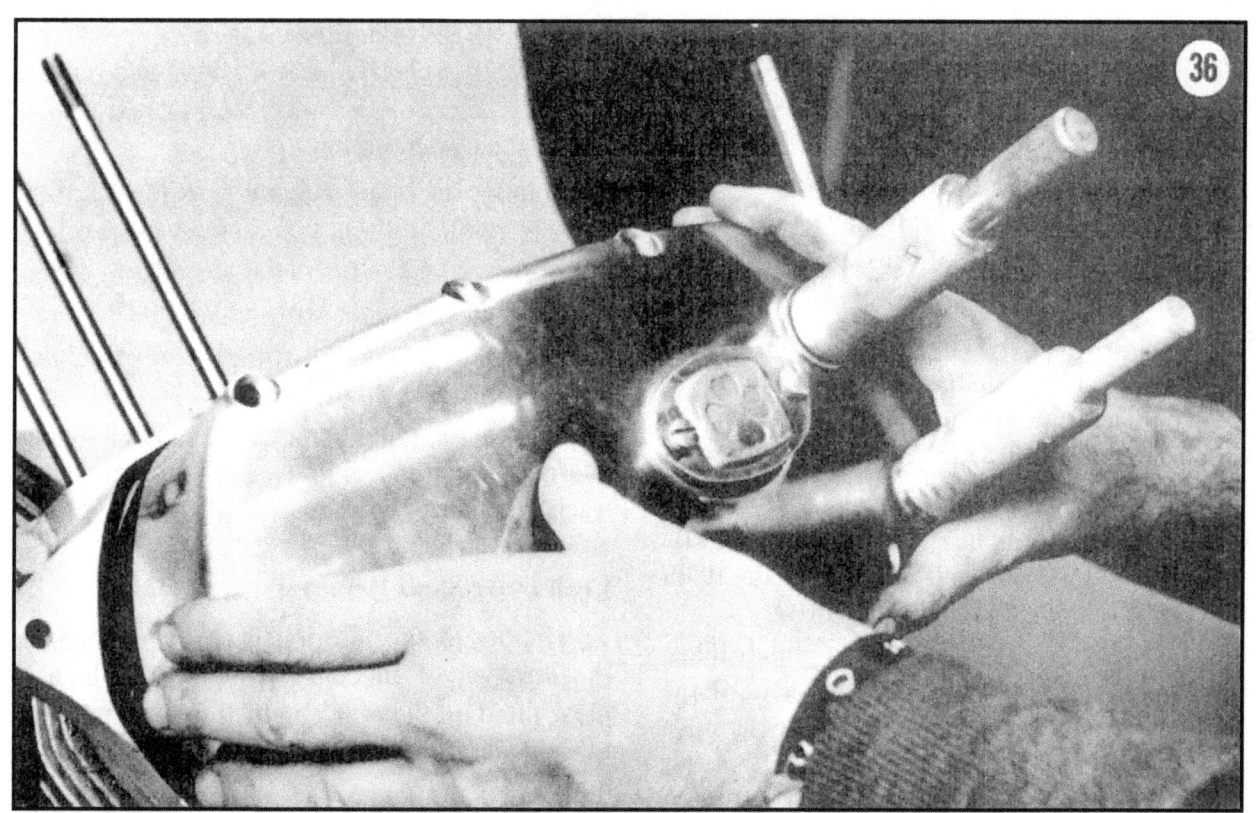

3. Remove the cotter pins and clutch spring nuts with a slotted screwdriver (or with needle nosed pliers, using great care). A slotted screwdriver is easily made by cutting a notch in the blade of a large screwdriver. See **Figure 38**.

4. Remove all clutch plates. It may be necessary to lift out the last plate with the aid of 2 screwdrivers.

5. Two pushrods, through the center of the transmission main shaft, are separated by a small ball bearing. Tilt the engine so that the primary drive side is facing downward. Remove the left-hand pushrod with one hand while holding your other hand under the clutch assembly. Catch the ball bearing as it rolls out of the main shaft. Pull out the right-hand pushrod.

6. Use a special tool, fitted in the clutch hubs, to rotate the clutch counterclockwise until the handle of the tool is against the top of the cush drive assembly. See **Figure 39**. An Ossa dealer can supply you with this convenient tool.

7. Remove the clutch nut.

8. Leave the special tool in position and remove the cush drive Allen nut, lockwasher, outer spring stop, and outer coupling cam.

9. Remove the inner clutch hub. If there is difficulty in removing this hub, caused by previous applications of Loctite, heat the region where the hub joins the main shaft with a torch.

10. Remove the engine sprocket, outer clutch hub, and primary chain as a unit.

11. Remove the inner race of the clutch needle bearing, the inner hub spacer, and the large washer from the transmission shaft.

Cush Drive Shaft Removal

1. The use of special tools is recommended for the removal of the cush drive shaft which is press fitted on the crankshaft. It may be possible to improvise or borrow the tools needed.

2. Screw a thread protector (a special tool) into the crankshaft threads. See **Figure 40**.

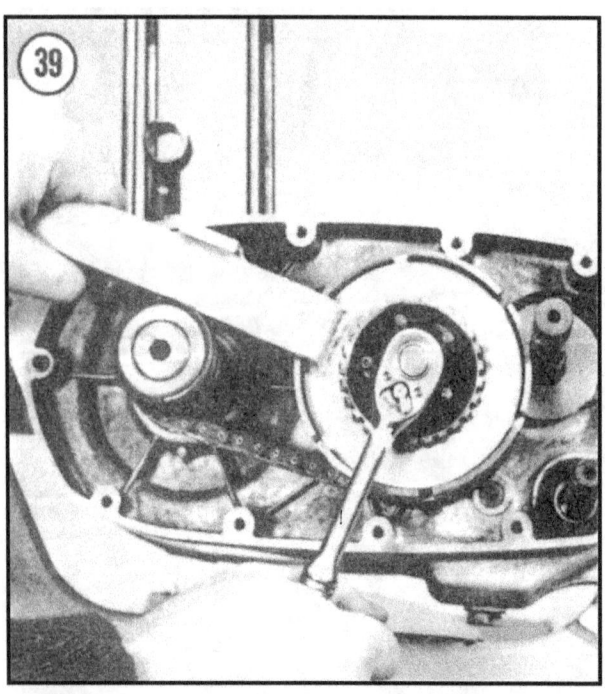

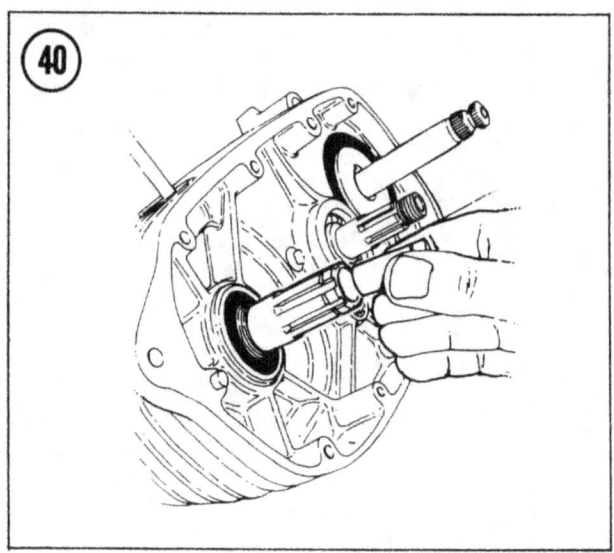

3. Put a wrench (a special tool) on the cush drive shaft. See **Figure 41**.

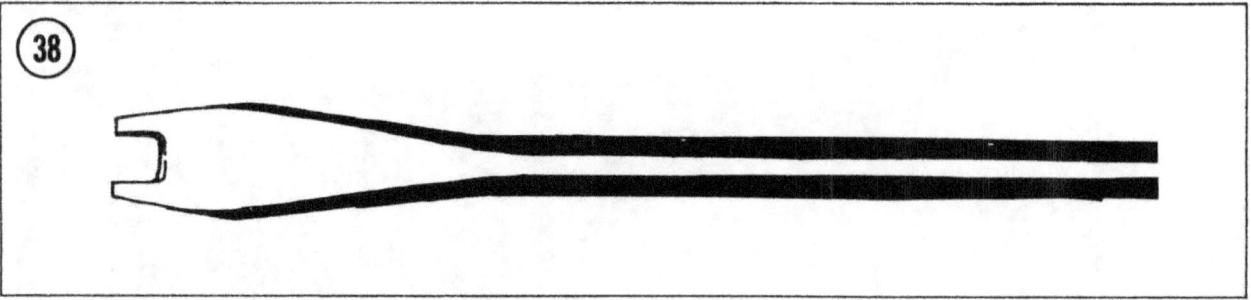

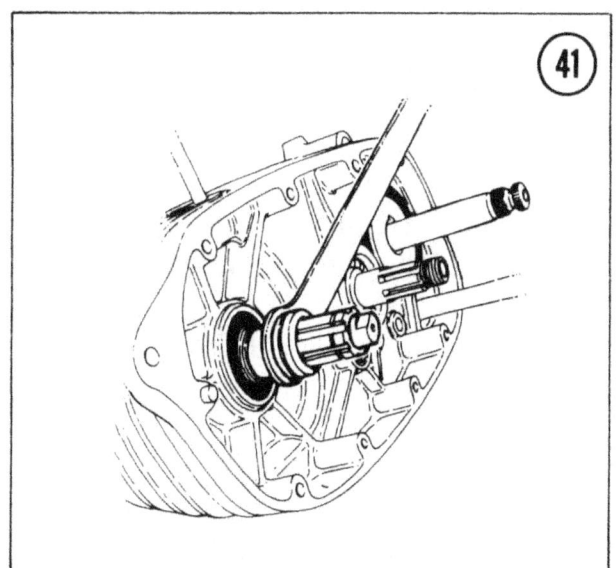

4. Install a shaft puller (a suitable one is available from an Ossa dealer) on the cush drive shaft; the groove around the top of the cush drive shaft should be accessible after the puller is installed. Fit the 2 collars and turn the puller handle until the puller is tight against the collars.

5. Turn the puller handle, while holding the wrench stationary, until the cush shaft breaks loose from the crankshaft.

6. Remove the wrench, puller, thread protector, and cush drive shaft.

Kickstarter Assembly Removal

1. Remove the snap ring from the kickstarter shaft with snap ring pliers; discard the ring for a new one.

2. Remove the looped end of the kickstarter return spring from the case mount with a large screwdriver.

3. Disengage the other end of the kickstarter return spring from the kickstarter shaft, with needle nose pliers, and remove the spring and washer.

4. If further disassembly of the engine is needed, proceed with the instructions given in the section, *Splitting the Crankcases*, in this chapter. Otherwise, continue with *Cleaning and Inspection*.

Cleaning and Inspection

1. Clean all parts with solvent and blow dry with compressed air.

2. Inspect all parts and components for wear, damage, cracks, or deterioration. If in doubt, replace the suspect part with a new one.

Kickstarter Assembly Installation

1. Turn the kickstarter shaft counterclockwise, by hand, to its limit of rotation; the long slot on the shaft should be facing upward.

2. Position large washer and kickstarter spring on the shaft and put the end of the spring into the slot on the kickstarter shaft. The looped end of the spring faces the front.

3. Insert a long drift into the spring's loop (**Figure 42**); turn the spring 1½ turns and install the loop into the retaining boss at the rear of the case. Be careful not to cut your fingers.

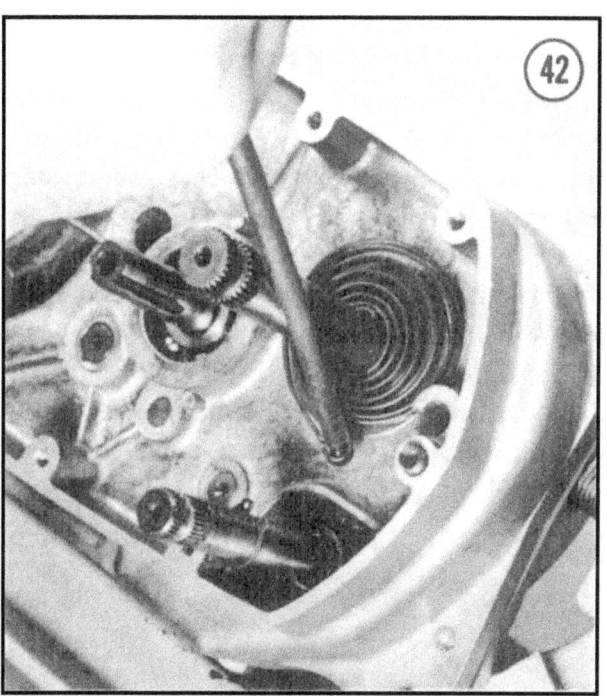

4. Install the other washer and a new snap ring on the shaft above the spring. Be sure that the sharp edge of the snap ring is toward the left end of the shaft.

5. Install the kickstarter lever on the shaft and test the action of the shaft and return spring. Remove the lever.

Cush Drive Shaft Installation

1. Install the washer and inner clutch hub spacer on the transmission main shaft against the bearing.

2. If inspection reveals wear of the clutch needle bearing inner race, replace the entire needle bearing assembly with a new one. Oil the inner race and install it on the main shaft against the clutch hub spacer.

3. If the entire needle bearing assembly is to be removed, remove the needle bearing from the outer clutch hub. A socket with a short extension can serve as a drift. Insert the drift into the rear of the outer hub and press the needle bearing out with a vise.

4. Install a new needle bearing into the outer hub by reversing the above procedure. The bearing must be flush with the front surface of the hub.

5. The primary side crankshaft and cush drive shaft have an interference fit; therefore, be sure that all oil and grease have been removed from these 2 parts. Install the cush drive shaft on the crankshaft and tap it with a soft mallet to seat it.

6. Inspect the 2 sprockets and the slots for the clutch plates on the outer clutch hub for wear or damage. See Figure 4, Chapter Two, for an illustration of sprocket wear and damage. If any wear or damage is visible, replace the part with a new one.

7. Fit the chain on the 2 sprockets and install the 3 parts as a unit on the shafts with the outer clutch hub on the transmission main shaft. See **Figure 43**.

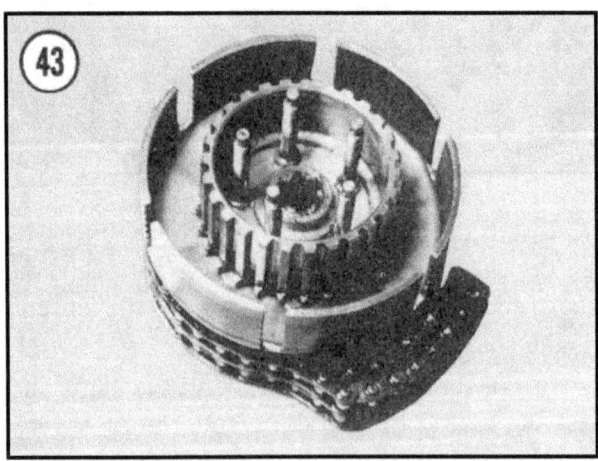

8. Check the play in the chain midway between the 2 sprockets by measuring the total movement of the chain in a direction perpendicular to itself. If the movement is more than ⅝ in., replace the chain with a new one.

9. Install the inner clutch hub on the main shaft. Use Loctite on the threads, and install the washer and nut on the shaft, finger-tight.

10. Install the cush drive cam on the cush drive shaft.

11. Measure the cush drive spring. If it is less than 1.4 in. (36mm), replace it with a new one.

12. Install the spring and spring stop on the shaft. Use care in aligning the splines.

13. Install the cush drive nut; use Loctite on the threads.

14. Install the clutch holding tool, described in Step 6 of *Clutch Removal*, on the hubs and rotate the hub clockwise until the handle of the tool rests against the cush drive shaft. The handle will be on the opposite side of the cush shaft, from that shown in Figure 39. Torque the cush drive nut to 65-70 ft.-lb. (9.0-9.7 mkg).

Clutch Installation

1. Leave the special tool in position and torque the clutch hub nut to 65-70 ft.-lb. (9.0-9.7 mkg). Remove the tool.

2. Check to see that the inner hub rotates while the outer hub remains stationary.

3. Check each clutch plate for wear or damage. Check each plate for warpage by laying it on a sheet of plate glass. Replace any doubtful parts.

4. The 3 types of plates in each clutch assembly are thick steel plate, thin steel plate, and friction plate. See **Figure 44**. Each clutch driving plate has friction pads bonded to both sides. Inspect the pads; if any of the pads are worn flush with the grooves separating them, replace all of the clutch driving plates with new ones.

5. Install the one thick steel plate in the clutch assembly.

6. Alternately install a friction plate and a thin steel plate until the last plate (a thin steel plate) is installed.

7. Install the clutch pressure plate.

8. Install the spring cups through the holes in the pressure plate and fit them down over the studs in the inner hub.

9. Measure the length of the clutch springs. If any one is less than 1.170 in. (29.7mm), replace the entire set of springs.

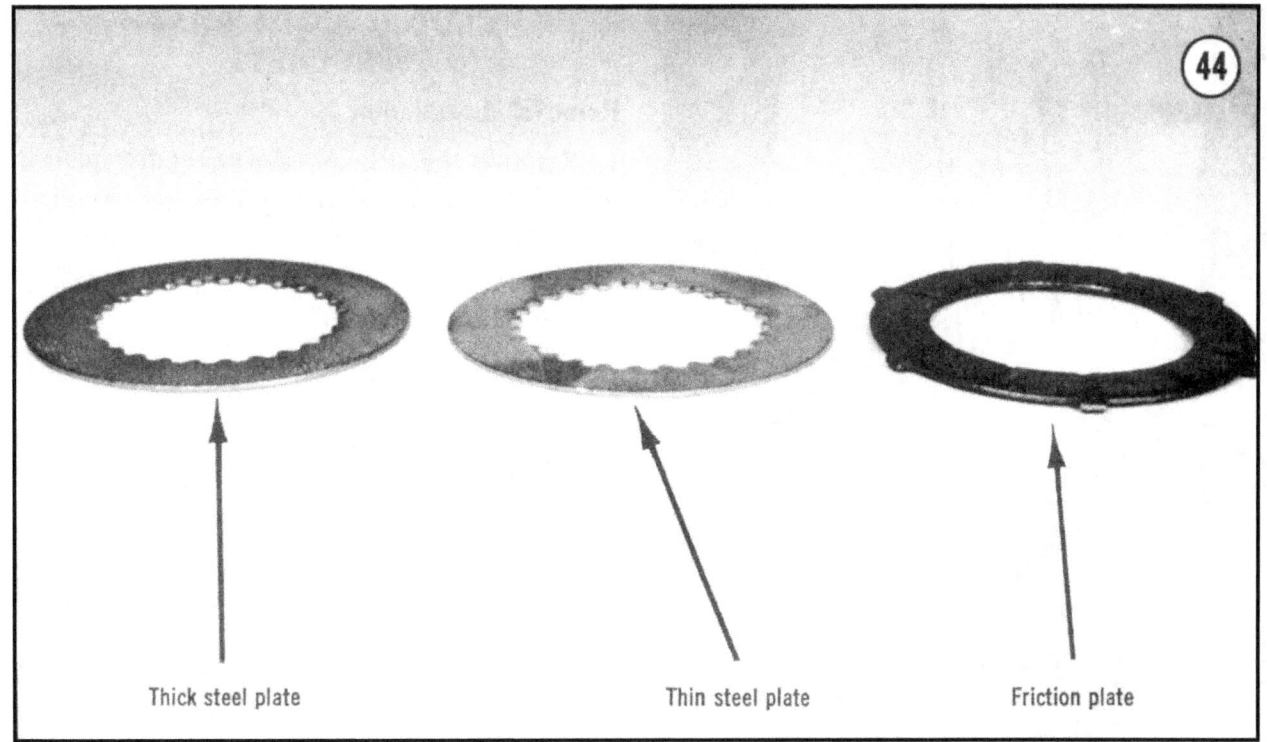

Thick steel plate   Thin steel plate   Friction plate

10. Install the springs in the cups and the spring nuts on the studs. Align the slots in the nuts with the holes in the studs. Cotter pins or safety wires will be installed in these holes later but do not install them now.

11. In order to check the operation of the clutch, it is necessary to install the magneto side engine case and clutch actuating components temporarily. Turn the engine to yield access to the magneto side and remove the seal from the center of the fifth driven gear.

12. Check both clutch pushrods for wear or damage. Replace if necessary.

13. Install the pushrods through the end of the fifth driven gear with the ball bearing between them.

14. Install the small seal in the fith driven gear.

15. Remove the actuating arm. See **Figure 45**.

16. Clean all components and the case thoroughly. Coat components with grease and install them. Grease the clutch actuating plunger heavily to hold it in place.

17. Install positioning dowels in engine case.

18. Install the magneto side engine cover.

19. Install the kickstarter lever on the shaft.

20. Clamp the lower rear engine mount flange in a vise with soft jaws.

21. Attach a special tool (obtained from an Ossa dealer) to the clutch actuating lever. See **Figure 46**. Move it to the left until the clutch pressure plate is disengaged and hold it there.

22. Push the kickstarter down to turn the pressure plate. Check to see if the pressure plate turns evenly. If it wobbles, the springs are not adjusted evenly. If necessary, follow Step 23 below to correct.

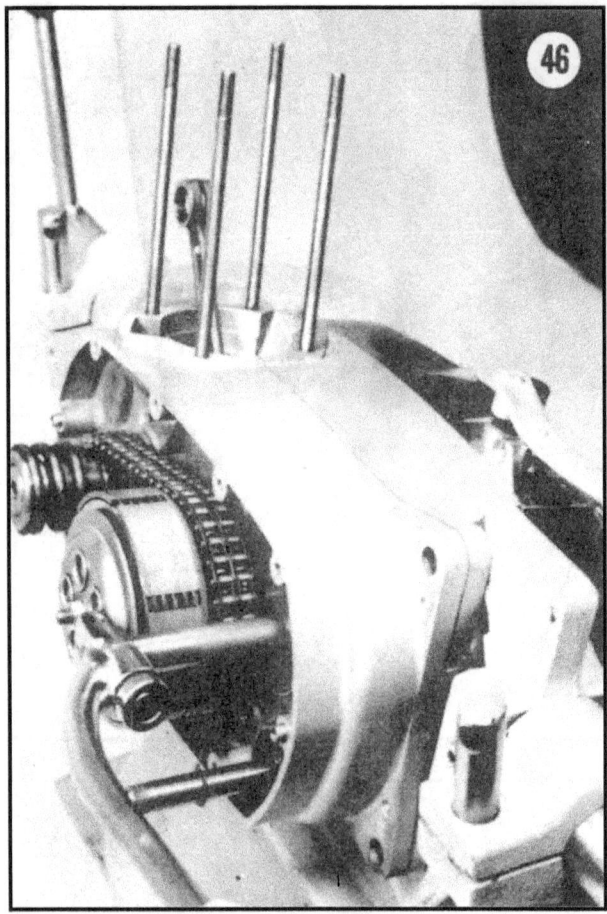

23. Mark the point where the pressure plate is farthest from the other clutch plates. Release the clutch and turn the nuts, or nuts, closest to the mark inward ½ turn. Repeat this procedure until the pressure plate runs evenly.

24. If the clutch is somewhat worn so that the nuts must be turned in to the point where cotter pins will not hold them in position, the rotation of the clutch will loosen the nuts and cause difficulty with the clutch. Also, there will be a tendency for the clutch to be hard to operate and to drag when it is disengaged. It may be necessary to install new plates to gain satisfactory operation.

25. Install cotter pins or safety wires.

26. Remove the magneto side cover. Be sure not to lose the actuating plunger.

27. Install the flat and spring washers on the selector shaft against the snap ring.

28. Be sure that the engine case positioning dowels are in good condition.

29. Follow Steps 3-10 in the section, *Primary Cover Installation*, in this chapter to complete reassembly of the primary side of the engine.

CLUTCH AND ENGINE SPROCKETS

Removal/Installation

1. Remove the primary cover, clutch plates, pushrods, and inner clutch hub as described under *Clutch Removal*.

2. Remove the engine sprocket, outer clutch hub, and primary chain as a unit.

3. Clean thoroughly with solvent and blow dry with compressed air.

4. Inspect the 2 sprockets and slots for the clutch plates on the outer clutch hub for wear or damage. See Figure 4, Chapter Two, for an illustration of sprocket wear and damage. If any wear or damage is visible, replace the part with a new one.

5. Fit the chain on the 2 sprockets and install the 3 parts as a unit on the shafts with the outer clutch hub on the transmission main shaft. See Figure 43.

6. Check the play in the chain midway between the 2 sprockets by measuring the total movement of the chain in a direction perpendicular to itself. If the movement is more than ⅝ in., replace the chain with a new one.

7. Continue reassembly in the reverse order of disassembly.

PRIMARY CHAIN INSPECTION

See the previous section for instructions on inspection of the primary chain.

BREAKING IN A REBUILT ENGINE

A rebuilt engine requires the same care and break-in as a new engine because most of the parts are new. Never over-rev or allow the engine to labor at low speeds. Change the transmission oil after 300-500 miles (480-800 km). New parts shed the scraps of metal which are left after machining operations. Check the ignition timing after the initial break-in period and tighten all nuts and bolts.

CHAPTER SEVEN

TRANSMISSION, CRANKSHAFT, AND BEARINGS

TRANSMISSION

Operation

An understanding of the functioning of key systems of a motorcycle is of value in home servicing and repairing and in the ownership and enjoyment of riding. This chapter enables the home mechanic to identify the components of the power transfer system and to understand the role each component plays in the overall function.

The clutch, which is fitted to the left end of the main shaft, delivers power to the transmission. The main shaft has 5 gears on it (**Figures 1 and 2**), one of which can be made to slide along the main shaft to engage the gear on its left by means of engaging dogs, i.e., small pegs, on the sides of the gears. The main shaft also has a sliding dog which is a gear engaging component but is not a gear.

The 2 geared shafts in the transmission are the main shaft, described above, and the countershaft. The countershaft provides for the changing of gear ratio. It also has a gear which can be made to slide along the countershaft to engage the gear on either the left or right side of itself. See Figures 1 and 2.

There are 3 shifting forks in the transmission, 2 on the main shaft and one on the countershaft, which move the sliding gears and the sliding dog to the desired position. See **Figure 3**. The shifting forks are mounted on the shifter shaft and can be made to slide along the shaft. The forks fit into grooves on the sliding gears and sliding dog; the grooves allow the sliding gear or sliding dog to rotate while being held in position along their shaft by the forks.

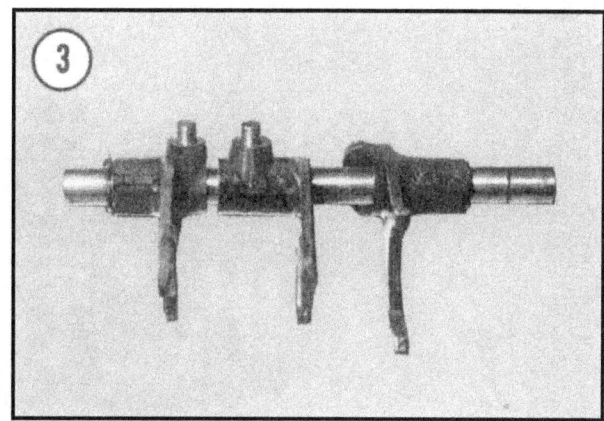

The shifting drum actuates the shifting forks. See **Figure 4**. Each of the 3 shifting forks has a small round peg which fits into one of the 3 grooves in the drum, i.e., one peg per groove. Rotation of the drum causes the shifting forks to move on the shifting fork shaft so as to engage the desired gear. The grooves in the drum are designed so that only one fork moves at a time

Main shaft 3rd gear
Sliding dog
Main shaft 1st gear
Main shaft 2nd gear
Main shaft 4th gear
5th driven gear
Main shaft
Countershaft
Countershaft 1st gear
Transfer gear
Countershaft 2nd gear
Countershaft 4th gear
Countershaft 3rd gear
TRANSMISSION

A
B
C
D
F
E
Main shaft
Yes
No
Yes
No
Yes
No
No
Yes
No
Yes
Yes
Countershaft
A′
B′
C′
D′
E′

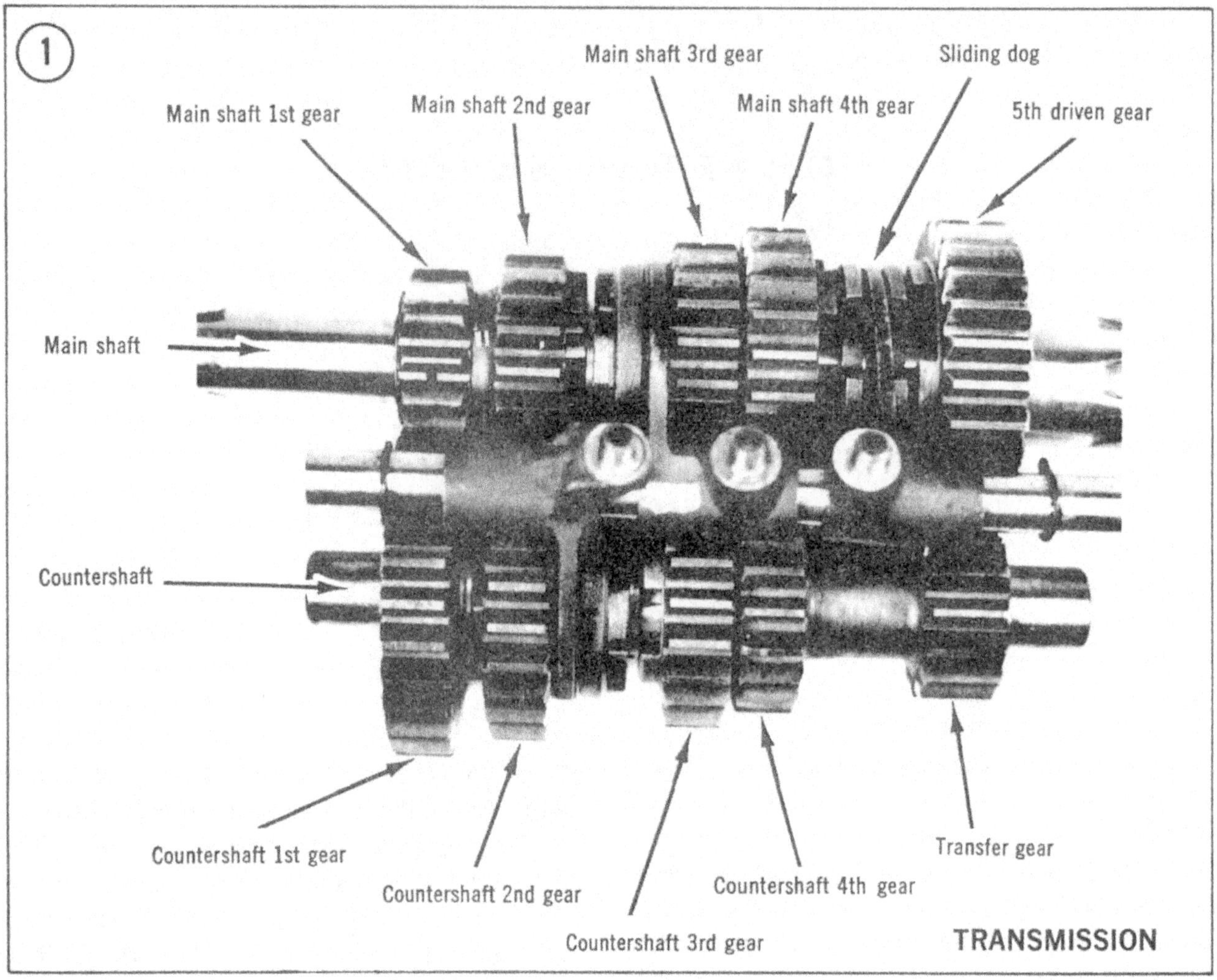

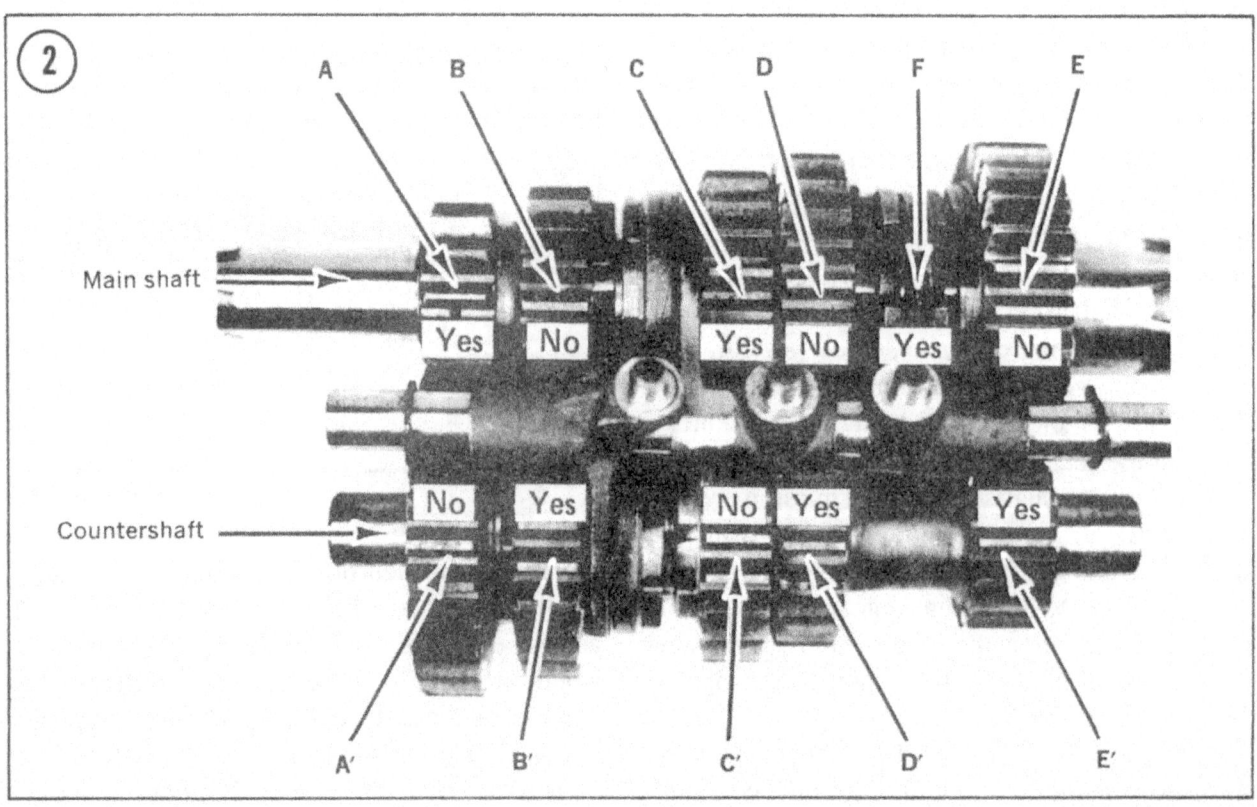

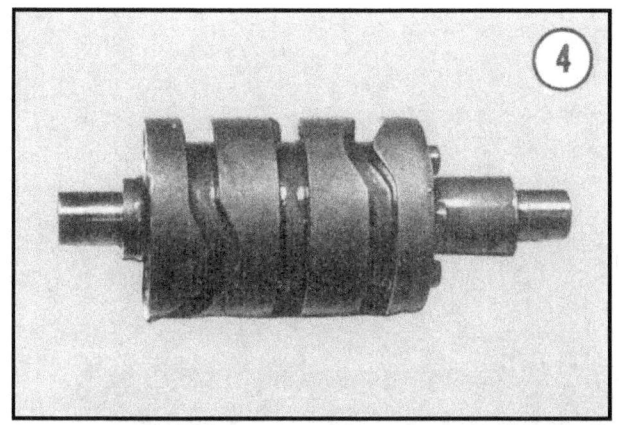

and so that only one gear or one sliding dog is engaged at a time.

The shifting drum has detent holes in the right end surface, one of which is smaller than the others. Each of the larger holes corresponds to a gear and the small one corresponds to neutral. When the transmission is in a gear, a spring loaded plunger is seated in the corresponding detent hole and holds the drum fixed so that the motorcycle is prevented from being jarred out of gear. The detent assembly comprises the plunger spring, screw, and a sealing washer. See **Figure 5**. The assembly fits into a hole located at the lower right rear side of the right engine case.

The drum is caused to turn by utilizing the round pegs selectors pins (round pegs) which are located on the left end surface of the drum. See Figure 4.

The selector shaft assembly comprises the selector shaft, the foot shift lever, the selection return spring, and the spring loaded selector pawl. See **Figure 6**. The foot shift may be bolted to either end of the selector shaft which protrudes from both sides of the engine.

Moving the foot shift lever rotates the selector shaft which causes the selector pawl to engage one of the selector pins on the end of the shifting drum and turns the drum to the next gear position. The selector shaft assembly is able, by design, to turn the drum enough for one gear change, up or down, only. The selector spring puts the selector shaft back in its original position when the foot shift lever is released and the spring loaded selector pawl fits on the next selector pin, in preparation for the subsequent change of gears.

The starting system is the foot operated, kick

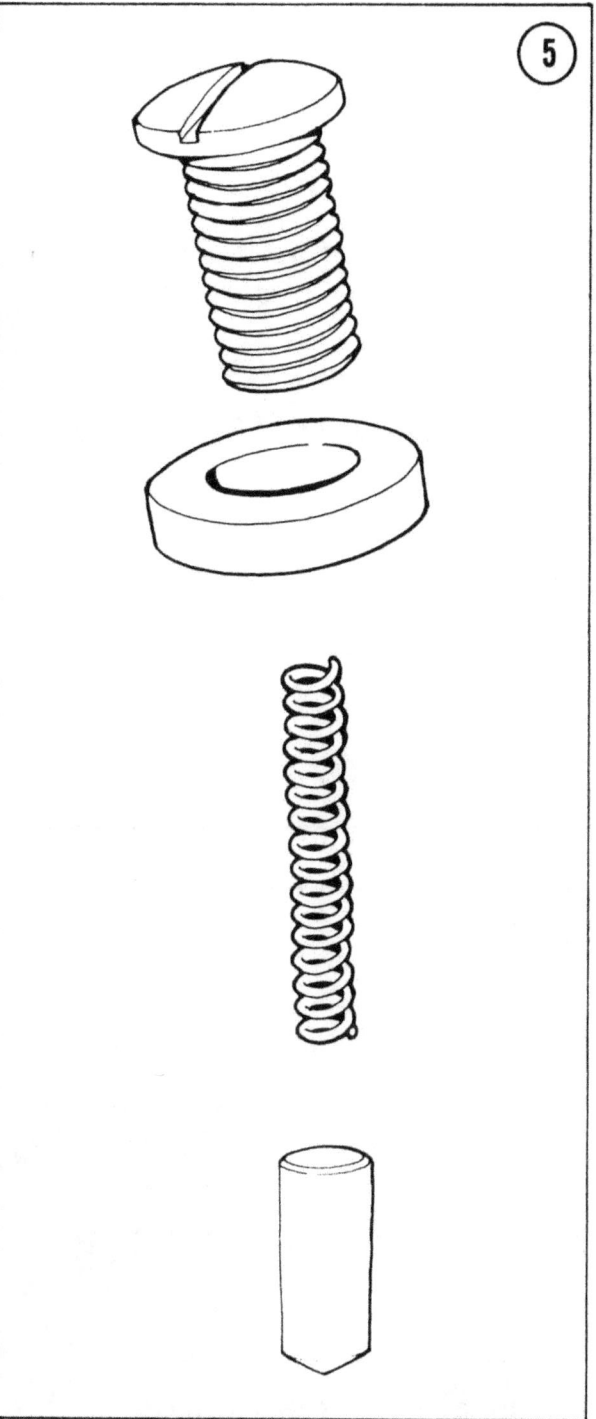

type. The kickstarter assembly comprises the kickstarter shaft, a spring loaded ratchet cam, a driving gear, a return spring, a foot lever, and a bolt. See **Figure 7**. The bolt fits into the right engine case. The driving gear is always meshed with a gear on the main shaft. The teeth on the ratchet cam and on the face of the driving gear are meshed only while the kickstarter is being used; while engaged, they turn in one direction only. While the kickstarter is not being used, a ramp on the cam is trapped behind the stop bolt.

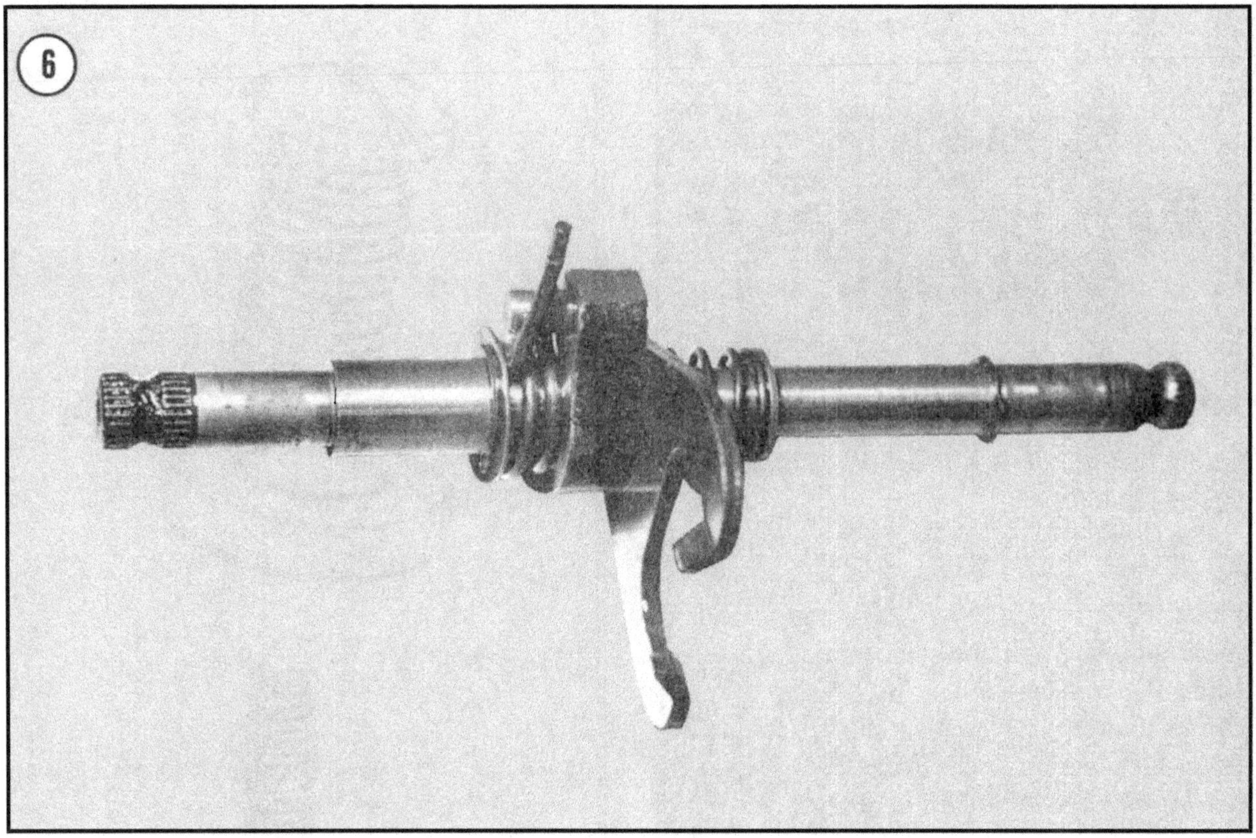

6

7

Operation of the kickstarter lever causes the ramp on the ratchet to move from behind the stop bolt and the ratchet to move to the left and mesh teeth with the driving gear. Continued movement of the kickstarter lever then causes rotation of the main shaft and, through the clutch and primary drive, rotation of the crankshaft. Because of the way the teeth on the ratchet and on the face of the driving gear are cut, the driving gear cannot cause the ratchet to turn when the engine starts. Releasing the kickstarter lever lets the return spring move the shaft and ratchet back to their disengaged position.

Transfer of Power

A knowledge of the way power is transferred through the transmission to the drive chain can be of substantial help in locating problems which may occur in the operation of the motorcycle.

Figure 1 shows the complete transmission assembly with the name for each part. Figure 2 is the same view of the transmission assembly but with a letter instead of the name of the gear. Each gear on the main shaft has the same letter designation as its opposing gear on the countershaft except that the letter for the countershaft gear has the prime mark (') added. For example, the main shaft 4th gear is denoted by the letter (D) and its opposing gear, countershaft 4th gear is denoted by (D'). Use of a letter, instead of the proper name for each gear, makes the text appreciably easier to understand.

In Figure 2, the transmission is in neutral. Each gear on the main shaft is meshed with its opposing gear on the countershaft. They remain meshed at all times. Even when a sliding gear moves, it will still be at least 60% meshed with its opposing gear. The Ossa transmission is thus called a "constant mesh transmission."

There is a word YES or NO superimposed on each gear in Figure 2. YES means that the gear is locked to the shaft either by splines or by being an integral part of the shaft; NO means that the gear is not locked. Remember this for the following discussion.

The following paragraphs describe what happens when the gears are shifted and how power is transferred through a 5-speed transmission when it is in gear. Assume that the transmission is in neutral initially, as shown in Figure 2. Pushing the foot shift lever down shifts the transmission from neutral to first gear. Grooves in the rotating drum slide the shifting fork connected to gear (B') to the left. The engaging dogs on the left of gear (B') fit into the slots on the right of gear (A') and engages gear (A'). See **Figure 8**. The other shifting forks do not move. Power enters the transmission through the main shaft. Gear (A) is locked to the main shaft and transmits the power to gear (A') on the countershaft. Gear (A') is not locked to the countershaft but gear (B') is and because gear (A') and gear (B') are now engaged, the countershaft turns. Gear (E') is locked to the countershaft; it transmits the power to gear (E) which is not locked to the main shaft. The drive sprocket, which is mounted to the right side face of gear (E), therefore turns.

Shifting from first to 2nd gear is done by pulling the foot shift liver up. Gear (B') moves to the right, thus disengaging from gear (A'). Gear (C) moves to the left and engages gear (B). See **Figure 9**. Gear (C') is not locked to the countershaft; it turns freely with gear (C). Power is transmitted from gear (C) to gear (B) to gear (B') which is locked to the countershaft. The countershaft turns gear (E'), which is locked to the shaft, and gear (E') turns gear (E) and the drive sprocket.

Shifting from 2nd to 3rd gear is effected by pulling the foot shift lever up. Gear (C) disengages from gear (B). Gear (B') engages gear (C'). See **Figure 10**. Power is transmitted from gear (C), which is locked to the main shaft, to gear (C') and thus to gear (B'). Gear (C') is not locked to the countershaft but it is engaged to gear (B') which is locked. Gear (E') turns gear (E) and the drive sprocket.

Shifting from 3rd to 4th gear is effected by pulling the foot shift lever up. Gear (B') disengages from gear (C'). The sliding dog (F) engages gear (D). See **Figure 11**. Power is transmitted from the main shaft to the sliding dog (F), which is locked to the main shaft and to gear (D), which is engaged by the sliding dog (F). Gear (D) turns gear (D') which is locked to the countershaft, thus turning gear (E') and (E) and the drive sprocket.

1st GEAR

Shifting from 4th to 5th gear is effected by pulling the foot shift lever up. The sliding dog (F) disengages from gear (D) and engages gear (E). See **Figure 12**. Because both sliding dog (F) and gear (E) are locked to the main shaft, power is transmitted directly, by passing the countershaft, and the main shaft turns gear (E) and the drive sprocket. There is no gear reduction in 5th gear; the gear ratio is 1:1.

The gear ratio is equal to the number of revolutions the clutch must make in order to cause one revolution of the drive sprocket. For example, to determine the gear ratio for 2nd gear: divide the number of teeth on gear (B′) by the number of teeth on gear (B) and record the resulting figure; divide the number of teeth on gear (E) by the number of teeth on gear (E′) and record the resulting figure; multiply the 2 resulting figures together to get the 2nd gear ratio.

Shifting from first gear to neutral is effected by lifting the foot shift lever to the position where a slight click is felt. The neutral position is midway between the positions for first and 2nd gear. Shifting from 2nd gear to neutral is effected by pushing downward on the foot shift lever to the position where a slight click is felt.

Removal

1. Follow procedures for engine, primary cover, and clutch removal and for splitting the crankcases is given in Chapter Six under *Engine Removal/Installation*.

2. Position the right hand engine case to provide for convenient access to the transmission shafts and gears. See **Figure 13**.

3. Remove the center case gasket and discard it.

4. Remove the slotted plastic breather tube.

5. Turn the kickstarter shaft clockwise until the whole assembly is clear for removal. Remove the assembly; retain the shim washers on both ends of the shaft.

6. Pull out the selector shaft.

7. Grab the transmission main shaft and countershaft with one hand and the shift drum and shift fork shaft with the other to remove the

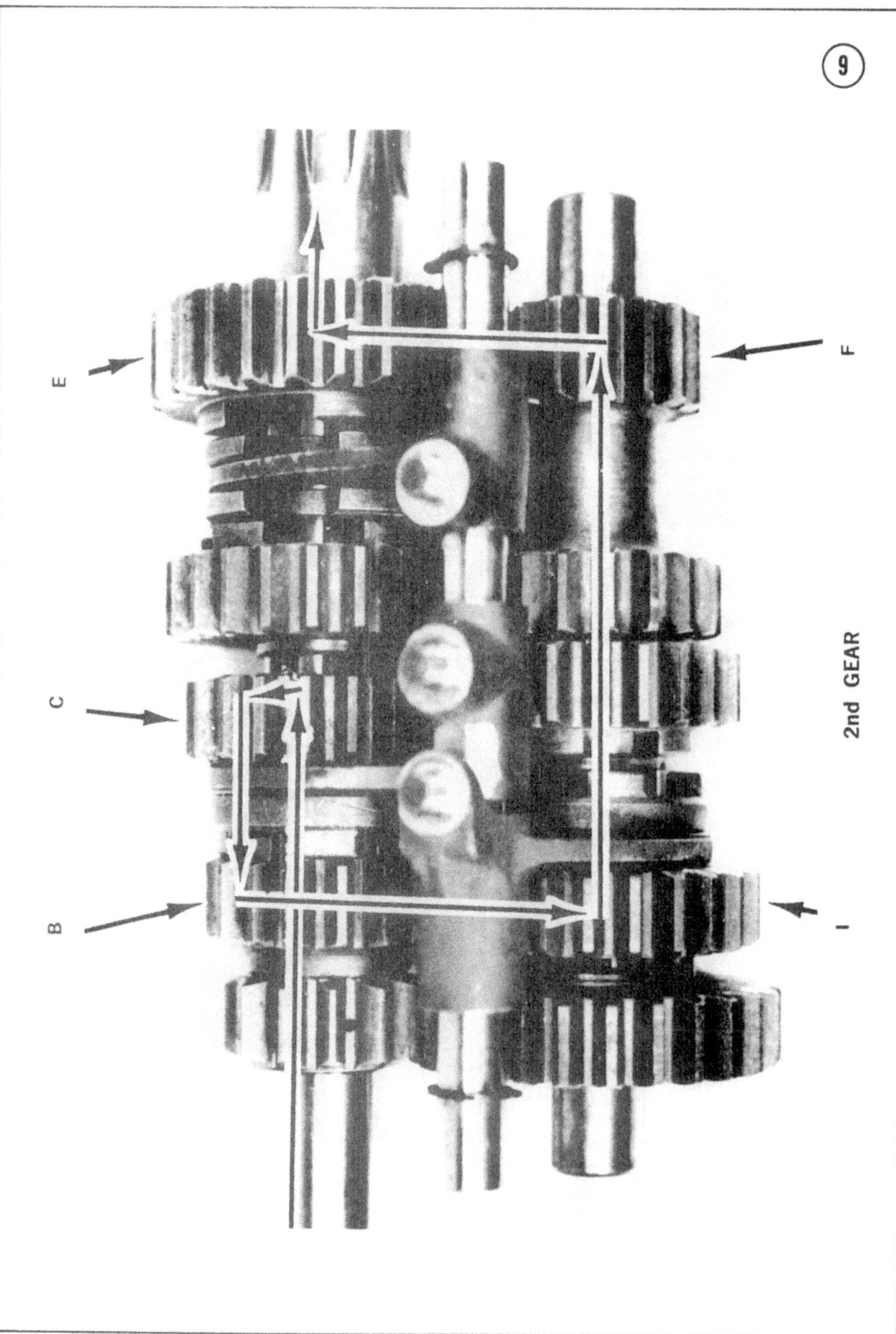

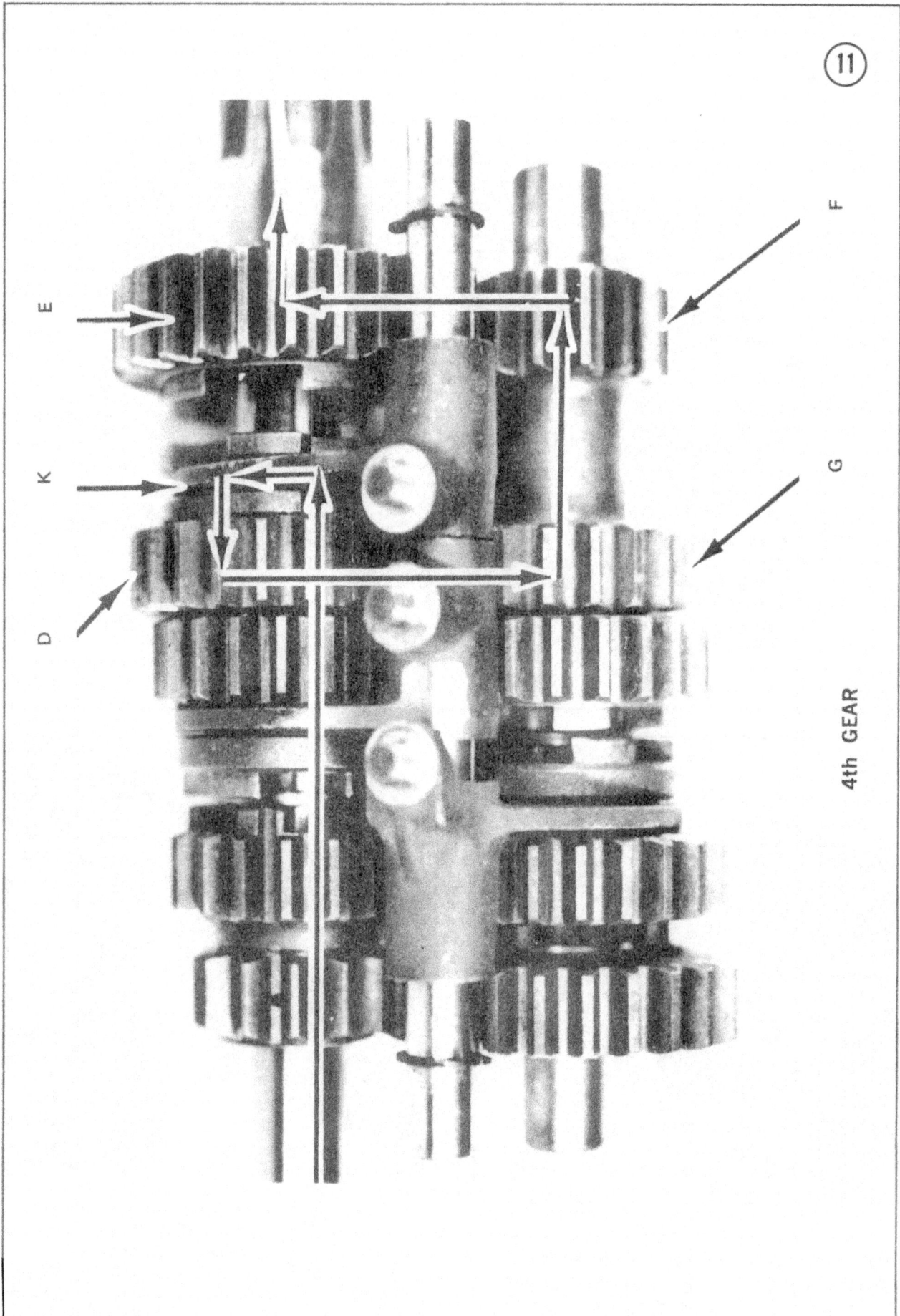

4th GEAR

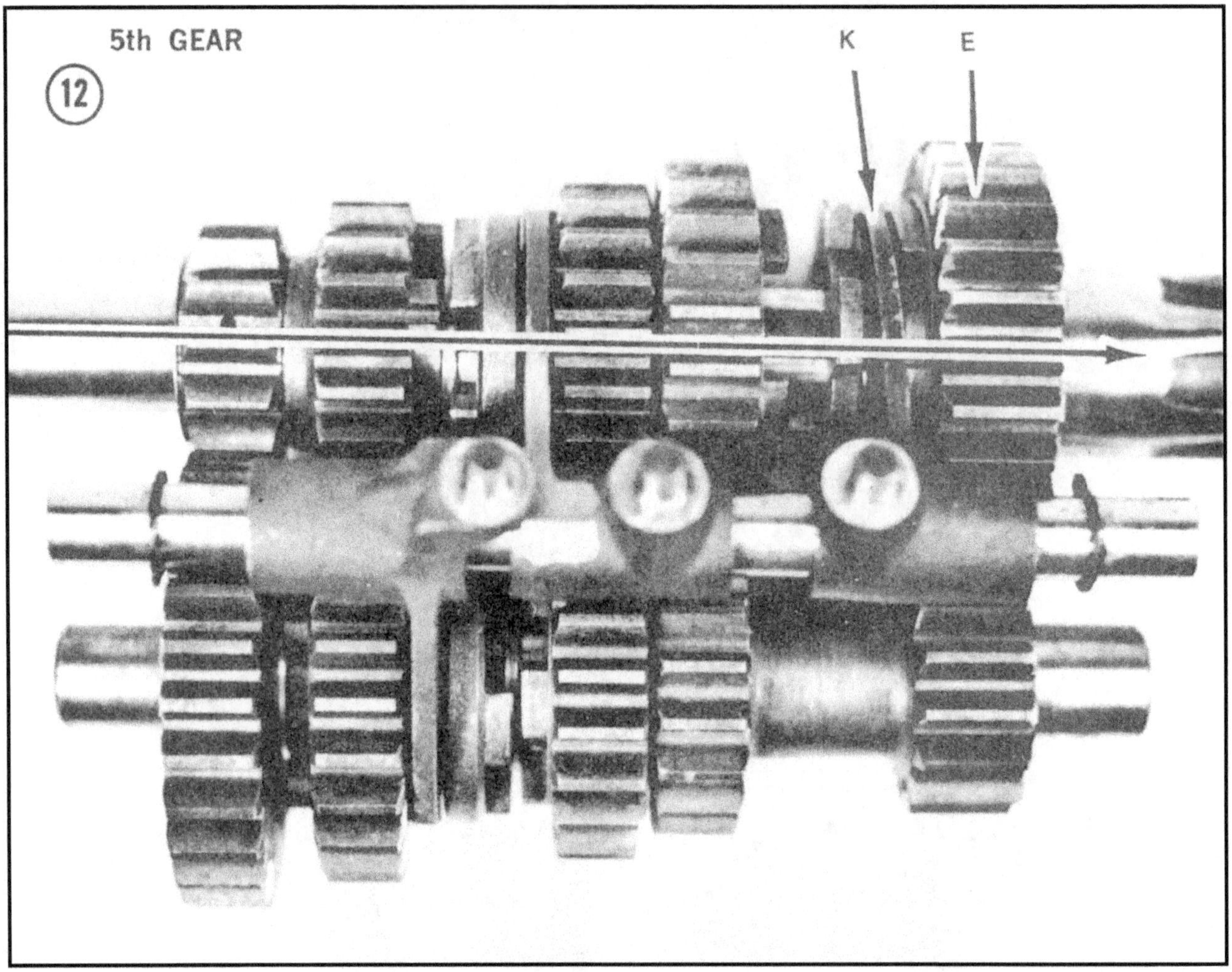

5th GEAR

(12)

(13)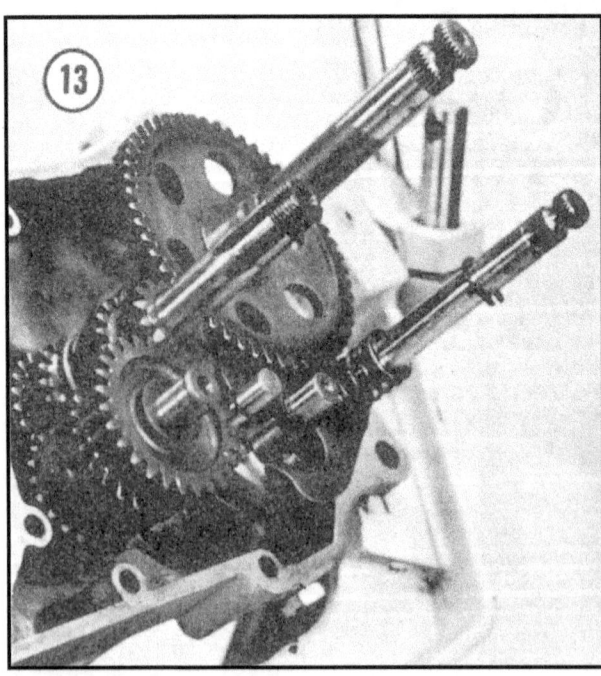

(14)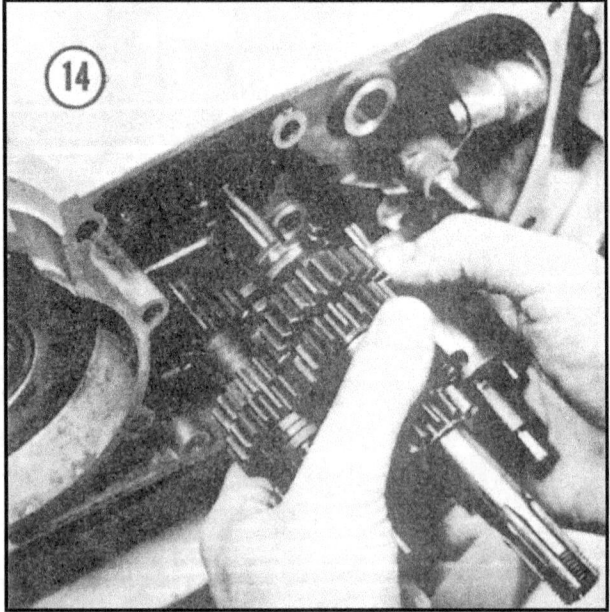

shafts and gears as a package. See **Figure 14**. Retrieve all shims and tag them for installation or place them on the proper shaft. The 5th driven gear on the main shaft (Figure 2) will remain in the case.

8. Remove the needle bearings and spacer from the 5th driven gear.

9. Pry up the sprocket nut tab washer on the outside of the right case.

10. Remove the sprocket by using a sprocket spanner and a sprocket nut wrench. Turn clockwise to loosen and remove this left hand threaded nut. See **Figure 15**.

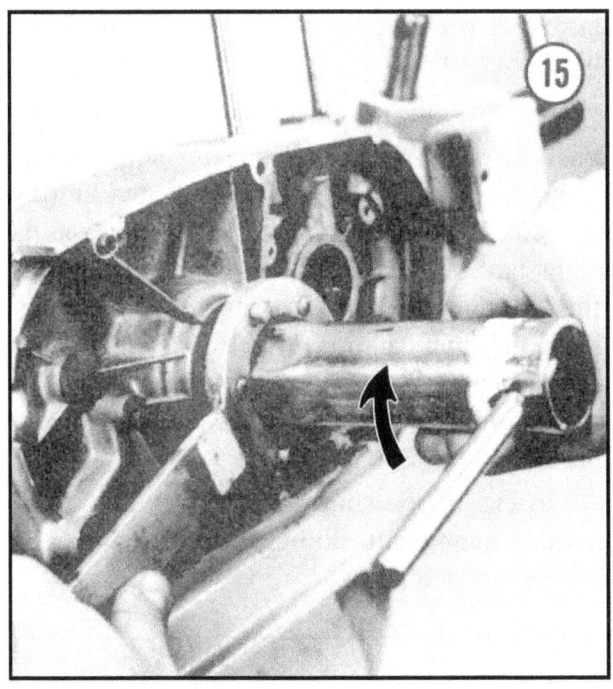

11. Tap the end of the 5th driven gear until it is free. Use a soft mallet.

12. Remove the sprocket distance spacer from inside the transmission oil seal.

13. Pry the small oil seal from the center of the 5th driven gear with one of the clutch pushrods.

Cleaning and Inspection

1. Clean all parts thoroughly in solvent and blow dry.

2. Carefully check all parts for wear, damage, or deterioration. Check the teeth on all gears for wear or damage.

3. Replace any part which has a thrust or friction surface showing a blue color. The blue color means that the part has been excessively hot.

4. Check the engaging dogs of all gears and the 4th and 5th gear sliding dogs. If a dog has rounded edges, replace it.

5. Check the freedom of the sliding gears to move back and forth on their shafts, along with the engaging dog. Be sure that there is no binding on the shaft.

6. In the case of broken gear teeth or a foreign object in the transmission causing it to seize, check the main shaft and countershaft for straightness. Put the shaft in a set of machinist's centers (see **Figure 16**) fitted with a dial indi-

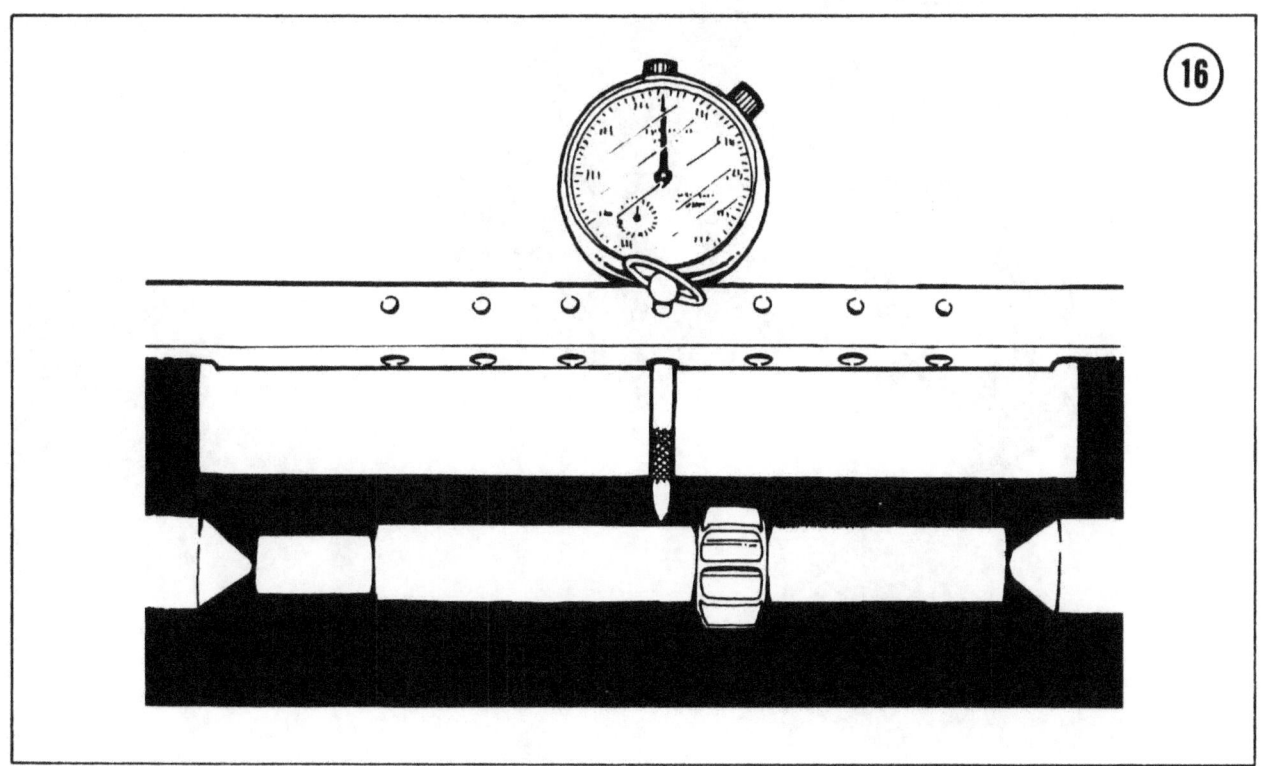

cator. Put the dial indicator on the middle of the shaft and rotate the shaft slowly. If it shows a runout of more than 0.001 in. (0.025mm), replace it. Also, carefully check all bearings and bushings in the transmission. Replace any doubtful part.

7. The countershaft 3rd gear and the main shaft 2nd and 4th gears are secured by lock rings in grooves on the shafts. Check the lock rings for up and down movement or side play on the shaft. Replace any that are not snugly fitted.

8. Check each shifting fork carefully for wear or damage. Only the 2 thrust pads on the ends of the fork should make contact with the sliding gear or dog. If there is *any* indication of contact by any other part of the fork, replace the fork.

9. Check the freedom of the shifting forks to move back and forth on the shifting fork shaft. Be sure that there is no binding.

10. Check the shifting fork shaft for wear or damage.

11. Measure the thickness (i.e., the dimension parallel to the shifting fork shaft) of each thrust pad on each fork. If any measurement is less than 0.148 in. (3.76mm), replace the fork. See **Figure 17**.

12. The shifting fork fits into grooves in the sliding gears and the sliding dog. See **Figure 18**. Measure the width of these grooves; if any groove is wider than 0.170 in. (4.32mm), replace the part.

13. The left shifting fork (the 1st and 3rd gear fork) fits into a groove on the countershaft sliding gear. See **Figure 19**. The center shifting fork (the 2nd gear fork) fits into a groove on the main shaft sliding gear. The right shifting fork (the 4th and 5th gear fork) fits into a groove in the main shaft sliding dog. Remove the snap rings from both ends of the shifting fork shaft with snap ring pliers and remove the forks from the shaft.

14. Insert the left shifting fork into the groove in the countershaft sliding gear. Be sure it is inserted right side up.

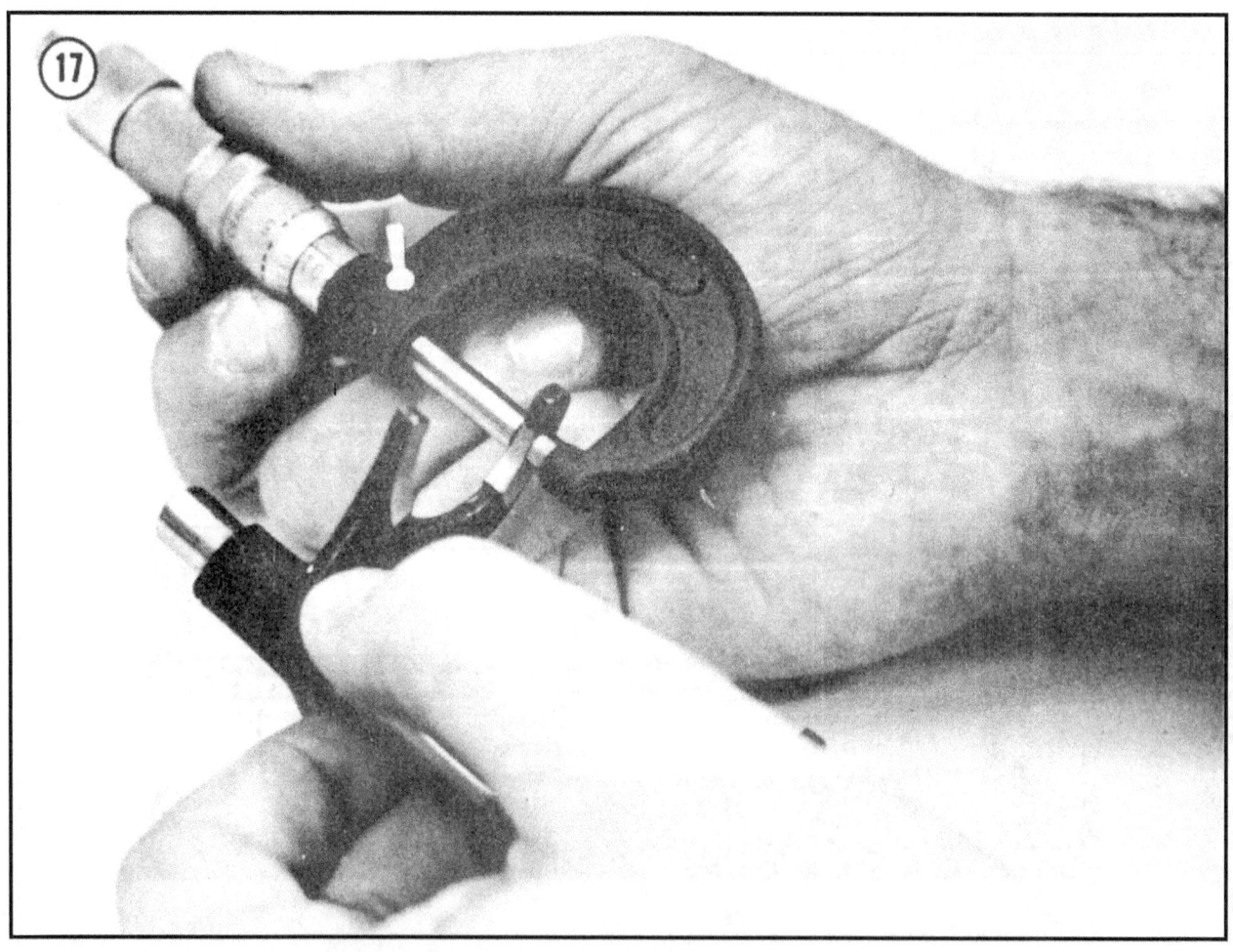

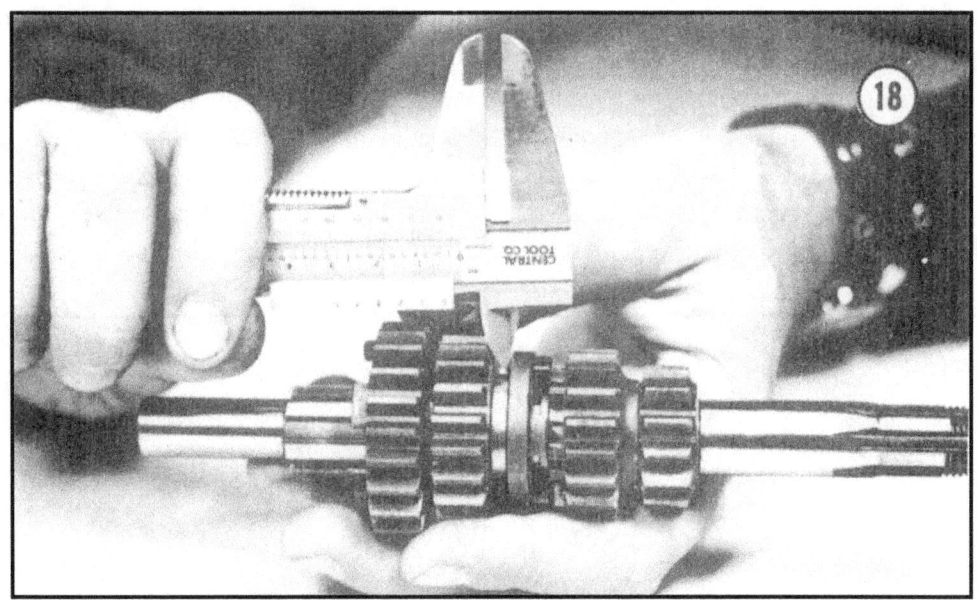

15. Measure the side clearance of the fork in the gear groove with a feeler gauge. Make the clearance measurement on both sides of both thrust pads. If any measurement is more than 0.020 in. (0.508mm), replace the shifting fork. See **Figure 20**.

16. Repeat Steps 13 and 14 with the center fork in the groove on the main shaft sliding and the right fork in the groove on the main shaft sliding dog. Maximum clearance is 0.020 in. (0.508mm) in all cases.

17. Measure the diameter of the peg, which fits into the proper groove in the shifting drum, on each shifting fork. Record the diameters and

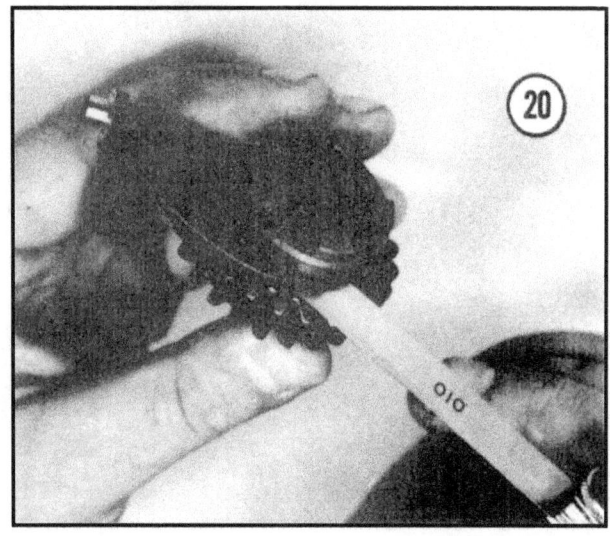

indicate for which fork the measurement was made. The purpose of the present set of measurements is to determine the amount of side play a shifting fork will have when it is engaged in a particular gear. Therefore the width of the grooves in the shifting drum will have to be determined at the critical positions specified below. Excessive side play in a shifting fork can be the cause of a transmission jumping out of gear or it can cause missed shifts.

18. Measure the width of the left groove (the groove nearest the face of the drum with the pegs) at the tips of the 2 vees in the groove. See **Figures 21 and 22**. The vee with a tip nearer the

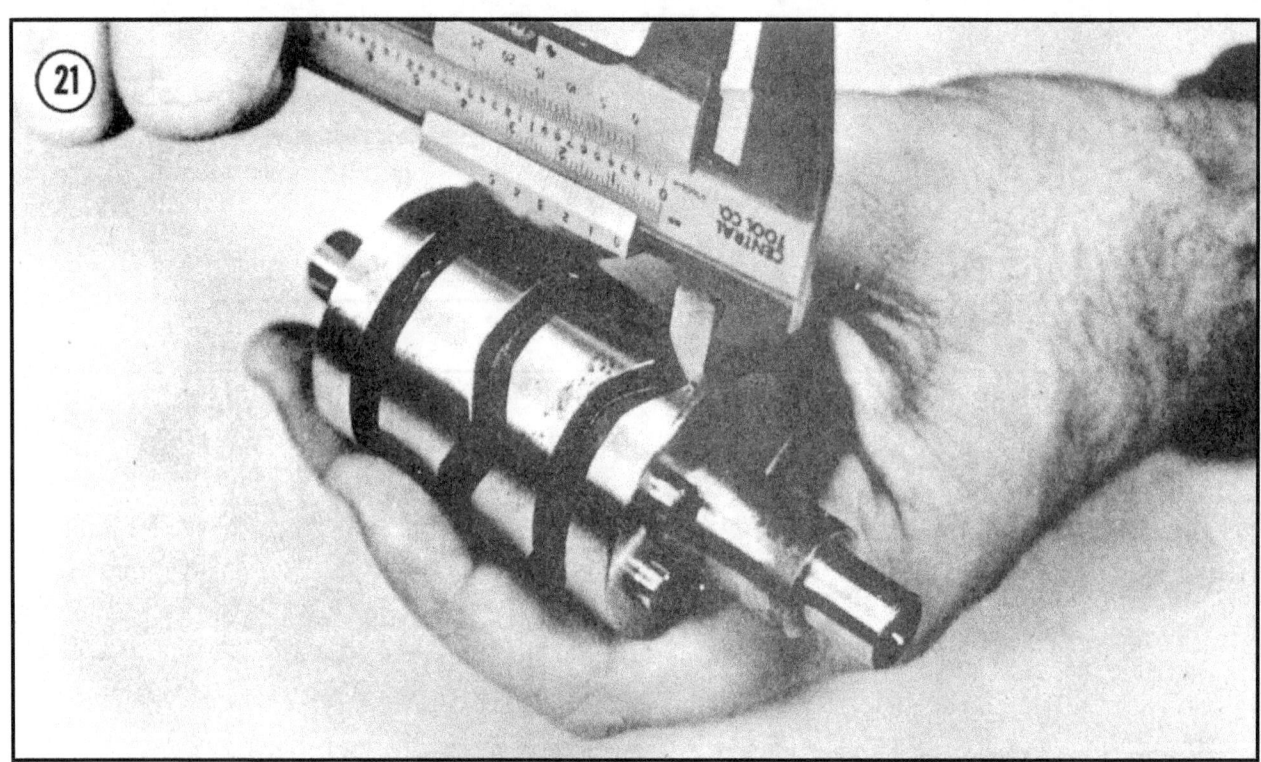

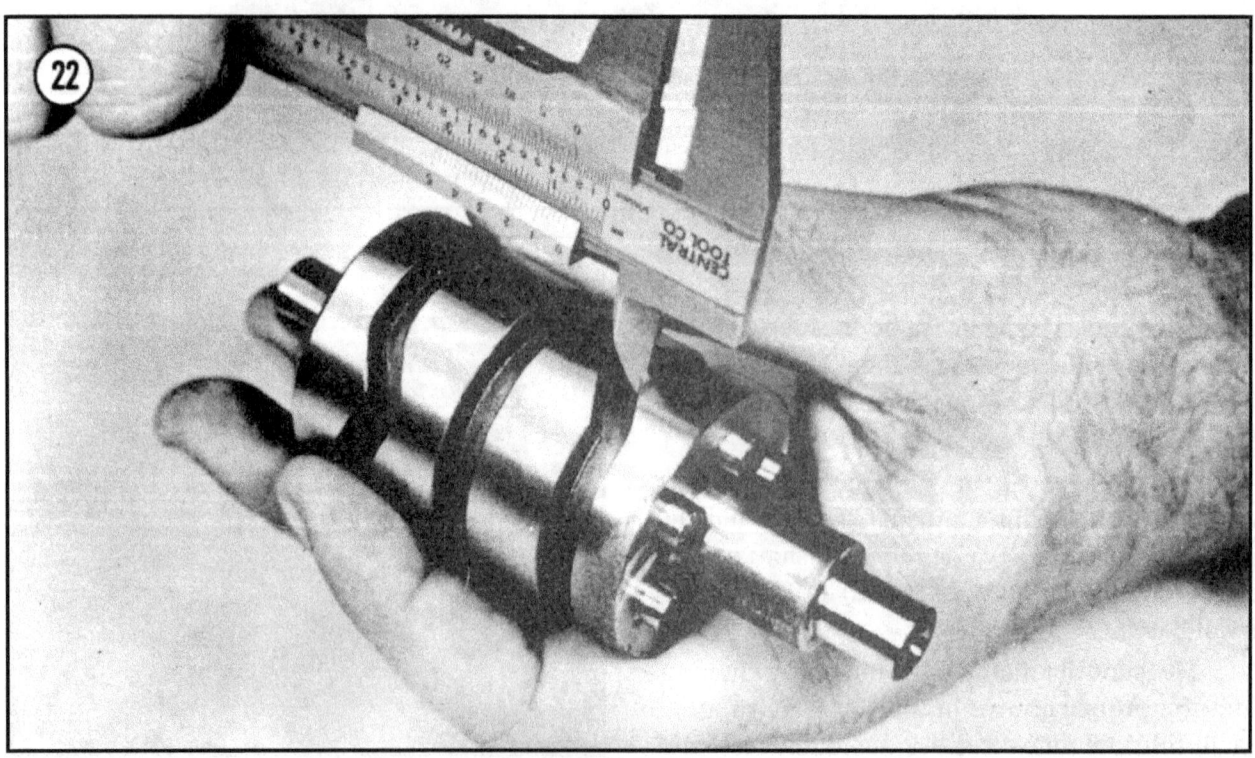

end of the drum is the 1st gear position; the other vee is the 3rd gear position. Record these 2 measurements which relate to the left fork.

19. Measure the width of the center groove at the tip of the single vee in the groove. See **Figure 23**. Record this measurement; it relates to the center fork. This vee is 2nd gear position.

20. Make one measurement of the width of the right groove (the groove nearest the face of the drum with the detent holes) at the tip of the vee. See **Figure 24**. Make another measurement of the width of the groove at the end of the groove (the end nearer the vee). See **Figure 25**. Record these 2 measurements; they relate to the right fork. Th first one is the 4th gear position and the last one is the 5th gear position.

21. For all 5 measurements taken above, subtract the diameter of the corresponding fork peg; if the difference is more than 0.008 in. (0.203mm) for any measurement, replace the appropriate fork.

22. If any of the groove width measurements taken above is more than 0.0244 in. (0.620mm), replace the drum.

23. Check the selector shaft and components for wear or damage. Check the condition of the splines on the end of the shaft and check the shaft for straightness. Check the tips of the

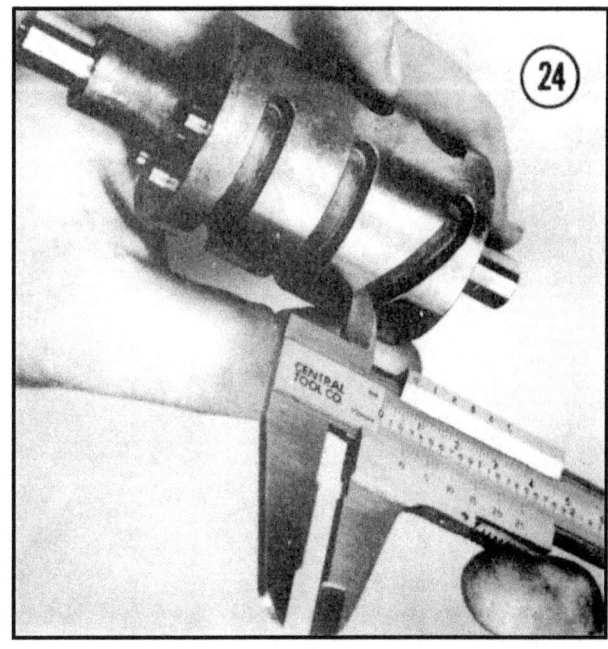

selector pawl for wear or chipping. Check the freedom of movement of the pawl by pulling it toward the left end of the shaft. Release the pawl and see if the pawl spring returns the pawl properly. Replace any defective or worn parts.

24. Check the selector shaft spring; it should be tight against the pin pressed into the housing of the shaft. Replace the spring if it is defective.

25. Check the snap rings and the lock ring on the shaft for wear or damage. Be sure they are installed and seated properly.

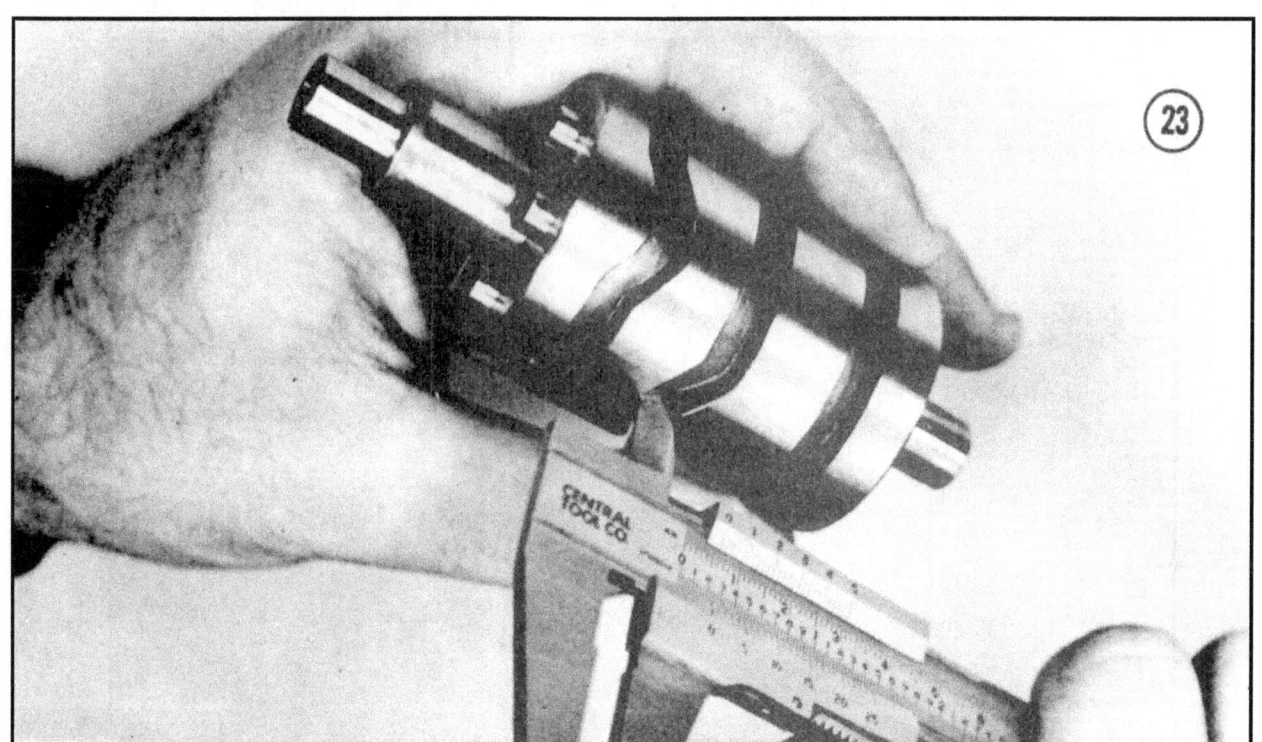

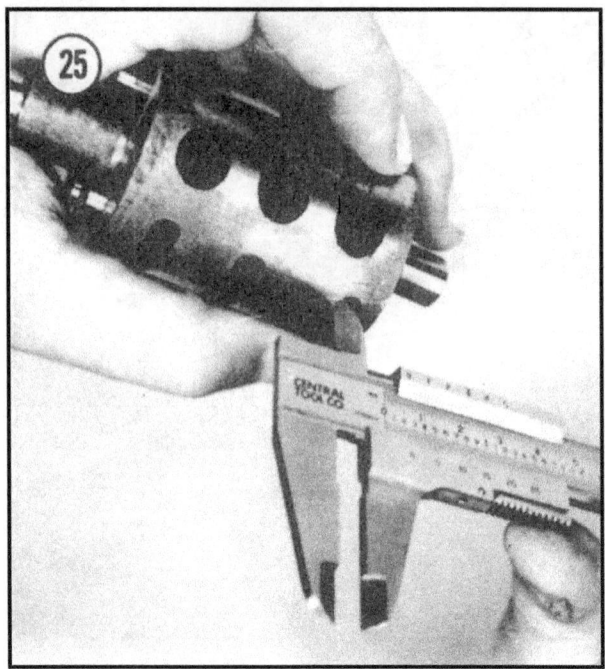

washers from outside the case and unscrew the stop bolt.

29. Check the stop bolt for wear or damage. Replace if necessary. Install the stop bolt with Loctite on the threads. The bottom of the head of the bolt should be approximately 0.080 in. (2mm) from the case shoulder. Install the washers and locknut (with Loctite) and torque the nut to 20 ft.-lb. (0.28 mkg).

30. Check the selector return spring anchor pin for wear or damage; be sure it is tight in the case. If a new one is installed, use Loctite on the threads.

31. Carefully check all bearings and bushings for wear or damage. Replace any doubtful part.

> NOTE: *To continue work on the transmission requires that the transmission components be assembled in place. If new bearings or bushings are needed, proceed to the section,* Crankshaft and Bearings, *in this chapter; if not continue with transmission work, as detailed below.*

26. Check the splines on the end of the kickstarter shaft. Check the teeth on the kickstarter driving gear; check to see that the gear rotates freely on the shaft.

27. Check the matching teeth on the ratchet cam and the driving gear. See **Figure 26**. Check to see that the cam will move along the shaft approximately 0.4 in. (1cm) toward the right end of the shaft and return by spring pressure.

28. Remove the kickstarter stop bolt in the rear of the case. See **Figure 27**. Remove the nut and

Installation

1. Install the gears on the main shaft. Be sure the lock rings are seated properly.

2. Install the gears on the countershaft. Be sure the lock rings are seated properly. The counter-

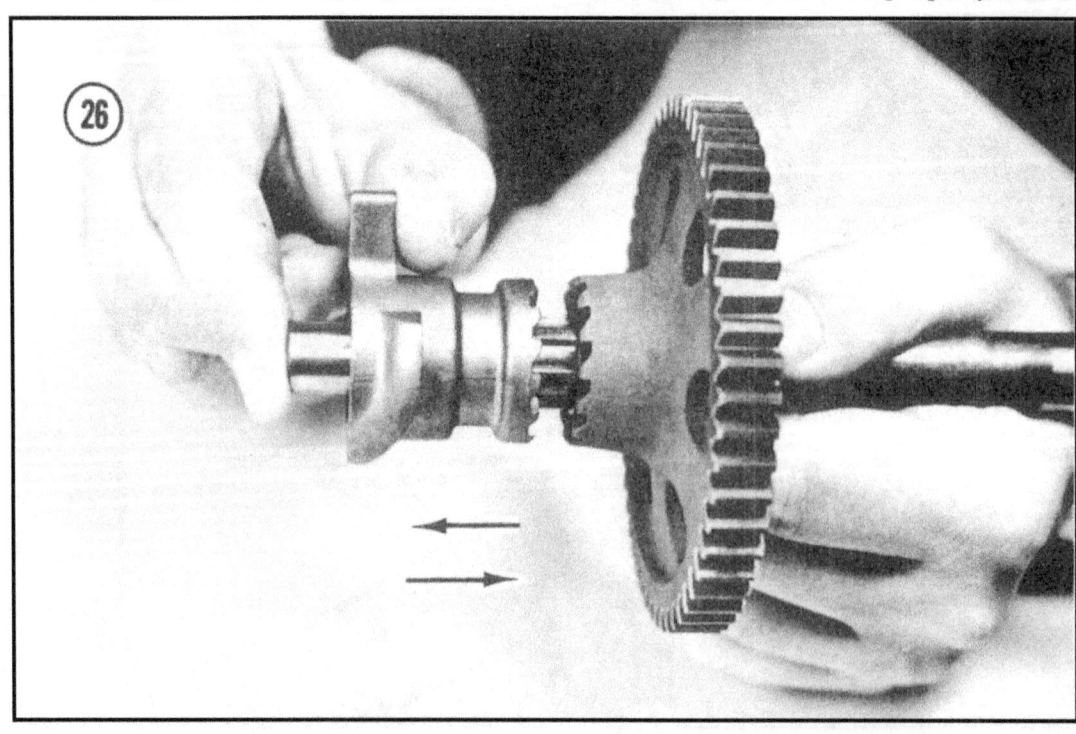

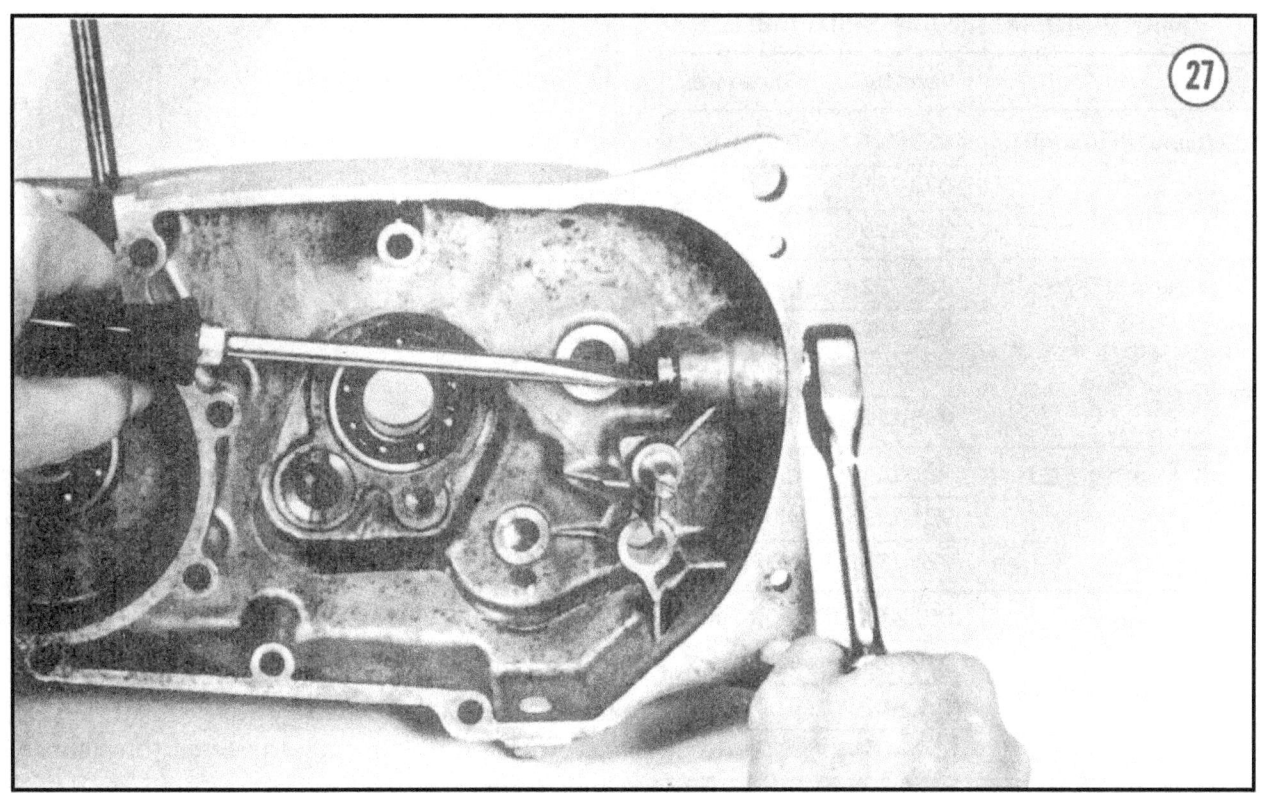

shaft 1st gear, see Figure 1, is an idling gear which rides on a caged needle bearing. Install the flat spacer washer, the needle bearing, and the gear over the bearing. See **Figure 28**. There are 3 needle bearings used in the transmission. See **Figure 29**. Use the widest one in this step.

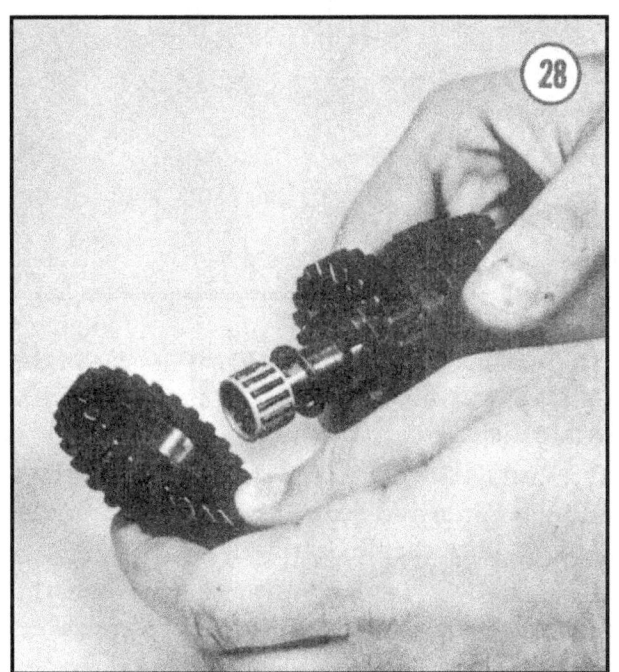

3. Refer to **Table 1** for the part numbers and sizes of all transmission shims.

4. Put the original shims back on the shafts. Install the assembled countershaft with its shims in the right engine case.

5. Install the crankcase positioning dowels and install a new center gasket on the right crankcase mating face.

6. Install the left crankcase and tighten 5 or more engine case screws.

Table 1 TRANSMISSION SHIM TABLE

	Part No.	Thickness
Left end of layshaft	033-176-I	0.002 in.
	033-176-II	0.004 in.
	033-176-IV	0.008 in.
Right end of layshaft & Right end of kickstarter shaft	033-292-I	0.002 in.
	033-292-II	0.004 in.
	033-292-IV	0.008 in.
	033-292-X	0.020 in.
Left end of main shaft	921-111	0.002 in.
	921-112	0.004 in.
	921-113	0.008 in.
Shift drum	050-404-I	0.002 in.
	050-404-II	0.004 in.
	050-404-IV	0.008 in.
	050-404-X	0.020 in.
Left end of kickstarter shaft	911-139-II	0.004 in.
	911-139-IV	0.008 in.
	911-139-X	0.020 in.
Crankshaft shims	991-139-II	0.004 in.
	991-139-IV	0.008 in.
	991-139-X	0.020 in.

7. The left end of the countershaft is exposed through the bushing in the left engine case. Measure the end play of the countershaft with a dial gauge or vernier caliper. Reach in through the center of the main shaft bearing with a hooked tool and hook the 4th gear on the countershaft. The play will be measured by pulling the shaft forward with the tool and pushing it away with the far right hand gear. If a dial indicator is used, attach it to the left engine case. The plunger should touch the left end of the countershaft and be parallel to it. If a vernier caliper is used, lay a strong, straightedged strip of metal across the engine case and use it as a reference line. See **Figure 30**. Measure the end play by moving the countershaft to the right and left as far as it will go.

8. Adjust the end play to 0.010-0.015 in. (0.254-0.381mm) by adding or subtracting

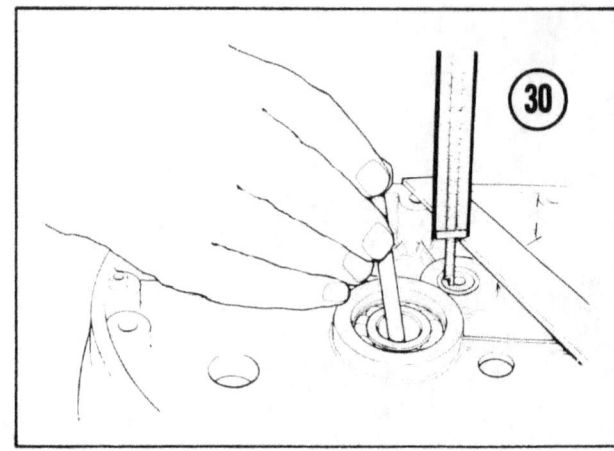

shims. Remove the left engine case to add or take away shims. Install the case and check the end play again. When end play is correctly adjusted, remove the countershaft.

9. Check the end play of the shifting drum with the caliper. See **Figure 31**. Move the drum back and forth with your finger inserted through the hole in the case. The end play should be 0.008-0.012 in. (0.20-0.30mm); shim accordingly. Remove the shifting drum after shimming.

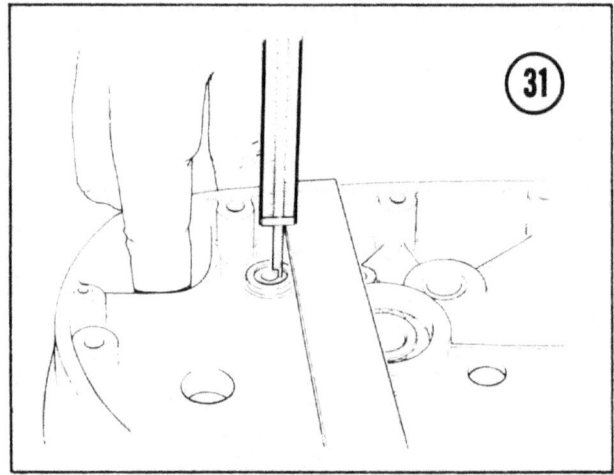

10. Install the main shaft 5th driven gear in the right transmission bearing by tapping it in with a soft mallet.

11. Install one of the main shaft needle bearings into the 5th driven gear. Install a 10mm spacer and the other needle bearing.

12. Install the main shaft and shims into the gear and install the left case on the center gasket.

13. Use the vernier caliper to measure the distance from the end of the main shaft to the inner ball bearing race, with the shaft all the way to the right. See **Figure 32**.

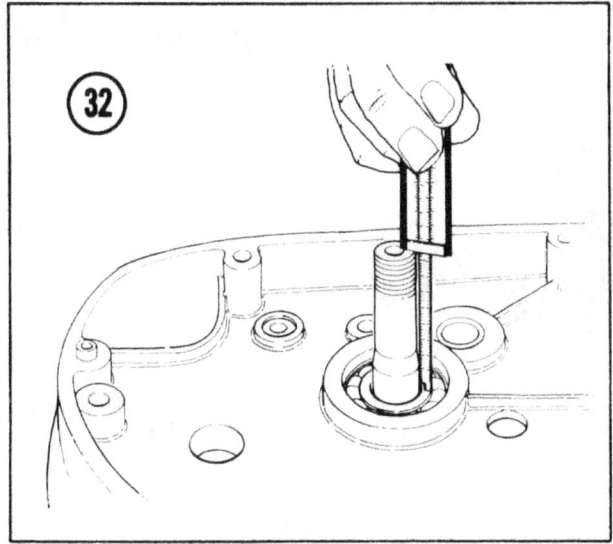

14. If the main shaft cannot be moved to the left by hand, install the clutch hub and nut on the shaft and pull it to the left. Carefully remove the hub and measure the position of the main shaft. End play should be 0.020-0.035 in. (0.51-0.89mm) but it is not critical. Record the amount of end play for future reference.

15. Remove the left case and main shaft and install the complete kickstarter assembly in the right case with the pointed end of the ratchet cam facing upward. Be sure the kickstarter shaft has at least a 0.040 in. (1.02mm) thick washer on each end.

16. Turn the kickstarter shaft counterclockwise until it stops or binds. If it binds before the shaft reaches its stop, there are too many shims on the right end of the shaft. Remove one shim at a time from the right end until it operates freely. When it operates properly, the ratchet cam will catch behind the stop bolt, disengaging the ratchet mechanism.

17. Install the left case with the gasket between cases. Tighten at least 5 screws.

18. Turn the shaft clockwise until it stops. Pull the shaft back and forth and measure end play. It should be 0.060-0.080 in. (1.52-2.03mm). The amount of play is not critical but correct it, if necessary, by adding or removing the large diameter shims on the left end of the shaft.

19. Now that the amount of shimming is known for each shaft, determine which end of each shaft they should go on.

20. Install the shifting forks on their shaft. See **Figure 33**. Install 2 new snap rings on the shaft with the sharp edges facing inward.

21. Install the 2 needle bearings in the main shaft 5th driven gear with the 10mm spacer between them.

22. Make a spacer with a thickness equal to the end play of the main shaft recorded in Step 14 above. Extra shims from the left end of the countershaft may be used to make the spacer. See **Figure 34**. Install the spacer on the right end of the main shaft.

23. Position the right engine case so that when

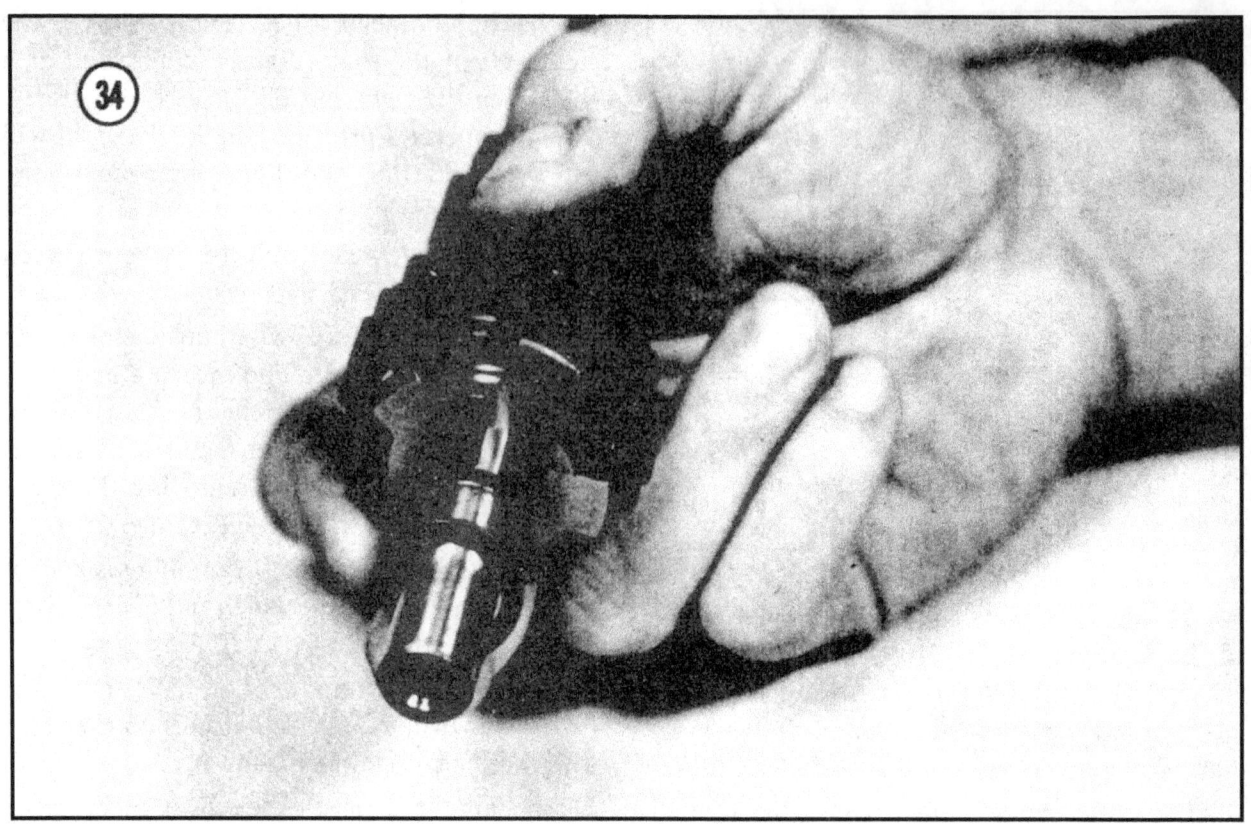

the transmission assembly is installed the shafts will be pointing straight up.

24. Install the transmission assembly as a unit in the right engine case (the reverse of the way it was removed). See **Figure 35**. Push all components to the right side of the case and be sure all parts turn freely.

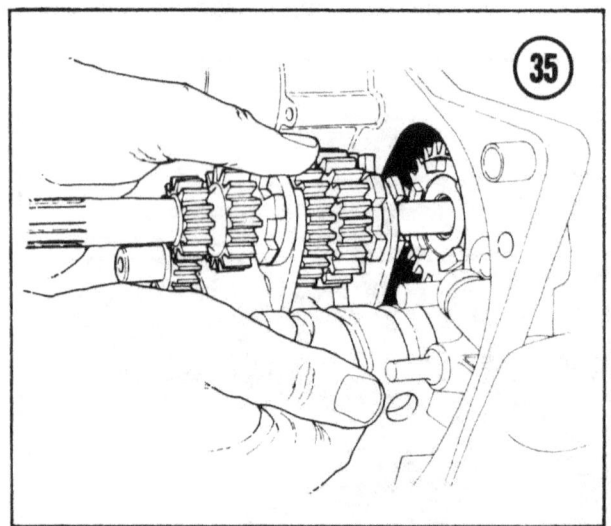

25. In order to check gear engagement, the shift drum will have to be turned by hand. Rotating the main shaft while turning the shifting drum to change gears, allows the engaging dogs to move into alignment and mesh with the other gear.

26. Turn the shifting drum counterclockwise to its limit to put the transmission into 1st gear position. See **Figure 36**. Be sure the engaging dogs in every gear position are engaged for at least 75% of their length.

27. Turn the shifting drum clockwise and rotate the main shaft until 2nd gear position is reached. Check the engaging dogs amount of engagement.

28. Repeat Step 27 for 3rd and 4th gear positions. Because of the temporary spacer installed on the main shaft, 5th gear cannot be properly engaged at this time.

29. If there is too little or too much gear engagement in any gear position, check the following possibilities.

   a. If a shifting fork is bent, the fitted sliding gear or sliding dog will have moved too far in one direction and not far enough in the other.

   b. If the shifting drum is shimmed too much on one side and not enough on the other, all of the sliding gears and the sliding dog will have moved too far in one direction

and not far enough in the other. Correct by moving some of the shims from one end to the other until engagement is correct in all gear positions.

c. If the main shaft is shimmed too much on one side and not enough on the other, the main shaft sliding gear and sliding dog will have moved too far in one direction and not far enough in the other. Action of the countershaft sliding gear would not be affected. Correct by moving the shims until the engagement is proper.

d. If the countershaft is shimmed too much on one side and not enough on the other, the countershaft sliding gear will have moved too far in one direction and not far enough in the other. Correct by moving the shims until the engagement is proper.

As long as a single shim is retained on the left end of the countershaft, all of the other shims on the other shafts may be moved to the right end if necessary.

Normally, the Ossa transmission will give no difficulty in shifting and in engagement no matter where these very thin shims are installed. Except for the example of a bent shifting fork, the above examples are rare and extreme.

30. Turn the shifting drum counterclockwise to the 1st gear position.

31. Install the detent assembly in the right case and turn it in 2 or 3 turns while holding the shifting drum all the way to the right. See **Figure 37**. Be careful not to allow the force of the detent spring to move the shifting drum to the left while screwing in the detent assembly. As the detent assembly is being screwed in, the shifting drum will turn slightly to line up the detent hole in the drum with the detent plunger. While the detent plunger is holding the shift drum in the 1st gear position, check the engagement of the dogs. If the engagement is not the same as when checked previously while in the 1st gear position, replace the shifting drum.

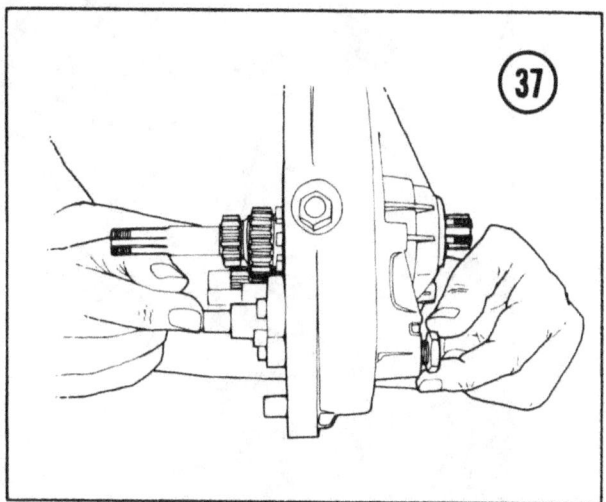

32. Remove the detent assembly and turn the shifting drum to the 2nd gear position. Screw in the detent assembly until the plunger engages

the hole on the shifting drum. Check the engagement and compare with the previously measured engagement. If the engagement is too little, replace the shifting drum.

33. Install the selector shaft assembly while the transmission is still in the 2nd gear position and the detent assembly is in place. Be sure the selector shaft is properly seated and that the return spring is on the anchor pin.

34. If the 2 shifting drum selector pins between the tips of the selector pawl are not centered between the pawl tips, correct by bending the selector return spring until the pins are centered. Be sure the spring ends have a snug fit on the anchor pin after bending. See **Figure 38**.

35. Repeat the above checking procedures for the selector and detent assemblies in 3rd gear and in 4th gear. If the location of the selector pins on the shifting drum varies from one gear position to another or if the detent installation results in poor gear engagement, replace the shifting drum.

36. Remove all the transmission components and the spacers from the right end of the main shaft. Install the components in the right case again and repeat the above checking procedures for the selector and detent assemblies in the 5th gear position.

37. Remove the detent assembly and all the transmission components. Install the shifting and selector shaft assembly in the right case. Be careful to install the shifting drum shims properly.

38. Use a feeler gauge to measure the clearance between the back of the selector pawl tips and the end of the shifting drum. See **Figure 39**. The clearance should be 0.015-0.080 in. (0.381-2.03mm); if it exceeds these limits, check the selector mechanism for straightness or damage. Too little clearance can be corrected with shims on the right end of the selector shaft. Use the same type shim as used on the left end of the countershaft. Too much clearance requires replacing the selector assembly.

39. Continue reassembly in the reverse order of disassembly.

CRANKSHAFT AND BEARINGS

Removal

The removal and installation of all bearings and bushings in the engine must be done without the application of any force.

> NOTE: *Driving or pressing the bearings in or out will damage the bearings and perhaps the cases to a degree which would necessitate discarding*

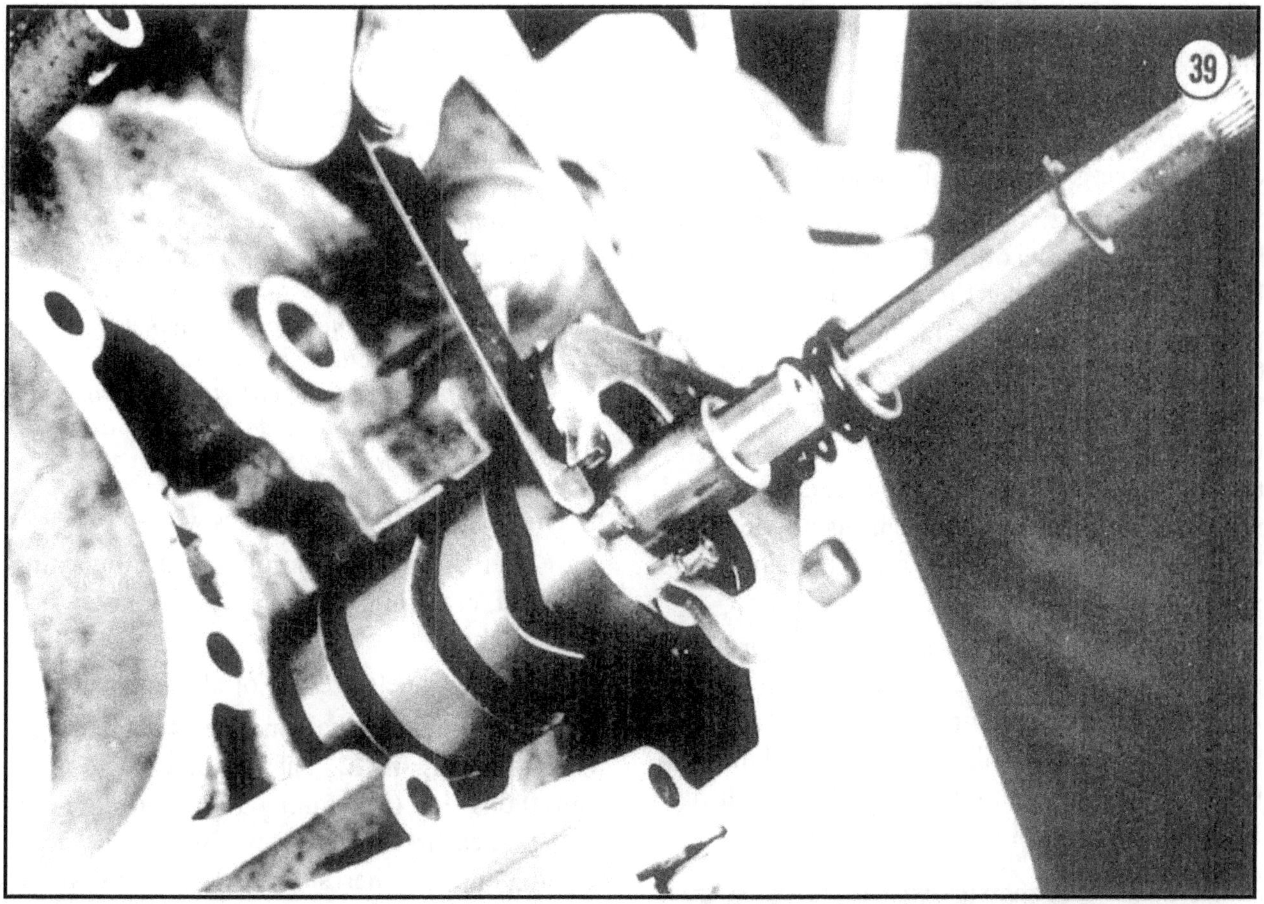

them. Always heat the engine cases for removal or installation of bearings and bushings. Difficulty in removing them means that the cases have not been heated long enough. Do not apply force.

1. Put the primary side engine case in an oven or electric stove or apply heat with a torch until the case temperature is 250-300°F (121-149°C). If a torch is used, be sure to keep the torch moving to heat the entire case evenly. Be careful not to overheat; excessive temperature may cause distortion of the cases. Keep the flame of the torch away from the crankshaft seals if they are to be reused. It is recommended, however, that these inexpensive crankshaft seals be replaced with new ones every time the crankshaft is removed or the crankcases are split.

2. After heating the left case, protect your hands with a cloth wrapped around the magneto side drive shaft and remove the crankshaft assembly from the case; the right side (primary side) main bearing will remain on the crankshaft. If there is difficulty in pulling the crankshaft out, place the case on a wooden box with the crankshaft hanging straight down and tap the end of the primary side drive shaft with a soft mallet to remove the crankshaft. See **Figure 40**.

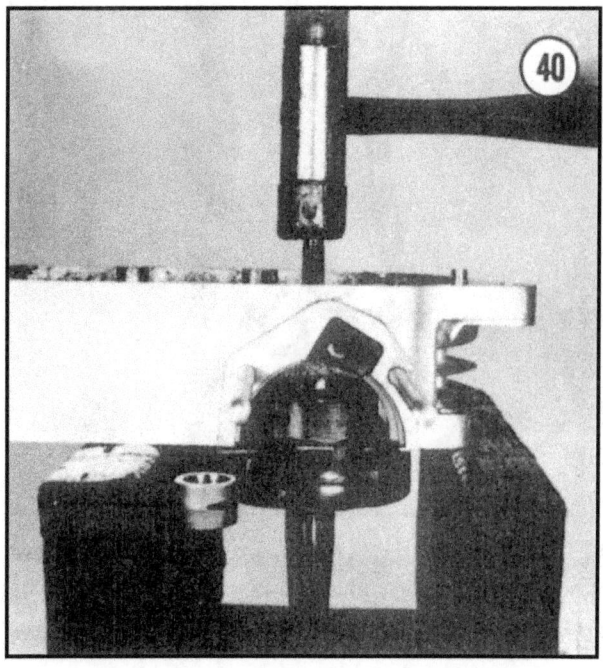

3. If a new transmission main shaft bearing or countershaft bushing in the primary side engine case is to be installed, remove the old one while

the cases are still heated. Push out or gently tap out the bearing with a soft mallet. Push out or use a drift to gently tap out the bushing.

4. Heat the magneto side case and gently tap out the bearings with a mallet and drift.

5. The countershaft bushing is in a dead-end hole on the inside of the magneto side case. Remove it by holding the case over a wooden surface with the bushing facing downward and tapping the case against the wooden surface. The bushing will fall out if the case is sufficiently heated.

6. Tap out the crankshaft seals and the transmission drive bearing seal from inside the cases with a mallet and a drift. A socket and an extension will serve as a drift.

7. Remove the main bearing from the primary side of the crankshaft with 2 large screwdrivers or 2 pry bars. See **Figure 41**. The balls or the races in the bearing will most likely be damaged by the prying. Do not reuse the bearing if it has been removed. Replace it with a new one.

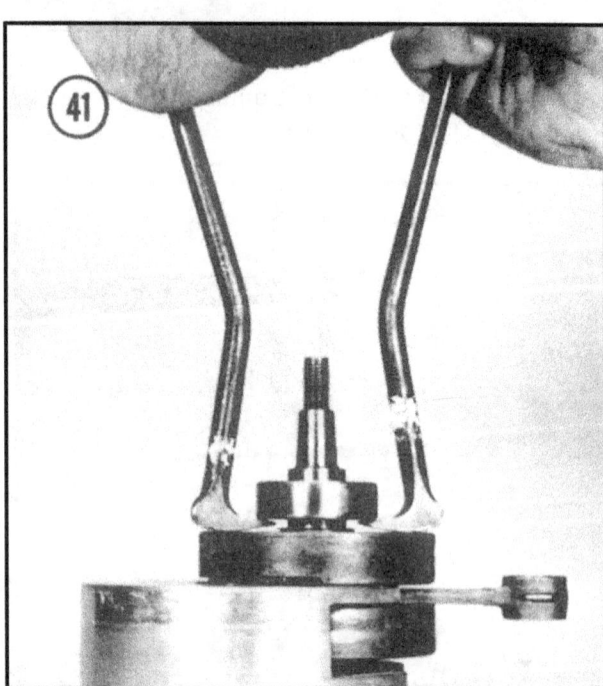

8. If there are any shimming washers between the primary side main bearing and the flywheel, remove them and tag them for identification.

Cleaning and Inspection

1. Clean all parts and the cases with solvent and blow dry with compressed air.

NOTE: *Much inspection but very few repairs relating to the crankshaft can be done by the home mechanic. Many special tools and much equipment are required, including a 15 ton press, a fixture for pressing apart the flywheels, an alignment jig for pressing them together again, and a set of machinist's centers fitted with 2 dial indicators to check for alignment after crankshaft reassembly. If these tools are not on hand along with the ability to use them properly, take the crankshaft to an Ossa dealer for inspection and repair.*

2. The crankshaft needs repairs when:
   a. There is a worn or damaged connecting rod, crankpin, bearing, flywheel, or wristpin hole.
   b. The flywheels are out of alignment.

3. Mount the crankshaft in a set of machinist's centers. See **Figure 42**. There should be no more than 0.001 in. (0.025mm) runout of the flywheels, measured at the point where the main bearings fit on either side of the crankshaft. If the runout is more, or if misalignment of the crankshaft is suspected, the complete assembly must be inspected and repaired.

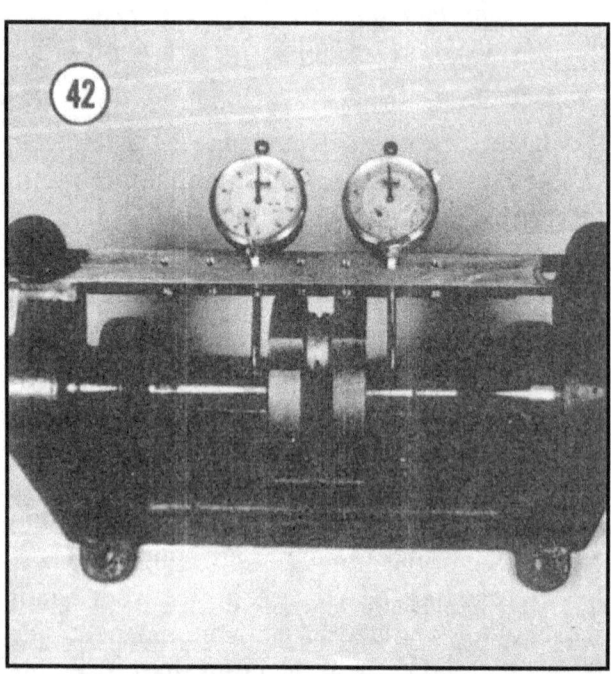

4. Check for roughness in the big end rod bearing or any perceptible up and down play in the connecting rod. If either roughness or play is detected, replace the big end bearing as an

assembly, including a new connecting rod, crankpin, rollers, and roller cage.

5. Clean the small end of the connecting rod, the wrist pin, and the wrist pin bearing. Inspect for wear or damage.

6. Install the wrist pin bearing in the small end of the connecting rod and install the wrist pin so that it is centered on the bearing as it would be if the piston were installed. See **Figure 43**.

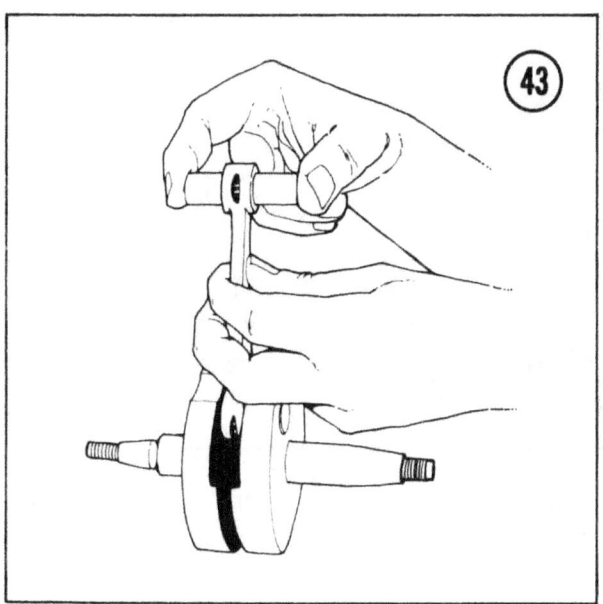

7. Hold the rod steady and try to move the wrist pin in all directions to check for play. If there is any detectable play in this assembly, replace the wrist pin and bearing and check it again.

8. If no play is now evident, the old connecting rod assembly can be used with the new wrist pin and bearing. If there is still play, the entire assembly must be replaced.

Crankshaft Alignment

If the crankshaft and engine cases are to be used again, and if the crankshaft alignment and end play are considered satisfactory, omit Steps 1 through 8 and proceed with Step 9 below.

If a different crankshaft or new engine cases are being installed, it is recommended that the end play and alignment of the crankshaft be checked; proceed with Step 1 below.

1. The connecting rod big end has considerable side clearance for lubrication. The crankshaft end play must be correct and the connecting rod must be centered between the flywheels to prevent side loading of the main bearings and the connecting rod and to avoid having the connecting rod strike the flywheels. Make a dummy bearing out of a used bearing in good condition. Sand the inner and outer races until the bearing will fit in the engine case while the case is cool and will allow the crankshaft to slide within the inner race.

2. Install the shims and the dummy bearing on the left drive shaft. See **Figure 44**.

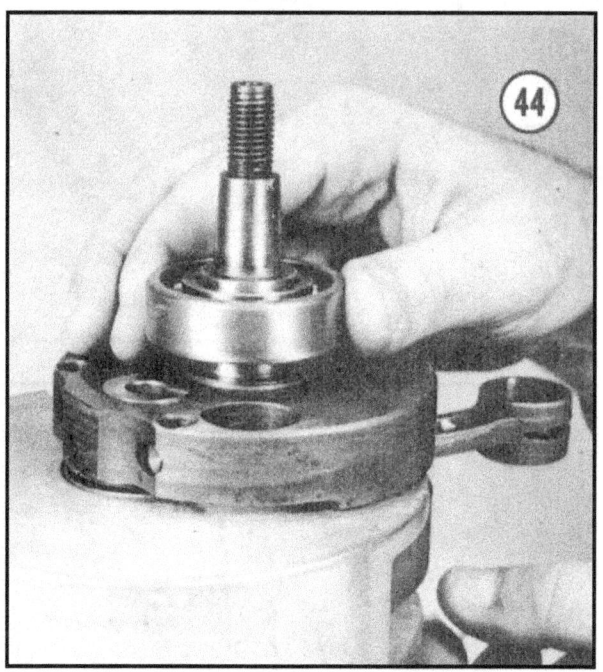

3. Install the crankshaft into the left case and be sure that the dummy bearing is seated against the mounting boss. See **Figure 45**.

4. Install the shims on the right main bearing and hold them in place with grease.

5. Install the left case against the right case, with the right end of the crankshaft through the right main bearing. Tap the left case with a soft mallet until it seats.

6. Install at least 5 engine case screws in the magneto side case and tighten them snugly; do not tighten firmly.

7. Tap on the right end of the crankshaft with a soft mallet to move it to the left as far as it will go.

8. Measure the distance from the right end of the crankshaft to the inner race of the main bearing with a vernier caliper. See **Figure 46**.

9. Tap the left end of the crankshaft with a soft mallet to move it to the right as far as it will go.

Dummy bearing

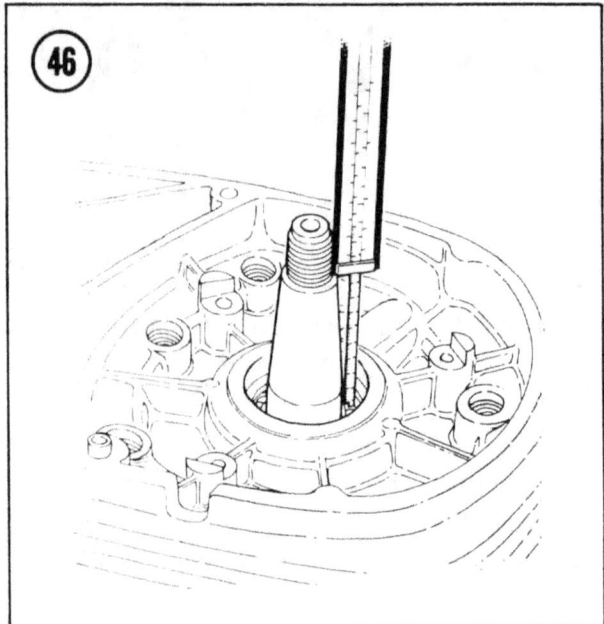

13. Install the cylinder over the piston and push it down firmly against the crankcase. See **Figure 47**.

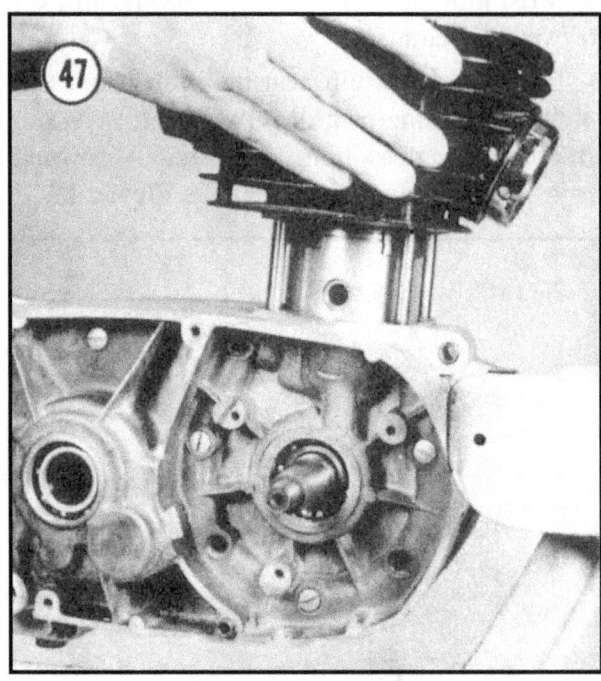

14. Turn the crankshaft 3 or 4 revolutions and stop with the piston at top dead center.

15. Insert a flexible probe type flashlight and a small dentist's mirror in the intake port. See **Figure 48**. Shine the light at the mirror and angle it so the light is reflected onto the connecting rod big end. Check as to how well the rod is centered on the crankpin.

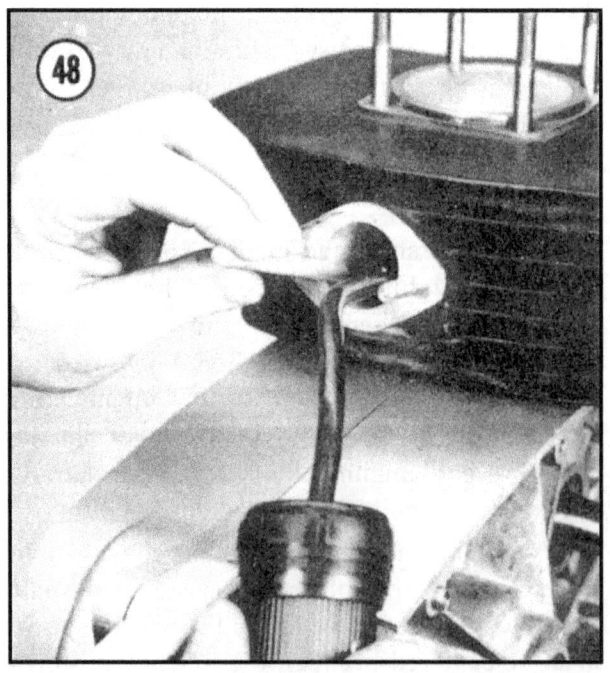

10. Measure the distance from the right end of the crankshaft to the inner race of the main bearing again; determine the end play. The crankshaft end play should be 0.004-0.008 in. (0.102-0.203mm).

11. Add or remove shims to correct the end play, if necessary. Try to have an equal total thickness of shims on each end.

12. Install the wrist pin bearing, the piston without the rings, and the wrist pin on the connecting rod.

16. If the rod is closer to one side of the crank, remove the cylinder and separate the cases. Move an estimated number of shims from one end of the crankshaft to the other end.

17. Install the assembly again as detailed above and again check the centering of the connecting rod on the crankpin. Repeat this procedure until the rod is centered.

18. Remove the cylinder and piston and separate the cases.

19. Remove the shims and tag them for later installation.

20. Remove the dummy bearing.

Installation

1. Put the crankshaft in a vise with soft jaws, with the left drive shaft pointing straight up.

2. Install the shims on the drive shaft.

3. Install the new bearing on the drive shaft and push it down as far as possible by hand. Be sure that the bearing has "C3" stamped on the outer race. See **Figure 49**. There is a slight difference between the left and right main bearings.

4. Place a length of pipe over the drive shaft and against the inner race of the bearing. See **Figure 50**. Tap the pipe with a hammer until the bearing seats against the shims. Be sure not to exert any force on the outer race.

5. Check the engine cases thoroughly for wear or damage from the previous bearings.

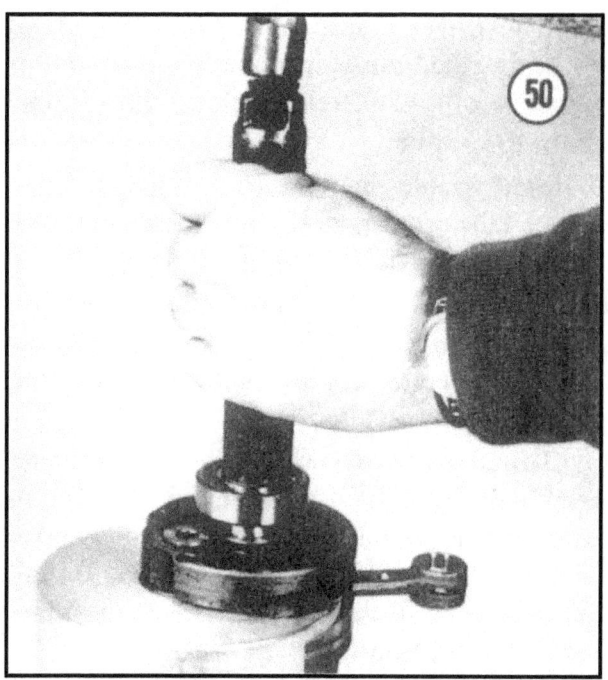

6. Heat the right engine case in an oven to 250-300°F (121-149°C). If the heating is done with a torch, keep the flame moving evenly and rapidly over the case. Do not overheat the case; excessive temperature may cause distortion of mating surfaces.

7. Position the heated case with the inside facing up and insert the bearing with the fingers. See **Figure 51**. Push it down until it seats against the boss.

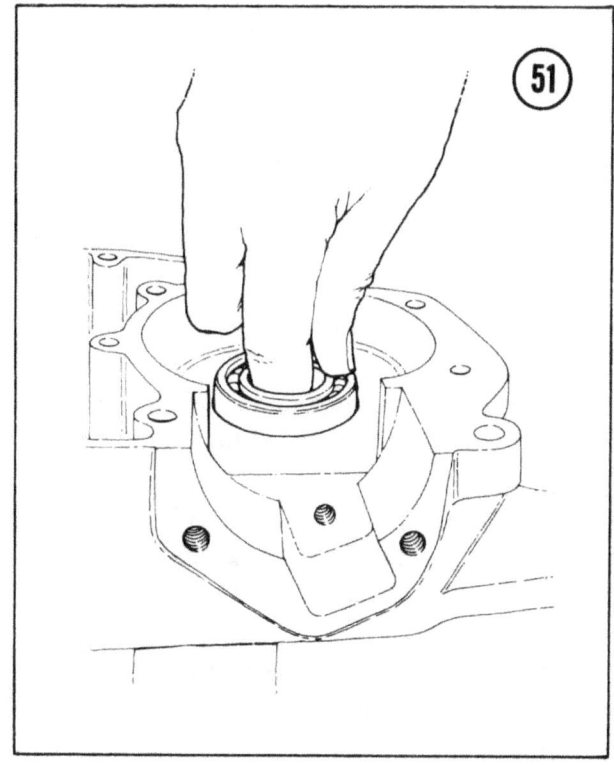

8. Do not drive or press any bearings into place. If a bearing will not seat properly, gently tap it out and cool it while reheating the case. Insert the bearing again.

9. Install countershaft bronze bushing following the same procedure. Heat the case and push the bushing into the case until it bottoms.

10. After the bearings and bushings are installed, let the case sit for at least 10 minutes while the parts reach the same temperature and are securely in place.

11. Turn the case over while it is still warm and install new oil seals. If possible, put the seal in place by hand. If not, use a block of wood and a hammer to tap the seal in. See **Figure 52**. Install the seals either flush with the case or not more than 1/16 in. below it.

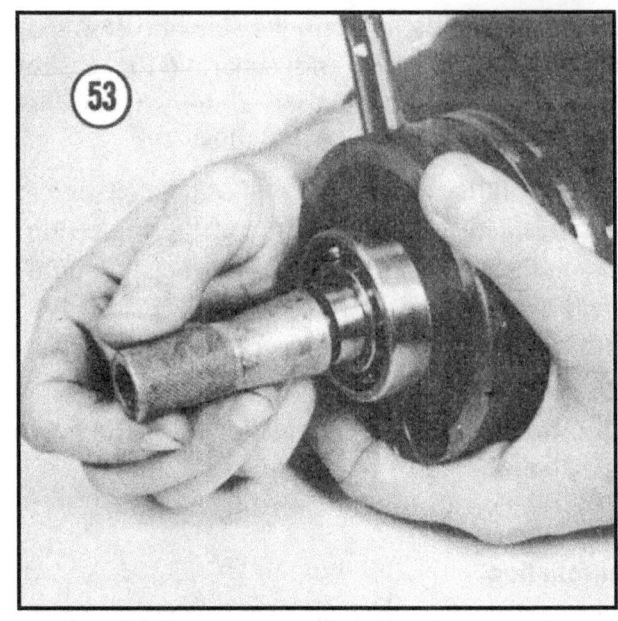

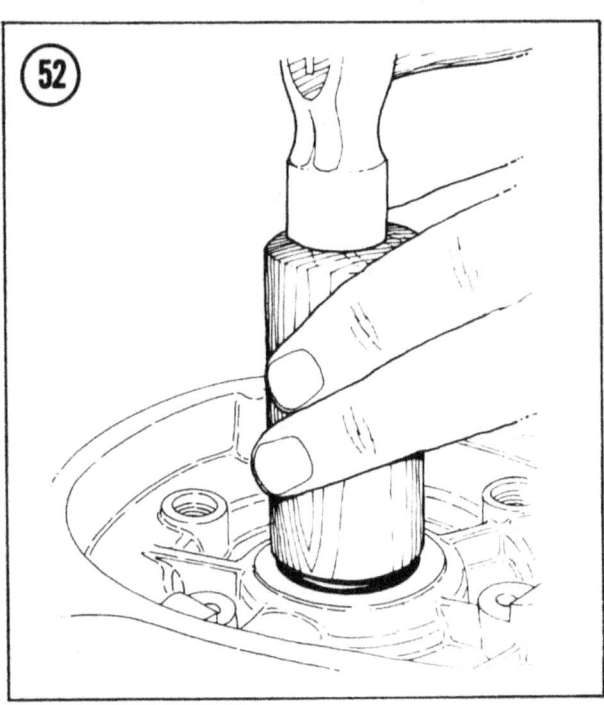

12. Heat the left engine case as detailed in Step 6.

13. Position the case on the bench with the inside facing down and install the crankshaft oil seal as detailed in Step 11.

14. Turn the warm case over with the inside facing up and install the transmission main shaft bearing and countershaft bushing. Be sure they seat properly.

15. Position the warm case vertically with the studs pointing upward.

16. Install the oil seal protector over the left end of the crankshaft. See **Figure 53**.

17. Hold the crank by the right drive shaft (see **Figure 54**) and the case with the other hand. Support the connecting rod with your thumb.

18. Install the left drive shaft into the case; be sure the bearing seats against its mounting boss.

19. Remove the oil seal protector.

20. Set the case on a box with the right drive shaft pointing upward and the left shaft not touching anything. Let it cool to room temperature.

21. Refer to Chapter Six to complete engine assembly.

CHAPTER EIGHT

CHASSIS

FRAME

The frame itself does not require any type of periodic maintenance other than occasional spot checking near tube junctures for signs of cracking or metal fatigue. Some earlier Stiletto models had a tendency to develop a crack in the frame at the spot indicated in **Figure 1**. Check this area frequently. If the motorcycle has been involved in an accident, regardless of severity, it should be checked by a shop for bends or fractures. Sometimes, damage is so slight that it escapes visual inspection. The only reliable detection method may be by magnafluxing which is a process using magnetic force fields and iron particles to detect tiny fractures. Also, inspect the entire frame if unusual vibration shows up suddenly.

Complete dismantling is seldom necessary unless the frame has been damaged in an accident, through rough usage, or by abuse. Most critical assemblies can be removed for repair or left on the motorcycle for adjustment. Refer to **Figures 2 and 3** for exploded illustrations of the chassis.

FRONT FORK AND STEERING COMPONENTS

The front suspension and steering are critical parts of the motorcycle for the rider's safety. A

loose fork stem, worn steering bearings, or bent fork tubes can cause serious steering and handling problems at high speeds. Proper care of a bike requires compliance with the scheduling chart and instructions given in Chapter Two. Promptly diagnose and correct any problem by referring to Chapter Three, *Troubleshooting*.

> NOTE: *The fork can be serviced without removing the fork tube assembly from the motorcycle. To do so simply omit the steps in the following procedure relating to removal of the fork leg unit from the motorcycle.*

Removal

See the exploded illustration of the suspension components given in **Figure 4**.

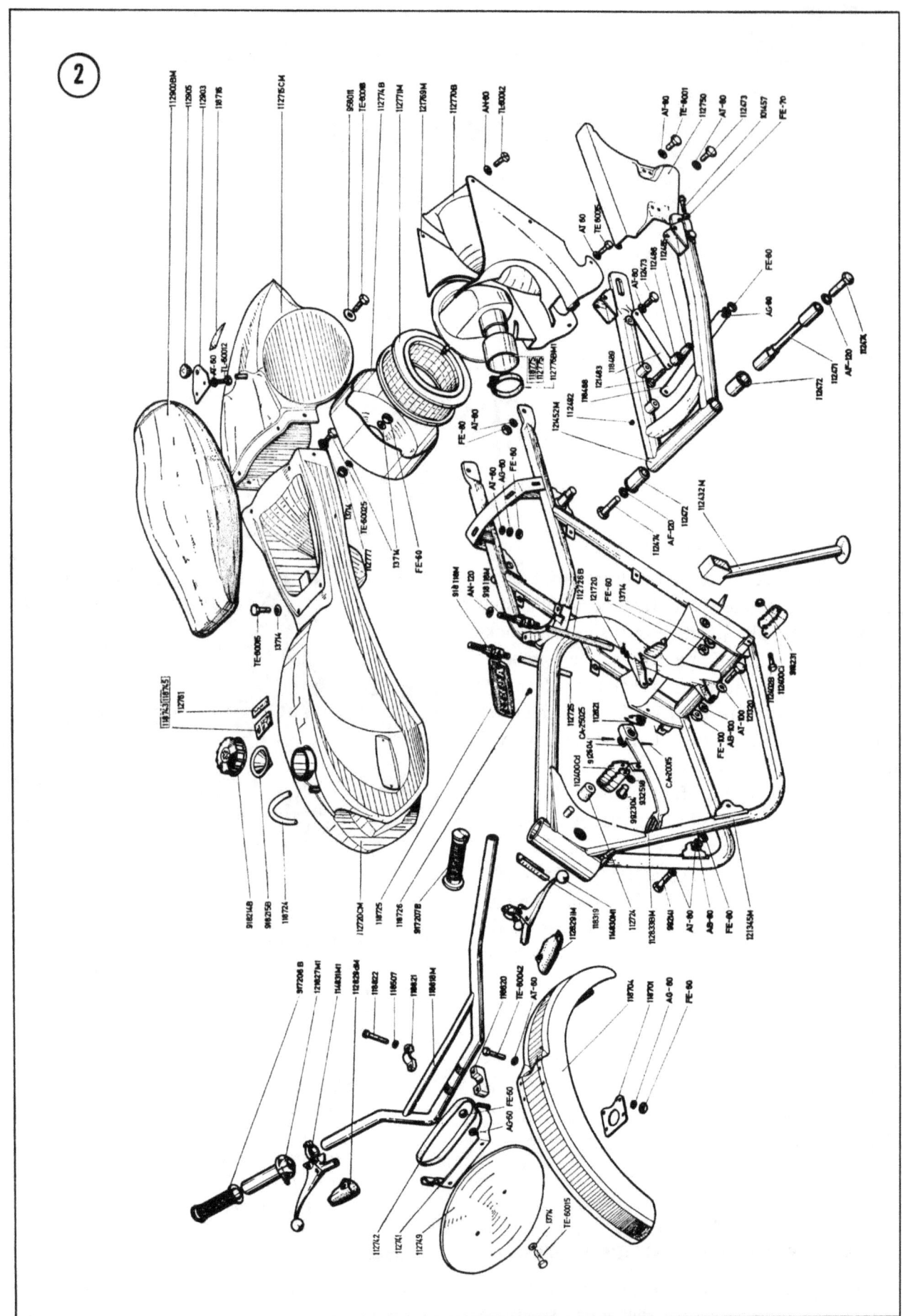

FRAME — 250 AS-71 STILETTO

Part Number	DESCRIPTION	Quantity
13.714	Washer, engine protector, rear fender, gas tank	12
101.457	Bolt, rear wheel adjuster	2
112.400 Cd	Right front footpeg	1
112.400 Ci	Left front footpeg	1
112.402 B	Footpeg shaft	2
112.432 M	Side stand	1
112.471	Swing arm axle	1
112.472	Bushing swing arm	2
112.473	Bolt chain guide	2
112.474	Bolt swing arm	2
112.485	Spacer chain guide	1
112.486	Pin chain guide	1
112.492	Rubber plug swing arm	1
112.715 CM (*)	Fender rear	1
112.720 CM (*)	Gas tank	1
112.724	Rubber washer tank mount	2
112.725	Fuel line right	1
112.726 B	Fuel line left	1
112.741	Bracket number plate	1
112.742	Rubber «O» ring	1
112.749 (*)	Number plate	1
112.750	Chain guard	1
112.761	Decal «Scrambler»	1
112.770 B (*)	Shell left	1
112.771 M	Air filter	1
112.774 B (*)	Filter cover	1
112.775	Tube filter (for 250-AS)	1
112.776 BMI	Clamp carburetor and filter	2
112.777	Nut air filter	1
112.821	Brake pedal return spring	1
112.829 dM	Cable dust protector right	1
112.829 iM	Cable dust protector left	1
112.833 BM	Brake lever assembly	1
112.900 BM	Seat	1
112.903	Seat mount	1
112.905	Seat nut	4
114.830 MI	Clutch lever assembly	1
114.831 MI	Brake lever assembly	1
118.319	Specifications label (Frame)	1
118.488	Front bracket chain guide	2
118.489	Rear bracket chain guide	4
118.507	Washer handlebar bolt	1
118.701	Mount front fender	1
118.704 (*)	Front fender	1
118.716	Decal «Stiletto»	2
118.724	Tube breather	1
118.725	Tank badge «OSSA»	2
118.726	Bolt, tank badge	4
118.743	Decal «250 cc»	1
118.745	Decal «175 cc»	1
118.775	Tube filter (for 175-AS)	1

Part Number	DESCRIPTION	Quantity
118.818 M	Handlebar	1
118.820	Handlebar mount	2
118.821	Handlebar clamp	2
118.822	Handlebar bolt	4
118.845	Spark plug label (Handlebar)	1
121.320	Bolt engine	2
121.345 M	Frame assembly	1
121.452 M	Swing arm assembly	1
121.483	Bolt chain guide	4
121.720	Clip fuel line	1
121.769 M	Shell right	1
121.827 MI	Twist grip assembly	1
912.604	Washer brake pedal	1
917.206 B	Rubber grip throttle	1
917.207 B	Rubber grip handlebar	2
918.118 M	Petcock assembly	1
918.214 B	Gas cap	1
918.215 B	Rubber seal	2
918.231	Footpeg nut	1
932.518	Washer brake pedal	2
958.011	Washer rear fender	1
992.141	Engine mounting bolt	2
992.304	Clevis pin rear brake	1

COMMON PARTS

Part Number	DESCRIPTION	Quantity
AB-80	Spring washer	2
AB-100	Spring washer	2
AF-120	Washer swing arm	2
AG-60	Washer fenders and number plate	10
AG-80	Washer chain guide	1
AN-60	Washer shell	5
AN-120	Washer fender, shell, number plate and seat	2
AT-60	Washer engine, chain guide, fenders and chain guard	12
AT-80	Washer rear engine mount	9
AT-100	Cotter pin brake cable	2
CA-20.015	Cotter pin brake pedal	1
CA-25.025	Nut fenders, shell, air filter and number plate	13
FE-60	Nut adjusting bolt	2
FE-70	Nut engine mount, fender rear	5
FE-80	Nut rear engine mount	2
FE-100	Bolt gas tank, shell and number plate	7
TE-60.015	Bolt rear fender	4
TE-60.025	Bolt front fender	4
TE-60.042	Bolt chain guide	1
TE-80.015	Bolt rear fender	2
TE-80.018	Bolt shell and seat	6
TL-60.012		

(*) When ordering these parts, specify the color

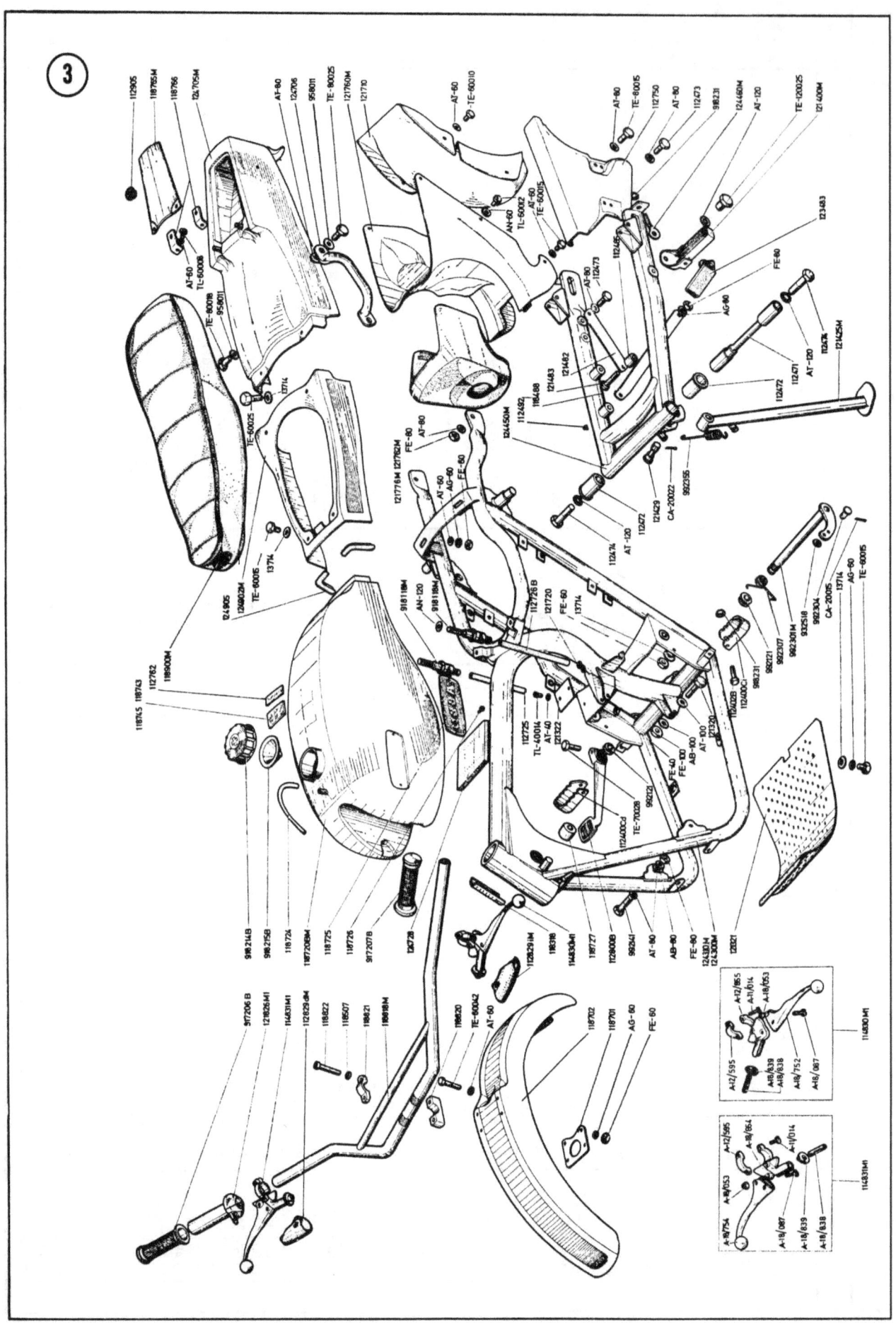

FRAME – 250 AE-72 PIONEER

Part Number	DESCRIPTION	Quanti.	Part Number	DESCRIPTION	Quanti.	Part Number	DESCRIPTION	Quanti.
13.714	Washer, engine protector, rear fender, gas tank	12	121.400 M	Passenger footpeg	2	A-18-854	Brake lever mount	1
112.400 Cd	Right front footpeg	1	121.425 M	Side stand assembly	1	A-18-855	Clutch lever mount	1
112.400 Ci	Left front footpeg	1	121.429	Side stand axle	1			
112.402 B	Footpeg shaft	2	121.482	Rear bracket chain guide	1		COMMON PARTS	
112.471	Swing arm axle	1	121.483	Bolt chain guide	1			
112.472	Bushing, swing arm	2	121.710	Auxiliary rear fender	4			
112.473	Bolt, chain guide	2	121.720	Clip fuel line	1			
112.474	Bolt, swing arm	1	121.760 M ng	Plastic shell	1	AB-80	Spring washer	2
112.485	Spacer chain guide	1	121.762 M	Carburetor dust cover, 250 cc.	1	AB-100	Spring washer	2
112.492	Rubber plug swing arm	1	121.776 M	Twistgrip assembly	2	AG-60	Washer engine protector, and fenders	10
112.725	Fuel line right	1	121.826 Ml	Rubber, cable protector	1	AG-80	Washer chain guide	1
112.726 B	Fuel line left	1	123.483	Frame 250 cc.	1	AN-60	Washer plastic shell	4
112.750	Chain guard	1	124.300 M	Frame 175 cc.	1	AN-120	Washer petcock	2
112.762	Enduro decal	1	124.310 M	Swing arm assembly	2	AT-40	Washer	2
112.800 B	Brake pedal	1	124.450 M	Rear wheel adjuster	1	AT-60	Washer fenders,schell, and seat	13
112.829 dM	Right cable dust protector	1	124.460 M	Fender rear	1	AT-80	Washer engine, chain guide, fenders and chain guard	10
112.829 iM	Left cables dust protector	1	124.705 M br	Side hand grip	2	AT-100	Engine washer	2
112.905	Seat nut	2	124.706	Rubber rest. gas tank	1	AT-120	Washer passenger footpegs and swing arm	4
114.830 Ml	Clutch lever assembly	1	124.728	Seat mount	1	CA-20.015	Cotter pin brake arm	1
114.831 Ml	Brake lever assembly	1	124.902 M br	Gasket seat mount	1	CA-20.022	Cotter pin side stand shaft	1
118.318	Specifications label (Frame)	1	124.905	Rubber grip throttle	2	FE-40	Nut	2
118.488	Front bracket chain guide	1	917.206 B	Rubber grip handlebar	1	FE-60	Nut fenders and schell	8
118.507	Washer handlebar bolt	4	917.207 B	Petcock assembly	2	FE-80	Nut engine mount, chain guide, and rear fender	5
118.701	Front fender mount	1	918.118 M	Gas cap	1	FE-100	Nut rear engine mount	2
118.702 br	Fender front	1	918.214 B	Rubber seal	1	TE-60.010	Bolt auxiliary fender	3
118.720 BMbr2	Gas tank	1	918.215 B	Footpeg nut and adjusting bolt	4	TE-60.015	Bolt engine protector, gas tank and shell	8
118.724	Tube breather	1	918.231	Washer brake pedal	2	TE-60.025	Bolt rear fender	4
118.725	Tank badge OSSA	2	932.518	Washer rear fender	4	TE-60.042	Bolt front fender	4
118.726	Bolt, tank badge	4	958.011	Bushing brake shaft	2	TE-70.028	Bolt brake pedal	1
118.727	Rubber washer tank mount	2	992.121	Engine mounting bolt	2	TE-80.015	Bolt chain guard	1
118.743	Decal 250 cc.	2	992.141	Rear brake lever assembly	1	TE-80.018	Bolt rear fender	1
118.745	Decal 175 cc.	1	992.301 M	Clevis pin rear brake	1	TE-80.025	Bolt rear fender	1
118.765 Mbr	Tool box cover	1	992.304	Brake pedal return spring	1	TE-120.025	Bolt passenger footpegs	2
118.766	Mount tool box cover	2	992.307	Side stand spring	1	TL-40.014	Bolt	2
118.818 M	Handlebar	1	992.355	Bolt, air clamp	4	TL-60.008	Bolt seat munt	2
118.820	Mount handlebar	2	A-11-014	Clamp air lever and clutch lever	2	TL-60.012	Bolt shell	4
118.821	Handlebar clamp	2	A-12-595	Nut, lever bolt	2			
118.822	Bolt, handlebar	4	A-18-053	Bolt, lever mount	2			
118.849	Regulation label (Handlebar)	1	A-18-087	Clutch lever	1			
118.900 M	Seat	1	A-18-752	Brake lever	1			
121.320	Bolt engine	2	A-18-754	Adjusting bolt	2			
121.321	Engine protector	1	A-18-838	Adjusting nut	1			
121.322	Rubber plate	1	A-18-839					

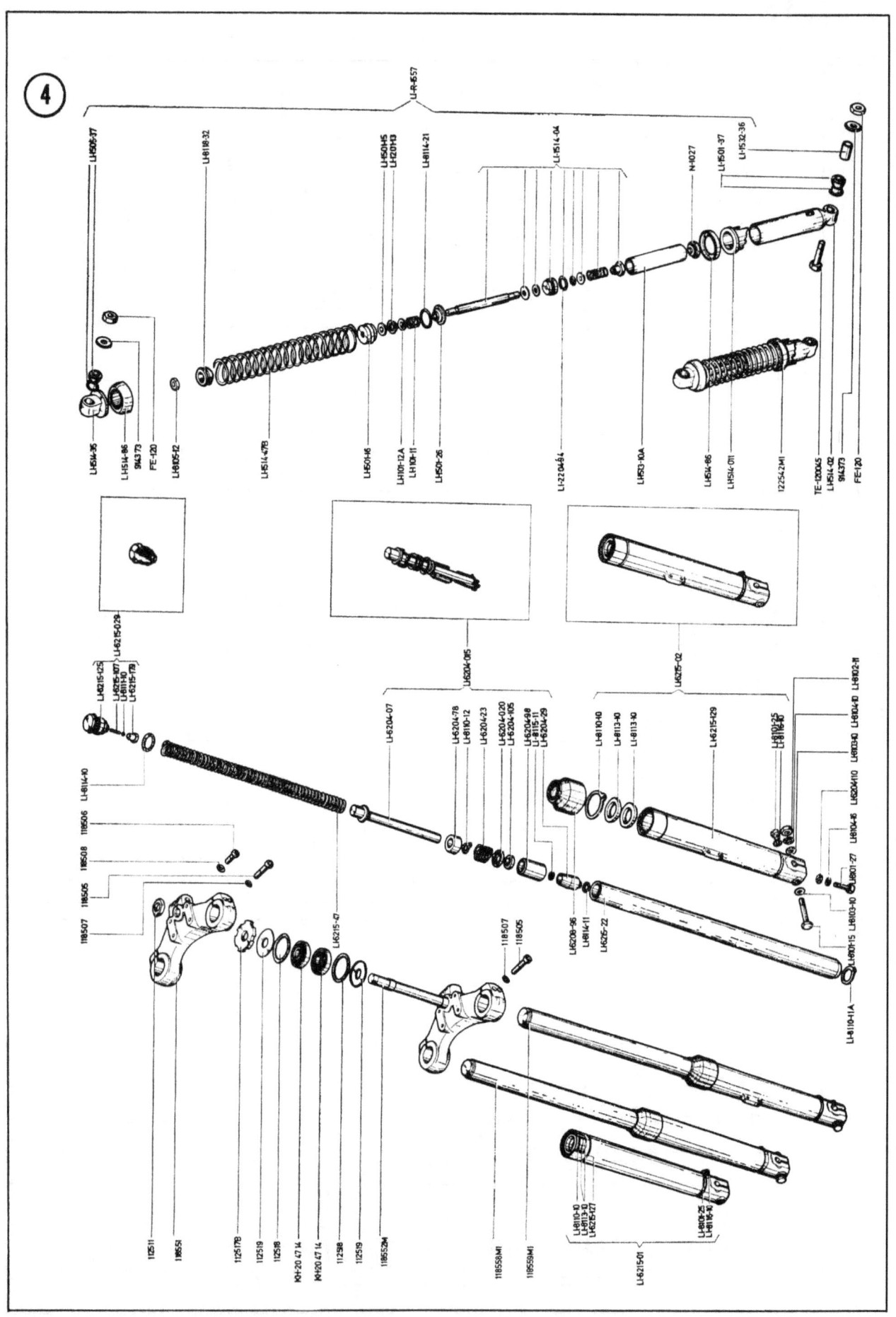

SUSPENSION COMPONENTS

Part Number	DESCRIPTION	Quanti.	Part Number	DESCRIPTION	Quanti	Part Number	DESCRIPTION	Quanti.
Ll-1101-11	Spring seal	2	Ll-6215-107	Spring stanchion plug	2	118.551	Top yoke	1
Ll-1101-12A	Guide spring seal	2	Ll-6215-125	Stanchion plug	2	118.552 M	Bottom yoke with stem	1
Ll-1201-13	Spring washer	2	Ll-6215-127	Right tank assembly	1	118.558 Ml	Suspension assembly right	1
Ll-1501-15	Oil seal	2	Ll-6215-129	Left tank assembly	1	118.559 Ml	Suspension assembly left	1
Ll-1501-16	Adjuster	2	Ll-6215-179	Bolt stanchion plug	2	122.542 Ml	Shock absorber assembly	2
Ll-1501-26	Guide	2	Ll-8101-15	Bolt M8 x 60	2	914.373	Washer schock absorber	4
Ll-1505-37	Silentblock	2	Ll-8101-25	Bolt	2			
Ll-1513-10A	Silentblock	2	Ll-8101-27	Allen bolt M8 x 25	2		COMMON PARTS	
Ll-1514-02	Inner tube	2	Ll-8102-11	Nut M8	2			
Ll-1514-04	Oil tank	2	Ll-8103-10	Polished washer	4			
Ll-1514-011	Pump assembly	1	Ll-8104-10	Spring washer	2	FE-120	Nut shock absorber	3
Ll-1514-35	Regulating bushing	2	Ll-8104-16	Spring washer	2	KH-20-47-14	Bearing assembly	2
Ll-1514-47 B	Top grip	2	Ll-8105-12	Bottom nut	2	TE-120.045	Bolt, shock absorber	2
Ll-1514-86	Spring	2	Ll-8110-10	Security ring I-47	2			
Ll-1532-36	Housing for spring	4	Ll-8110-11A	«O» ring 1-30	2			
Ll-R-1557	Bushing silentblock	2	Ll-8110-12	Security ring E-16	2			
Ll-2204-94	Spare part kit	—	Ll-8111-10	Ball Ø 3,5	2			
Ll6204-015	Rings for pump	2	Ll-8113-10	Oil seal 35.47.7	4			
Ll-6204-020	Damper assembly	2	Ll-8114-10	Stanchion «O» ring 26 x 32 x 3	2			
Ll-6204-07	«O» Ring	2	Ll-8114-11	Stanchion «O» ring 12 x 17 x 2,5	2			
Ll-6204-23	Valve tube	2	Ll-8114-21	Washer	2			
Ll-6204-29	Retaining spring	2	Ll-8115-11	Washer	2			
Ll-6204-78	Valve	2	Ll-8116-10	Washer	2			
Ll-6204-98	Pump	2	Ll-8118-32	Rubber stop	2			
Ll-6204-105	Cylinder valve mount	2	N-1027	Valve assembly	2			
Ll-6204-110	Washer valve	2	112,511	Nut steering shaft	1			
Ll-6208-96	Washer damper bolt	2	112.517 B	Nut steering adjuster	1			
Ll-6215-01	Dust cover	1	112.518	Felt washer	2			
Ll-6215-02	Right tank assembly	1	112.519	Dust cover	2			
Ll-6215-029	Left tank assembly	2	118.505	Bolt stanchion tube	8			
Ll-6215-22	Stanchion plug	2	118.506	Bolt steering shaft	1			
Ll-6215-47	Stanchion tube	2	118.507	Washer, stanchion tube bolt	8			
	Spring		118.508	Washer, steering shaft bolt	1			

1. Drain the fork oil as detailed in Steps 1-3 of the *Fork Oil Changing* section of Chapter Two.

2. Raise the front wheel clear of the ground by placing a block or stand under the engine.

3. Loosen the front brake cable completely.

4. Detach the front brake cable from the front brake arm and pull the cable up, free of the cable stop.

5. Remove the brake anchor strap from the left fork leg.

6. Remove the large nut and washer (22mm) from the axle.

7. Remove the axle pinch bolt from both fork legs (see **Figure 5**).

8. Remove the axle.

9. Remove the wheel.

10. *Pioneer and Plonker models*: Disconnect the speedometer drive from the cable; remove the drive unit.

11. *Pioneer models*: Loosen the bolts holding the headlight brackets to the fork tubes. Remove the fork tube cap and remove the speedometer and bracket; screw the cap nut back in place by hand.

12. *Plonker models*: Loosen the bolts holding the headlight brackets to the fork tubes. Remove the bolts holding the fender and speedometer unit to the fork legs.

13. *Stiletto and TT models*: Remove the front number plate.

14. Loosen (do *not* remove) the fork tube cap nuts.

15. Loosen (do *not* remove) the 8 clamp pinch bolts holding the 2 triple clamps (**Figure 6**).

16. Remove each fork tube in turn by pulling it down from the triple clamps (**Figure 7**). If necessary, lightly tap the cap nut with a soft mallet to facilitate removal of the tube.

17. Remove the handlebars. Leaving the cables attached to the handlebars is optional.

18. Remove the gas tank breather tube from the steering stem.

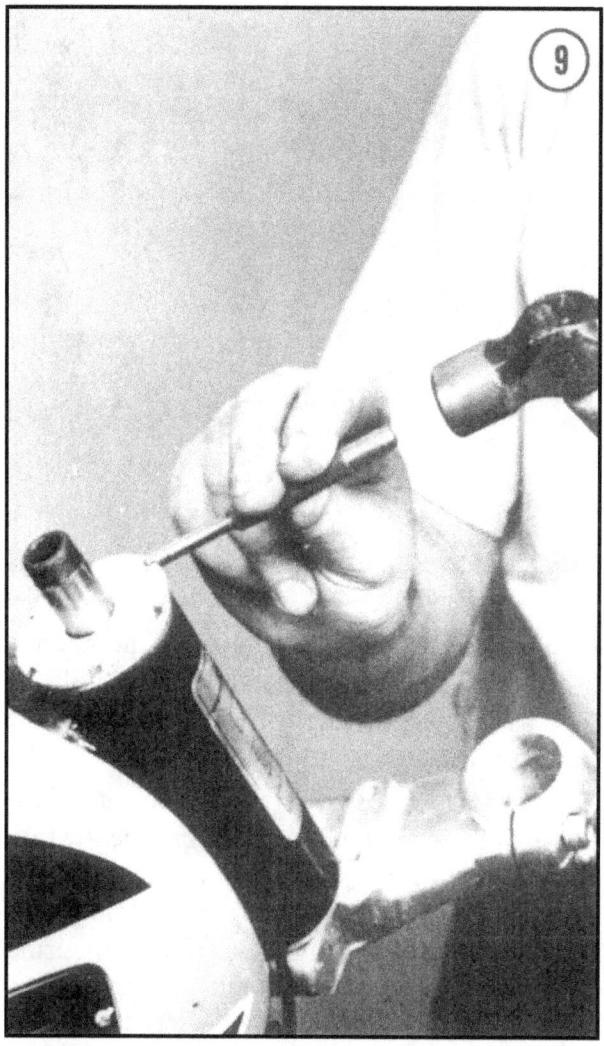

19. Remove the nut located on top of the upper triple clamp.

20. Loosen the pinch bolt located on the upper triple clamp.

21. Remove the upper triple clamp from the steering stem. If necessary, lightly tap the clamp upward with a soft mallet to aid in removal (**Figure 8**).

22. Remove the securing bolts and the front fender.

23. Remove the steering shaft collar nut with dust shield and felt washer from the steering shaft. It will probably be necessary to loosen the collar nut (right-hand thread) with a punch and mallet (**Figure 9**).

24. Lightly tap the top of the steering shaft with a soft mallet to free it. Hold the lower triple clamp and remove the steering shaft from the bottom.

25. Remove the inner race, rollers, and cage of the upper steering bearing.

26. If the condition of the bearing in the lower triple clamp is suspect, place the lower triple clamp upside down in a soft jawed vise and remove the bearing by tapping the dust shield with a hammer and punch (**Figure 10**). Install a *new* bearing and *new* dust shield.

27. Remove each outer steering race, in turn, by tapping gently around the lip of the race with a

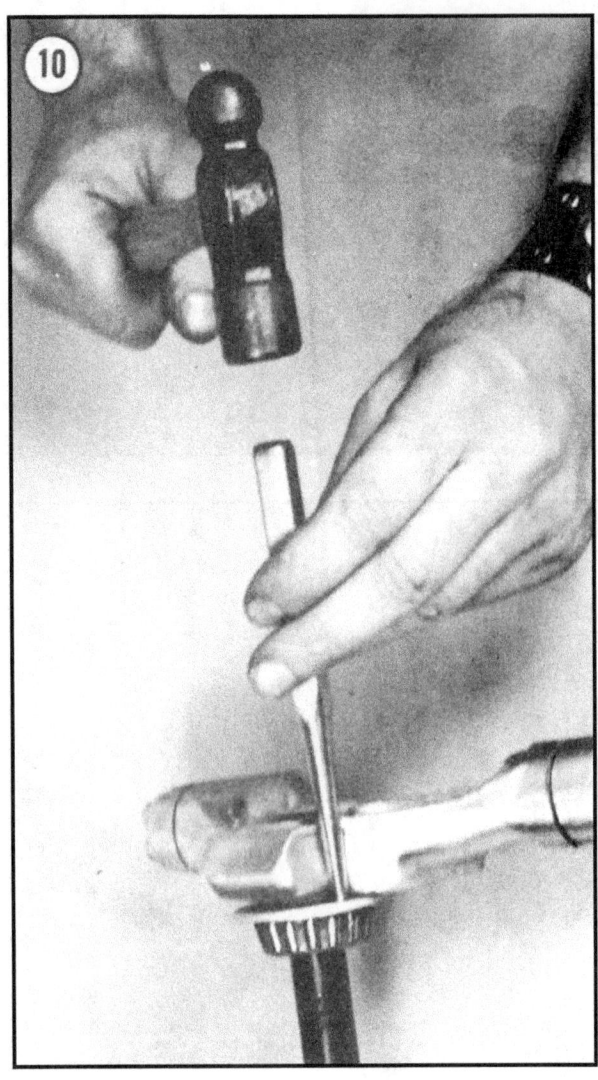

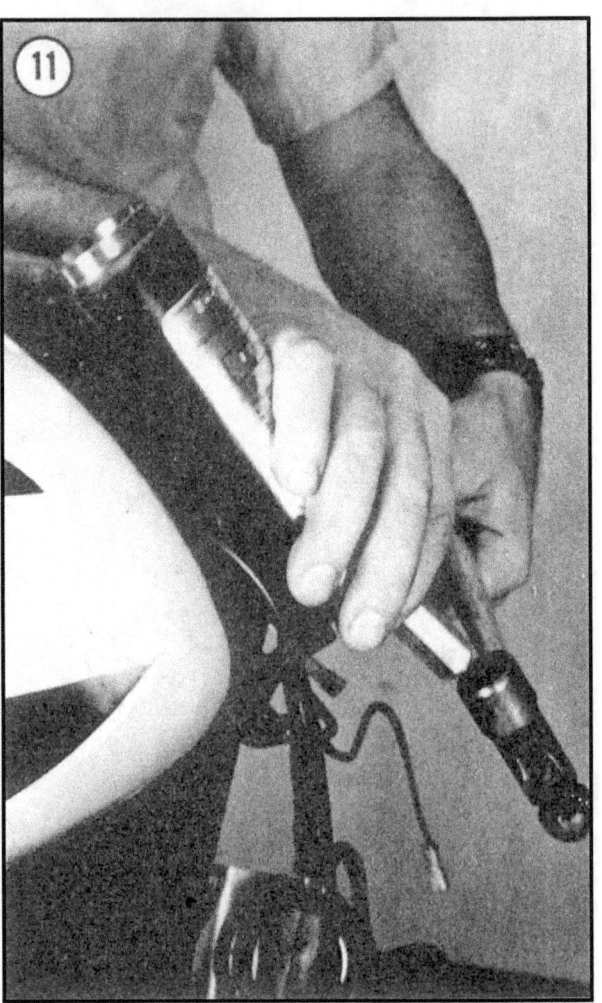

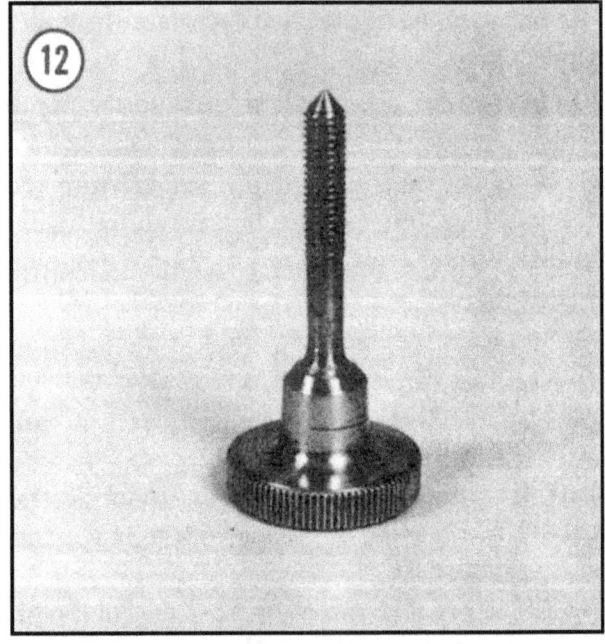

long punch from the opposite end of the steering head (**Figure 11**). Be very careful not to tilt the race as it is driven out to avoid distorting the inside of the steering head.

28. Remove the bolt from the bottom end of the fork leg. If the aluminum pedestal inside the fork tube turns with the bolt and prevents removal of the bolt it will be necessary to lock the pedestal in place while removing the bolt. To do so, grind the tip of a bolt, which has 6mm x 1 threads and is threaded for more than ¾ in., to a point (at an angle of approximately 45°). A machinist's precision in grinding is not necessary (**Figure 12**). Screw the pointed bolt into the fork leg oil drain hole (**Figure 13**) until it touches the damper assembly inside the fork tube; turn the bolt approximately ½ turn more to lock the pedestal in place. Remove the bolt from the bottom end of the fork leg and remove the pointed bolt from the drain hole.

29. Remove the fork leg from the fork tube.

30. Remove the oil seal snap rings and oil seals from the fork legs using a pair of internal snap ring pliers, if available.

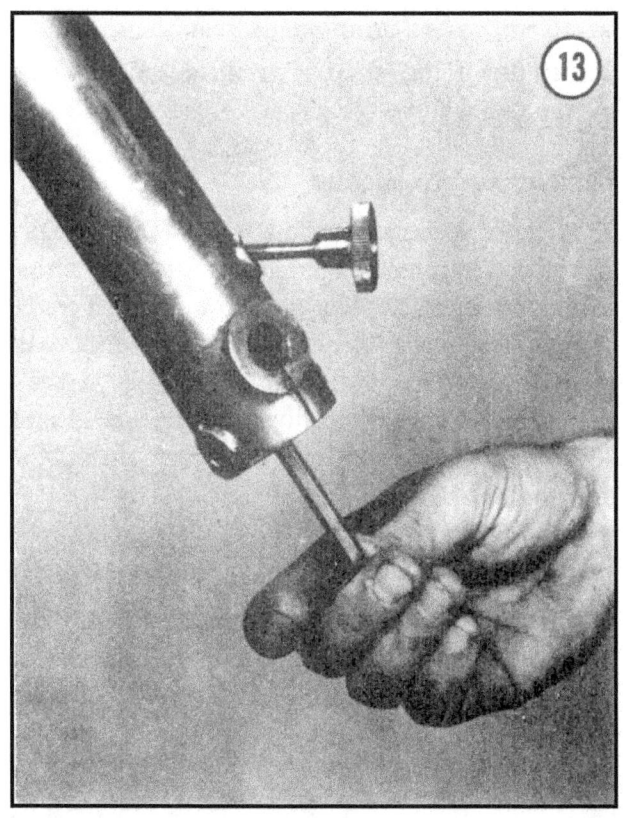

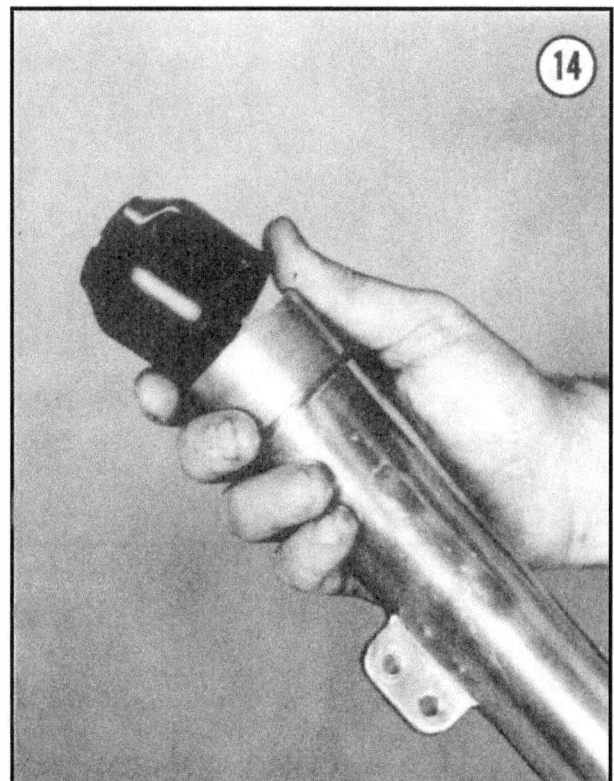

31. Remove the fork tube cap nut and the fork spring.

32. Measure the free length of the spring. Pioneer springs should measure 17.36-17.48 in. (44.09-44.40cm). Plonker springs should measure 17.00-17.12 in. (43.18-43.48cm). Stiletto springs should measure 17.59-17.71 in. (44.68-44.96cm). Install new springs in both legs if either one is too short.

33. Remove the rubber dust wiper from the fork leg (**Figure 14**). Check it carefully for wear or damage. If in doubt, replace it.

34. Remove the snap ring from the bottom of the fork tube; use internal snap ring pliers, if available.

35. Remove the damper assembly from the bottom of the tube.

36. Measure the free length of the rebound spring (**Figure 15**). If it measures less than one inch, replace it.

37. Inspect the damper valve disc (a large washer type disc with 8 drilled holes) and the attached spring wave washer very carefully for wear or damage (**Figure 16**). Also check the wave washer for looseness on the disc. If in doubt, replace it.

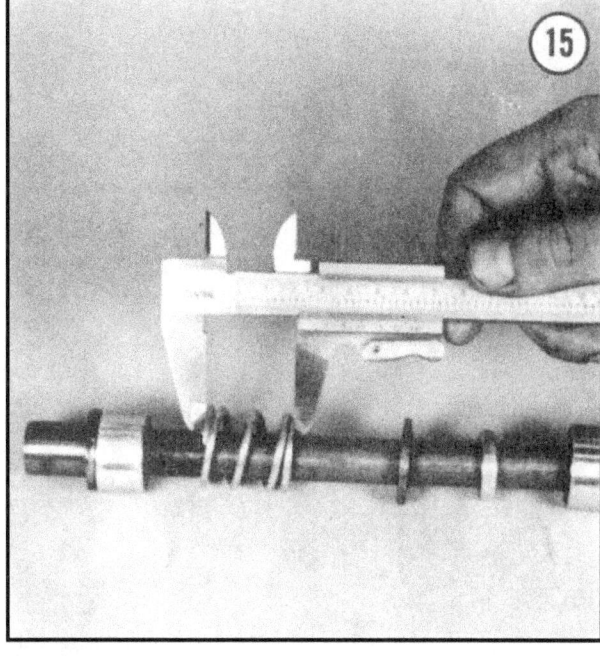

38. Remove the aluminum pedestal from the damper shaft by following Steps 39 through 41.

39. Screw the axle pinch bolt into the base of the damper shaft aluminum pedestal.

40. Install the damper assembly in the bottom of the fork tube; do not install the snap ring.

41. Invert the fork tube and use a mallet to tap the head of the axle pinch bolt until the damper shaft and pedestal separate (**Figure 17**).

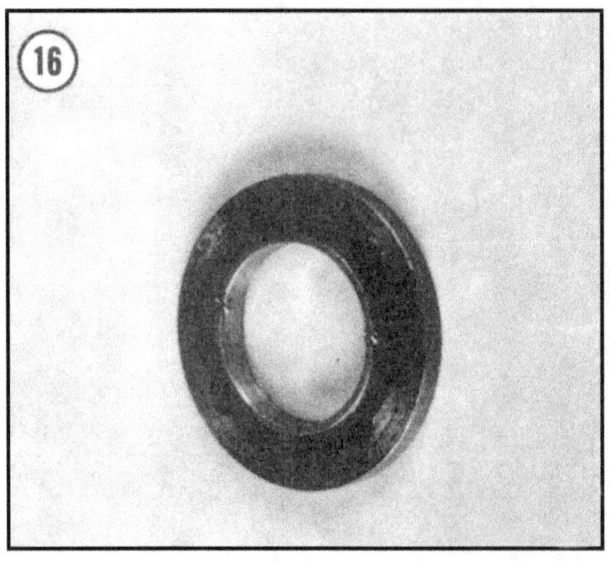

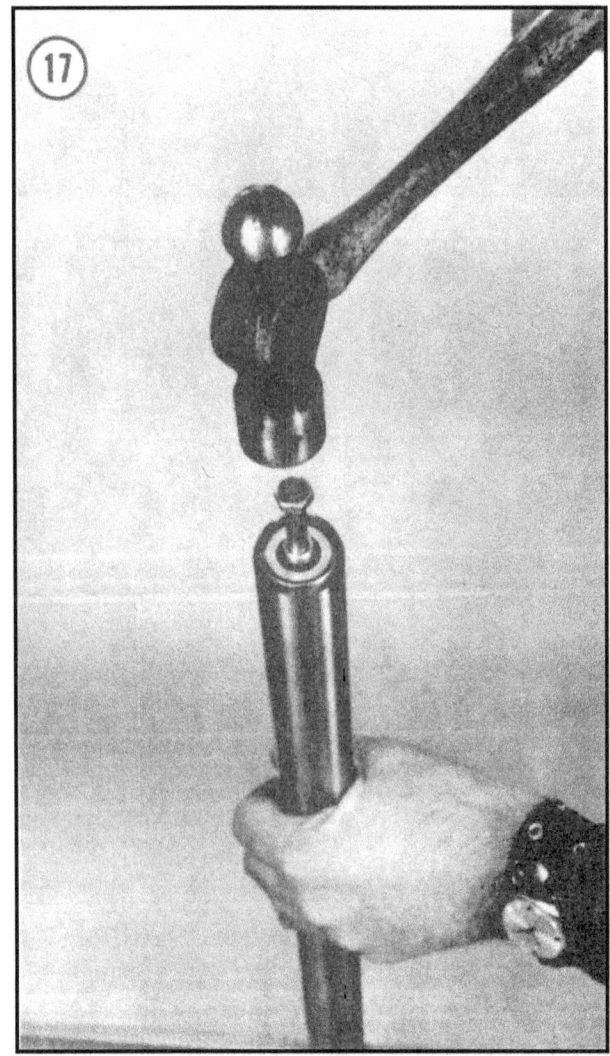

44. Remove the components from the shaft.

45. Remove the snap ring from the damper piston and remove the piston from the shaft.

Cleaning and Inspection

In general, inspect all parts for wear, cracks, deterioration, or damage; clean parts with kerosene or cleaning solvent and blow dry with compressed air; pack bearings in grease; and coat washers and seals with grease. Detailed instructions for reassembly follow. If there is doubt about the condition of any part, install a new one.

Installation

1. Install the outer steering races in the steering head using a soft mallet and punch (**Figure 18**). *Do not tilt* the steering races while driving them in.

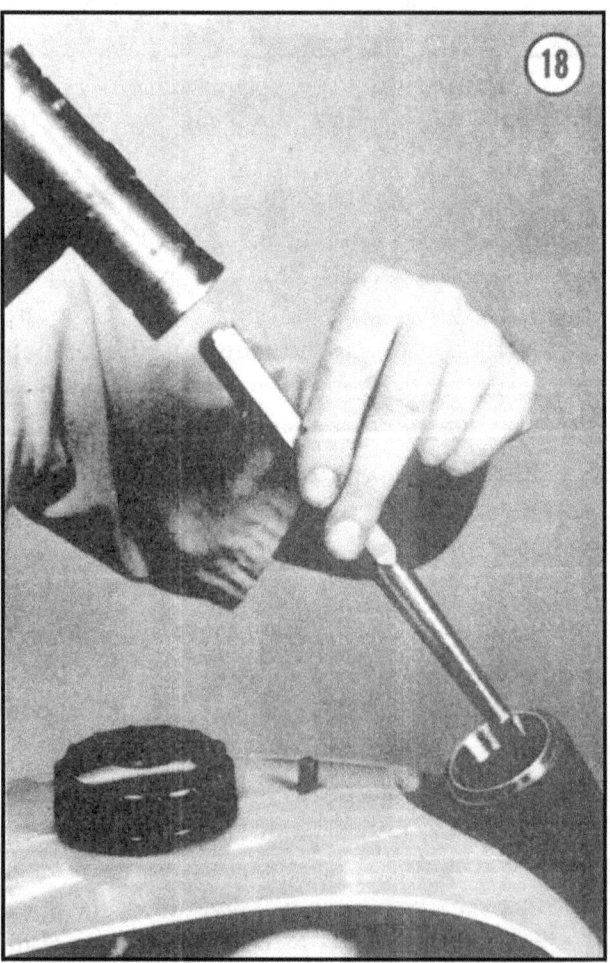

42. Remove the damper assembly from the fork tube.

43. Remove the axle pinch bolt from the damper shaft.

2. Place a new dust shield on the steering shaft.

3. Coat the felt washer with grease and place it on the dust cover.

4. Pack the lower steering bearing rollers with grease and install in the lower triple clamp with a pipe placed down over the steering shaft and resting on the inner race (**Figure 19**). Use a plastic mallet to tap the pipe until bearing is seated.

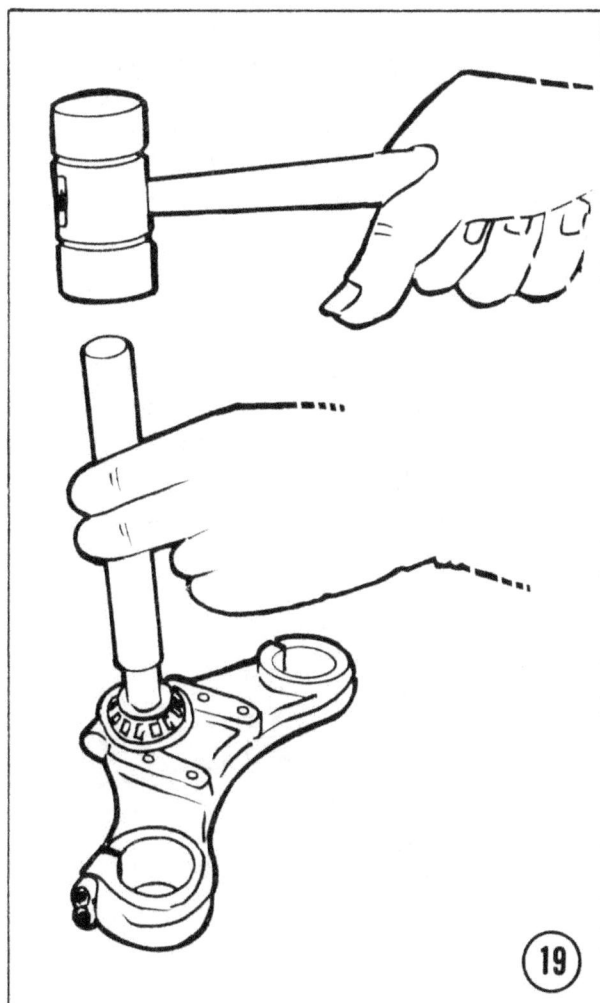

5. Insert the steering shaft into the steering head from the bottom.

6. Position the greased felt washer and dust cover on the shaft and screw the steering shaft collar nut onto the shaft as far as possible by hand.

7. Use a mallet and punch as shown in Figure 9 (except change the direction of impact so as to cause tightening of the nut) to tighten the nut an additional 1/8 turn.

8. Use a soft mallet to apply a sharp tap upward on the bottom triple clamp and downward on the steering shaft.

9. Check the movement of the bottom triple clamp by rotating it. If it is too loose, tighten the collar nut. If it is too tight, unscrew the collar nut slightly. Again, tap the bottom triple clamp and the steering shaft and check the movement of the bottom triple clamp. Repeat until the movement feels right. Even after assembly is completed, it may be necessary to adjust the steering bearings again.

10. Install the upper triple clamp and nut. Do not tighten the nut.

11. Install the fender on the lower triple clamp. The thick washer is fitted under the bolt head. Fit the flat fender mount plate under the nuts. Use Loctite, or similar compound, on the threads and torque the nuts to 6 ft.-lb. (0.8 mkg). On Pioneer models, install the horn and ignition switch bracket under the 2 forward fender mounting bolts (see **Figure 20**).

Assembly

1. Install the damper piston on the damper shaft; the recessed end of the piston must be toward the bottom of the shaft (**Figure 21**).

2. Install a new snap ring (with square edge facing outward) in the shaft groove.

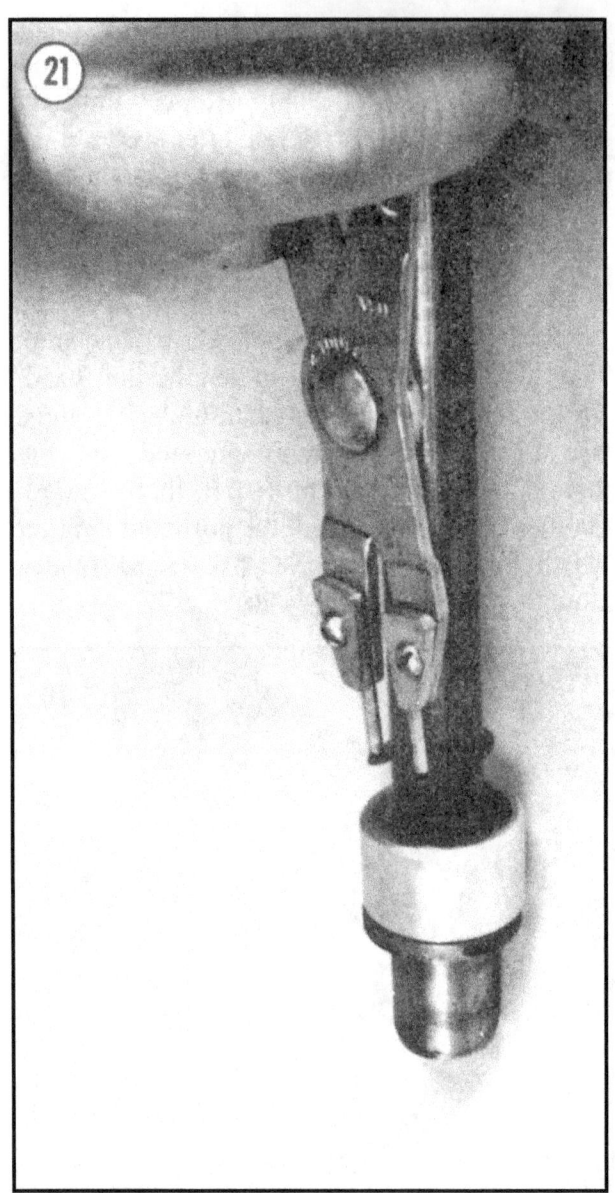

8. Insert the damper assembly into the fork tube from the bottom. Install a new snap ring; be sure that the square edge of the snap ring faces the bottom of the fork tube.

WARNING
Care should be taken in installing any snap ring properly. Be particularly careful to install the snap ring at the bottom of the damper assembly correctly; it holds the front wheel on the motorcycle when the wheel is off the ground.

9. Grease and install a new oil seal in the fork leg with the open side of the seal facing the bottom of the fork leg. Use a drift to gently drive the seal in until it seats in its mounting boss. A socket with an extension attached can serve as a drift (**Figure 22**).

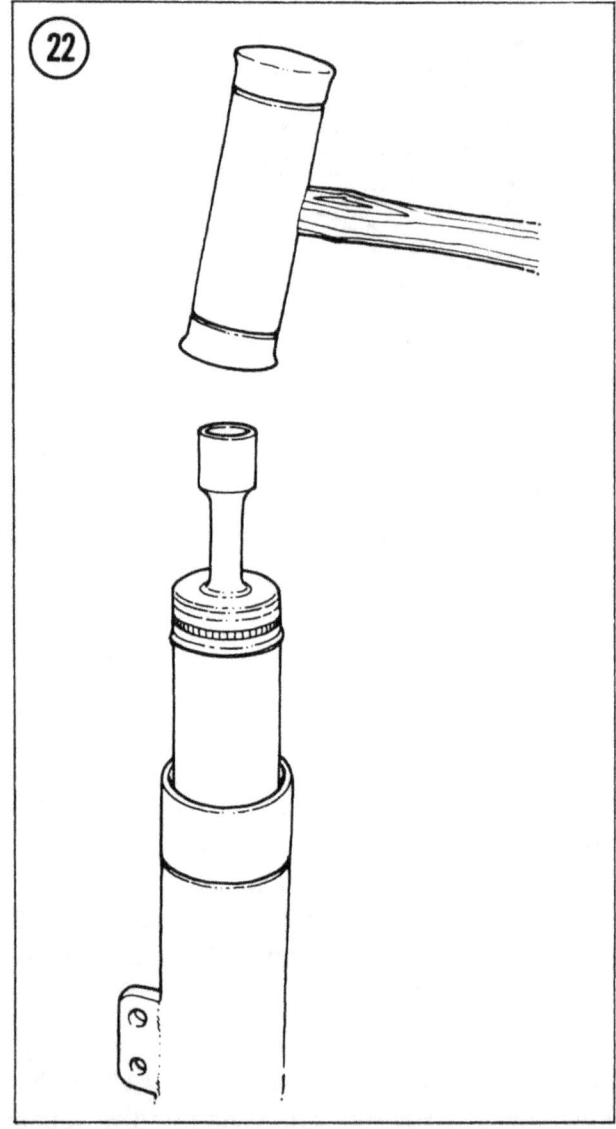

3. Hold the shaft inverted and position the rebound spring against the damper piston.

4. Place the damper valve disc (with its spring washer away from the rebound spring), the aluminum valve disc washer (fitted into the recessed end of the cylinder), and the damper cylinder on the shaft.

5. Insert a new rubber washer inside the damper pedestal and set the pedestal upright on a hard, flat surface.

6. Heat the pedestal to 150-200°F (66-93°C) with a torch.

7. Push the bottom end of the damper shaft into the pedestal until it is fully seated and maintain the downward pressure until the pedestal cools sufficiently to become tight on the shaft.

10. Install a new snap ring in the fork leg with the square edge facing upward (**Figure 23**).

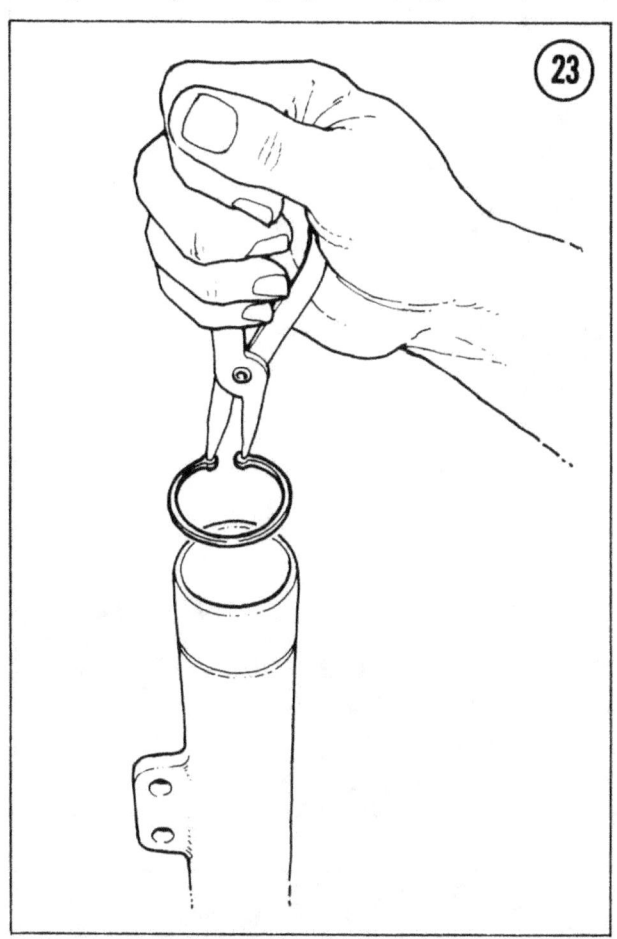

11. Check the condition of the O-ring on the fork cap nuts. Install a new O-ring if in doubt about the old one.

12. Insert the fork spring into the top of the fork tube and screw in the cap nut by hand.

13. Place a new O-ring in the groove on the bottom of the damper pedestal. It may be necessary to use a small amount of grease to hold it in place.

14. Lightly coat the fork leg oil seals and fork tubes with oil and push the tube into the fork leg until it bottoms.

15. Place the lockwasher and flat washer on the Allen bolt and screw it in from the bottom of the fork leg; tighten securely. It may be necessary to use the special pointed bolt described in Step 28 of *Front Fork Removal* to hold the pedestal locked in place while tightening the Allen bolt. See **Figure 24**.

16. Remove the pointed bolt, if used. Install the drain plug screw with its fiber washer.

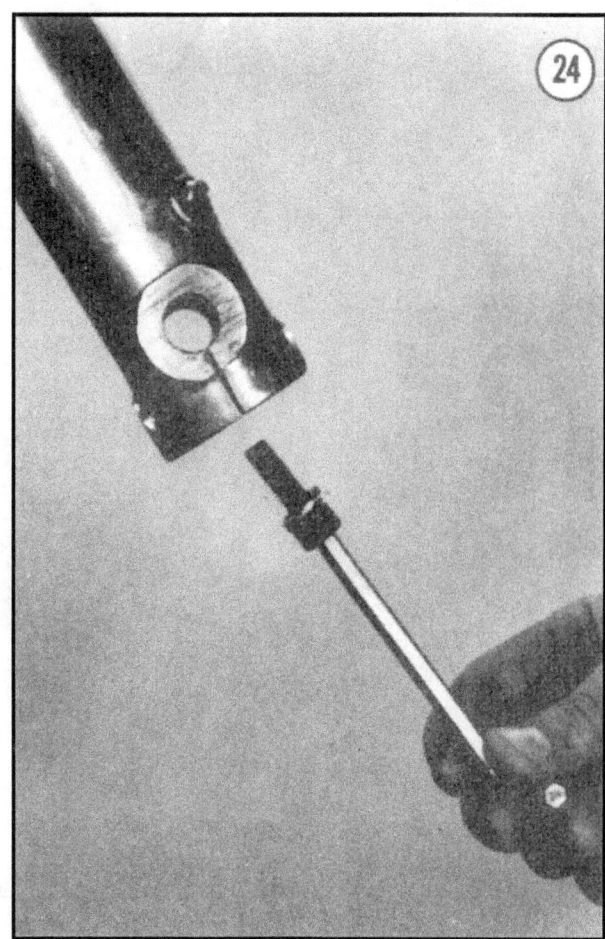

After both fork legs have been assembled per the above instructions, proceed with assembly of the front suspension as detailed below.

17. Oil the inside of the fork seals and rubber dust covers and install them over the tops of the fork legs.

18. *Pioneer and Stiletto models*: Install the fork tube up through the triple clamps from the bottom with the mounting lug, for the brake anchor strap, on the left fork leg facing forward. On the Pioneer model, the tube passes through the headlight mounting bracket between the triple clamps (**Figure 25**).

19. *Plonker models*: Install the fork tube up through the triple clamps from the bottom and through the headlight mounting bracket between the triple clamps (Figure 25). Be sure that the flat side of the axle mounting boss is fitted toward the hub and that the drain screw faces the rear.

20. Check to see that the top of the tube (not the cap nut) is flush with the top of the upper triple clamp.

㉕

21. Screw in one of the top triple clamp pinch bolts by hand; do not tighten securely.

22. Install the other fork tube by following Steps 17 through 21.

23. *Plonker models*: Install the front fender. Use the rear lug on the left leg to hold the speedometer and bracket. Torque the nuts to 10 ft.-lb. (1.4 mkg).

24. *Pioneer and Stiletto models*: Place the wheel in position with the brake assembly on the left. The speedometer drive is on the right side of the hub and the flat spacer washer on the left. Install the axle from the right side.

25. *Plonker models (1972 and later)*: Place the wheel in position. The speedometer drive is on the left side of the hub. Install the axle from the left side.

26. Check to see that the driving tabs of the speedometer drive unit are fitted into the recesses in the hub (**Figure 26**).

27. All models except 5-speed Plonkers have 2 flat axle washers. Place the thick one between the hub and fork leg and the thin one under the

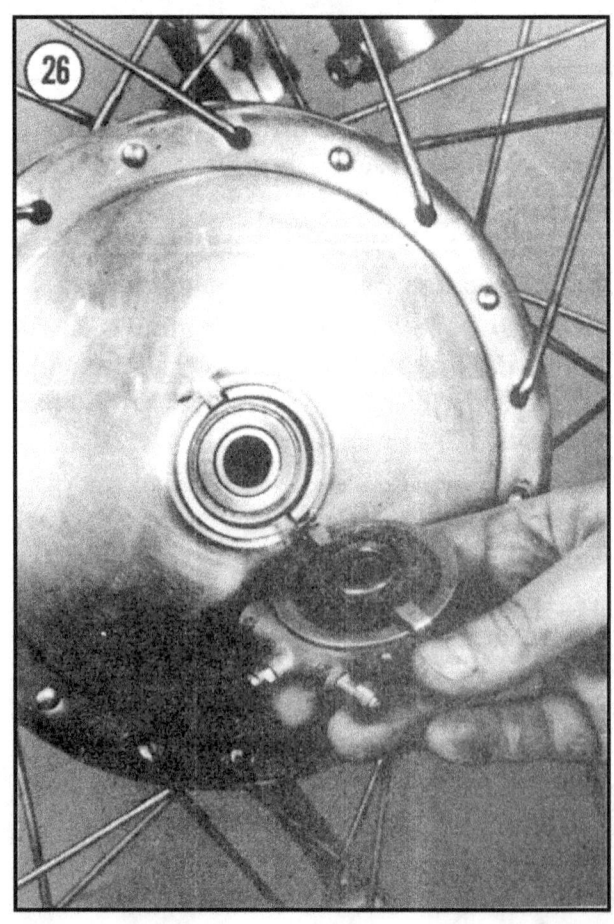

axle nut. See **Figure 27**. Tighten the axle nut by hand.

28. Install the brake anchor strap on the fork lug. Put Loctite on the nut threads and torque to 6 ft.-lb. (0.8 mkg).

29. Install the axle pinch bolts with the bolt heads toward the front. Tighten by hand.

30. *Plonker models*: Attach the speedometer cable to the hub drive unit.

31. Put both wheels on the ground. Clamp the front wheel with your knees and turn the fork tubes until the wheel is perpendicular to the triple clamps. Tighten the triple clamp pinch bolts with a torque of 10 ft.-lb. (1.4 mkg).

32. Torque the steering shaft pinch bolt on the top triple clamp to 15 ft.-lb. (2.1 mkg).

33. Torque the top triple clamp nut to 35 ft.-lb. (4.8 mkg).

34. Hold the axle and torque the axle nut to 60 ft.-lb. (8.3 mkg) for all models except the Plonker which requires 50 ft.-lb. (6.9 mkg).

35. Torque the left axle pinch bolt on all models except the Plonker and the right pinch bolt on the Plonker to 15 ft.-lb. (2.1 mkg). Pump the forks up and down several times to align the fork legs on the axle. Torque the remaining axle pinch bolt to 15 ft.-lb. (2.1 mkg).

36. *Pioneer and Plonker models*: Tighten the headlight mounting brackets.

37. *Stiletto models*: Install front number plate.

38. Move the forks back and forth. If the steering is tight, proceed to Step 40.

39. Have someone hold the rear brake on with both wheels on the ground. Hold the front wheel with one hand and the junction of the top triple clamp and steering head with the other hand (**Figure 28**). Try to push the wheel back and forth as it would move if the motorcycle were rolling forward and backward. If there is any play at the top of the steering head, proceed to Step 40.

40. Tightness or play in the prior 2 steps mean that the steering bearings will have to be readjusted. Loosen the top triple clamp nut and all top triple clamp pinch bolts. Adjust the shaft collar (**Figure 29**) with a hammer and punch. Tighten or loosen the steering head bearings as

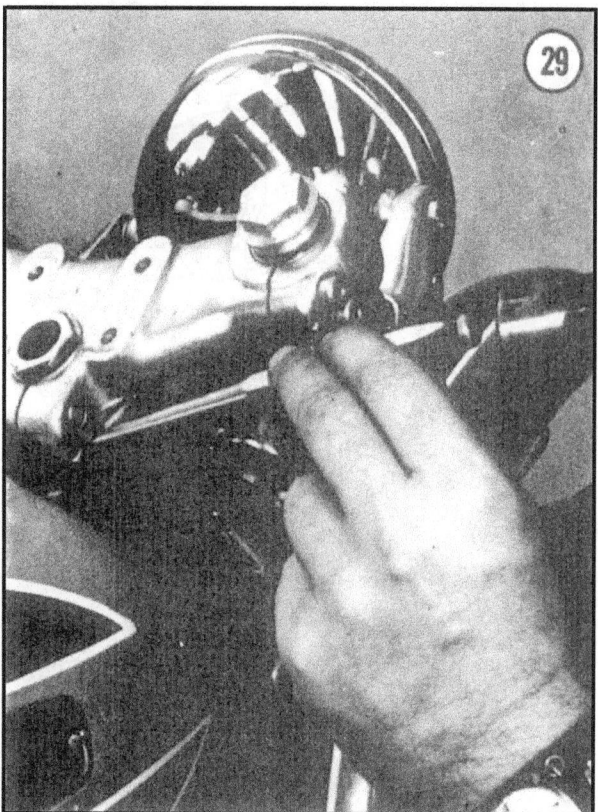

detailed previously. Tighten the top triple clamp nut and bolts.

41. Install the handlebars and torque the bolts to 10 ft.-lb. (1.4 mkg).

42. Fill the forks with 190-200cc of SAE 30 motor oil as detailed in the section, *Fork Oil Changing*, in Chapter Two.

43. Install the gas tank breather hose in the end of the steering shaft.

44. *Pioneer models*: Install the speedometer bracket on top of the right fork tube and secure it with the cap nut torqued to 50 ft.-lb. (6.9 mkg). Install the speedometer cable in the drive unit on the front hub.

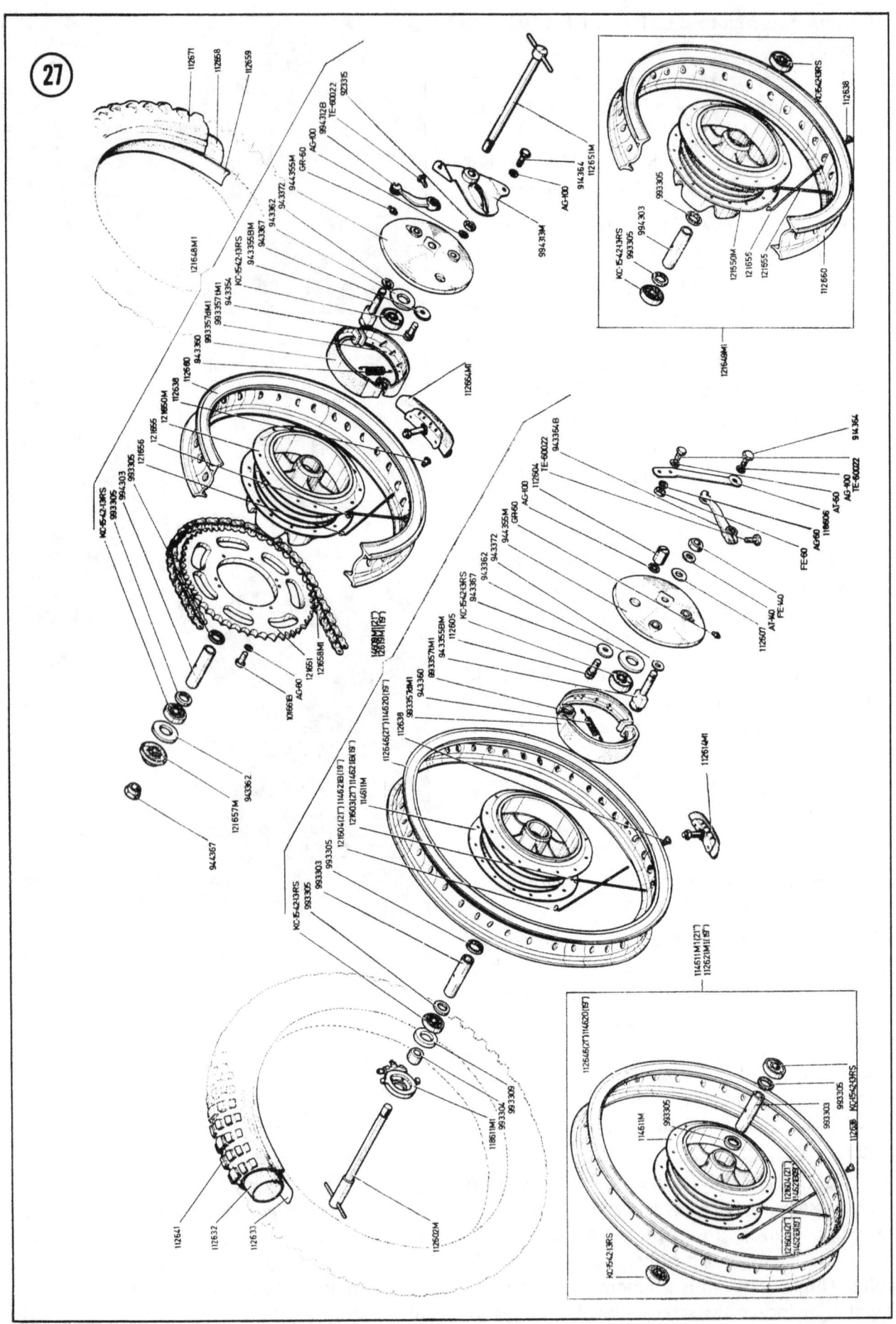

FRONT AND REAR WHEELS

Part Number	DESCRIPTION	Quantity
101.661 B	Bolt rear sprocket	8
112.602 M	Front axle assembly	1
112.604	Nut backing plate shaft	1
112.605	Shaft backing plate	1
112.607	Spacer front wheel	1
112.614 MI	Tire valve	2
112.619 MI	Front hub assembly 19" with brake	1
112.621 MI	Front hub assembly 19"	1
112.632	Innertube	1
112.633	Rubber innertube	1
112.638	Spoke nipples	72
112.641	Front tire	1
112.646	Rim, 21"	1
112.651 M	Rear axle assembly	1
112.658	Innertube	1
112.659	Rubber innertube	1
112.660	Rim	1
112.664 MI	Tire valve	2
112.671	Rear tire	1
114.609 MI	Front hub assembly with brake 21"	1
114.611 MI	Front hub (21") assembly	1
114.611 M	Front hub	1
114.620	Rim, 19"	1
114.621 B	Spokes for 19" wheel	36
118.606	Arm anchor plate	1
118.611 MI	Speedo drive assembly	1
121.603	Spokes (innerside) front wheel	18
121.604	Spokes (outerside) front wheel	18
121.648 MI	Rear hub assembly with brake	1
121.649 MI	Rear hub assembly	1
121.650 M	Rear hub	1
121.651	Rear sprocket	1
121.655	Spokes (innerside) rear wheel	18
121.656	Spokes (outerside) rear wheel	18
121.657 M	Bearing cover rear wheel	1
121.658 MI	Secondary chain	2
914.364	Bolt anchor plate	1
923.315	Nut backing plate	1
943.354	Bolt backing plate	1
943.355 BM	Brake cam assembly	2

Part Number	DESCRIPTION	Quantity
943.360	Spring brake shoe	4
943.362	Felt washer	3
943.364 B	Front brake arm	1
943.367	Thrust washer	2
943.372	Washer brake cam	2
944.355 M	Backing plate	2
944.367	Nut rear axle	1
993.303	Spacer front wheel	1
993.304	Spacer bushing front wheel	4
993.305	Aligning washer spacer tube	1
993.309	Felt washer	2
993.357 dMI	Front leading brake shoe	2
993.357 tMI	Trailing brake shoe	1
994.303	Spacer tube rear wheel	1
994.312 B	Rear brake arm	1
994.313 M	Anchor plate rear wheel	1

COMMON PARTS

Part Number	DESCRIPTION	Quantity
AG-60	Washer anchor arm	2
AG-80	Washer rear sprocket	8
AG-100	Washer backing plate	4
AT-60	Washer Front anchor arm	2
AT-140	Washer front axle	1
GR-60	Grease Fitting	2
FE-60	Nut front anchor arm	2
FE-140	Nut front axle	1
KC-15-42-13RS	Wheel bearing with dust cover	4
TE-60022	Bolt, brake arm and anchor arm	4

SWING ARM

Removal/Installation

An exploded illustration of the swing arm is shown in Figures 2 and 3. The 2 types of swing arm mountings used on the Ossa motorcycle are shown in **Figure 30**. The older type is the lower one illustrated.

1. Remove the rear wheel as detailed under *Wheels* in this chapter.

2. Remove the shocks as detailed in the section, *Rear Shocks*, of this chapter.

3. Check the swing arm for lateral movement, as shown in **Figure 31**, by trying to move it from side to side. If the bolts are tight and there is movement, the bushings may be faulty. Typical symptoms of worn swing arm bushings are shimmy, wander, and wheel hop.

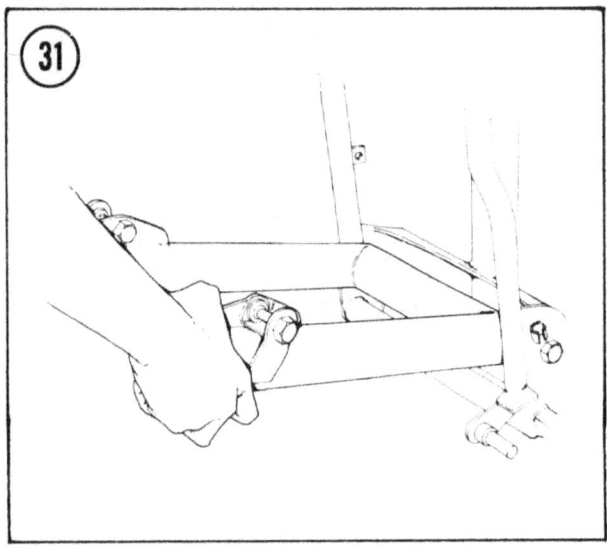

4. For bikes with the older type through bolt, remove the nut and drive the bolt out. Install new bushings and check again for lateral movement. If looseness persists, thin shims can be inserted between the swing arm and the frame until a smooth working assembly is obtained. See **Figure 32**.

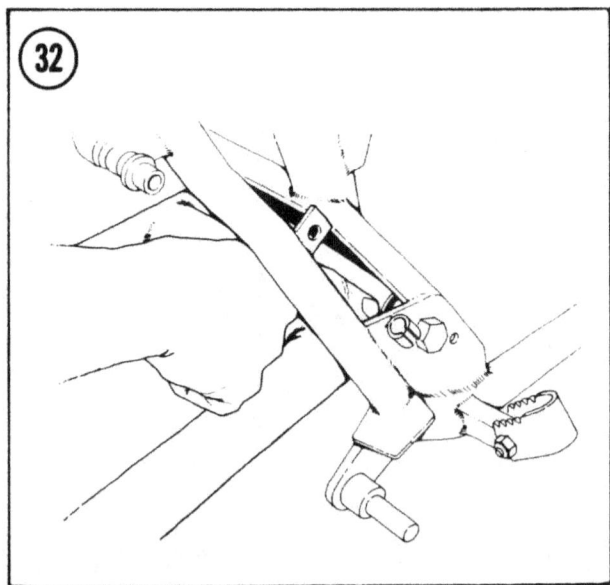

5. Ossa models with the newer mounting method use short bolts which screw into the swing arm pivot shaft. Remove the 2 bolts, drive out the pivot shaft, and inspect the bushings for wear. The nylon bushings used in the new method rarely wear out.

6. A recommended safety measure, especially for competition bikes, is to safety-wire the swing arm bolts to small holes drilled through the

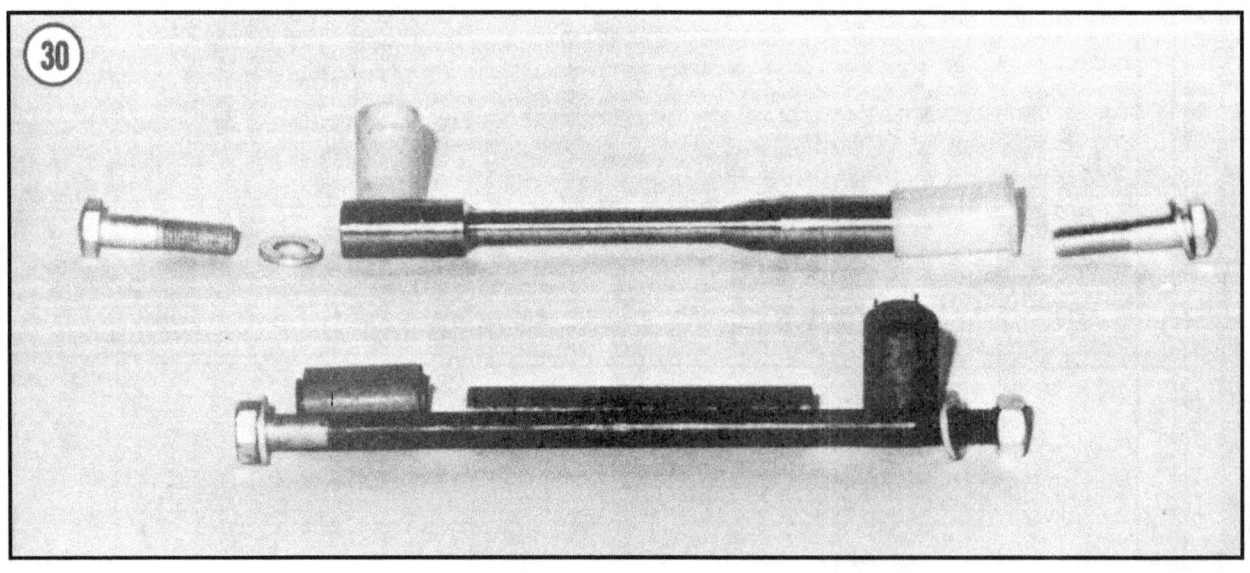

adjacent frame gusset to prevent their working loose.

7. Reassemble in reverse order of disassembly.

REAR SHOCKS

Disassembly/Assembly

1. Support the motorcycle under the engine to relieve pressure on the shocks.

2. Remove the bolts securing the shocks to the frame at the top and the swing arm at the bottom.

3. The illustrations are for Betor shocks but the instructions apply also to Telesco shocks. Place the top of the shock in the jaws of a strong vise (**Figure 33**).

4. Grasp the shock cover and pull against spring pressure (as shown in Figure 33) to move the shock cover down and insert a wrench between the cover and the top shock mount. Loosen the nut which locks the top mount on the shock absorber shaft.

5. Unscrew the top mount. Remove the cover and spring.

6. Test the shock by moving the plunger in and out. There should be no indication of binding but there must be damping action along the plunger's total travel. If there is damping or resistance along only a portion of the plunger's travel, the shock may be low on oil. If the plunger binds along any portion of its travel, the shaft is bent and must be replaced. Straightening is possible in an emergency, but replacement is recommended.

7. Check for indications of leaking oil. Further disassembly is necessary only if oil must be added or if the plunger is bent. A shock repair kit should be installed.

8. Remove the seal holder cap nut. See **Figure 34**.

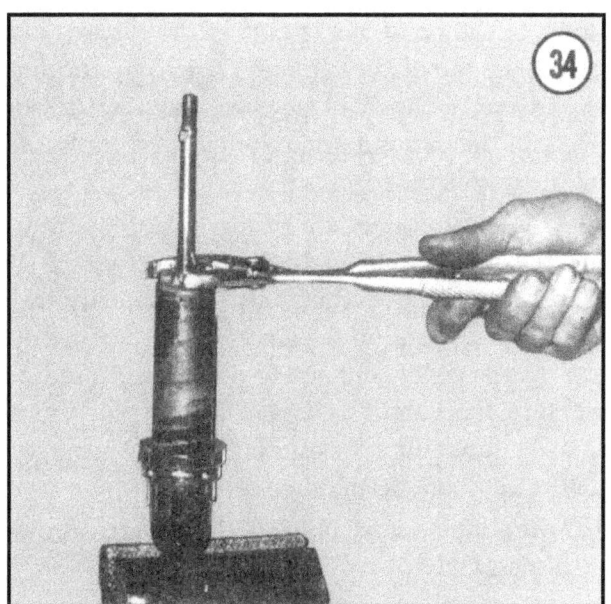

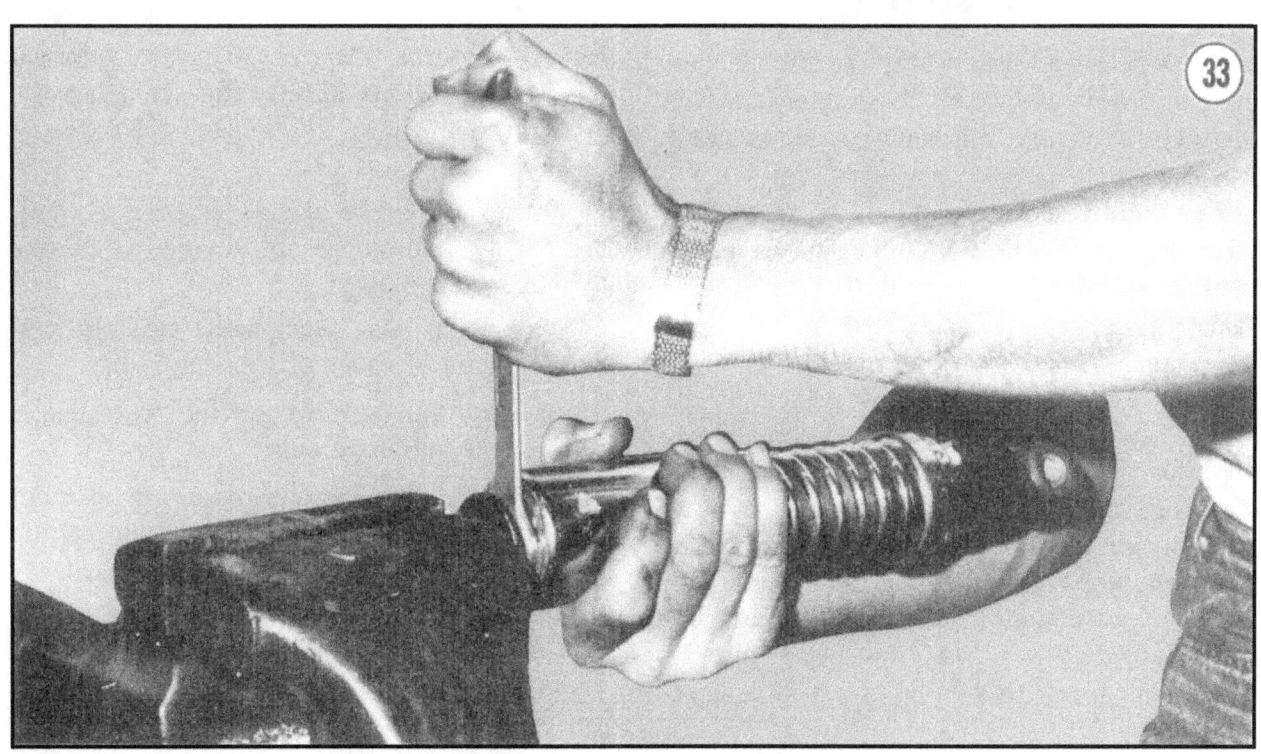

9. Remove the seal and install a new one or install a rebuild kit (available from Ossa dealers), as needed. Refer to **Figure 35**, page 132 for the correct order of reassembly if the kit comes without directions.

10. Follow procedures carefully in reassembling to avoid leaving air in the system. Pour 70cc of shock oil (5 weight is recommended for normal use) into the shock and screw the cap nut in until it is approximately ⅔ of the way into the shock tube. Slowly push the shaft down, expelling air and any excess oil, until the shaft is all the way down. If the shaft does not go down to the point where part of the threads are below the top of the cap nut, loosen the cap nut slightly until the shaft goes all the way down. Tighten the cap nut securely and pull the shaft all the way to the top.

11. Check the shock for proper action by moving the plunger up and down as described in Step 6 above. If it functions satisfactorily, replace the locknut on the shaft, install the spring and shock cover and screw on the top mount. Be sure the rubber bumpers are in place and that the top mount locknut is tightened securely before remounting the shocks.

12. Continue reassembly in the reverse order of disassembly.

WHEELS

The wheels and brakes are very critical components on any motorcycle. No matter how well the bike is running, if it can't be ridden safely it is useless.

The front brake must supply more braking effort than the rear to stop in the shortest possible distance, hence the front brake linings wear faster. Proper maintenance will assure safe operation.

Balance and shimmy are more critical on the front wheel than the rear. The front wheel affects all other handling aspects of the bike. Both wheels should be checked for balance, shimmy, (side-to-side play), wobble (out-of-round), run-out, and proper tire inflation. Many of these problems go unnoticed at low speeds but become dangerous at high speeds. See Figure 27 for exploded views of both front and rear wheel assemblies.

Front Wheel Removal/Installation

1. Support the front wheel clear of the ground by placing a block or stand under the engine.

2. Loosen the front brake cable completely.

3. Detach the front brake cable from the front brake arm and pull the cable up, free of the cable stop.

4. Remove the brake anchor strap from the left fork leg.

5. Remove the large nut and washer (22mm) from the axle.

6. Remove the axle pinch bolt from both fork legs. See Figure 5.

7. Remove the axle.

8. Remove the wheel.

9. *Pioneer and Stiletto models*: Place the wheel in position with the brake assembly on the left. The speedometer drive is on the right side of the hub and the flat spacer washer on the left. Install the axle from the right side.

10. *Plonker models (1972 and later)*: Place the wheel in position. The speedometer drive is on the left side of the hub. Install the axle from the left side.

11. Check to see that the driving tabs of the speedometer drive unit are fitted into the recesses in the hub. See Figure 26.

12. All models except 5-speed Plonkers have 2 flat axle washers. Place the thick one between the hub and fork leg and the thin one under the axle nut. See Figure 27. Tighten the axle nut by hand.

13. Install the brake anchor strap on the fork lug. Put Loctite on the nut threads and torque to 16 ft.-lb. (2.2 mkg).

14. Install the axle pinch bolts with the bolt heads toward the front. Tighten by hand.

15. *Plonker models*: Attach the speedometer cable to the hub drive unit.

16. Hold the axle still and torque the axle nut to 60 ft.-lb. (8.3 mkg) for all models except the Plonker which requires 50 ft.-lb. (6.9 mkg).

17. Torque the left axle pinch bolt on all models except the Plonker and the right pinch bolt on the Plonker to 15 ft.-lb. (2.1 mkg).

18. Pump the forks up and down several times

to align the fork legs on the axle. Torque the remaining axle pinch bolt to 15 ft.-lb. (2.1 mkg).

Rear Wheel Removal/Installation

1. Loosen the rear brake adjustment and disconnect the cable.
2. Disconnect the rear chain at the master link.
3. Remove the axle nut and pull the axle out.
4. Pull the wheel to the rear to remove it.
5. When installing the rear wheel, be sure to fit the brake anchor into the anchor plate before installing the axle.
6. Insert the axle and install the axle nut finger-tight.
7. Reconnect the chain. Face the closed end of the master link in the direction of chain rotation.
8. Adjust free play of the chain using the adjusters which bear against the axle. Adjust to approximately one inch of free play in the chain's longest run with a rider seated on the bike.
9. Check the straightness of the chain by sighting along the top run of the chain from a distance behind the bike. Change the chain adjusters as necessary and recheck chain free play.
10. Tighten the axle nut and recheck chain alignment and free play.
11. Reconnect the rear brake.

Runout and Wobble

1. Support the wheel firmly by the axle in such a way that it is free to rotate.
2. Position a dial indicator to make contact with the rim of the wheel. See **Figure 36**. A piece of wire, bent to touch the rim at its maximum point of runout, and a feeler gauge can be used as a substitute for approximate truing.
3. Observe the dial indicator as the wheel is rotated through one complete revolution. A standard value for both wobble and runout is 0.02 in. (0.5mm). The maximum permissible limit is 0.08 in. (2mm).
4. Adjust the spokes until runout is within acceptable limits. Start with a spoke opposite a high point and work around the wheel in either direction.

5. Repeat the above procedure with the dial indicator touching the rim so as to measure wobble (out-of-roundness). Correct, if necessary, by adjusting the spokes.

Balance

An unbalanced wheel can be hazardous. Depending on the degree of unbalance and the speed of the motorcycle, the rider may experience anything from a mild vibration to a violent shimmy which may result in loss of control. Balance weights are applied to the spokes on the light side of the wheel to correct this condition.

Before you attempt to balance the wheel, check to be sure that the wheel bearings are in good condition and properly lubricated, and that the brakes do not drag, so that the wheel rotates freely.

1. Mount the wheel on a fixture such as the one in **Figure 37** so it can rotate freely.

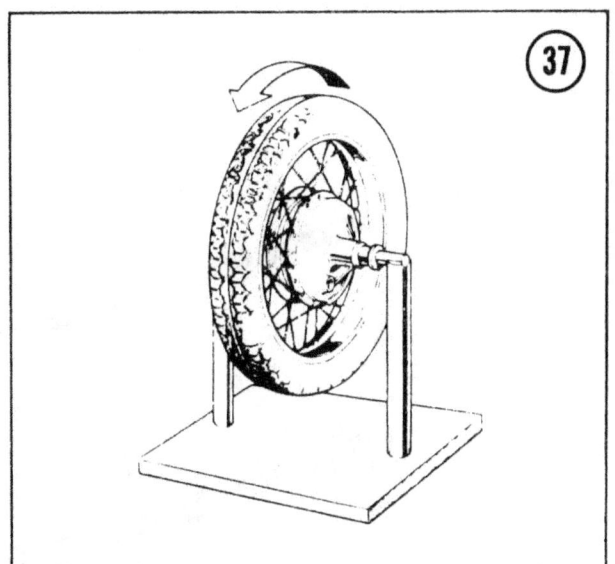

2. Give the wheel a spin and let it coast to a stop. Mark the tire at the lowest point.
3. Spin the wheel several more times. If the wheel keeps coming to a rest at the same point it is out of balance.
4. Attach a weight to the upper—or light—side of the wheel at the spoke (**Figure 38**). Weights come in 4 sizes: 5, 10, 15, and 20 grams.

Experiment with different weights until the wheel, when spun, comes to rest at a different position each time.

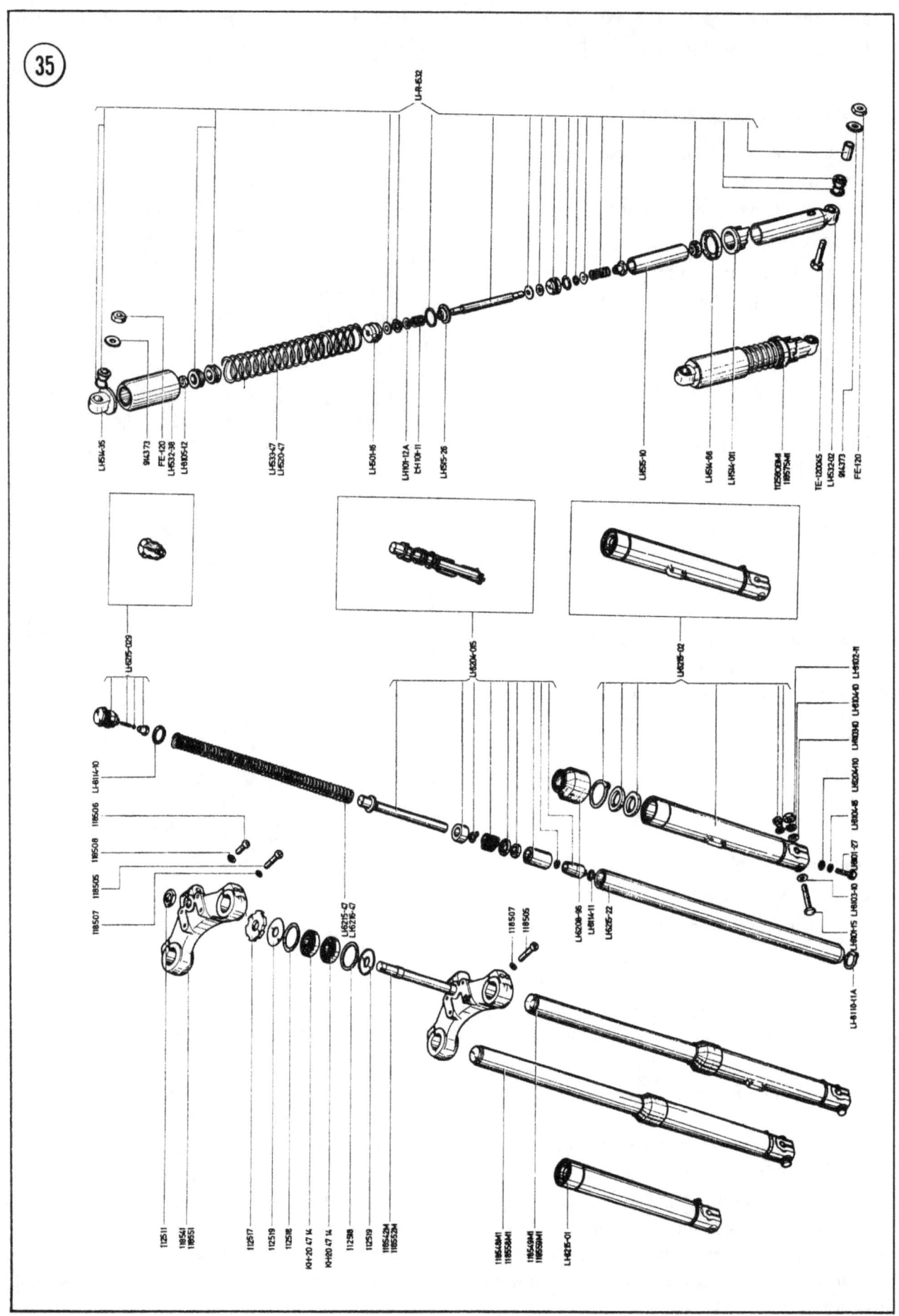

SUSPENSION COMPONENTS

Part Number	Description	Quantity	Part Number	Description	Quantity
LI-1101-11	Spring seal	2	LI-8110-11A	«O» ring 1-30	2
LI-1101-12A	Guide spring seal	2	LI-8114-10	Stanchion «O» ring 26 x 32 x 3	2
LI-1501-16	Adjuster	2	LI-8114-11	Stanchion «O» ring 12 x 17 x 2,5	2
LI-1514-011	Regulating bushing	2	112.511	Nut steering shaft	1
LI-1514-35	Top grip	2	112.517	Nut steering adjuster	1
LI-1514-86	Housing for spring	2	112.518	Felt washer	2
LI-1515-10	Inner tube	2	112.519	Dust cover	2
LI-1515-26	Guide	2	112.580 BMI	Shock absorber assembly (for 175 and 250 AS71)	2
LI-1520-47	Spring (for 175 and 250 AS71)	2	118.505	Bolt stanchion tube	8
LI-R-1532	Spare part kit	2	118.506	Bolt steering shaft	1
LI-1532-02	Oil tank	2	118.507	Washer, stanchion tube bolt	8
LI-1532-38	Cover	2	118.508	Washer, steering shaft bolt	1
LI-1533-47	Spring (for 175-250 AE71 and 250 E71)	2	118.541	Top yoke (for 175 and 250 AS71)	1
LI-6204-015	Damper assembly	2	118.542 M	Bottom yoke with stem (for 175 and 250 AS71)	1
LI-6204-110	Washer damper bolt	2	118.548 MI	Suspension assembly left (for 175 and 250 AS71)	1
LI-6208-96	Dust cover	2	118.549 MI	Suspension assembly right (for 175 and 250 AS71)	1
LI-6215-01	Right tank assembly	1	118.551	Top yoke (for 175-250 AE71 and 250 E71)	1
LI-6215-02	Left tank assembly	1	118.552 M	Bottom yoke with stem (for 175-250 AE71 and 250 E71)	1
LI-6215-029	Stanchion plug	2	118.558 MI	Suspension assembly right (for 175-250 AE71 and 250 E71)	1
LI-6215-22	Stanchion tube	2	118.559 MI	Suspension assembly left (for 175-250 AE71 and 250 E71)	1
LI-6215-47	Spring (for 175-250 AE71 and 250 E71)	2	118.575 MI	Shock absorber assembly (for 175-250 AE71 and 250 E71)	2
LI-6216-47	Spring (for 175 and 250 AS-71)	2	914.373	Washer schock absorber	4
LI-8101-15	Bolt M8 x 60	2			
LI-8101-27	Allen bolt M8 x 25	2		COMMON PARTS	
LI-8102-11	Nut M8	2			
LI-8103-10	Polished washer	4	FE-120	Nut shockabsorber	4
LI-8104-10	Spring washer	2	KH-20-47-14	Bearing assembly	2
LI-8104-16	Spring washer	2	TE-120.045	Bolt, shokabsorber	2
LI-8105-12	Bottom nut	2			

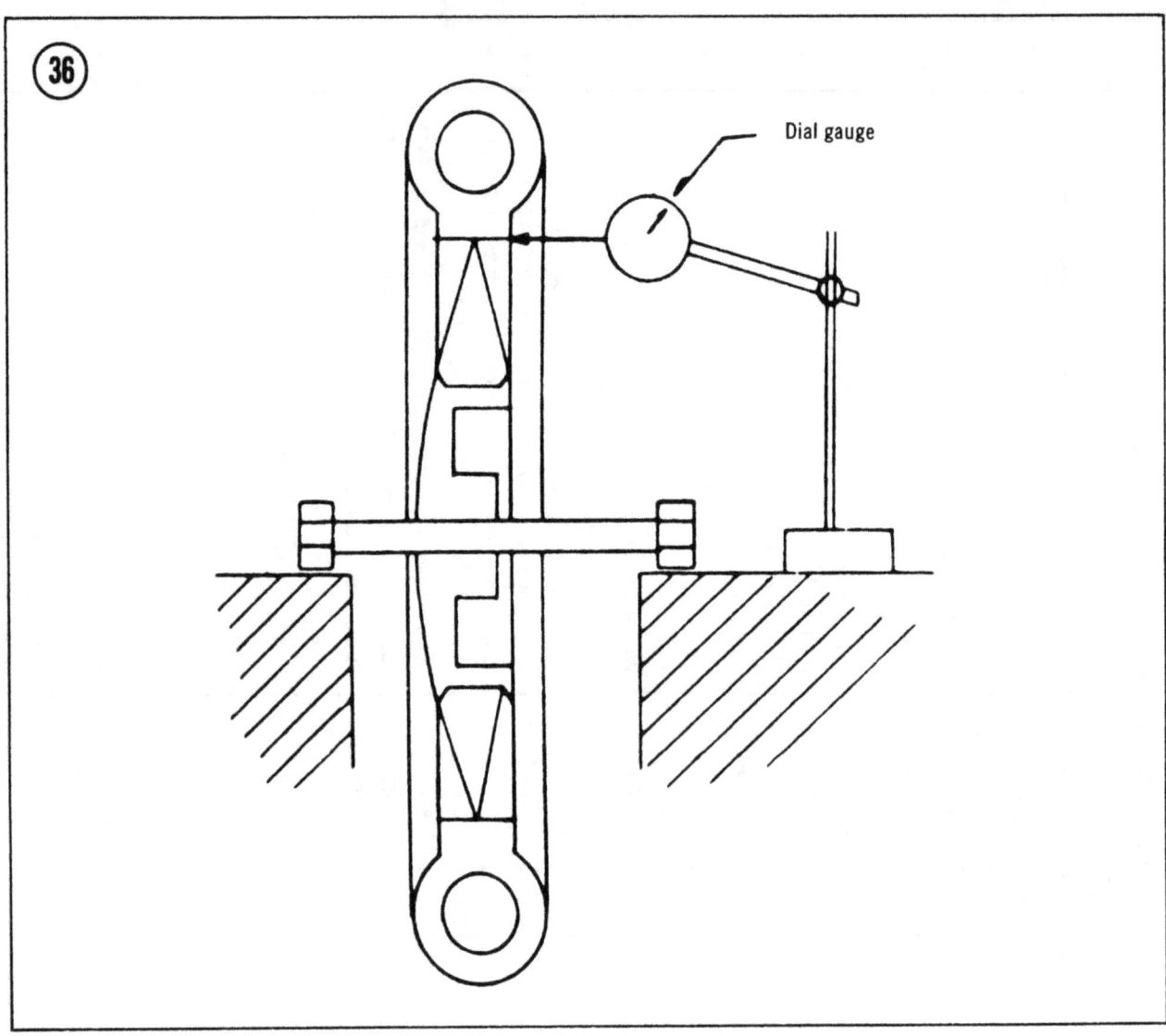

SPOKES

The spokes support the weight of the motorcycle and rider, and transmit tractive and braking forces, as shown in **Figure 39**. Diagram A illustrates action of the spokes as they support the machine. Tractive forces are shown in Diagram B. Braking forces are shown in Diagram C.

Check the spokes periodically for looseness or binding. A bent or otherwise faulty spoke will adversely affect neighboring spokes, and should therefore be replaced immediately.

The "tuning fork" method of checking spoke tightness is simple and works well. Tap each spoke with a spoke wrench or shank of a screwdriver and listen to the tone. A tightened spoke will emit a clear, ringing tone, and a loose spoke will sound flat. All spokes in a correctly tightened wheel will emit tones of similar pitch but not necessarily the same precise tone.

Bent or stripped spokes should be replaced as soon as they are detected. Unscrew the nipple from the spoke and depress the nipple into the rim far enough to free the end of the spoke, taking care not to push the spoke all the way in. Remove the damaged spoke from the hub and use it to match a new spoke of identical length. If necessary, trim the new spoke to match the original and dress the end of the threads with a die. Install the new spoke in the hub and screw on the nipple, tightening it until the spoke's tone is similar to the tone of the other spokes on the wheel. Periodically check the new spoke; it will stretch and must be retightened several times before it takes its final set.

Spokes tend to loosen as the bike is ridden. Retighten each spoke one turn, beginning with those on one side of the hub, then those on the other side. Tighten the spokes on a new bike

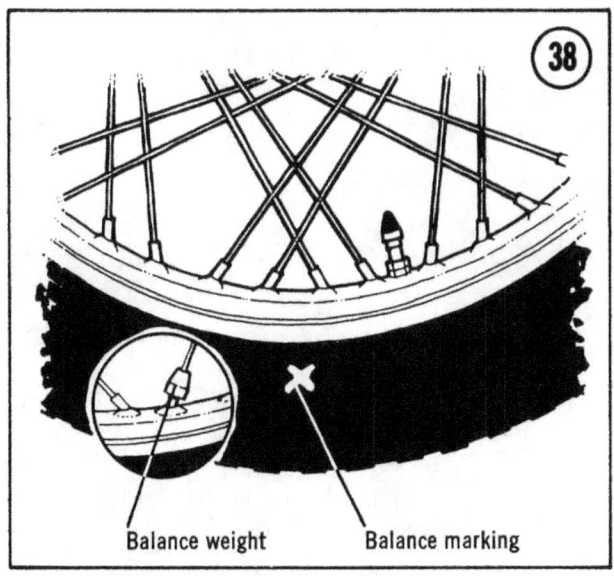
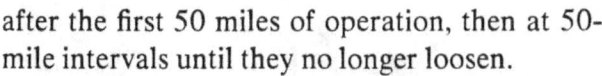

after the first 50 miles of operation, then at 50-mile intervals until they no longer loosen.

If the bike is subjected to particularly severe service, as in off-road or competition riding, check the spokes frequently.

WHEEL BEARINGS

Wheel bearings require cleaning often, especially if the bike is used off-road or in competition. Rinsing well with solvent and regreasing will generally restore bearings to proper service. Bearing service is the same for both wheels.

Removal/Installation

1. Remove the wheel as detailed under *Wheel* in this chapter.
2. Lift out the backing plate. See **Figure 40**.
3. Carefully heat the hub to 300°F (**Figure 41**).
4. Remove the bearings by tapping the hub or entire wheel on a hard surface.
5. Clean and grease the bearings or replace with new ones if wear is obvious.
6. Install by heating the hub to 300°F and gently tapping them in place. Be sure to insert the spacer tube between the 2 bearings. See Figure 27. The bearings fit against a shoulder in the hub; they will sound solid when tapped if properly installed.

Wheel bearings may be installed with either side facing in unless one side is shielded; the shielded side faces out.

7. Oil the felt washer which fits over the axle and install the wheel as detailed previously.
8. Check to see that the wheel turns freely after the axle nut is tightened snugly. Binding is usually caused by prior overtightening of the axle nuts which causes a slight collapse of the spacer

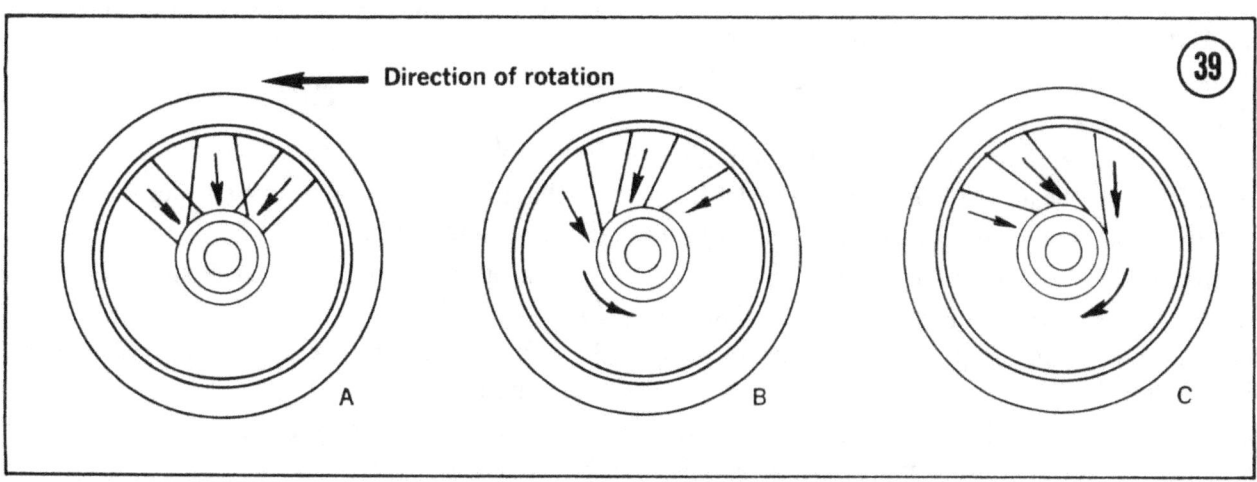

tube between the bearings. Installation of a new spacer tube will usually cure the problem.

BRAKES

Brake service is the same on front and rear wheels.

1. Remove either wheel as detailed under *Wheel* in this chapter.

2. Lift out the backing plate. See Figure 40.

3. Remove the nut from the backing plate bolt. See **Figure 42**.

4. Remove the bolt from the brake actuating arm. Remove the arm. See **Figures 43 and 44**.

5. Push the brake cam and backing plate bolt out of the backing plate. See **Figure 45**.

6. Inspect the brake shoes. Measure the lining at its thinnest point. Replace if the measurement is less than 1/16 in.

7. Check the brake lining surfaces carefully for scoring, oil-residue, or glazing. Glaze can be removed by roughing the lining surface with a wire brush.

8. Clean the cam and grease it with a high-temperature grease for smooth brake action. Be sure to check under the brake actuating arm for a buildup of dirt at the point where it contacts the backing plate and clean if necessary.

9. During reassembly, be sure the washer fits over both brake shoes. See **Figure 46**.

10. Reassemble in reverse order of disassembly.

TIRE

Removal

1. Place the wheel on a soft surface to prevent damage to the hub.

2. If a puncture is suspected, inspect the tread for sharp objects.

3. Remove the valve core and the valve stem retaining nut.

4. Break the bead free of the rim by stepping on it from both sides.

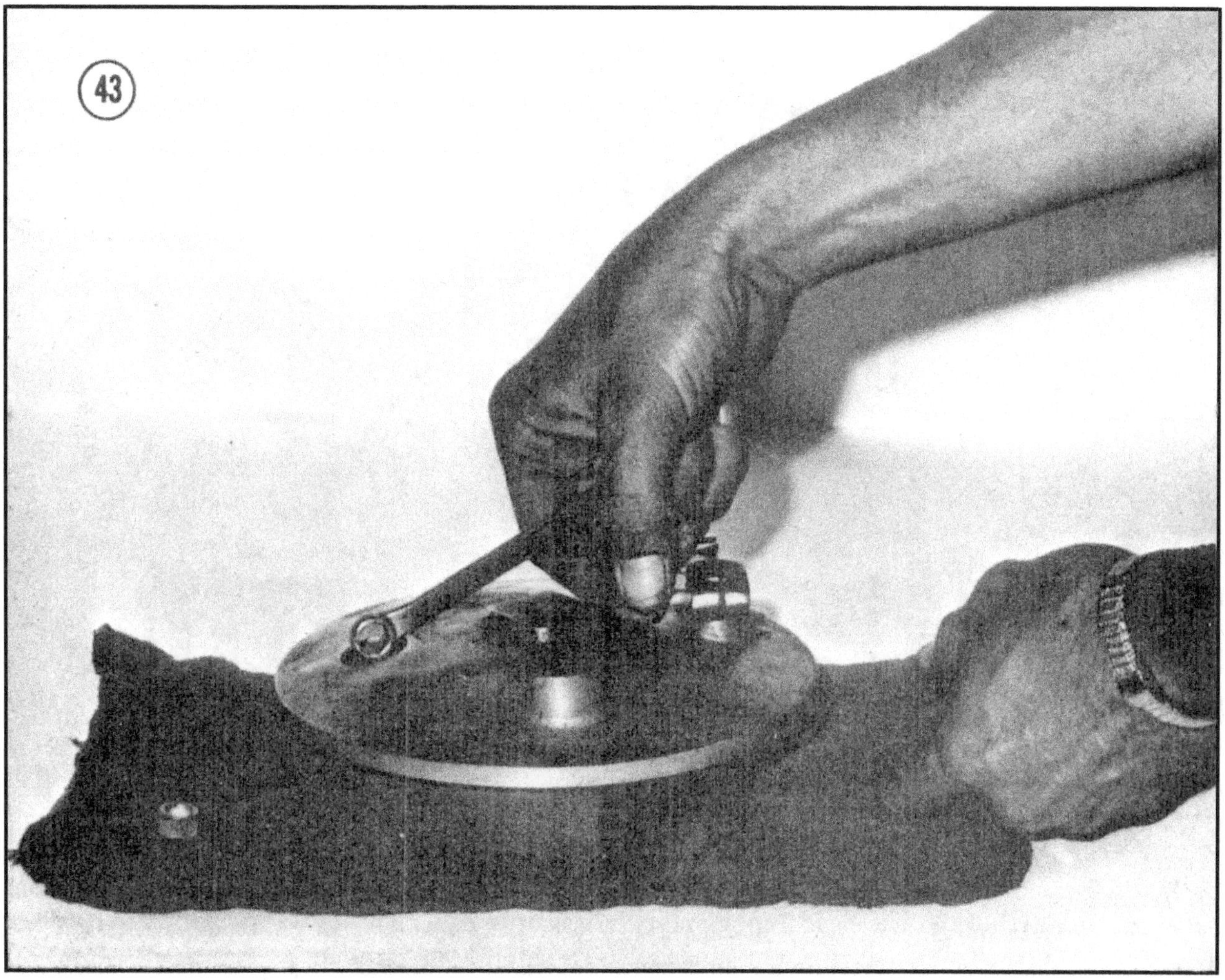

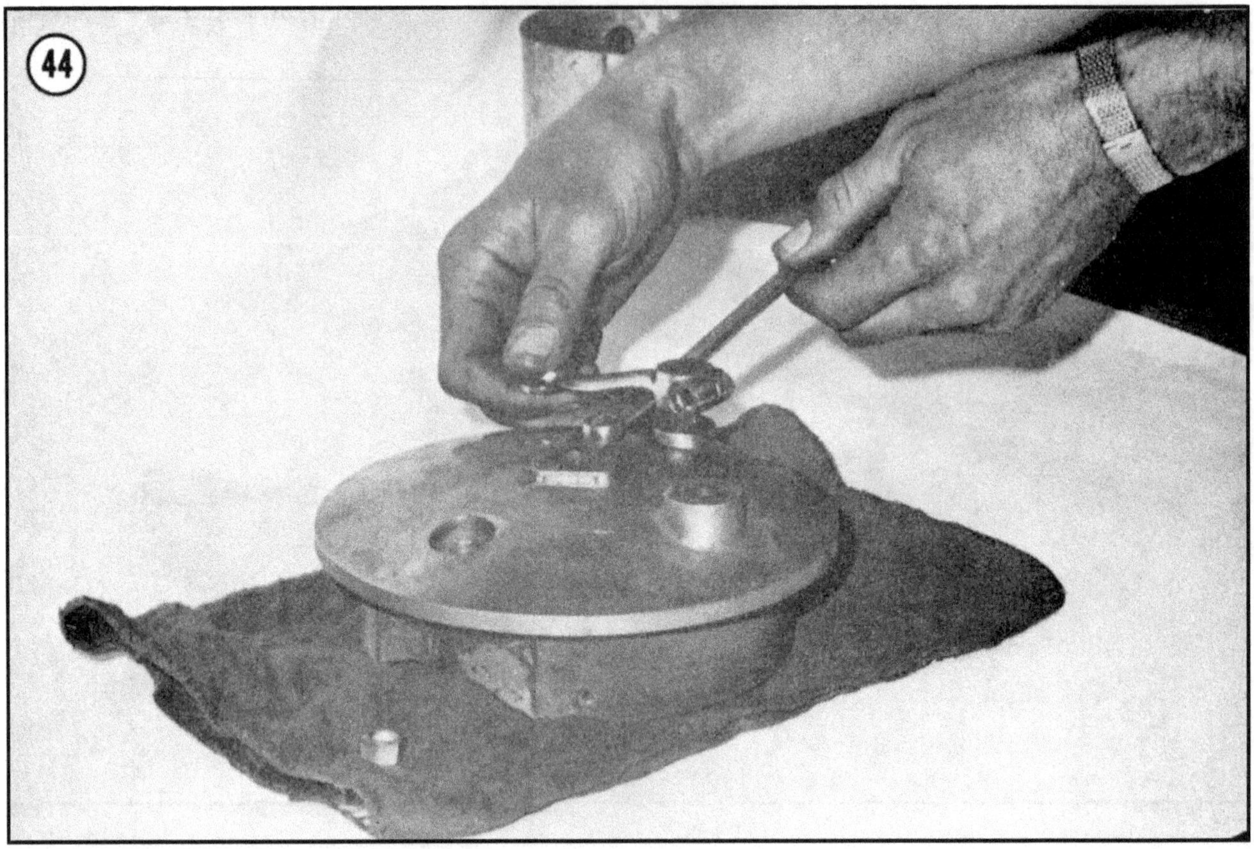

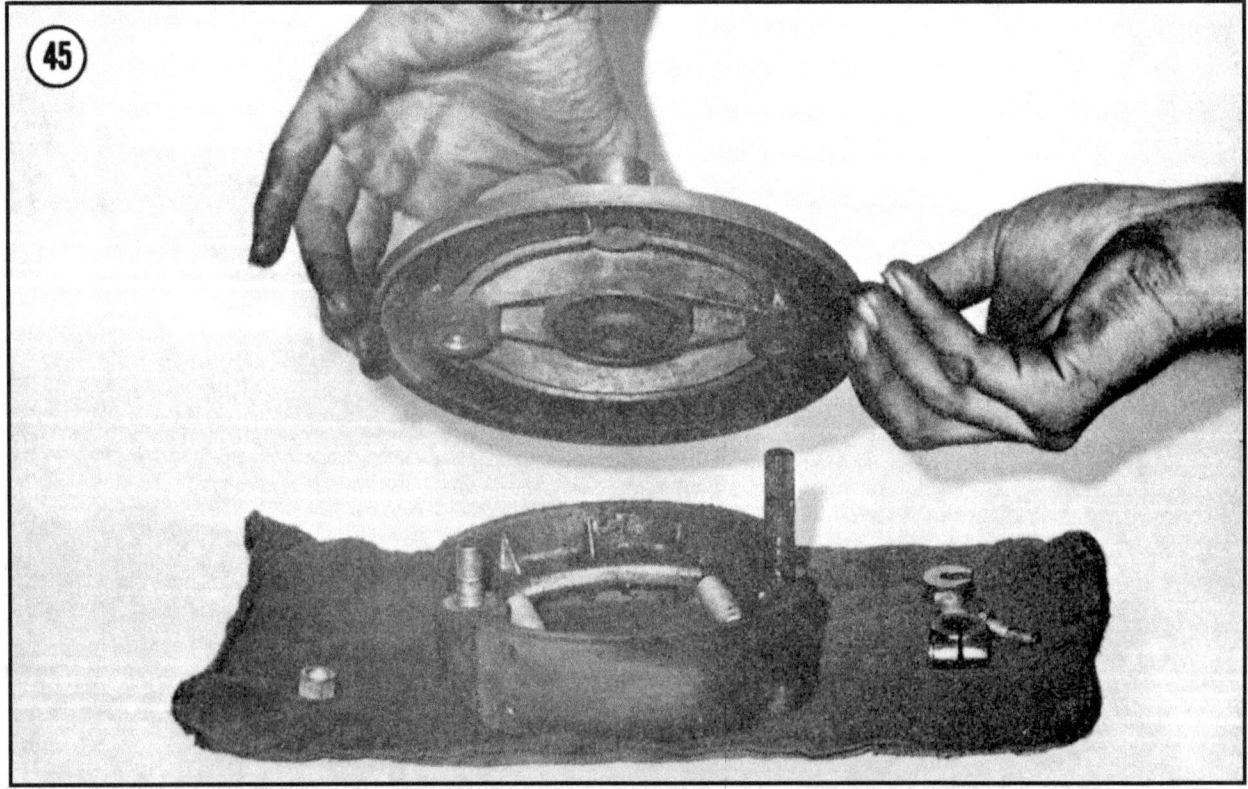

5. Insert 2 small tire irons 4 to 6 inches apart between the rim and the tire bead at the valve location.

6. Pry in and down with the irons, moving only one iron at a time until the bead is free of the rim all the way around.

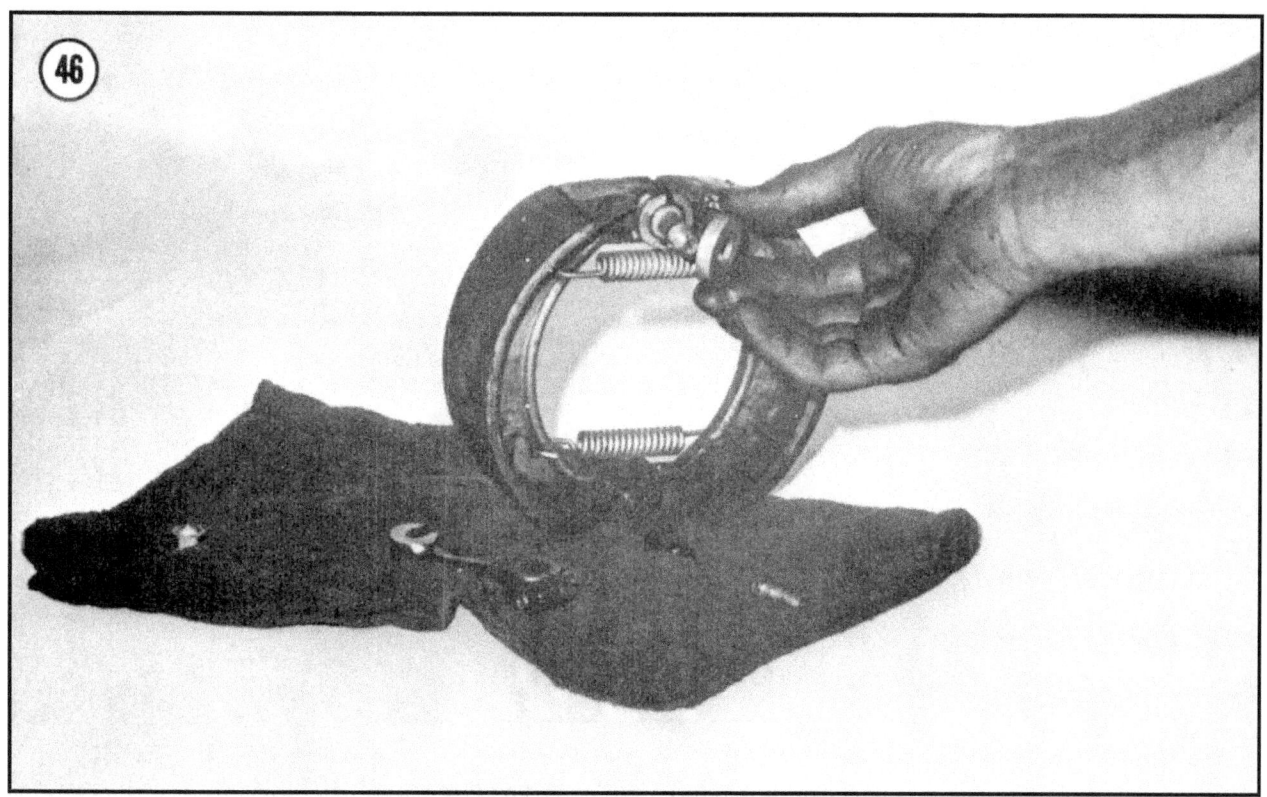

7. Pull the inner tube out of the tire casing.

Installation

1. Inflate the new inner tube slightly, leaving the valve core in place.

2. Make sure the inner strip that protects the tube is in good condition and is centered over the spoke nipples.

3. Insert the tube into the tire casing with the valve stem and the tire balance mark aligned with the hole in the rim.

4. Insert the valve stem through the hole in the rim and partially tighten the retaining nut. Remove the valve core.

5. Coat the bead surfaces and the edge of the rim with tire mounting solution (liquid dishwashing detergent is a good substitute).

6. Push the tire into place with your feet. Start on the far side of the rim from the valve and work in opposite directions around the wheel with your heels.

7. Force the last bit of bead into place with a soft-headed mallet. Do not use tire irons or screwdrivers which could damage the tube.

8. Insert the valve core. Inflate the tire to 10 psi over the recommended pressure to seat the bead against the rim. Deflate completely and reinflate to standard pressure. Check for leaks.

EXHAUST PIPE

Carbon deposits can form in the exhaust pipe and cause a loss in engine efficiency and power. The easiest way to remove these deposits is to run a piece of used drive chain through the pipe. Another method is to chuck a length of wire cable, with one end flared, in an electric drill. Run the wire through the pipe a few times.

APPENDIX

SPECIFICATIONS

SPECIFICATIONS AND DATA

	250 Stiletto MX	250 Stiletto TT	250 Pioneer	250 Plonker/Explorer	175 Stiletto	175 Pioneer
Engine						
Type	2-cycle	2-cycle	2-cycle	2-cycle	2-cycle	2-cycle
Number of cylinders	One	One	One	One	One	One
Bore	72mm	72mm	72mm	72mm	60.9mm	60.9mm
Stroke	60mm	60mm	60mm	60mm	60mm	60mm
Displacement	244cc	244cc	244cc	244cc	175cc	175cc
Compression ratio	12.3 to 1	13.4 to 1	12.3 to 1	9.8 to 1	13.0 to 1	10.2 to 1
Carburetor						
Make	IRZ	IRZ	IRZ	IRZ	IRZ	IRZ
Type	Double needle	Double needle	Double needle	Single needle	Double needle	Double needle
Venturi diameter	33mm	33mm	29mm	27mm	29mm	29mm
Mid-range main jet size	76	96	68 ①, 75 ②	N/A	80	82
Hi-speed main jet size	115	108	106 ①, 105 ②	110	90	100
Pilot jet size	40	40	40 ①, 53 ②	48	40	35
Slide	No. 4	No. 4	No. 4	No. 5	No. 4	No. 6
Electrics						
Ignition	Flywheel magneto	Flywheel magneto	Flywheel magneto	Flywheel magneto	Flywheel magneto	Flywheel magneto
Lighting	None	None	Battery	Direct AC	None	Battery
Lighting system voltage	None	None	6 V	6 V	None	6 V
Ignition system	Pointless solid state electronic	Pointless solid state electronic	Pointless solid state electronic	Pointless solid state electronic	Pointless solid state electronic	Pointless solid state electronic
Spark plug	NGK B10EN or equivalent	NGK B10EN or equivalent	NGK B9ES or equivalent	NGK B8ES or equivalent	NGK B10EN or equivalent	NGK B9ES or equivalent
Gearing						
Primary drive ratio	2.26:1	2.26:1	2.26:1	2.26:1	2.26:1	2.26:1
1st gear ratio	2.62:1	1.99:1	3.60:1	4.31:1	2.62:1	3.60:1
2nd gear ratio	1.80:1	1.48:1	2.44:1	3.24:1	1.80:1	2.44:1
3rd gear ratio	1.43:1	1.21:1	1.81:1	2.40:1	1.34:1	1.81:1
4th gear ratio	1.10:1	1.04:1	1.35:1	1.62:1	1.10:1	1.35:1
5th gear ratio	1:1	1:1	1:1	1:1	1:1	1:1
Gearbox sprocket	12 teeth	12 teeth	12 teeth	12 teeth	12 teeth	11 teeth
Rear wheel sprocket	53 teeth	53 teeth	40 teeth	46 teeth	53 teeth	40 teeth
Gearbox oil capacity	1 quart	1 quart	1 quart	1 quart	1 quart	1 quart

① 1971 models ② 1972 and later models

(continued)

SPECIFICATIONS AND DATA (continued)

	250 Stiletto MX	250 Stiletto TT	250 Pioneer	250 Plonker/Explorer	175 Stiletto	175 Pioneer
Gearing (continued)						
Gearbox lubricant	Full bore—SAE 80W racing gearbox lubricant or its equivalent, or SAE 30W motor oil	Full bore—SAE 80W racing gearbox lubricant or its equivalent, or SAE 30W motor oil	Full bore—SAE 80W racing gearbox lubricant or its equivalent, or SAE 30W motor oil	Full bore—SAE 80W racing gearbox lubricant or its equivalent, or SAE 30W motor oil	Full bore—SAE 80W racing gearbox lubricant or its equivalent, or SAE 30W motor oil	Full bore—SAE 80W racing gearbox lubricant or its equivalent, or SAE 30W motor oil
Primary chain						
Brand	Joresa 2032-50	Joresa 2032-50	Joresa 2032-50	Joresa 2032-50	Joresa 2032-50	Joresa 2032-50
Pitch	3/8 in.-double row	3/8 in.-double row	3/8 in.-double row	3/8 in.-double row	3/8 in.-double row	3/8 in.-double row
Width	0.225	0.225	0.225	0.225	0.225	0.225
Rear chain						
Brand	Joresa 520	Joresa 520	Joresa 520	Joresa 520	Joresa 520	Joresa 520
Pitch	5/8 in.	5/8 in.	5/8 in.	5/8 in.	5/8 in.	5/8 in.
Front suspension						
Type	Betor telescopic	Betor telescopic	Betor telescopic	Betor telescopic	Betor telescopic	Betor telescopic
Travel	6 1/2 in.	6 1/2 in.	6 1/2 in.	7 in.	6 1/2 in.	6 1/2 in.
Lubricant	200cc 5W per leg	200cc 5W per leg	200cc 5W per leg	200cc 5W per leg	200cc 5W per leg	200cc 5W per leg
Rear suspension						
Type	Betor 5-way adjustable	Betor 5-way adjustable	Betor 5-way adjustable	Betor 5-way adjustable	Betor 5-way adjustable	Betor 5-way adjustable
Travel	3 1/2 in.	3 1/2 in.	3 1/2 in.	3 1/2 in.	3 1/2 in.	3 1/2 in.
Wheels and tires						
Front tire	3.00 x 21 knobby	3.50 x 19 trials	3.00 x 21 knobby	2.75 x 21 trials	3.00 x 21 knobby	3.00 x 21 trials
Rear tire	4.00 x 18 knobby	4.00 x 18 knobby	4.00 x 18 knobby	4.00 x 18 trials	4.00 x 18 knobby	4.00 x 18 trials
Tire pressures (psi)						
Front	8-10	8-10	8-10	4-6	8-10	8-10
Rear	10-15	10-15	10-15	6-8	10-15	10-15
Brakes						
Type	Internal expanding, single leading shoe	Internal expanding, single leading shoe	Internal expanding, single leading shoe	Internal expanding, single leading shoe	Internal expanding, single leading shoe	Internal expanding, single leading shoe
Drum diameter	158mm	158mm	158mm	122mm	158mm	158mm
General data						
Wheelbase	54.5 in.	54.5 in.	54.5 in.	51 in.	54.5 in.	54.5 in.
Minimum ground clearance	7 in.	6 in.	10 in.	10 1/2 in.	7 in.	10 in.
Dry weight	233 lb.	236 lb.	242 lb.	197 lb.	228 lb.	242 lb.
Fuel tank capacity	2.6 gal.	2.6 gal.	3 gal.	1.5 gal.	2.6 gal.	3 gal.
Reserve capacity	0.5 gal.	0.5 gal.	0.5 gal.	0.3 gal.	0.5 gal.	0.5 gal.

SPECIFICATIONS AND DATA

	250 Phantom	175 Phantom	125 Phantom	250 Super Pioneer	175 Super Pioneer	125 Super Pioneer
Engine						
Size	250cc	175cc	125cc	250cc	175cc	125cc
No. of cylinders	One	One	One	One	One	One
Type	2-cycle	2-cycle	2-cycle	2-cycle	2-cycle	2-cycle
Bore	72mm	60.9mm	54mm	72mm	60.9mm	54mm
Stroke	60mm	60mm	54mm	60mm	60mm	54mm
Displacement	244cc	175cc	N/A	244cc	175cc	N/A
Compression ratio	N/A	N/A	N/A	N/A	N/A	N/A
Piston sizes available	Standard	Standard	Standard	Standard	Standard	Standard
	1st over (+0.2mm)	1st over (+0.2mm)	1st over (+0.2mm)	1st over (+0.2mm)	1st over (+0.2mm)	1st over (+0.2mm)
	2nd over (+0.4mm)	2nd over (+0.4mm)	2nd over (+0.4mm)	2nd over (+0.4mm)	2nd over (+0.4mm)	2nd over (+0.4mm)
	3rd over (+0.6mm)	3rd over (+0.6mm)	3rd over (+0.6mm)	3rd over (+0.6mm)	3rd over (+0.06mm)	3rd over (+0.6mm)
Horsepower (hp @ rpm)	33 @ 5,500/ 26 @ 6,500	27 @ 6,500	21 @ 7,500	21 @ 6,500	17 @ 6,500	15 @ 7,500
Carburetor						
Make	Bing	Bing	Bing	Amal	Amal	Amal
Type	54 Series	54 Series	54 Series	Concentric	Concentric	Concentric
Mid-range main jet size	165	165	165	N/A	N/A	N/A
Hi-speed main jet size	280	280	280	N/A	N/A	N/A
Pilot jet size	40	40	40	N/A	N/A	N/A
Slide	N/A	N/A	N/A	N/A	N/A	N/A
Electrics						
Ignition (typical)	Flywheel magneto	Flywheel magneto	Flywheel magneto	Flywheel magneto	Flywheel magneto	Flywheel magneto
Lighting	None/direct AC	None	None	None/direct AC	Battery	Battery
Lighting system voltage	None/6V	None	None	6V	6V	6V
Ignition system (typical)	Pointless solid state electronic	Pointless solid state electronic	Pointless solid state electronic	Pointless solid state electronic	Pointless solid state electronic	Pointless solid state electronic
Spark plug	NGK B8EN, B9EN, or equivalent	NGK B8EN, B9EN, or equivalent	NGK B8EN, B9EN, or equivalent	NGK B8EN, B9EN, or equivalent	NGK B8EN, B9EN, or equivalent	NGK B8EN, B9EN, or equivalent
Gearing						
Primary drive ratio	2.26:1	2.26:1	2.26:1	2.26:1	2.26:1	2.26:1
1st gear ratio	1.26:1	1.26:1	1.26:1	3.52:1	3.52:1	3.52:1
2nd gear ratio	1.92:1	1.92:1	1.92:1	2.39:1	2.39:1	2.39:1
3rd gear ratio	1.43:1	1.43:1	1.43:1	1.78:1	1.78:1	1.78:1
4th gear ratio	1.17:1	1.17:1	1.17:1	1.33:1	1.33:1	1.33:1

(continued)

SPECIFICATIONS AND DATA (continued)

	250 Phantom	175 Phantom	125 Phantom	250 Super Pioneer	175 Super Pioneer	125 Super Pioneer
Gearing (continued)						
5th gear ratio	1.1:1	1.1:1	1.1:1	1.1:1	1.1:1	1.1:1
Gearbox sprocket	12 teeth	12 teeth	12 teeth	11 teeth	11 teeth	11 teeth
Rear wheel sprocket	53 teeth	53 teeth	53 teeth	43 teeth	40 teeth	40 teeth
Gearbox oil capacity	1 quart	1 quart	1 quart	1 quart	1 quart	1 quart
Gearbox lubricant	①	①	①	①	①	①
Primary chain						
Brand	Joresa 2032-50	Joresa 2032-50	Joresa 2032-50	Joresa 2032-50	Joresa 2032-50	Joresa 2032-50
Pitch	3/8 in.-double row	3/8 in.-double row	3/8 in.-double row	3/8 in.-double row	3/8 in.-double row	3/8 in.-double row
Rear chain						
Brand	Joresa 520	Joresa 520	Joresa 520	Joresa 520	Joresa 520	Joresa 520
Pitch	5/8 in.	5/8 in.	5/8 in.	5/8 in.	5/8 in.	5/8 in.
Front suspension						
Type	Betor telescopic	Betor telescopic	Betor telescopic	Betor telescopic	Betor telescopic	Betor telescopic
Travel	6 1/2 in.	6 1/2 in.	6 1/2 in.	6 1/2 in.	6 1/2 in.	6 1/2 in.
Oil type (typical)	①	①	①	①	①	①
Quantity per leg	200cc	200cc	200cc	200cc	200cc	200cc
Rear suspension						
Type	Betor 5-way adjustable	Betor 5-way adjustable	Betor 5-way adjustable	Betor 5-way adjustable	Betor 5-way adjustable	Betor 5-way adjustable
Travel	3 1/2 in.	3 1/2 in.	3 1/2 in.	3 1/2 in.	3 1/2 in.	3 1/2 in.
Wheels and tires						
Front tire	3.50 x 21 knobby	3.50 x 21 knobby	3.50 x 21 knobby	3.50 x 21 knobby	3.50 x 21 knobby	3.50 x 21 knobby
Rear tire	4.50 x 18 knobby	4.50 x 18 knobby	4.50 x 18 knobby	4.50 x 18 knobby	4.50 x 18 knobby	4.50 x 18 knobby
Tire pressures	8-10 front / 10-15 rear	8-10 front / 10-15 rear	8-10 front / 10-15 rear	8-10 front / 10-15 rear	8-10 front / 10-15 rear	8-10 front / 10-15 rear
Brakes						
Type (typical)	Internal expanding, single leading shoe	Internal expanding, single leading shoe	Internal expanding, single leading shoe	Internal expanding, single leading shoe	Internal expanding, single leading shoe	Internal expanding, single leading shoe
Drum diameter	158mm	158mm	158mm	158mm	158mm	158mm
General data						
Wheelbase	54 3/4 in. / 55 1/2 in.	54 3/4 in.	54 3/4 in.	54 3/4 in.	54 3/4 in.	54 3/4 in.
Dry weight	197 lb. / 207 lb.	194 lb.	190 lb.	209 lb.	206 lb.	202 lb.
Fuel tank capacity	2.6 gal.	2.6 gal.	2.6 gal.	3 gal.	3 gal.	3 gal.
Reserve capacity	0.5 gal.	0.5 gal.	0.5 gal.	0.5 gal.	0.5 gal.	0.5 gal.

① Full bore—80W racing gearbox lubricant or its equivalent, or SAE 30W motor oil

SUPPLEMENT

1977-1978 SERVICE INFORMATION

The following supplement provides procedures unique to the 1977 and later Ossa motorcycles. All other service procedures are identical to earlier models.

The headings in this supplement correspond to those in the main portion of this book. If a change is not included in the supplement, there are no changes affecting the 1977 and later models.

Use the data in this supplement, in conjunction with the procedures outlined in the various chapters in the main body of this manual, for these late model motorcycles.

CHAPTER ONE

GENERAL INFORMATION

Radical change is not a characteristic of the Ossa factory; gradual evolution seems to be standard operating procedure for this small Spanish motorcycle manufacturer.

The 1977-1978 Ossa lineup uses the same basic one-cylinder, two-stroke engine design that it has for years, making maintenance and overhaul easy for anyone who has ever worked on an Ossa engine. For instance, the engine used in the newest 310 Mountaineer is the same as that used in the newest 250 Super Pioneer 250, except that the bore and stroke has been increased to obtain 310cc.

Most 1977-1978 modifications resulted from suggestions from Ossa's factory riders and their customers. The end result is a rugged, highly efficient motorcycle for the dedicated amateur or expert rider.

Refer to **Table 1** for specifications and data on the latest Ossa lineup. Also, refer to the following remarks covering the individual models.

250cc Super Pioneer

This enduro bike is basically unchanged from previous Super Pioneers, except for modifications to the suspension system (none of which affect the various maintenance procedures outlined in the front of this book).

The suspension, front and rear, has been changed somewhat to provide longer wheel travel (7 in. in front, thanks to a Betor fork; and 4¾ in. in the rear, with its adjustable gas Betor shocks).

The frame is made of chrome moly tubing and covered with epoxy paint, resulting in light weight, immense strength, and long wear.

A large diameter conical front hub is used (the same one used on late model Ossa M-X and enduro bikes) in conjunction with Akront alloy rims. Rear spokes are now a hefty ⅛ in. in diameter. Identical brake rims are used in both front and rear (30mm wide x 150mm diameter). Pirelli tires are standard.

The standard engine for 1977-1978 is Ossa's 250cc "Stage II" which provides more mid-range and top-end torque (in exchange for perhaps 5% less low-end torque) than the 1976 engine.

> NOTE: *The 1976 "Stage I" engine can be ordered on 1977-1978 models, for those of you who feel that you need more low-end torque and less mid-range and top end.*

A Bing carburetor (with choke) replaces the Amal carburetor used on the original Super Pioneer models. The Motoplate pointless electronic ignition is standard.

310 Mountaineer

This model is virtually identical to the 250cc Super Pioneer except that the bore and stroke has been enlarged to obtain 310cc. Other than that, a white paint job distinguishes the 310 Mountaineer from the Super Pioneer.

The extra displacement provides the tractability needed for open class enduro racing (and at 217 lbs., it is the lightest open class enduro bike available).

Table 1 SPECIFICATIONS AND DATA

	250 Super Pioneer	250 Six Day	GPIII
Engine	2-stroke single	2-stroke single	2-stroke single
Bore	72mm	72mm	72mm
Stroke	60mm	60mm	60mm
Displacement	244cc	244cc	244cc
Compression ratio	14:1	N/A	14.9:1
Carburetion	32mm Bing	36mm Bing	38mm Bing
Ignition	Magneto CDI	Magneto CDI	Magneto CDI
Brakes	30mm x 150mm	30mm x 122mm (front); 30mm x 150mm (rear)	30mm x 150mm
Wheelbase	55.5 in.	55.5 in.	57.6 in.
Dry weight	217 lb.	207 lb.	207 lb.
Transmission	5-speed	5-speed	5-speed
Gearing			
1st	3.60:1	2.78:1	2.12:1
2nd	2.45:1	1.92:1	1.74:1
3rd	1.82:1	1.43:1	1.43:1
4th	1.35:1	1.17:1	1.17:1
5th	1:1	1:1	1:1

	310 Mountaineer	BLT Plonker
Engine	2-stroke single	2-stroke single
Bore	77mm	77mm
Stroke	65mm	65mm
Displacement	310cc	310cc
Compression ratio	12.9:1	N/A
Carburetion	32mm Bing	26mm Mikuni
Ignition	Magneto CDI	Magneto CDI
Brakes	30mm x 150mm	30mm x 150mm
Wheelbase	55.5 in.	52 in.
Dry weight	217 lb.	195 lb.
Transmission	5-speed	5-speed
Gearing		
1st	3.60:1	4.31:1
2nd	2.45:1	3.46:1
3rd	1.82:1	2.40:1
4th	1.35:1	1.62:1
5th	1:1	1:1

BLT Plonker

This excellent trials bike is very similar to previous Plonker models, except that the 250cc engine has been enlarged to 310cc (as in the 310 Mountaineer).

250cc Six Day

This model is new for 1978, but is derived from the Desert Phantom. Plastic fenders, gas tank, and side fenders by Hoss are standard, as well as a special ISDT air filter system, also by Hoss.

The front fork travel is a whopping 8 inches; gas shock absorbers are used at the rear.

Again, the engine is the tried-and-true 250cc 2-stroke unit used in the Super Pioneer, with its 72mm x 60mm bore and stroke, resulting in 244cc. A 36mm Bing carburetor is used; the ignition is Motoplate electronic.

GP III

This 250cc M-Xer is a "Works" version of the GP II (which was introduced in 1976 and called a "76½," which in turn was derived from the GP I, which was introduced in 1975). It is a bike for the serious M-X rider.

A new 5-port cylinder and 4-fin cylinder design is used for improved cylinder cooling and extra power. Other than that, the basic engine is the same as other late model 250cc Ossa engines. Refer to Chapter Six, this supplement, for exploded views of the engine.

The chassis features Betor leading axle front forks, with 9½ in. of travel; a redesigned swing arm (lengthened 1³⁄₁₆ in.) in conjunction with forward mounted gas shocks which results in 8¾ in. of rear wheel travel; large diameter conical front hub with torque arm; chrome moly frame; rear brake arm and brake pedal made of forged aluminum; flexible fenders; new-style gas tank; spring loaded, reinforced footpegs; new chain guide with replaceable wear block; new roller-type chain tensioner; heavier spokes; and improved rear wheel bearing protection.

CHAPTER SIX

ENGINE

250 Super Pioneer

Refer to **Figure 1** for an exploded view of the Ossa 250 Super Pioneer engine. Service procedures are similar to previous engines (refer to Chapter Six in the front of this book).

CHAPTER EIGHT

CHASSIS

FRAME

250 Super Pioneer

Refer to **Figure 2** (pages 152-153) for an exploded view of the Ossa 250 Super Pioneer frame. Service procedures are similar to previous models (refer to Chapter Six in the front of this book).

FRONT FORK AND STEERING COMPONENTS

250 Super Pioneer

Refer to **Figure 3** (pages 154-155) for an exploded view of the Ossa 250 Super Pioneer front fork and steering components. Service procedures are similar to previous models (refer to Chapter Six in the front of this book).

WHEELS

250 Super Pioneer

Refer to **Figure 4** (pages 156-157) for an exploded view of the Ossa 250 Super Pioneer wheel assemblies. Service procedures are similar to previous models (refer to Chapter Six in the front of this book).

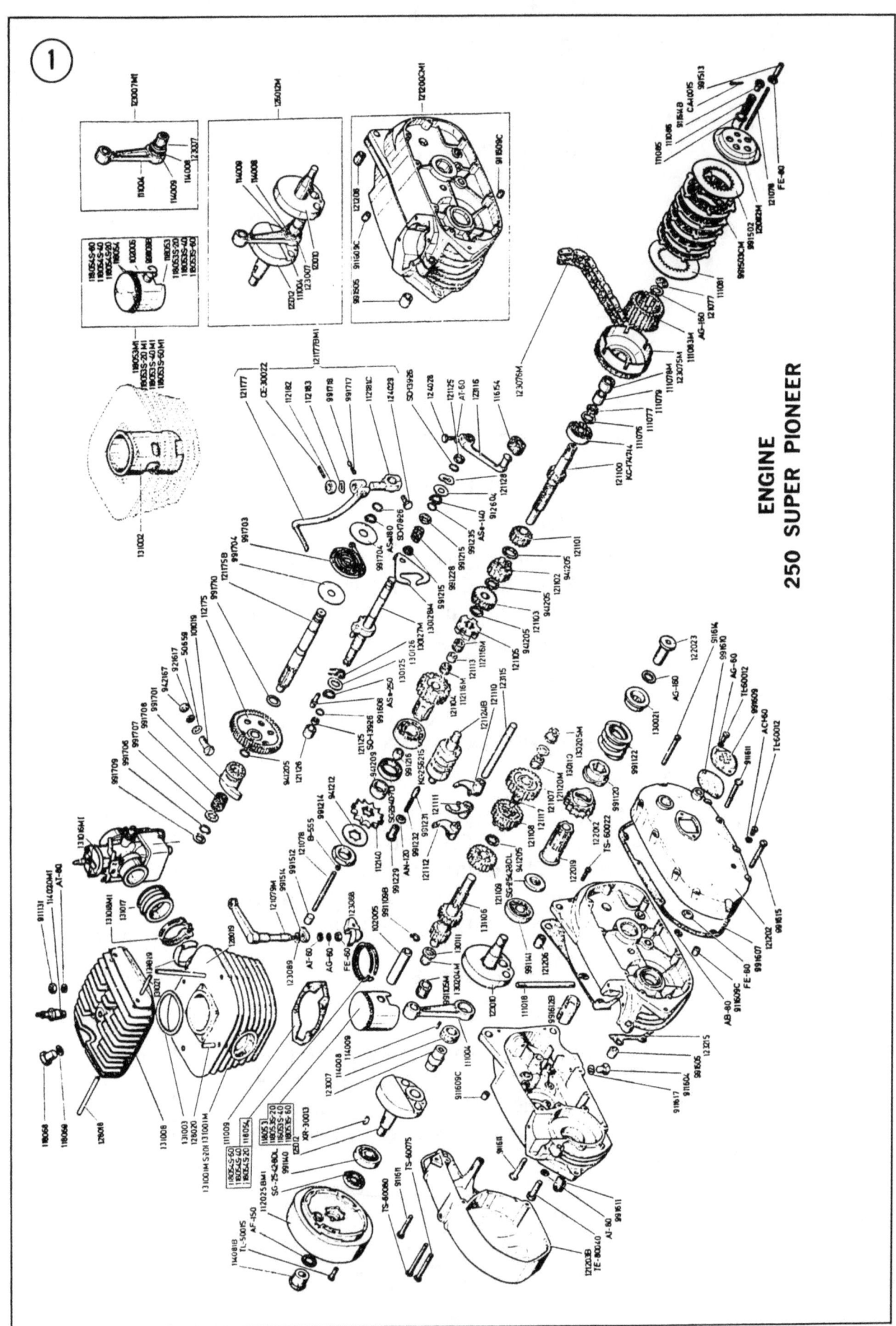

ENGINE 250 SUPER PIONEER

Part Number	DESCRIPTION	Quant.
33 176 II IV X	Shim washer layshaft	1
33 292 II IV X	Shim washer layshaft	1
50 404 II IV X	Shim washer selector	1
50 659	Washer stop bolt kick	1
101 019	Bolt kick	1
102 005	Wristpin	1
111 004	Connecting rod	1
111 009	Cylinder gasket	1
111 018	Stud, cylinder head	4
111 076	Thrust washer	1
111 077	Spacer	1
111 078 M	Needle brg.	1
111 079	"O" ring	1
111 081	Clutch plate inner	5
111 083 M	Clutch hub assembly	1
111 085	Cup clutch spring	1
111 086	Clutch spring	5
112 025 BMI	Flywheel magneto	1
112 116 M	Needle brg. cage 5 th. gear	2
112 140	Countershaft sprocket	1
112 175	Kickstarter driving gear	1
112 181 C	Kick lever support	1
112 182	Support kick lever ring	1
112 183	Spring washer lever	1
114 008	Cage big end bearing	1
114 009	Roller big end bearing	14
114 020 M	Nut magneto flywheel	1
114 081 B	Rubber footshift lever	1
116 154	Spark plug assembly	1
118 053 S 20 MI	Piston assembly 1st oversize	1
118 053 S 40 MI	Piston assembly 2nd oversize	1
118 053 S 60 MI	Piston assembly 3rd oversize	1
118 053	Piston	1
118 053 S 20	Piston 1st oversize	1
118 053 S 40	Piston 2nd oversize	1
118 053 S 60	Piston 3rd oversize	1
118 054	Piston ring	2
118 054 S 20	Piston ring 1st oversize	1
118 054 S 40	Piston ring 2nd oversize	1
118 054 S 60	Piston ring 3rd oversize	1
118 068	Compression release plug	1
118 069	Compression release basket	1
120 077	Nut clutch hub	1
120 078	Clutch rod	1
120 079 M	Clutch arm assembly	1
121 100	Main shaft	1
121 101	Gear 2nd main shaft	1
121 102	Gear 3rd main shaft	1
121 103	Gear 4th main shaft	1
121 104	Gear 5th main shaft	1
121 105	Dog wheel 4th and 5th gear	1
121 107	Gear 1st lay shaft	1
121 108	Gear 2nd layshaft	1
121 109	Gear 3rd layshaft	1
121 110	Shifting fork 1st and 3rd	1
121 111	Shifting fork 2nd	1
121 112	Shifting fork 4th and 5th	1
121 113	Spacer 5th gear	1
121 117	Washer 1st gear	1
121 120 M	Needle brg 1st gear	1
121 124 BM	Selector body assembly	1
121 125	Dust cover selector shaft	1
121 126	Plug selector shaft	1
121 175 BM	Shaft kickstarter	1
121 177 BMI	Kickstarter lever assembly	1
121 177	Kickstarter lever	1

Part Number	DESCRIPTION	Quant.
121 200 CM1	Engine cases assembly	1
121 202	Clutch cover	1
121 203 B	Magneto cover	1
121 206	Bushing	2
122 012	Engine sprocket	1
122 019	Shaft cush drive	1
122 023	Allen nut cush drive	1
123 007 MI	Cankshaft pin	1
123 010	Connecting rod asse.	1
123 075 M	Flywheel clutch side	1
123 076 M	Primary chain assem.	1
123 082 M	Primary chain	1
123 088	Clutch cover	1
123 089	Clutch cam protector	1
123 115	"O" ring and clutch axle	5
123 116	Shifting fork shaft	1
123 215	Gearshift lever	1
124 028	Gasket center case	1
124 029	Bolt, gear lever	1
125 012 M	Flywheel magneto	1
125 016 MI	Crankshaft assembly	1
128 018	Bolt kickstarter lever	1
128 019	Long anti-noise rubber, cylinder head	1
128 020	Long anti-noise rubber, cylinder	1
130 021	Short anti-noise rubber, cylinder	2
130 110	Cush drive stop	1
130 111	Left washer, layshaft	1
130 125	Right washer, layshaft	1
130 126 M	Spring, selector	1
130 127	Washer, selector	1
130 128 M	Selector shaft assembly	1
130 204 M	Selector fork assembly	1
130 205 M	Right needle bushing, layshaft	1
131 001 MS 20	Left needle bushing, layshaft	2
131 002	Cylinder assembly 1st oversize	1
131 003	Cylinder sleeve	1
131 008	Head gasket	1
131 016 MI	Cylinder head	1
131 017	Carburettor	1
131 018 MI	Rubber mount	2
131 019	Clamp for carburettor rubber mount	4
131 021	Short anti-noise rubber, cylinder head	4
131 106	Layshaft	1
911 131	Nut cylinder head	5
911 139 II IV X	Shim washer	1
911 604 B	Slotted nut clutch spring	4
911 609 C	Drain plug	1
911 611	Locating dowel	1
911 614	Bolt, engine cases	15
911 617	Screw	4
912 604	Gasket drain plug	1
921 111	Washer selector shaft	1
921 112	Shim washer mainshaft 0.05	1
921 113	Shim washer mainshaft 0.1	1
921 617	Shim washer mainshaft 0.2	5
941 205	Washer	1
941 212	Circlip	1
942 167	Spacer countershaft sprocket	2
991 105 M	Washer countershaft sprocket	1
991 109 B	Nut stop bolt	1
991 120	Rod brg. cage	1
991 122	Piston circlip	1
	Coupling cush drive	1
	Spring cush drive	1

Part Number	DESCRIPTION	Quant.
911 139 II IV X	Shim washer	1
991 140	Right main brg	1
991 141	Left main brg	1
991 214	Nut countershaft sprocket	2
991 215	Spring stop bolt selector	1
991 216	Oil seal	1
991 228	Spring	1
991 229	Guide selector	1
991 231	Anchor pin selector	1
991 232	Spring	1
991 235	Retaining ring	1
991 502	Clutch plate	5
991 503 CM	Clutch plate	5
991 512	Plunger clutch arm	1
991 513	Clutch regulating screw	1
991 514	Clutch cam	1
991 605	Locating dowel engine case	2
991 607	Gasket clutch cover	1
991 608	Anchor pin	1
991 609	Inspection cover	1
991 610	Inspection cover gasket	1
991 611	Grommet rubber	1
991 612 B	Tube breather	1
991 615	Screw engine cover primary side	2
991 701	Ratchet kickstarter	1
991 703	Spring kickstarter	1
991 704	Washer kickstarter spring	1
991 706	Circlip kickstarter shaft	1
991 707	Stop kickstarter spring	1
991 708	Thrust washer kickstarter engage	1
991 709	Spring kickstarter kickstarter shaft	1
991 717	Thrust washer kickstarter gear	1
991 718	Spring lever pin	1
	Pin kick lever	1

COMMON PARTS

Part Number	DESCRIPTION	Quant.
AB 80	Spring washer engine cases	1
AC1 60	Washer oil lever screw	1
At 150	Washer magneto	2
AG-60	Lock washer clutch arm. Inspection cover	2
AG-160	Washer cush drive hub	3
AN-120	Flat washer	4
ASe-140	Snap. ring selector	5
ASe-180	Snap ring selector and kickstarter	2
ASe-250	Snap ring selector spring	5
AT-60	Clutch arm washer	5
AT.80	Washer head and engine cases	2
B 555	Clutch rod ball	1
CA 15 015	Clutch bolt cotter pin	1
CE.30.022	Kick suport pin	1
FE 60	Nut clutch arm nut	2
FE 80	Nut clutch and engine	1
KC.17 47 14	"O" ring selector shaft	1
KC.25-52-15	"O" ring kickstarter	1
SG-25 42-8-DL	Engine bolt	2
SG.29 40.7-DL	Clutch cover and oil lever bolt	3
SO.139.26	Engine case bolt	3
SO.178.26	Bolt magneto cover	3
TE 80040	Screw magneto back plate	2
TL-50 015	Clutch cover and oil lever bolt	2
TS 60 022	Engine case bolt	2
TS 60 075	Bolt magneto cover	2
TS 60 080	Bolt magneto cover	1
XR 30 013	Magneto key	1

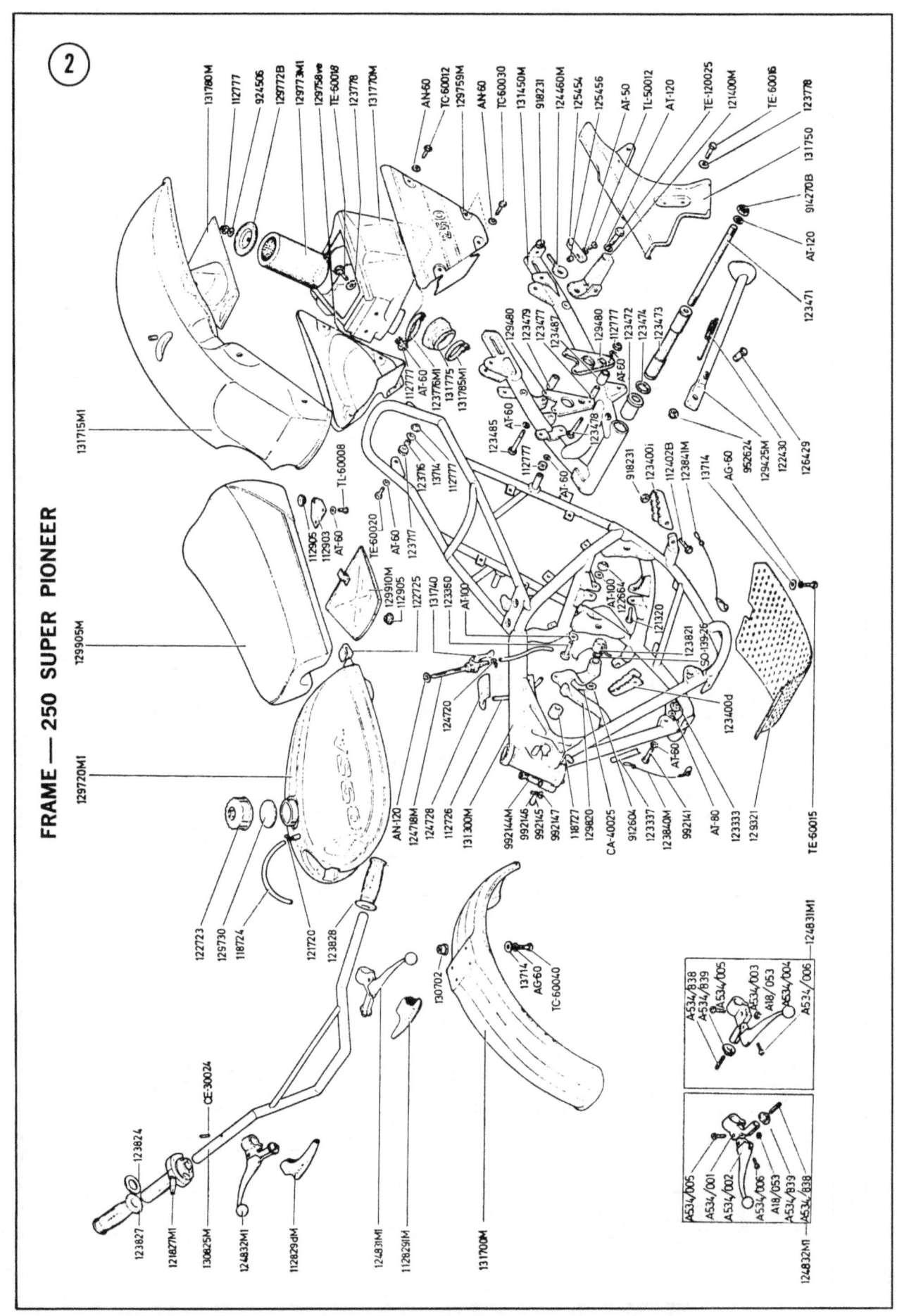

FRAME — 250 SUPER PIONEER

Part Number	DESCRIPTION	Quanti
13.714	Washer, engine protector, rear fender, gas tank, plastic shell	20
112.402 B	Footpeg shaft	2
112.726	Right fuel line from tank to carb.	1
112.777	Nut, chain guide, fender seat and shell	18
112.829 dM	Right dust protector	1
112.829 iM	Left dust protector	1
112.903	Seat mount	1
112.905	Nut, tool box and rear seat	2
118.319	Identification lable (only for USA)	1
118.724	Tube breather, tank	1
118.727	Rubber washer tank mount	2
121.320	Bolt, engine (bottom)	1
121.400 M	Passenger footpeg	2
121.720	Clip fuel line	3
121.827 Ml	Throttle assembly	1
122.430	Spring, side stand	1
122.664	Nut, engine mount	2
122.723	Gas cap	1
122.725	Gasket, gas tank-seat	1
123.333	Nut, engine mount	2
123.337	Decal, frame specifications	1
123.360	Bolt engine (top)	1
123.400 d	Right footpeg	1
123.400 i	Left footpeg	1
123.471	Rear swing arm axle	1
123.472	Bushing rear swing arm	2
123.473	Swing arm spacer	1
123.474	Circlip spacer.	2
123.477	Chain guide spacer	1
123.478	Nut, chain guide spacer	2
123.479	Chain guide spacer mount	2
123.485	Nut, chain guide	1
123.487	Bearing, chain guide	1
123.716	Tube spacer, fender and plast. shell	8
123.717	Sliemblock, fender and plastic shell	8
123.776 MI	Clamp, from rubber tube to filter	5
123.778	Washer shell	1
123.821	Rubber stop, brake pedal	1
123.823	Washer, rubber grip throttle	2
123.824	Nut, footpeg and adjusting bolt	4
123.828 (*)	Rubber grip throttle (right)	1
123.840 M	Wire brake pedal	2

Part Number	DESCRIPTION	Quanti
123.841 M	Wire gear pedal	1
124.460 M	Rear wheel tension assembly	2
124.718 M	Petcock assembly	2
124.720	Clip fuel line	2
124.728	Rubber rest gas tank	1
124.831 Ml	Clutch lever assem.	1
124.832 Ml	Brake lever assem.	1
125.454	Stop side stand	2
125.456	Tube side stand stop	1
126.429	Side stand axle	1
129.321	Skid plate	1
129.425 M	Side stand assembly	2
129.480	Chain guide	1
129.718	Decal, rear fender	1
129.720 Mldr	Petrol tank assembly	2
129.726	Decal, petrol tank	1
129.727	Decal top tank (first)	2
129.730	Rubber seal, petrol tank	1
129.758 dr	Plastic shell (right)	1
129.759 Mdr	Plastic shell assembly (left)	1
129.763	Decal left plastic shell	2
129.772 B	Air filter cover	1
129.773 Ml	Air filter assembly	1
129.820	Brake lever	2
129.905 M	Seat assembly	1
129.910 M	Tool box cover	1
130.702	Spacer, front fender	4
130.825 M	Handlebar	1
131.300 M	Frame assembly	1
131.450 M	Rear swing arm assembly	1
131.700	Front fender	2
131.715 Mldr	Rear fender assembly	2
131.728 d	Right side decal	1
131.728 i	Left side decal	1
131.735	Ossa decal	2
131.740	Left fuel line from tank to carb.	2
131.750	Chain guard	1
131.770 Mng	Air filter mount assembly	1
131.775	Rubber tube from air filter to carb	1
131.780 M	Inlet silencer cover assembly	1
131.785 Ml	Clamp, rubber tube to carburettor	2
912.604	Washer brake pedal	1
914.270 B	Nut, swing arm axle	2
918.231	Nut, footpeg and adjusting bolt	4
924.506	Washer, filter cover	1
952.624	Nut, side plate	1
992.141	Bolt, front engine mounting	1

Part Number	DESCRIPTION	Quanti
992.144 M	Steering lock	1
992.145	Steering lock cover	1
992.146	Rivet	1
992.147	Washer	2
A-18/053	Nut, handle bolt	1
A-534/001	Brake lever mount	1
A-534/002	Brake lever	1
A-534/003	Clutch lever mount	1
A-534/004	Clutch lever clutchand	1
A-534/005	Bolt, brake levers	2
A-534/006	Bolt, clutch and brake lever mount	4
A-534/838	Adjusting bolt	2
A-534/839	Locknut adjusting bolt	2
	STANDARD	
AG-60	Washer front fender	8
AN-60	Washer plastic shells and fenders	8
AN-120	Washer, petcock	2
AT-50	Washer side stand	2
AT-60	Washer, fenders shells seat and filter mount	18
AT-80	Washer, front engine mount	4
AT-100	Washer, rear engine mount	4
AT-120	Washer, passenger footpegs and swing arm	4
CE-30.024	Cotter pin, handlebar	4
CA-40.025	Cotter pin brake pedal	1
SO-139-26	"O" ring brake pedal	1
TE-60.015	Bolt, engine protector	2
TE-60.016	Bolt, chain guard	7
TE-60.018	Bolt, filter mount	3
TE-60.020	Bolt, rear fender	4
TE-60.040	Bolt, front fender	4
TE-120.025	Bolt, passenger footpeg	2
TL-50.012	Bolt, side stand stop	2
TL-60.008	Bolt, seat mount	2
TC-60.012	Bolt, shells and rear fender	6
TC-60.030	Bolt, shells	2

(*) To mount it, it must be impregnated with EC 1368 adhesive of 3 M COMPANY or an equivalent.

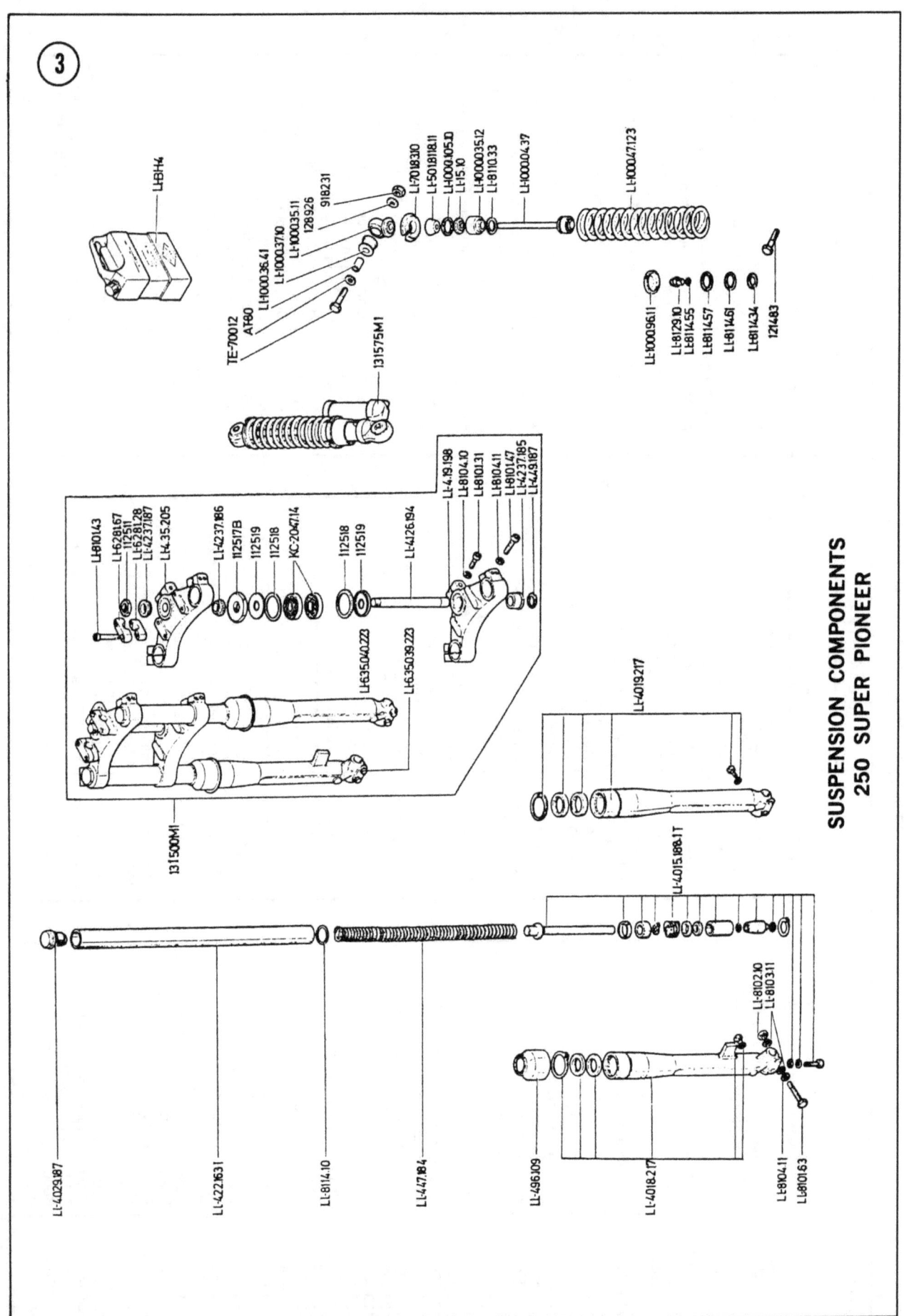

SUSPENSION COMPONENTS 250 SUPER PIONEER

Part Number	Description	Quantity	Part Number	Description	Quantity
				SHOCK ABSORBER	
112.511	Nut, steering shaft	1			
112.517 B	Nut, steering adjuster	1			
112.518	Felt washer	2	121.483	Bolt, shock absorber	4
112.519	Dust cover	2	128.926	Top washer, shock absorber	2
131.500 MI	Front fork assembly	1	131.575 BMI	Shock absorber assembly	2
KH-20-47-14	Ball bearing assembly	2	918.231	Nut, shock absorber	2
LL-422.163-I	Stanchion tube	2	AT-80	Washer, shock absorber	8
LL-419.198	Bottom yoke	1	TE-70.012	Top bolt, shock absorber	2
LL-435.205	Top yoke	1	LL-15-10	Oil seal	2
LL-447.184	Spring	2	LL-501-8118-11	Rubber top	2
LL-449.187	"O" ring	1	LL-701-83-10	Washer, top grip	2
LL-496.109	Dust cover	2	LL-1000-035-12	Guide assembly	2
LL-635-039-223	Right suspension assembly	1	LL-1000-04-37	Plunger assembly	2
LL-635-040-223	Left suspension assembly	1	LL-1000-35-11	Top grip	2
LL-4.015-188.1-T	Valve assembly	2	LL-1000-36-41	Bushing silentblock	4
LL-4.018-217	Right tank assembly	1	LL-1000-37-10	Bottom silentblock	4
LL-4.019-217	Left tank assembly	1	LL-1000-47-123	Spring	2
LL-4.029-187	Stanchion plug assembly	2	LL-1000-96-11	Dust cover vase	2
LL-4.126-194	Steering stem	1	LL-1000-105-10	Washer, oil seal	2
LL-4.237-185	Bushing bottom yoke	1	LL-8.110-33	"O" ring	2
LL-4.237-186	Bushing top yoke	1	LL-8.114-34	"O" ring	2
LL-4.237-187	Bushing top yoke	1	LL-8.114-55	"O" ring	4
LL-6.281-28	Boss, handlebar	2	LL-8.114-57	"O" ring	2
LL-6.281-67	Boss, handlebar	2	LL-8.114-61	"O" ring	2
LL-8.101-31	Allen bolt M8 x 30	2	LL-8.129-10	Valve	2
LL-8.101-43	Allen bolt M8 x 50	4	LL-BH-4	Oil vase	1
LL-8.101-47	Allen bolt M6 x 30	8			
LL-8.101-63	Bolt M6 x 50	4			
LL-8.102-10	Nut M6 x 1	2			
LL-8.103-11	Polished washer "6"	8			
LL-8.104-10	Spring washer "8"	2			
LL-8.104-11	Spring washer "6"	12			
LL-8.114-10	"O" ring	2			

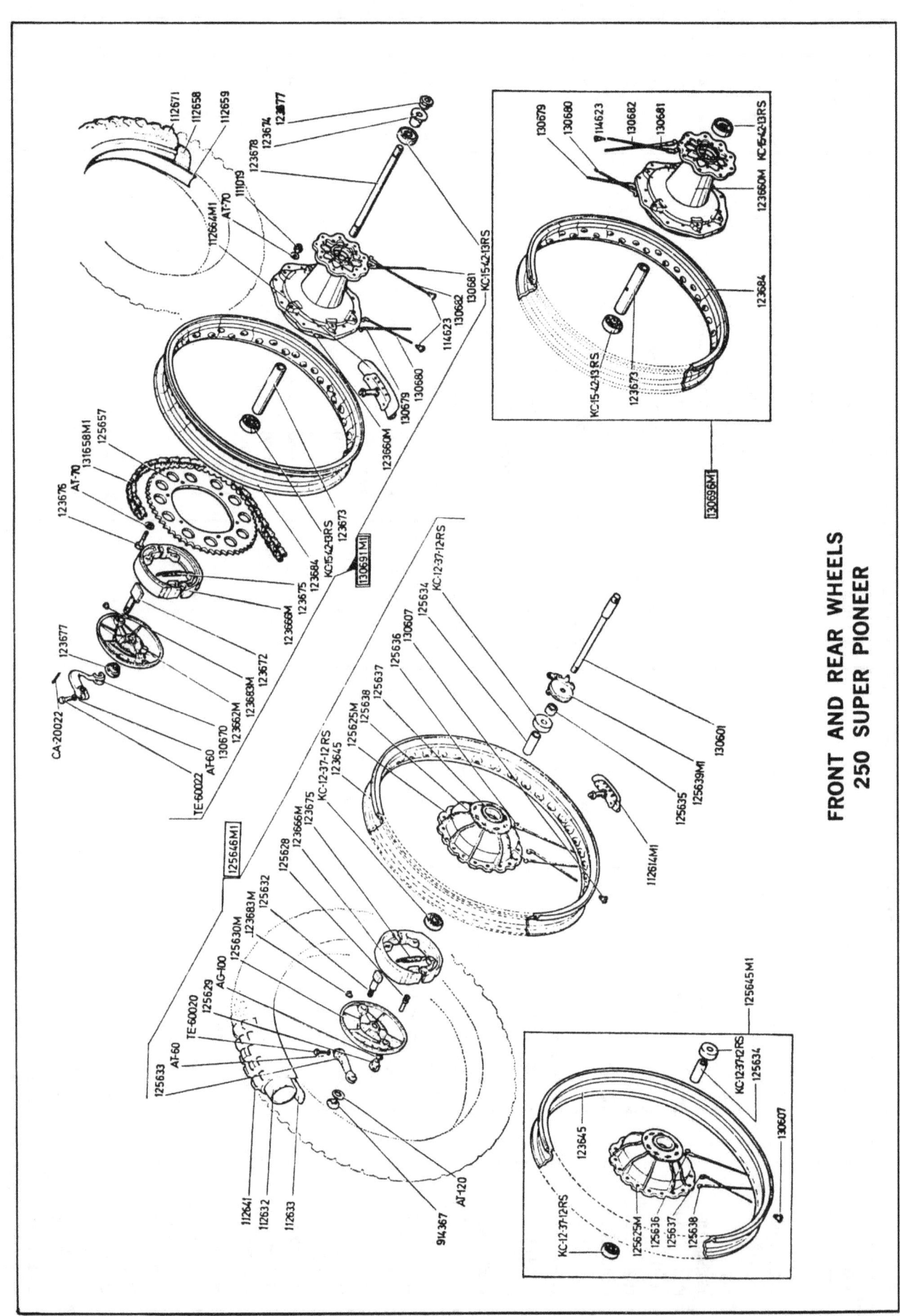
FRONT AND REAR WHEELS
250 SUPER PIONEER

FRONT AND REAR WHEELS 250 SUPER PIONEER

Part Number	DESCRIPTION	Quantity	Part Number	DESCRIPTION	Quantity
111.019	Lock nut, brake shoe	2	125.636	Front wheel spoke	18
112.614 MI	Tyre dog	1	125.637	Spoke (inner side) front wheel (brake side)	9
112.632	Inner tube	1	125.638	Spoke (outer side) front wheel (brake side)	9
112.633	Rubber inner tube	1	125.639 MI	Speedometer plug	1
112.641	Front tyre	1	125.645 MI	Front hub assembly	1
112.658	Inner tube	1	125.646 MI	Front hub and brake assembly	1
112.659	Rubber inner tube	2	125.657	Rear sprocket	1
112.664 MI	Tyre dog	1	130.601	Front wheel axle	1
112.671	Rear tyre	1	130.607	Spoke nipple	36
114.623	Spoke nipples	36	130.670	Rear brake lever	1
123.645	Rim	1	130.679	Short spoke, rear wheel (brake side)	9
123.660 M	Rear hub assembly	1	130.680	Long spoke, rear wheel (brake side)	9
123.662 M	Backing plate (rear)	4	130.681	Short spoke, rear wheel (tyre dog side)	9
123.666 M	Brake shoe assembly	1	130.682	Long spoke, rear wheel (tyre dog side)	9
123.672	Brake cam	1	130.691 MI	Rear hub and brake assembly	1
123.673	Spacer tube rear wheel	1	130.696 MI	Rear hub assembly	1
123.674	Spacer, rear wheel	4	131.658 MI	Secondary chain	1
123.675	Spring, brake shoe	4	914.367	Spoke nipple	1
123.676	Bolt, rear sprocket	6			
123.677	Nut, rear wheel axle	2			
123.678	Rear wheel axle	1			
123.683 M	Greaser brake cam	2	AT-60	Washer, brake lever	2
123.684	Rim	1	AT-70	Washer, rear sprocket	12
125.625 M	Front hub assembly with brake	1	AT-120	Washer, wheel axle	1
125.628	Backing plate, pivot	1	AG-100	Spring washer, backing plate pivot	1
125.629	Nut, backing plate pivot	1	CA-20.022	Cotter pin, brake arm	1
125.630 M	Backing plate assembly	1	KC-12-37-12RS	Wheel bearing with dust cover	2
125.632	Brake cam	1	KC-15-42-13RS	Wheel bearing with dust cover	2
125.633	Front brake lever	1	TE-60.020	Bolt, front brake lever	1
125.634	Front wheel spacer tube	1	TE-60.022	Bolt, rear brake lever	1
125.635	Front wheel spacer bushing	1			

NOTES

INDEX

A

Air cleaner 13

B

Battery
   Charging 46-47
   Inspection and service 46
   Installation 47
   Removal 45
   Safety precautions 45-46
   Tune-up 13
Bearings (see Crankshaft and bearings)
Brake lever 12
Brakes 24, 136

C

Carburetor
   Adjusting procedures 41
   Cleaning parts 41
   Disassembly and assembly (Bing) 38-41
   Disassembly and assembly (IRZ) 36-37
   Double-needle model (IRZ) 35
   Final test and adjustment 43-44
   Float mechanism 30
   Initial test and adjustment 42-43
   Jet needle adjustment 41-42
   Main fuel system 32-34
   Main jet adjustment 42
   Needle jet adjustment 42
   Overhaul frequency 35-36
   Pilot system 30-32
   Throttle valve adjustment 41
   Tickler system 35
   Tune-up adjustment 19
Charging system troubleshooting 25-26
Chassis
   Brakes 136
   Exhaust pipe 139
   Frame 109, 149, 152-153
   Front fork and steering
      components 109-128, 149, 154-155
   Rear shock 129-130
   Spokes 134-135
   Swing arm 128-129
   Tires 136-139
   Wheel bearings 135-136
   Wheels 130-133, 149, 156-157
Clutch, cush drive shaft, and kickstarter
   Clutch installation 78-80
   Clutch removal 74-76
   Clutch troubleshooting 23-24
   Cush drive shaft installation 77-78
   Cush drive shaft removal 76-77
   Inspection 77
   Kickstarter 77
Clutch sprocket 80
Compression ratio, determination of 149
Compression test 16-17
Control cables 12
Controls, location of 6
Crankcase, splitting 71-73
Crankshaft and bearings
   Cleaning and inspection 104-105
   Crankshaft alignment 105-107
   Installation 107-108
   Removal 102-104
Cush drive shaft (see Clutch, cush drive
   shaft and kickstarter)
Cylinder and piston
   Cylinder liner installation 67-68
   Cylinder liner removal 66-67
   Inspection and installation 64-66
   Piston seizure 23
   Removal 63-64

D

Decarbonization 19
Drive chain 7-10

E

Electrical system
   Battery 45-47
   Headlight 55-56
   Ignition coil 55
   Ignition switch 55
   Ignition system 47-55
   Taillight, indicator light, and horn 56
   Troubleshooting 24
   Wiring diagram 48-49
Engine
   Breaking in a rebuilt engine 80
   Clutch and engine sprockets 80
   Clutch, cush drive shaft, and kickstarter .. 74-80
   Crankcase, splitting 71-73
   Cylinder and piston 63-69
   Magneto 69-71
   Operation 57-62
   Primary cover 74
   Removal and installation 62-63
   Servicing engine in frame 62
Exhaust pipe 139

F

Flat spots 23
Frame 109, 149, 152-153

Front fork and steering components
    Assembly 121-127, 149, 154-155
    Cleaning and inspection 120
    Installation 120-121
    Oil change 10-12
    Removal 109-120
Fuel system
    Air filter 13
    Carburetor adjustment 41-44
    Carburetor operation 30-35
    Carburetor overhaul 35-41
    Fuel strainer 13
    Gas tank 44
Fuse 27

G

General information 1-6, 146-148

H

Headlight 55-56
Horn 14, 27, 56
Horsepower and torque, conversion formula 149

I

Idling, poor 23
Ignition system
    Coil 55
    Description 47
    Electronic ignition cautions and
      maintenance 54
    Operation 54
    Switch 55
    Timing, static 17-18
    Timing, strobe 18-19
    Troubleshooting 24-25
Indicator light 56

K

Kickstarter (see Clutch, cush drive shaft,
  and kickstarter)

L

Lights 14, 26-27, 55-56
Lubrication (see Maintenance and lubrication)

M

Magneto
    Installation 70-71
    Removal 69-70
Maintenance and lubrication
    Air cleaner 13
    Battery 13
    Brake lever 12

    Carburetor 19
    Compression test 16-17
    Control cables 12
    Decarbonization 19
    Drive chain 7-10
    Electrical equipment 14
    Engine tune-up 13
    Fork oil 10-12
    Fuel strainer 13
    Ignition timing 17-19
    Intervals 7
    Oil changing 7
    Rear sprocket 10
    Spark plug 14-16
    Speedometer cable 12
    Tools 7
    Winter storage 19-20
Manual organization 1-2
Misfiring 23

O

Oil changing 7
Overheating 23

P

Parts replacement 4
Piston (see Cylinder and piston)
Power loss 23
Primary cover 74

S

Safety hints 3
Serial numbers 6
Service hints 2-3
Service information, 1977-1978 models 145
Shock absorber, rear 129-130
Spark plug 14-15
Specifications and data 141-144, 147
Speedometer cable 12
Spokes 134-135
Sprocket, rear 10
Sprockets, clutch and engine 80
Starting difficulties 22
Storage 19-20
Supplies, expendable 6
Swing arm 128-129

T

Taillight 56
Tire 136-139
Tools 4-6
Transmission
    Cleaning and inspection 91-96
    Installation 96-102
    Operation 81-85

Removal 86-91
　　Transfer of power 85-86
　　Troubleshooting 24
Troubleshooting
　　Brakes 24
　　Charging system 25-26
　　Clutch 23-24
　　Electrical 24
　　Fuse 27
　　Horn 27
　　Ignition switch 25
　　Ignition system 24-25
　　Lights 26-27
　　Operating difficulties 23-24
　　Operating requirements 21-22
　　Starting difficulties 22
　　Transmission 24
　　Troubleshooting guide 28-29
Tune-up
　　Air cleaner 13
　　Battery 13
　　Carburetor 19
　　Compression test 16-17
　　Decarbonization 19
　　Electrical equipment 14
　　Fuel strainer 13
　　General information 13
　　Ignition timing 17-19
　　Spark plug 14-16

V

Vibration, excessive 23

W

Wheel bearings 135-136
Wheels 130-131, 149, 156-157
Wiring diagram 48-49

VELOCEPRESS MANUALS – MOTORCYCLE BY MAKE

AJS 1932-1948 SINGLES & TWINS 250cc THRU 1000cc (BOOK OF)
AJS 1945-1956 SINGLES RIGID & SPRTING FACTORY WSM & PARTS
AJS 1945-1960 SINGLES MODELS 16 & 18 350cc & 500cc (BOOK OF)
AJS 1948-1956 TWINS MODELS 20 & 30 FACTORY WSM & PARTS
AJS 1955-1965 SINGLES MODELS 16 & 18 350cc & 500cc (BOOK OF)
AJS 1957-1966 SINGLES & TWINS (ALL) FACTORY WSM
AJS 1959-1969 G80CS G85CS & P11 OFF ROAD FACTORY WSM
AJS 1968-1974 STORMER FACTORY WSM & PARTS LIST
ARIEL UP TO 1932 (BOOK OF)
ARIEL 1932-1939 PREWAR MODELS (BOOK OF)
ARIEL 1933-1951 (WORKSHOP MANUAL)
ARIEL 1939-1960 4 STROKE SINGLES (BOOK OF)
ARIEL 1958-1964 LEADER & ARROW FACTORY WSM & PARTS LIST
ARIEL 1958-1964 LEADER & ARROW (BOOK OF)
BMW R26 R27 (1956-1967) FACTORY WORKSHOP MANUAL
BMW R50 R50S R60 R69S (1955-1969) FACTORY WORKSHOP MANUAL
BMW R50/5 R60/5 R75/5 (1969-1973) FACTORY WORKSHOP MANUAL
BRIDGESTONE 90 SERIES FACTORY WSM & PARTS CATALOGUE
BRIDGESTONE 175 SERIES FACTORY WSM & PARTS CATALOGUE
BRIDGESTONE 350 SERIES FACTORY WSM & PARTS CATALOGUES
BSA SERVICE SHEETS MASTER CATALOGUE ALL MODELS 1945-1967
BSA BANTAM D1 TO D7 1948-1966 FACTORY SERVICE SHEETS MANUAL
BSA BANTAM ALL MODELS FROM 1948 ONWARDS (BOOK OF)
BSA BANTAM D14 FACTORY SERVICE MANUAL
BSA DANDY FACTORY WORKSHOP MANUAL (COMPILATION)
BSA SINGLES & V-TWINS UP TO 1926 inc. 1927 SUPPLEMENT (BOOK OF)
BSA SINGLES & V-TWINS UP TO 1930 (BOOK OF)
BSA SINGLES & V-TWINS UP TO 1935 (BOOK OF)
BSA SINGLES & V-TWINS 1936-1939 (BOOK OF)
BSA C10, C11 & C12 1945-1958 FACTORY SERVICE SHEETS MANUAL
BSA OHV & SV SINGLES CONCENTRIC 1945-1959 (BOOK OF)
BSA C15 & B40 1958-1967 FACTORY SERVICE SHEETS MANUAL
BSA OHV & SV SINGLES 250cc (ONLY) 1954-1970 (BOOK OF)
BSA B31, B32, B33 & B34 1945-60 FACTORY SERVICE SHEETS MANUAL
BSA OHV SINGLES 350 & 500cc 1955-1967 (BOOK OF)
BSA M20, M21 & M33 1945-1963 FACTORY SERVICE SHEETS MANUAL
BSA TWINS A7 & A10 1948-1962 FACTORY SERVICE SHEETS MANUAL
BSA TWINS A7 & A10 1948-1962 (BOOK OF)
BSA TWINS A50 & A65 1962-1965 FACTORY WORKSHOP MANUAL
BSA TWINS A50 & A65 1962-1969 (SECOND BOOK OF)
BULTACO 125cc to 37cc SINGLES 1968-1979 WORKSHOP MANUAL
CZ 125cc to 380cc SINGLES 1967-1974 WORKSHOP MANUAL
DOUGLAS 1929-1939 PREWAR ALL MODELS (BOOK OF)
DOUGLAS 1948-1957 POSTWAR ALL MODELS FACTORY SHOP MANUAL
DUCATI 160cc, 250cc & 350cc OHC MODELS FACTORY SHOP MANUAL
HODAKA 90cc,100cc & 125cc SINGLES 1964-1978 WORKSHOP MANUAL
HONDA 50cc ALL MODELS UP TO 1970 INC MONKEY & TRAIL (BOOK OF)
HONDA 90cc ALL MODELS UP TO 1966 (BOOK OF)
HONDA TWINS & SINGLES 50cc THRU 305cc 1960-1966 (BOOK OF)
HONDA TWINS ALL MODELS 125cc THRU 450cc UP TO 1968 (BOOK OF)
HONDA C100 50cc SUPER CUB O.H.C. 1959-1962 FACTORY WSM
HONDA C110 50cc SPORT CUB O.H.C. 1960-1962 FACTORY WSM
HONDA 50-65-70-90cc O.H.C. SINGLES 1959-1983 WSM
HONDA 100-125cc SINGLES CB/CD/CL/SL/TL 1970-1984 FACTORY WSM
HONDA 125-150cc TWINS C/CS/CB/CA 1959-1966 FACTORY WSM
HONDA 125-160-175-200cc TWINS 1965-1978 WORKSHOP MANUAL
HONDA 250-305cc TWINS C/CS/CB 1961-1968 FACTORY WSM
HOHDA 250-350cc TWINS CB/CL/SL 1968-1973 FACTORY WSM
HONDA 250-360cc TWINS CB/CL/CJ 1974-1977 FACTORY WSM
HONDA 350F & 400F 4-CYLINDER 1972-1977 FACTORY WSM
HONDA 450cc TWINS CB/CL 1965-1974 K0 TO K7 WORKSHOP MANUAL
HONDA 500cc & 550cc 4-CYL 1971-1978 FACTORY WORKSHOP MANUAL
HONDA 750cc SHOC 4-CYL 1969-1978 K0~K8 WORKSHOP MANUAL
HUSQVARNA 125cc to 450cc SINGLES 1965-1975 WORKSHOP MANUAL
INDIAN PONYBIKE, BOY RACER & PAPOOSE ILL PARTS LIST & SALES LIT

VELOCEPRESS MANUALS – SCOOTERS BY MAKE

BSA SUNBEAM SCOOTER WORKSHOP MANUAL 1959-1965
BSA SUNBEAM SCOOTER 1959-1965 (BOOK OF)
LAMBRETTA 1947-1957 ALL 125 & 150cc MODELS (BOOK OF)
LAMBRETTA 1957-1970 LI & TV MODELS (SECOND BOOK OF)
NSU PRIMA 1956-1964 ALL MODELS (BOOK OF)
TRIUMPH TIGRESS SCOOTER WORKSHOP MANUAL 1959-1965
TRIUMPH TIGRESS SCOOTER (BOOK OF)
VESPA 1951-1961 (BOOK OF)
VESPA 1955-1963 125 & 150cc & GS MODELS (SECOND BOOK OF)
VESPA 1955-1968 GS & SS (BOOK OF)
VESPA 1963-1972 90, 125 & 150cc (THIRD BOOK OF)

VELOCEPRESS MANUALS – MOPEDS & MOTORIZED BICYCLES

CYCLEMOTOR (BOOK OF)
NSU QUICKLY 1953-1963 ALL MODELS (BOOK OF)
PUCH MAXI N & S MAINTENANCE & REPAIR (3 MANUAL COMPILATION)
RALEIGH MOPEDS 1960-1969 (BOOK OF)

www.VelocePress.com

J.A.P. ENGINES 1927-1952 & MOTORCYCLES 1934-1952 (BOOK OF)
KAWASAKI TRIPLES 1968-1980 ALL MODELS 250cc to 750cc WSM
MAICO 250cc to 501cc 1968-1978 WORKSHOP MANUAL
MATCHLESS 1931-1939 ALL MODELS 250cc THRU 990cc (BOOK OF)
MATCHLESS 1945-1956 RIGID & SPRING FACTORY WSM & PARTS
MATCHLESS 1945-1956 SINGLES G3 & G80 350cc & 500cc (BOOK OF)
MATCHLESS 1948-1956 TWINS G9 & G11 FACTORY WSM & PARTS
MATCHLESS 1955-1966 SINGLES G3 & G80 350cc & 500cc (BOOK OF)
MATCHLESS 1957-1966 SINGLES & TWINS (ALL) FACTORY WSM
MONTESA 1962-1978 125cc to 360cc ALL MODELS WORKSHOP MANUAL
NEW IMPERIAL ALL SV & OHV FROM 1935 ONWARDS (BOOK OF)
NORTON 1932-1939 PREWAR MODELS (BOOK OF)
NORTON 1932-1947 (BOOK OF)
NORTON 1938-1956 (BOOK OF)
NORTON 1945-1963 MODELS 16H, Big4, ES2, 19 & 50 WSM'S & PARTS
NORTON 1955-1963 MODELS 19, 50 & ES2 (BOOK OF)
NORTON 1948-1970 DOMINATOR TWINS FACTORY WSM'S & PARTS
NORTON 1955-1965 DOMINATOR TWINS (BOOK OF)
NORTON 1960-1970 TWIN CYLINDER FACTORY WORKSHOP MANUAL
NORTON 1970-1975 COMMANDO 850 & 750cc FACTORY WSM
NORTON 1975-1978 MK 3 COMMANDO 850 cc FACTORY WSM
OSSA 1971-1978 125cc, 175cc, 250cc, 310cc WSM
PANTHER 1932-1958 LIGHTWEIGHT MODELS 250 & 350cc (BOOK OF)
PANTHER 1938-1966 HEAVYWEIGHT MODELS 600 & 650cc (BOOK OF)
PENTON-KTM-SACHS 1968-1975 100cc & 125cc WORKSHOP MANUAL
PENTON-KTM 1972-1975 175cc, 250cc & 400cc WSM & PARTS MANUALS
PENTON-KTM 1972-1979 125cc to 400cc ENGINE WSM & PARTS MANUAL
RALEIGH MOTORCYCLES 1919-1933 (BOOK OF)
ROYAL ENFIELD 1934-1946 SINGLES & V TWINS (BOOK OF)
ROYAL ENFIELD 1937-1953 SINGLES & V TWINS (BOOK OF)
ROYAL ENFIELD 1946-1962 SINGLES (BOOK OF)
ROYAL ENFIELD 1948-1962 350cc & 500cc PRE-UNIT BULLET WSM
ROYAL ENFIELD 1948-1963 500cc TWINS FACTORY WORKSHOP MANUAL
ROYAL ENFIELD 1952-1963 700cc TWINS FACTORY WORKSHOP MANUAL
ROYAL ENFIELD 1956-1966 250cc CRUSADER & 350cc NEW BULLET WSM
ROYAL ENFIELD 1958-1966 250cc & 350cc SINGLES (SECOND BOOK OF)
ROYAL ENFIELD 1962-1970 INTERCEPTOR WSM'S & PARTS (Compilation)
RUDGE 1933-1939 (BOOK OF)
SACHS 1968-1975 100cc & 125cc ENGINES WSM & M/CYCLE PARTS LIST
SUNBEAM 1928-1939 (BOOK OF)
SUNBEAM 1946-1957 S7 & S8 (BOOK OF)
SUZUKI 50cc & 80cc UP TO 1966 (BOOK OF)
SUZUKI T10 1963-1967 FACTORY WORKSHOP MANUAL
SUZUKI T20 & T200 1965-1969 FACTORY WORKSHOP MANUAL
SUZUKI TWINS 1962 ONWARDS 125-500cc WORKSHOP MANUAL
TRIUMPH 1935-1949 SINGLES & TWINS (BOOK OF)
TRIUMPH 1937-1961 SINGLES SV & OHV 250cc-600cc + TERRIER & CUB
TRIUMPH 1945-1955 PRE-UNIT 350cc, 500cc & 650cc TWINS WSM No.11
TRIUMPH 1945-1959 TWINS (BOOK OF)
TRIUMPH 1956-1969 TWINS (BOOK OF)
TRIUMPH 1956-1962 PRE-UNIT 500cc & 650cc TWINS WSM No.17
TRIUMPH 1957-1963 UNIT CONSTRUCTION 350-500cc WSM No.4
TRIUMPH 1963-1974 UNIT CONSTRUCTION 350-500cc FACTORY WSM
TRIUMPH 1963-1970 UNIT CONSTRUCTION 650cc FACTORY WSM
TRIUMPH 1968-1974 TRIDENT T150 & T150V FACTORY WSM
TRIUMPH 1971-1973 650cc OIL-IN-FRAME FACTORY WSM
TRIUMPH 1973-1978 750cc BONNEVILLE & TIGER FACTORY WSM
TRIUMPH 1979-1983 750cc T140, TR7 & TR65 FACTORY WSM
VELOCETTE 1925-1970 ALL SINGLES & TWINS (BOOK OF)
VELOCETTE 1933-1952 MOV-MAC-MSS RIGID FRAME FACTORY WSM
VELOCETTE 1953-1960 MAC SPRING FRAME WSM & ILL PARTS LIST
VELOCETTE 1954-1971 MSS-VENOM-THRUXTON-VIPER FACTORY WSM
VILLIERS ENGINE UP TO 1959 INC. 3 WHEELERS (BOOK OF)
VILLIERS ENGINE UP TO 1969 (BOOK OF)
VINCENT 1935-1955 (WORKSHOP MANUAL)
YAMAHA 1961-1967 YA5 & YA6 (WORKSHOP MANUAL & ILL PARTS LIST)
YAMAHA 1968-1971 DT1 & MX SERIES Inc. GYT WORKSHOP MANUAL
YAMAHA 1971-1972 JT1& JT2 (WORKSHOP MANUAL & ILL PARTS LIST)

VELOCEPRESS MANUALS - THREE WHEELER'S

BOND MINICAR THREE WHEELER 1948-1967 (BOOK OF)
BMW ISETTA FACTORY WORKSHOP MANUAL
BSA THREE WHEELER (BOOK OF)
RELIANT REGAL THREE WHEELER 1952-1973 (BOOK OF)
VINTAGE MORGAN THREE WHEELER (BOOK OF)

VELOCEPRESS TECHNICAL BOOKS – MOTORCYCLE

1930'S BRITISH MOTORCYCLE CARBS & ELEC COMPONENTS (BOOK OF)
1930'S BRITISH MOTORCYCLE ENGINES (OVERHAUL & MAINTENANCE)
1930'S BRITISH MOTORCYCLE GEARBOXES & CLUTCHES (BOOK OF)
CATALOG OF BRITISH MOTORCYCLES (1951 MODELS)
LUCAS ELECTRONICS BRITISH M/CYCLES REPAIR & PARTS (1950-1977)
MOTORCYCLE ENGINEERING (P.E. Irving)
MOTORCYCLE ROAD TESTS 1949-1953 (Motor Cycle Magazine UK)
SPEED AND HOW TO OBTAIN IT (Motor Cycle Magazine UK)
TUNING FOR SPEED (P.E. Irving)
WIPAC (COMBO) MANUAL NUMBER 3 + M/CYCLE & SCOOTER MANUAL

www.ingramcontent.com/pod-product-compliance
Lightning Source LLC
Chambersburg PA
CBHW080739300426
44114CB00019B/2631